Albert Schwegler, Julius H. Seelye, Henry B. Smith

A history of philosophy in epitome by Dr. Albert Schwegler

Albert Schwegler, Julius H. Seelye, Henry B. Smith

A history of philosophy in epitome by Dr. Albert Schwegler

ISBN/EAN: 9783743356313

Hergestellt in Europa, USA, Kanada, Australien, Japan

Cover: Foto ©Thomas Meinert / pixelio.de

Manufactured and distributed by brebook publishing software (www.brebook.com)

Albert Schwegler, Julius H. Seelye, Henry B. Smith

A history of philosophy in epitome by Dr. Albert Schwegler

A

HISTORY OF PHILOSOPHY

IN EPITOME,

BY

DR. ALBERT SCHWEGLER.

TRANSLATED FROM THE ORIGINAL GERMAN,

BY

JULIUS H. SEELYE.

FIFTH EDITION.

NEW YORK:
D. APPLETON & COMPANY, 90, 92 & 94 GRAND ST.
LONDON: 16 LITTLE BRITAIN.
1869.

INTRODUCTORY NOTE

BY HENRY B. SMITH, D. D.

THE History of Philosophy, by Dr. Albert Schwegler, is considered in Germany as the best concise manual upon the subject from the school of Hegel. Its account of the Greek and of the German systems, is of especial value and importance. It presents the whole history of speculation in its consecutive order. Though following the method of Hegel's more extended lectures upon the progress of philosophy, and though it makes the system of Hegel to be the ripest product of philosophy, yet it also rests upon independent investigations. It will well reward diligent study, and is one of the best works for a text-book in our colleges, upon this neglected branch of scientific investigation. The translation is made by a competent person, and gives, I doubt not, a faithful ren dering of the original.

HENRY B. SMITH.

UNION THEOLOGICAL SEMINARY, NEW YORK, *Nov. 6, 1855.*

TRANSLATOR'S PREFACE.

Schwegler's History of Philosophy originally appeared in the "*Neue Encyklopädie für Wissenschaften und Künste.*" Its great value soon awakened a call for its separate issue, in which form it has attained a very wide circulation in Germany. It is found in the hands of almost every student in the philosophical department of a German university, and is highly esteemed for its clearness, conciseness, and comprehensiveness.

The present translation was commenced in Germany three years ago, and has been carefully finished. It was undertaken with the conviction that the work would not lose its interest or its value in an English dress, and with the hope that it might be of wider service in such a form

1

to students of philosophy here. It was thought especially, that a proper translation of this manual would
supply a want for a suitable text-book on this branch of
study, long felt by both teachers and students in our
American colleges.

The effort has been made to translate, and not to para-
phrase the author's meaning. Many of his statements
might have been amplified without diffuseness, and made
more perceptible to the superficial reader without losing
their interest to the more profound student, but he has so
happily seized upon the germs of the different systems,
that they neither need, nor would be improved by any
farther development, and has, moreover, presented them
so clearly, that no student need have any difficulty in apprehending them as they are. The translator has therefore endeavored to represent faithfully and clearly the
original history. As such, he offers his work to the
American public, indulging no hope, and making no efforts for its success beyond that which its own merits
shall ensure.   J. H. S.

SCHENECTADY, N. Y., *January,* 1856.

CONTENTS.

———•••———

xiv   CONTENTS.

HISTORY OF PHILOSOPHY.

SECTION I.

WHAT IS MEANT BY THE HISTORY OF PHILOSOPHY.

To philosophize is to reflect; to examine things, in thought.

Yet in this is the conception of philosophy not sufficiently defined. Man, as thinking, also employs those practical activities concerned in the adaptation of means to an end; the whole body of sciences also, even those which do not in strict sense belong to philosophy, still lie in the realm of thought. In what, then, is philosophy distinguished from these sciences, *e. g.* from the science of astronomy, of medicine, or of rights? Certainly not in that it has a different material to work upon. Its material is precisely the same as that of the different empirical sciences. The construction and disposition of the universe, the arrangement and functions of the human body, the doctrines of property, of rights and of the state—all these materials belong as truly to philosophy as to their appropriate sciences. That which is given in the world of experience, that which is real, is the content likewise of philosophy. It is not, therefore, in its material but in its form, in its method, in its mode of knowledge, that philosophy is to be distinguished from the empirical sciences. These latter derive their material directly from experience; they find it at hand and take it up just as they find it. Philosophy, on the other hand, is never satisfied with receiving that which is given simply as it is given, but rather follows it out to its ultimate grounds; it examines every individual thing in reference to a final principle, and considers it as one link in the whole chain of knowledge. In this way philosophy removes from the individual thing given in experience, its immediate, individual, and accidental character; from the sea of empirical individualities, it brings out that which is common to all; from the infinite and orderless mass of contingencies it finds that which is necessary, and throws over all a universal law. In short, philosophy examines the *totality* of experience in the form of an *organic system* in harmony with the laws of thought. From the above it is seen, that philosophy (in the sense we have given it) and the empirical sciences have a reciprocal influence; the latter conditioning the former, while they at the same time are conditioned by it. We shall, therefore, in the history of the world, no more find an absolute and complete philosophy, than a complete empirical science (*Empirik*). Rather is philosophy found only in the form of the different philosophical systems, which have successively appeared in the course of history, advancing hand in hand with the progress of the empirical sciences and the universal, social, and civil culture, and showing in their advance the different steps in the development and improvement of human science. The history of philosophy has, for its object, to represent the content, the succession, and the inner connection of these philosophical systems.

The relation of these different systems to each other is thus already intimated. The historical and collective life of the race is bound together by the idea of a spiritual and intellectual progress, and manifests a regular order of advancing, though not always continuous, stages of development. In this, the fact harmonizes with what we should expect from antecedent probabilities. Since, therefore, every philosophical system is only the philosophical expression of the collective life of its time, it follows that these different systems which have appeared in history will disclose one organic movement and form together one rational and internally connected (*gegliedertes*) system. In all their developments, we shall find one constant order, grounded in the striving of the spirit ever to raise itself to a higher point of consciousness and knowledge, and to recognize the whole spiritual and natural universe, more and more, as its outward being, as its reality, as the mirror of itself.

Hegel was the first to utter these thoughts and to consider the history of philosophy as a united process, but this view, which is, in its principle, true, he has applied in a way which would destroy the freedom of human actions, and remove the very conception of contingency, *i. e.* that any thing should be contrary to reason. Hegel's view is, that the succession of the systems of philosophy which have appeared in history, corresponds to the succession of logical categories in a system of logic. According to him, if, from the fundamental conceptions of these different philosophical systems, we remove that which pertains to their outward form or particular application, &c., there remain the different steps of the logical conceptions (*e. g.* being, becoming, existence, being *per se* (*fürsichseyn*) quantity, &c.). And on the other hand, if we take up the logical process by itself, we find also in it the actual historical process.

This opinion, however, can be sustained neither in its principle nor in its historical application. It is defective in its principle, because in history freedom and necessity interpenetrate, and, therefore, while we find, if we consider it in its general aspects, a rational connection running through the whole, we also see, if we look solely at its individual parts, only a play of numberless contingencies, just as the kingdom of nature, taken as a whole, reveals a rational plan in its successions, but viewed only in its parts, mocks at every attempt to reduce them to a preconceived order. In history we have to do with free subjectivities, with individuals capable of originating actions, and have, therefore, a factor which does not admit of a previous calculation. For however accurately we may estimate the controlling conditions which may attach to an individual, from the general circumstances in which he may be placed, his age, his associations, his nationality, &c., a free will can never be calculated like a mathematical problem. History is no example for a strict arithmetical calculation. The history of philosophy, therefore, cannot admit of an apriori construction; the actual occurrences should not be joined together as illustrative of a preconceived plan; but the facts, so far as they can be admitted, after a critical sifting, should be received as such, and their rational connection be analytically determined. The speculative idea can only supply the law for the arrangement and scientific connection of that which may be historically furnished.

A more comprehensive view, which contradicts the above-given Hegelian notion, is the following. The actual historical development is, very generally, different from the theoretical. Historically *e. g.* the State arose as a means of protection against robbers, while theoretically it is derived from the idea of rights. So also, even in the actual history of philosophy, while the logical (theoretical) process is an ascent from the abstract to the concrete, yet does the historical development of philosophy, quite generally, descend from the concrete to the abstract, from intuition to thought, and separates the abstract from the concrete in those general forms of culture and those religious and social circumstances, in which the philosophizing subject is placed. A *system* of philosophy proceeds synthetically, while the *history* of philosophy, *i. e.* the history of the thinking process proceeds analytically. We might, therefore, with great propriety, adopt directly the reverse of the Hegelian position, and say that what in reality is the first, is for us, in fact, the last. This is illustrated in the Ionic philosophy. It began not with being as an abstract conception, but with the most concrete, and most apparent, *e. g.* with the material conception of water, air, &c. Even if we leave the Ionics and advance to the being of the Eleatics or the becoming of the Heraclitics, we find, that these, instead of being pure thought determinations, are only unpurified conceptions, and materially colored intuitions. Still farther, is the attempt impracticable to refer every philosophy that has appeared in history to some logical category as its central principle, because the most of these philosophies have taken, for their object, the idea, not as an abstract conception, but in its realization as nature and mind, and, therefore, for the most part, have to do, not with logical questions, but with those relating to natural philosophy, psychology and ethics. Hegel should not, therefore, limit his comparison of the historical and systematic process of development simply to logic, but should extend it to the whole system of philosophical science. Granted that the Eleatics, the Heraclitics and the Atomists may have made such a category as the centre of their systems, and we may find thus far the Hegelian logic in harmony with the Hegelian history of philosophy. But if we go farther, how is it? How with Anaxagoras, the Sophists, Socrates, Plato, Aristotle? We cannot, certainly, without violence, press one central principle into the systems of these men, but if we should be able to do it, and could reduce *e. g.* the philosophy of Anaxagoras to the conception of " the end," that of the Sophists to the conception of " the appearance," and the Socratic Philosophy to the conception of " the good,"—yet even then we have the new difficulty that the historical does not correspond to the logical succession of these categories. In fact, Hegel himself has not attempted a complete application of his principle, and indeed gave it up at the very threshold of the Grecian philosophy. To the Eleatics, the Heraclitics and the Atomists, the logical categories of " being," " becoming," and being *per se* may be successively ascribed, and so far, as already remarked, the parallelism extends, but no farther. Not only does Anaxagoras follow with the conception of reason working according to an end, but if we go back before the Eleatics, we find in the very beginning of philosophy a total diversity between the logical and historical order. If Hegel had carried out his principle consistently, he should have thrown away entirely the Ionic philosophy, for matter is no logical category; he should have placed the Pythagoreans after the Eleatics and the Atomists, for in logical order the categories of quantity follow those of quality; in short, he would have been obliged to set aside all chronology. Unless this be done, we must be satisfied with a theoretical reproduction of the course which the thinking spirit has taken in its history, only so far as we can see in the grand stages of history a rational progress of thought; only so far as the philosophical historian, surveying a period of development, actually finds in it a philosophical acquisition,—the acquisition of a new idea: but we must guard ourselves against applying to the transition and intermediate steps, as well as to the whole detail of history, the postulate of an immanent conformity to law, or an organism in harmony with our own thoughts. History often winds its way like a serpent in lines which appear retrogressive, and philosophy, especially, has not seldom withdrawn herself from a wide and already fruitful field, in order to settle down upon a narrow strip of land, the limits even of which she has sought still more closely to abridge. At one time we find thousands of years expended in fruitless attempts with only a negative result;—at another, a fulness of philosophical ideas are crowded together in the experience of a lifetime. There is here no sway of an immutable and regularly returning law, but history, as the realm of freedom, will first completely manifest itself at the end of time as the work of reason.

SECTION II.

CLASSIFICATION.

A few words will suffice to define our problem and classify its elements. Where and when does philosophy begin? Manifestly, according to the analysis made in § I., where a final philosophical principle, a final ground of being is first sought in a philosophical way,—and hence with the Grecian philosophy. The Oriental— Chinese and Hindoo—so named philosophies,—but which are rather theologies or mythologies,—and the mythic cosmogonies of

Greece, in its earliest periods, are, therefore, excluded from our more definite problem. Like Aristotle, we shall begin the history of philosophy with Thales. For similar reasons we exclude also the philosophy of the Christian middle ages, or Scholasticism. This is not so much a philosophy, as a philosophizing or reflecting within the already prescribed limits of positive religion. It is, therefore, essentially theology, and belongs to the science of the history of Christian doctrines.

The material which remains after this exclusion, may be naturally divided into two periods; viz :—ancient—Grecian and Græco-Romanic—and modern philosophy. Since a preliminary comparison of the characteristics of these two epochs could not here be given without a subsequent repetition, we shall first speak of their inner relations, when we come to treat of the transition from the one to the other.

The first epoch can be still farther divided into three periods ; (1.) The pre-Socratic philosophy, *i. e.* from Thales to the Sophists inclusive ; (2.) Socrates, Plato, Aristotle ; (3.) The post-Aris· totelian philosophy, including New Platonism.

SECTION III.

GENERAL VIEW OF THE PRE-SOCRATIC PHILOSOPHY.

1. THE universal tendency of the pre-Socratic philosophy is to find some principle for the explanation of nature. Nature, the most immediate, that which first met the eye and was the most palpable, was that which first aroused the inquiring mind. At the basis of its changing forms,—beneath its manifold appearances, thought they, lies a first principle which abides the same through all change. What then, they asked, is this principle ? What is the original ground of things ? Or, more accurately, what element of nature is the fundamental element ? To solve this inquiry was the problem of the *Ionic* natural philosophers. One

proposes as a solution, water, another, air, and a third, an original chaotic matter.

2. The *Pythagoreans* attempted a higher solution of this problem. The proportions and dimensions of matter rather than its sensible concretions, seemed to them to furnish the true explanation of being. They, accordingly, adopted as the principle of their philosophy, that which would express a determination of proportions, *i. e.* numbers. " Number is the essence of all things," was their position. Number is the mean between the immediate sensuous intuition and the pure thought. Number and measure have, to be sure, nothing to do with matter only in so far as it possesses extension, and is capable of division in space and time, but yet we should have no numbers or measures if there were no matter, or nothing which could meet the intuitions of our sense. This elevation above matter, which is at the same time a cleaving to matter, constitutes the essence and the character of Pythagoreanism.

3. Next come the *Eleatics*, who step absolutely beyond that which is given in experience, and make a complete abstraction of every thing material. This abstraction, this negation of all division in space and time, they take as their principle, and call it pure being. Instead of the sensuous principle of the Ionics, or the symbolic principle of the Pythagoreans, the Eleatics, therefore, adopt an intelligible principle.

4. Herewith closes the analytic, the first course in the development of Grecian philosophy, to make way for the second, or synthetic course. The Eleatics had sacrificed to their principle of pure being, the existence of the world and every finite existence. But the denial of nature and the world could not be maintained. The reality of both forced itself upon the attention, and even the Eleatics had affirmed it, though in guarded and hypothetical terms. But from their abstract being there was no passage back to the sensuous and concrete; their principle ought to have explained the being of events, but it did not. To find a principle for the explanation of these, a principle which would account for the becoming, the event was still the problem. *Heraclitus* solved

it, by asserting that, inasmuch as being has no more reality than not being, therefore the unity of the two, or in other words the becoming, is the absolute principle. He held that it belonged to the very essence of finite being that it be conceived in a continual flow, in an endless stream. " Every thing flows." We have here the conception of original energy, instead of the Ionic original matter ; the first attempt to explain being and its motion from a principle analytically attained. From the time of Heraclitus, this inquiry after the cause of the becoming, remained the chief interest and the moving spring of philosophical development.

5. Becoming is the unity of being and not-being, and into these two elements is the Heraclitic principle consciously analyzed by the *Atomists*. Heraclitus had uttered the principle of the becoming, but only as a fact of experience. He had simply expressed it as a law, but had not explained it. The necessity for this universal law yet remained to be proved. WHY is every thing in a perpetual flow—in an eternal movement? From the dynamical combination of matter and the moving force, the next step was to a consciously determined distinction, to a mechanical division of the two. Thus Empedocles combining the doctrines of Heraclitus and Parmenides, considered matter as the abiding being, while force was the ground of the movement. But the Atomists still considered the moving mythic energies as forces ; Empedocles regarded them as love and hate ; and Democritus as unconscious necessity. The result was, therefore, that the becoming was rather limited as a means for the mechanical explanation of nature, than itself explained.

6. Despairing of any merely materialistic explanation of the becoming, *Anaxagoras* next appears, and places a world-forming Intelligence by the side of matter. He recognized mind as the primal causality, to which the existence of the world, together with its determined arrangement and design (*zweckmässigkeit*) must be referred. In this, philosophy gained a great principle, viz.—an ideal one. But Anaxagoras did not know how to fully carry out his principles. Instead of a theoretical comprehension of the universe—instead of deriving being from the idea, he grasped

again after some mechanical explanation. His "world forming reason" serves him only as a first impulse, only as a moving power. It is to him a *Deus ex machina*. Notwithstanding, therefore, his glimpse of something higher than matter, yet was Anaxagoras only a physical philosopher, like his predecessors Mind had not yet appeared to him as a true force above nature, as an organizing soul of the universe.

7. It is, therefore, a farther progress in thought, to comprehend accurately the distinction between mind and nature, and to recognize mind as something higher and contra-distinguished from all natural being. This problem fell to the *Sophists*. They entangled in contradictions, the thinking which had been confined to the object, to that which was given, and gave to the objective world which had before been exalted above the subject, a subordinate position in the dawning and yet infantile consciousness of the superiority of subjective thinking. The Sophists carried their principle of subjectivity, though at first this was only negative, into the form of the universal religious and political changing condition (*Aufklärung*).* They stood forth as the destroyers of the whole edifice of thought that had been thus far built until *Socrates* appeared, and set up against this principle of *empirical* subjectivity, that of the *absolute* subjectivity,—that of the spirit in the form of a free moral will, and the thought is positively considered as something higher than existence, as the truth of all reality. With the Sophist closes our first period, for with these the oldest philosophy finds its self-destruction (*Selbstauflösung*).

---

* This word literally means *clearing up*, but has a philosophical sense for which no precise equivalent is found in the English language. When used physically, it denotes that every obstruction which prevented the clear sight of the bodily eye is removed, and when used psychologically it implies the same fact in reference to our mental vision. The *Aufklärung* in philosophy is hence the clearing up of difficulties which have hindered a true philosophical insight. To express this, I know of no better word than the literal rendering, "*up-clearing*" or "*clearing up*," which the reader will find adopted in the following pages.—TRANSLATOR.

SECTION IV.

THE IONIC PHILOSOPHERS.

1. THALES.—At the head of the Ionic natural philosophers and therefore at the head of philosophy, the ancients are generally agreed in placing Thales of Miletus, a cotemporary of Crœsus and Solon; although this beginning lies more in the region of tradition than of history. The philosophical principle to which he owes his place in the history of philosophy is, that, "the principle (the primal, the original ground) of all things is water; from water every thing arises and into water every thing returns." But simply to assume water as the original ground of things was not to advance beyond his myth-making predecessors and their cosmologies. Aristotle, himself, when speaking of Thales, refers to the old "theologians,"—meaning, doubtless, Homer and Hesiod, —who had ascribed to Oceanus and Tethys, the origin of all things. Thales, however, merits his place as the beginner of philosophy, because he made the first attempt to establish his physical principle, without resorting to a mythical representation, and, therefore, brought into philosophy a scientific procedure. He is the first who has placed his foot upon the ground of a logical (*verständig*) explanation of nature. We cannot now say with certainty, how he came to adopt his principle, though he might have been led to it, by perceiving that dampness belonged to the seed and nourishment of things; that warmth is developed from moisture; and that, generally, moisture might be the plastic, living and life-giving principle. From the condensation and expansion of this first principle, he derives, as it seems, the changes of things, though the way in which this is done, he has not accurately determined.

The philosophical significance of Thales does not appear to extend any farther. He was not a speculative philosopher after a later mode. Philosophical book-making was not at all the order of his day, and he does not seem to have given any of his opinions a written form.   On account of his ethico-political wisdom, he is numbered among the so-named " seven wise men," and the characteristics which the ancients furnish concerning him only testify to his practical understanding.   He is said e. g. to have first calculated an eclipse of the sun, to have superintended the turning of the course of the Halys under Crœsus, &c.   When subsequent narrators relate that he had asserted the unity of the world, had set up the idea of a world-soul, and had taught the immortality of the soul and the personality of God, it is doubtless an unhistorical reference of later ideas to a stand-point, which was, as yet, far from being developed.

2. ANAXIMANDER.—Anaximander, sometimes represented by the ancients as a scholar and sometimes as a companion of Thales, but who was, at all events, younger than the latter, sought to carry out still farther his principles.   The original essence which he assumed, and which he is said to have been the first to name principle ($\dot{\alpha}\rho\chi\eta$), he defined as the " unlimited, eternal, and unconditioned," as that which embraced all things and ruled all things, and which, since it lay at the basis of all determinateness of the finite and the changeable, is itself infinite and undeterminate.   How we are to regard this original essence of Anaximander is a matter of dispute.   Evidently it was not one of the four common elements, though we must not, therefore, think it was something incorporeal and immaterial.   Anaximander probably conceived it as the original matter before it had separated into determined elements,—as that which was first in the order of time, or what is in our day called the chemical indifference in the opposition of elements.   In this respect his original essence is indeed " unlimited " and " undetermined," i. e. has no determination of quality nor limit of quantity, yet it is not, therefore, in any way, a pure dynamical principle, as perhaps the " friendship " and " enmity " of Empedocles might have been, but it was only a more philosophical expression for the same thought, which the old cosmogonies have attempted to utter in their representation of chaos.   Accordingly, Anaximander suffers the original opposition

of cold and warm, of dry and moist (*i. e.* the basis of the four elements) to be secreted from his original essence, a clear proof that it was only the undeveloped, unanalyzed, potential being of these elemental opposites.

3. ANAXIMENES.—Anaximenes, who is called by some the scholar, and by others the companion of Anaximander, turned back more closely to the view of Thales, in that he made air as the principle of all things. The perception that air surrounds the whole world, and that breath conditions the activity of life, seems to have led him to his position.

4. RETROSPECT.—The whole philosophy of the three Ionic sages may be reduced to these three points, viz:—(1.) They sought for the universal essence of concrete being; (2.) They found this essence in a material substance or substratum; (3.) They gave some intimation respecting the derivation of the elements from this original matter.

SECTION V.

PYTHAGOREANISM.

1. ITS RELATIVE POSITION.—The development of the Ionic philosophy discloses the tendency to abstract matter from all else; though they directed this process solely to the determined *quality* of matter. It is this abstraction carried to a higher step, when we look away from the sensible concretions of matter, and no more regard its *qualitative* determinateness as water, air, &c., but only direct our attention to its *quantitative* determinateness,—to its space-filling property. But the determinateness of quantity is number, and this is the principle and stand-point of Pythagoreanism.

2. HISTORICAL AND CHRONOLOGICAL.—The Pythagorean doctrine of numbers is referred to Pythagoras of Samos, who is said to have flourished between 540 and 500 B. C. He dwelt in the

latter part of his life at Crotonia, in Magna Grecia, where he founded a society, or, more properly, an order, for the moral and political regeneration of the lower Italian cities. Through this society, this new direction of philosophy seems to have been introduced,—though more as a mode of life than in the form of a scientific theory. What is related concerning the life of Pythagoras, his journeys, the new order which he founded, his political influence upon the lower Italian cities, &c., is so thoroughly interwoven with traditions, legends, and palpable fabrications, that we can be certain at no point that we stand upon a historical basis. Not only the old Pythagoreans, who have spoken of him, delighted in the mysterious and esoteric, but even his new-Platonistic biographers, Porphyry and Jamblichus, have treated his life as a historico-philosophical romance. We have the same uncertainty in reference to his doctrines, *i. e.* in reference to his share in the number-theory. Aristotle, *e. g.* does not ascribe this to Pythagoras himself, but only to the Pythagoreans generally, *i. e.* to their school. The accounts which are given respecting his school have no certainty till the time of Socrates, a hundred years after Pythagoras. Among the few sources of light which we have upon this subject, are the mention made in Plato's Phædon of the Pythagorean Philolaus and his doctrines, and the writings of Archytas, a cotemporary of Plato. We possess in fact the Pythagorean doctrine only in the manner in which it was taken up by Philolaus, Eurytas and Archytas, since its earlier adherents left nothing in a written form.

3. The Pythagorean Principle.—The ancients are united in affirming that the principle of the Pythagorean philosophy was number. But in what sense was this their principle—in a material or a formal sense? Did they hold number as the material of things, *i. e.* did they believe that things had their origin in numbers, or did they regard it as the archetype of things, *i. e.* did they believe that things were made as the copy or the representation of numbers? From this very point the accounts given by the ancients diverge, and even the expressions of Aristotle seem to contradict each other. At one time he speaks of Pythagorean-

ism in the former, and at another in the latter sense. From this circumstance modern scholars have concluded that the Pythagorean doctrine of numbers had different forms of development; that some of the Pythagoreans regarded numbers as the substances and others as the archetypes of things. Aristotle, however, gives an intimation how the two statements may be reconciled with each other. Originally, without doubt, the Pythagoreans regarded number as the material, as the inherent essence of things, and therefore Aristotle places them together with the Hylics (the Ionic natural philosophers), and says of them that "they held things for numbers" (*Metaph.* I., 5, 6). But as the Hylics did not identify their matter, *e. g.* water, immediately with the sensuous thing, but only gave it out as the fundamental element, as the original form of the individual thing, so, on the other side, numbers also might be regarded as similar fundamental types, and therefore Aristotle might say of the Pythagoreans, that "they held numbers to be the corresponding original forms of being, as water, air, &c." But if there still remains a degree of uncertainty in the expressions of Aristotle respecting the sense of the Pythagorean doctrine of numbers, it can only have its ground in the fact that the Pythagoreans did not make any distinction between a formal and material principle, but contented themselves with the undeveloped view, that, "number is the essence of things, every thing is number."

4. The carrying out of this Principle.—From the very nature of the "number-principle," it follows that its complete application to the province of the real, can only lead to a fruitless and empty symbolism. If we take numbers as even and odd, and still farther as finite and infinite, and apply them as such to astronomy, music, psychology, ethics, &c., there arise combinations like the following, viz.: one is the point, two are the line, three are the superficies, four are the extension of a body, five are the condition (*beschaffenheit*), &c.—still farther, the soul is a musical harmony, as is also virtue, the soul of the world, &c. Not only the philosophical, but even the historical interest here ceases, since the ancients themselves—as was unavoidable from the

2

arbitrary nature of such combinations—have given the most contradictory account, some affirming that the Pythagoreans reduced righteousness to the number three, others, that they reduced it to the number four, others again to five, and still others to nine. Naturally, from such a vague and arbitrary philosophizing, there would early arise, in this, more than in other schools, a great diversity of views, one ascribing this signification to a certain mathematical form, and another that. In this mysticism of numbers, that which alone has truth and value, is the thought, which lies at the ground of it all, that there prevails in the phenomena of nature a rational order, harmony and conformity to law, and that these laws of nature can be represented in measure and number. But this truth has the Pythagorean school hid under extravagant fancies, as vapid as they are unbridled.

The physics of the Pythagoreans possesses little scientific value, with the exception of the doctrine taught by Philolaus respecting the circular motion of the earth. Their ethics is also defective. What we have remaining of it relates more to the Pythagorean life, i. e. to the practice and discipline of their order than to their philosophy. The whole tendency of Pythagoreanism was in a practical respect ascetic, and directed to a strict culture of the character. As showing this, we need only to cite their doctrines concerning the transmigration of the soul, or, as it has been called, their "immortality doctrine," their notion in respect of the lower world, their opposition to suicide, and their view of the body as the prison of the soul—all of which ideas are referred to in Plato's Phædon, and the last two of which are indicated as belonging to Philolaus.

SECTION VI

THE ELEATICS.

1. RELATION OF THE ELEATIC PRINCIPLE TO THE PYTHAGO-REAN.—While the Pythagoreans had made matter, in so far as it is quantity and the manifold, the basis of their philosophizing, and while in this they only abstracted from the determined elemental condition of matter, the Eleatics carry the process to its ultimate limit, and make, as the principle of their philosophy, a total abstraction from every finite determinateness, from every change and vicissitude which belongs to concrete being. While the Pythagoreans had held fast to the form of being as having existence in space and time, the Eleatics reject this, and make as their fundamental thought the negation of all exterior and posterior. Only being is, and there is no not-being, nor becoming. This being is the purely undetermined, changeless ground of all things. It is not being *in* becoming, but it is being as exclusive of all becoming; in other words, it is pure being.

Eleaticism is, therefore, Monism, in so far as it strove to carry back the manifoldness of all being to a single ultimate principle; but on the other hand it becomes Dualism, in so far as it could neither carry out its denial of concrete existence, *i. e.*, the phenomenal world, nor yet derive the latter from its presupposed original ground. The phenomenal world, though it might be explained as only an empty appearance, did yet exist; and, since the sensuous perception would not ignore this, there must be allowed it, hypothetically at least, the right of existence. Its origin must be explained, even though with reservations. This contradiction of an unreconciled Dualism between being and existence, is the point where the Eleatic philosophy is at war with itself—though, in the beginning of the school—with *Xenophanes*, it does not yet appear. The principle itself, with its results, is only fully apparent in the lapse of time. It has three periods of formation, which successively appear in three successive generations. Its foundation belongs to *Xenophanes;* its systematic formation to *Parmenides;* its completion and partial dissolution to *Zeno* and *Melissus*—the latter of whom we can pass by.

2. XENOPHANES.—Xenophanes is considered as the originator of the Eleatic tendency. He was born at Colophon; emigrated to Elea, a Phocæan colony in Lucania, and was a younger cotemporary of Pythagoras. He appears to have first uttered the proposition—" every thing is one," without, however, giving any more explicit determination respecting this unity, whether it be one simply in conception or in actuality. Turning his attention, says Aristotle, upon the world as a whole, he names the unity which he finds, God. God is the One. The Eleatic " One and All " (ἐν καὶ πᾶν) had, therefore, with Xenophanes, a theological and religious character. The idea of the unity of God, and an opposition to the anthropomorphism of the ordinary views of religion, is his starting point. He declaimed against the delusion that the gods were born, that they had a human voice or form, and railed at the robbery, adultery, and deceit of the gods as sung by Homer and Hesiod. According to him the Godhead is wholly seeing, wholly understanding, wholly hearing, unmoved, undivided, calmly ruling all things by his thought, like men neither in form nor in understanding. In this way, with his thought turned only towards removing from the Godhead all finite determinations and predicates, and holding fast to its unity and unchangeableness, he declared this doctrine of its being to be the highest philosophical principle, without however directing this principle polemically against the doctrine of finite being, or carrying it out in its negative application.

3. PARMENIDES.—The proper head of the Eleatic school is Parmenides of Elea, a scholar, or at least an adherent of Xenophanes. Though we possess but little reliable information respecting the circumstances of his life, yet we have, in inverse proportion, the harmonious voice of all antiquity in an expression of reverence for the Eleatic sage, and of admiration for the depth of his mind, as well as for the earnestness and elevation

of his character. The saying—"a life like Parmenides," became afterwards a proverb among the Greeks.

Parmenides embodied his philosophy in an epic poem, of which we have still important fragments. It is divided into two parts. In the first he discusses the conception of being. Rising far above the yet unmediated view of Xenophanes, he attains a conception of pure single being, which he sets up as absolutely opposed to every thing manifold and changeable, *i. e.*, to that which has no being, and which consequently cannot be thought. From this conception of being he not only excludes all becoming and departing, but also all relation to space and time, all divisibility and movement. This being he explains as something which has not become and which does not depart, as complete and of its own kind, as unalterable and without limit, as indivisible and present though not in time, and since all these are only negative, he ascribes to it, also, as a positive determination— thought. Being and thought are therefore identical with Parmenides. This pure thought, directed to the pure being, he declares is the only true and undeceptive knowledge, in opposition to the deceptive notions concerning the manifoldness and mutability of the phenomenal. He has no hesitancy in holding that to be only a name which mortals regard as truth, viz., becoming and departing, being and not-being, change of place and vicissitude of circumstance. We must therefore be careful not to hold "the One" of Parmenides, as the collective unity of all concrete being.

So much for the first part of Parmenides' poem. After the principle that there is only being has been developed according to its negative and positive determinations, we might believe that the system was at an end. But there follows a second part, which is occupied solely with the hypothetical attempt to explain the phenomenal world and give it a physical derivation. Though firmly convinced that, according to reason and conception, there is only "the One," yet is Parmenides unable to withdraw himself from the recognition of an appearing manifoldness and change. Forced, therefore, by his sensuous perception to enter upon a discussion of the phenomenal world, he prefaces this second part of his poem with the remark, that he had now closed what he had to say respecting the truth, and was hereafter to deal only with the opinion of a mortal. Unfortunately, this second part has been very imperfectly transmitted to us. Enough however remains to show, that he explained the phenomena of nature from the mingling of two unchangeable elements, which Aristotle, though apparently only by way of example, indicates as warm and cold, fire and earth. Concerning these two elements, Aristotle remarks still farther that Parmenides united the warmth with being, and the other element with not-being.

It is scarcely necessary to remark that between the two parts of the Parmenidean philosophy—between the doctrine concerning being and the doctrine concerning appearance—there can exist no inner scientific connection. What Parmenides absolutely denies in the first part, and indeed declares to be unutterable, viz., the not-being, the many and the changeable, he yet in the second part admits to have an existence at least in the representation of men. But it is clear that the not-being cannot once exist in the representation, if it does not exist generally and every where, and that the attempt to explain a not-being of the representation, is in complete contradiction with his exclusive recognition of being. This contradiction, this unmediated juxtaposition of being and not-being, of the one and the many, *Zeno*, a scholar of Parmenides, sought to remove, by affirming that from the very conception of being, the sensuous representation, and thus the world of the not-being, are dialectically annihilated.

4. ZENO.—The Eleatic Zeno was born about 500 B. C.; was a scholar of Parmenides, and the earliest prose writer among the Grecian philosophers. He is said to have written in the form of dialogues. He perfected, dialectically, the doctrine of his master, and carried out to the completest extent the abstraction of the Eleatic One, in opposition to the manifoldness and determinateness of the finite. He justified the doctrine of a single, simple, and unchangeable being, in a polemical way, by showing up the contradictions into which the ordinary representations of the

phenomenal world become involved. While Parmenides affirms that there is only the One, Zeno shows in his well-known proofs (which unfortunately we cannot here more widely unfold), that the many, the changing, that which has relation to space, or that which has relation to time, is not. While Parmenides affirmed the being, Zeno denied the appearance. On account of these proofs, in which Zeno takes up the conceptions of extension, manifoldness and movement, and shows their inner contradictory nature, Aristotle names him the founder of dialectics.

While the philosophizing of Zeno is the completion of the Eleatic principle, so is it at the same time the beginning of its dissolution. Zeno had embraced the opposition of being and existence, of the one and the many, so abstractly, and had carried it so far, that with him the inner contradiction of the Eleatic principle comes forth still more boldly than with Parmenides; for the more logical he is in the denial of the phenomenal world, so much the more striking must be the contradiction, of turning, on the one side, his whole philosophical activity to the refutation of the sensuous representation, while, on the other side, he sets over against it a doctrine which destroys the very possibility of a false representation.

SECTION VII.

HERACLITUS.

1. Relation of the Heraclitic Principle to the Eleatic.—Being and existence, the one and the many, could not be united by the principle of the Eleatics; the Monism which they had striven for had resulted in an ill-concealed Dualism. Heraclitus reconciled this contradiction by affirming that being and not-being, the one and the many, existed at the same time as the becoming. While the Eleatics could not extricate themselves from the dilemma that the world is either being or not-being,

Heraclitus removes the difficulty by answering—it is neither be-ing nor not-being, because it is both.

2. HISTORICAL AND CHRONOLOGICAL.—Heraclitus, surnamed by later writers the obscure, was born at Ephesus, and flourished about 500 B. C. His period was subsequent to that of Xeno-phanes, though partially cotemporary with that of Parmenides. He laid down his philosophical thoughts in a writing "Concern-ing Nature," of which we possess only fragments. Its rapid transitions, its expressions so concise and full of meaning, the general philosophical peculiarity of Heraclitus, and the antique character of the earliest prose writings, all combine to make this work so difficult to be understood that it has long been a proverb. Socrates said concerning it, that "what he understood of it was excellent, and he had no doubt that what he did not understand was equally good; but the book requires an expert swimmer." Later Stoics and Academicians have written commentaries upon it.

3. THE PRINCIPLE OF THE BECOMING.—The ancients unite in ascribing to Heraclitus the principle that the totality of things should be conceived in an eternal flow, in an uninterrupted move-ment and transformation, and that all continuance of things is only appearance. "Into the same stream," so runs a saying of Heraclitus, "we descend, and at the same time we do not de-scend; we are, and also we are not. For into the same stream we cannot possibly descend twice, since it is always scattering and collecting itself again, or rather it at the same time flows to us and from us." There is, therefore, ground for the assertion that Heraclitus had banished all rest and continuance from the totality of things; and it is doubtless in this very respect that he accuses the eye and the ear of deception, because they reveal to men a continuance where there is only an uninterrupted change.

Heraclitus has analyzed the principle of the becoming still more closely, in the propositions which he utters, to account for the origin of things, where he shows that all becoming must be conceived as the product of warring opposites, as the harmonious union of opposite determinations. Hence his two well-known propositions : " Strife is the father of things," and " The One setting itself at variance with itself, harmonizes with itself, like the harmony of the bow and the viol." " Unite," so runs another of his sayings, " the whole and the not-whole, the coalescing and the not-coalescing, the harmonious and the discordant, and thus we have the one becoming from the all, and the all from the one."

4. THE PRINCIPLE OF FIRE.—In what relation does the principle of fire, which is also ascribed to Heraclitus, stand to the principle of the becoming? Aristotle says that he took fire as his principle, in the same way that Thales took water, and Anaximenes took air. But it is clear we must not interpret this to mean that Heraclitus regarded fire as the original material or fundamental element of things, after the manner of the Ionics. If he ascribed reality only to the becoming, it is impossible that he should have set by the side of this becoming, yet another elemental matter as a fundamental substance. When, therefore, Heraclitus calls the world an ever-living fire, which in certain stages and certain degrees extinguishes and again enkindles itself, when he says that every thing can be exchanged for fire, and fire for every thing, just as we barter things for gold and gold for things, he can only mean thereby that fire represents the abiding power of this eternal transformation and transposition, in other words, the conception of life, in the most obvious and effective way. We might name fire, in the Heraclitic sense, the symbol · or the manifestation of the becoming, but that it is also with him the substratum of movement, i. e. the means with which the power of movement, which is antecedent to all matter, serves it self in order to bring out the living process of things. In the same way Heraclitus goes on to explain the manifoldness of things, by affirming that they arise from certain hindrances and a partial extinction of this fire. The product of its extremest hindrance is the earth, and the other things lie intermediately between.

5. TRANSITION TO THE ATOMISTS.—We have above regarded the Heraclitic principle as the consequent of the Eleatic, but we

2*

might as properly consider the two as antitheses. While Heraclitus destroys all abiding being in an absolutely flowing becoming,
so, on the other hand, Parmenides destroys all becoming in an
absolutely abiding being; and while the former charges the eye
and the ear with deception, in that they transform the flowing
becoming into a quiescent being, the latter also accuses these
same senses of an untrue representation, in that they draw the
abiding being into the movement of the becoming. We can
therefore say that the being and the becoming are equally valid
antitheses, which demand again a synthesis and reconciliation.
But now can we say that Heraclitus actually and satisfactorily
solved the problem of Zeno? Zeno had shown every thing actual
to be a contradiction, and from this had inferred their not-being,
and it is only in this inference that Heraclitus deviates from the
Eleatics. He also regarded the phenomenal world as an existing
contradiction, but he clung to this contradiction as to an ultimate
fact. That which had been the negative result of the Eleatics,
he uttered as his positive principle. The dialectics which Zeno
had subjectively used against the phenomenal, he directed objectively as a proof for the becoming. But this becoming which the
Eleatics had thought themselves obliged to deny entirely, Heraclitus did not explain by simply asserting that it was the only
true principle. The question continually returned—why is all
being a becoming? Why does the one go out ever into the
.many? To give an answer to this question, i. e. to explain the
becoming from the pre-supposed principle of being, forms the
stand-point and problem of the *Empedoclean* and *Atomistic*
philosophy.

SECTION VIII.

EMPEDOCLES.

1. GENERAL VIEW.—Empedocles was born at Agrigentum, and is extolled by the ancients as a natural philosopher, physician and poet, and also as a seer and worker of miracles. He flourished about 440 B. C., and was consequently younger than Parmenides and Heraclitus. He wrote a doctrinal poem concerning nature, which has been preserved to us in tolerably complete fragments. His philosophical system may be characterized in brief, as an attempt to combine the Eleatic being and the Heraclitic becoming. Starting with the Eleatic thought, that neither any thing which had previously been could become, nor any thing which now is could depart, he sets up as unchangeable being, four eternal original materials, which, though divisible, were independent, and underived from each other. In this we have what in our day are called the four elements. With this Eleatic thought he united also the Heraclitic view of nature, and suffered his four elements to become mingled together, and to receive a form by the working of two moving powers, which he names unifying friendship and dividing strife. Originally, these four elements were absolutely alike and unmovable, dwelling together in a divine sphere where friendship united them, until gradually strife pressing from the circumference to the centre of the sphere (*i. e.* attaining a separating activity), broke this union, and the formation of the world immediately began as the result.

2. THE FOUR ELEMENTS.—With his doctrine of the four elements, Empedocles, on the one side, may be joined to the series of the Ionic philosophers, but, on the other, he is excluded from this by his assuming the original elements to be four. He is distinctly said by the ancients to have originated the theory of the four elements. He is more definitely distinguished from the old Ionics, from the fact that he ascribed to his four "root-elements" a changeless being, by virtue of which they neither arose from

each other nor departed into each other, and were capable of no change of essence but only of a change of state. Every thing which is called arising and departing, every change rests there-fore only upon the mingling and withdrawing of these eternal and fundamental materials; the inexhaustible manifoldness of being rests upon the different proportions in which these elements are mingled. Every becoming is conceived as such only as a change of place. In this we have a mechanical in opposition to a dynamic explanation of nature.

3. THE TWO POWERS.—Whence now can arise any becoming, if in matter itself there is found no principle to account for the change? Since Empedocles did not, like the Eleatics, deny that there was change, nor yet, like Heraclitus, introduce it in his matter, as an indwelling principle, so there was no other course left him but to place, by the side of his matter, a moving power. The opposition of the one and the many which had been set up by his predecessors, and which demanded an explanation, led him to ascribe to this moving power, two originally diverse directions, viz.: repulsion and attraction. The separation of the one into the many, and the union again of the many into the one, had in-dicated an opposition of powers which Heraclitus had already recognized. While now Parmenides starting from the one had made love as his principle, and Heraclitus starting from the many had made strife as his, Empedocles combines the two as the prin-ciple of his philosophy. The difficulty is, he has not sufficiently limited in respect to one another, the sphere of operation of these two directions of his power. Although to friendship belonged peculiarly the attractive, and to strife the repelling function, yet does Empedocles, on the other hand, suffer his strife to have in the formation of the world a unifying, and his friendship a dividing effect. In fact, the complete separation of a dividing and unify-ing power in the movement of the becoming, is an unmaintainable abstraction.

4. RELATION OF THE EMPEDOCLEAN TO THE ELEATIC AND HERACLITIC PHILOSOPHY.—Empedocles, by placing, as the prin-ciple of the becoming, a moving power by the side of his matter,

makes his philosophy a mediation of the Eleatic and Heraclitic principles, or more properly a placing of them side by side. He has interwoven these two principles in equal proportions in his system. With the Eleatics he denied all arising and departing, *i. e.* the transition of being into not-being and of not-being into being, and with Heraclitus he shared the interest to find an explanation for change. From the former he derived the abiding, unchangeable being of his fundamental matter, and from the latter the principle of the moving power. With the Eleatics, in fine, he considered the true being in an original and undistinguishable unity as a sphere, and with Heraclitus, he regarded the present world as a constant product of striving powers and oppositions. He has, therefore, been properly called an Eclectic, who has united the fundamental thoughts of his two predecessors, though not always in a logical way.

SECTION IX.

THE ATOMISTIC PHILOSOPHY.

1. ITS PROPOUNDERS.—Empedocles had sought to effect a combination of the Eleatic and Heraclitic principle—the same was attempted, though in a different way, by the Atomists, Leucippus and Democritus. Democritus, the better known of the two, was the son of rich parents, and was born about 460 B. C. in Abdera, an Ionian colony. He travelled extensively, and no Greek before the time of Aristotle possessed such varied attainments. He embodied the wealth of his collected knowledge in a series of writings, of which, however, only a few fragments have come down to us. For rhythm and elegance of language, Cicero compared him with Plato. He died in a good old age.

2. THE ATOMS.—Empedocles derived all determinateness of the phenomenal from a certain number of qualitatively determined and undistinguishable original materials, while the Atomists de-

rived the same from an originally unlimited number of constituent elements, or atoms, which were homogeneous in respect of quality, but diverse in respect of form. These atoms are unchangeable, material particles, possessing indeed extension, but yet indivisible, and can only be determined in respect of magnitude. As being, and without quality, they are entirely incapable of any transformation or qualitative change, and, therefore, all becoming is, as with Empedocles, only a change of place. The manifoldness of the phenomenal world is only to be explained from the different form, disposition, and arrangement of the atoms as they become, in various ways, united.

3. THE FULNESS AND THE VOID.—The atoms, in order to be atoms, *i. e.* undivided and impenetrable unities,—must be mutually limited and separated. There must be something set over against them which preserves them as atoms, and which is the original cause of their separateness and impenetrability. This is the void space, or more strictly the intervals which are found between the atoms, and which hinder their mutual contact. The atoms, as being and absolute fulness, and the interval between them, as the void and the not-being, are two determinations which only represent in a real and objective way, what are in thought, as logical conceptions, the two elements in the Heraclitic becoming, viz. being and the not-being. But since the void space is one determination of being, it must possess objective reality no less than the atoms, and Democritus even went so far as to expressly affirm in opposition to the Eleatics, that being is no more than nothing.

4. THE ATOMISTIC NECESSITY.—Democritus, like Empedocles, though far more extensively than he, attempted to answer the question—whence arise these changes and movements which we behold ? Wherein lies the ground that the atoms should enter into these manifold combinations, and bring forth such a wealth of inorganic and organic forms ? Democritus attempted to solve the problem by affirming that the ground of movement lay in the gravity or original condition of the material particles, and, therefore, in the matter itself, but in this way he only talked about the

question without answering it. The idea of an infinite series of causalities was thus attained, but not a final ground of all the manifestations of the becoming, and of change. Such a final ground was still to be sought, and as Democritus expressly declared that it could not lie in an ultimate reason ($\nu o \hat{\nu} \varsigma$), where Anaxagoras placed it, there only remained for him to find it in an absolute necessity, or a necessary pre-determinateness ($\dot{\alpha} \nu \acute{\alpha} \gamma \kappa \eta$). This he adopted as his " final ground," and is said to have named it chance ($\tau \acute{\nu} \chi \eta$), in opposition to the inquiry after final causes, or the Anaxagorean teleology. Consequent upon this, we find as the prominent characteristic of the later Atomistic school (Diagoras the Melier), polemics against the gods of the people, and a constantly more publicly affirmed Atheism and Materialism.

5. RELATIVE POSITION OF THE ATOMISTIC PHILOSOPHY.—Hegel characterizes the relative position of the Atomistic Philosophy as follows, viz. :—" In the Eleatic Philosophy being and not-being stand as antitheses,—being alone is, and not-being is not; in the Heraclitic idea, being and not-being are the same,—both together, *i. e.* the becoming, are the predicate of concrete being; but being and not-being, as objectively determined, or in other words, as appearing to the sensuous intuition, are precisely the same as the antithesis of the fulness and the void. Parmenides, Heraclitus and the Atomists all sought for the abstract universal; Parmenides found it in *being*, Heraclitus in the *process* of being *per se*, and the Atomists in the *determination* of being *per se*." So much of this as ascribes to the Atomists the characteristic predicate of being *per se* is doubtless correct,—but the real thought of the Atomistic system is rather analogous with the Empedoclean, to explain the possibility of the becoming, by presupposing these substances as possessing being *per se*, but without quality. To this end the not-being or the void, *i. e.* the side which is opposed to the Eleatic principle, is elaborated with no less care than the side which harmonizes with it, *i. e.* that the atoms are without quality and never change in their original elements. The Atomistic Philosophy is therefore a mediation between the Eleatic and the Heraclitic principles. It is Eleatic in affirming the undivided

being *per se* of the atoms ;—Heraclitic, in declaring their mul-
teity and manifoldness. It is Eleatic in the declaration of an
absolute fulness in the atoms, and Heraclitic in the claim of a
real not-being, *i. e.* the void space. It is Eleatic in its denial of
the becoming, *i. e.* of the arising and departing,—and Heraclitic
in its affirmation that to the atoms belong movement and a capacity for unlimited combinations. The Atomists carried out their
leading thought more logically than Empedocles, and we might
even say that their system is the perfection of a purely mechanical
explanation of nature, since all subsequent Atomists, even to our
own day, have only repeated their fundamental conceptions. But
the great defect which cleaves to every Atomistic system, Aristotle has justly recognized, when he shows that it is a contradiction, on the one hand, to set up something corporeal or space-filling
as indivisible, and on the other, to derive the extended from that
which has no extension, and that the consciousless and inconceivable necessity of Democritus is especially defective, in that it
totally banishes from nature all conception of design. This is
the point to which Anaxagoras turns his attention, and introduces
his principle of an intelligence working with design.

SECTION X.

ANAXAGORAS.

1. His Personal History.—Anaxagoras is said to have been
born at Clazomenæ, about the year 500 B. C.; to have gone to
Athens immediately, or soon after the Persian war, to have lived
and taught there for a long time, and, finally, accused of irreve-
rence to the gods, to have fled, and died at Lampsacus, at the age
of 72. He it was who first planted philosophy at Athens, which
from this time on became the centre of intellectual life in Greece.
Through his personal relations to Pericles, Euripides, and other
important men,—among whom Themistocles and Thucydides

should be named—he exerted a decisive influence upon the culture of the age. It was on account of this that the charge of defaming the gods was brought against him, doubtless by the political opponents of Pericles. Anaxagoras wrote a work " *Concerning Nature*," which in the time of Socrates was widely circulated.

2. HIS RELATION TO HIS PREDECESSORS.—The system of Anaxagoras starts from the same point with his predecessors, and is simply another attempt at the solution of the same problem. Like Empedocles and the Atomists so did Anaxagoras most vehemently deny the becoming. " The becoming and departing,"—so runs one of his sayings—" the Greeks hold without foundation, for nothing can ever be said to become or depart; but, since existing things may be compounded together and again divided, we should name the becoming more correctly a combination, and the departing a separation." From this view, that every thing arose by the mingling of different elements, and departed by the withdrawing of these elements, Anaxagoras, like his predecessors, was obliged to separate matter from the moving power. But though his point of starting was the same, yet was his direction essentially different from that of any previous philosopher. It was clear that neither Empedocles nor Democritus had satisfactorily apprehended the moving power. The mythical energies of love and hate of the one, or the unconscious necessity of the other, explained nothing, and least of all, the design of the becoming in nature. The conception of an activity which could thus work designedly, must, therefore, be brought into the conception of the moving power, and this Anaxagoras accomplished by setting up the idea of a world-forming intelligence (νοῦς), absolutely separated from all matter and working with design.

3. THE PRINCIPLE OF THE νοῦς.—Anaxagoras described this intelligence as free to dispose, unmingled with any thing, the ground of movement, but itself unmoved, every where active, and the most refined and pure of all things. Although these predicates rest partly upon a physical analogy, and do not exhibit purely the conception of immateriality, yet on the other hand

does the attribute of thought and of a conscious acting with design admit no doubt to remain of the decided idealistic character
of the Anaxagorean principle.   Nevertheless, Anaxagoras went
no farther than to enunciate his fundamental thought without
attempting its complete application.   The explanation of this is
obvious from the reasons which first led him to adopt his principle.   It was only the need of an original cause of motion, to
which also might be attributed the capacity to work designedly,
which had led him to the idea of an immaterial principle.   His
νοῦς, therefore, is almost nothing but a mover of matter, and in
this function nearly all its activity is expended.   Hence the universal complaint of the ancients, especially of Plato and Aristotle, respecting the mechanical character of his doctrine.   In
Plato's Phædon Socrates relates that, in the hope of being
directed beyond a simple occasioning, or mediate cause, he had
turned to the book of Anaxagoras, but had found there only a
mechanical instead of a truly teleological explanation of being.
And as Plato so also does Aristotle find fault with Anaxagoras in
that, while he admits mind as the ultimate ground of things, he
yet resorts to it only as to a *Deus ex machina* for the explanation
of phenomena, whose necessity he could not derive from the
causality in nature.   Anaxagoras, therefore, has rather postulated
than proved mind as an energy above nature, and as the truth and
actuality of natural being.

The further extension of his system, his doctrine concerning
the homoiomeria (constituent elements of things), which according
to him existed together originally in a chaotic condition until with
their separation and parting the formation of the world began—
can here only be mentioned.

4. ANAXAGORAS AS THE CLOSE OF THE PRE-SOCRATIC REAL-
ISM.—With the Anaxagorean principle of the νοῦς, *i. e.* with the
acquisition of an absolutely immaterial principle, closes the realistic period of the old Grecian Philosophy.   Anaxagoras combined together the principles of all his predecessors.   The infinite
matter of the Hylics is represented in his chaotic original mingling of things; the Eleatic pure being appears in the idea of the

νοῦς; the Heraclitic power of becoming and the Empedoclean moving energies are both seen in the creating and arranging power of the eternal mind, while the Democritic atoms come to view in the homoiomeria. Anaxagoras is the closing point of an old and the beginning point of a new course of development,—the latter through the setting up of his ideal principle, and the former through the defective and completely physical manner in which this principle was yet again applied.

SECTION XI.

THE SOPHISTIC PHILOSOPHY.

1. RELATION OF THE SOPHISTIC PHILOSOPHY TO THE ANAXA-GOREAN PRINCIPLE.—Anaxagoras had formed the conception of mind, and in this had recognized thought as a power above the objective world. Upon this newly conquered field the Sophistic philosophy now began its gambols, and with childish wantonness delighted itself in setting at work this power, and in destroying, by means of a subjective dialectic, all objective determinations. The Sophistic philosophy—though of far more significance from its relation to the culture of the age than from its philosophy—had for its starting principle the breach which Anaxagoras had commenced between the subjective and the objective,—the Ego and the external world. The subject, after recognizing himself as something higher than the objective world, and especially as something above the laws of the state, above custom and religious tradition and the popular faith, in the next place attempted to prescribe laws for this objective world, and instead of beholding in it the historical manifestation of reason, he looked upon it only as an exanimated matter, upon which he might exercise his will.

The Sophistic philosophy should be characterized as the clearing up reflection. It is, therefore, no philosophical system, for its doctrines and affirmations exhibit often so popular and even trivial

a character that for their own sake they would merit no place at
all in the history of philosophy. It is also no philosophical school
in the ordinary sense of the term,—for Plato cites a vast number
of persons under the common name of " Sophists,"—but it is an
intellectual and widely spread direction of the age, which had struck
its roots into the whole moral, political, and religious character
of the Athenian life of that time, and which may be called the
Athenian clearing up period.

2. RELATION OF THE SOPHISTIC PHILOSOPHY TO THE UNIVER-
SAL LIFE OF THAT AGE.—The Sophistic philosophy is, theoretically, what the whole Athenian life during the Peloponnesian war
was practically.   Plato justly remarks in his Republic that the
doctrines of the Sophists only expressed the very principles which
guided the course of the great mass of men of that time in their
civil and social relations, and the hatred with which they were
pursued by the practical statesmen, clearly indicates the jealousy
with which the latter saw in them their rivals and the destroyers
of their polity.   If the absoluteness of the empirical subject—*i. e.*
the view that the individual Ego can arbitrarily determine what
is true, right and good,—is in fact the theoretical principle of the
Sophistic philosophy, so does this in a practical direction, as an
unlimited Egoism meet us in all the spheres of the public and
private life of that age.   The public life had become an arena of
passion and selfishness; those party struggles which racked Athens
during the Peloponnesian war had blunted and stifled the moral
feeling; every individual accustomed himself to set up his own
private interest above that of the state and the common weal, and
to seek in his own arbitrariness and advantage the measuring rod
for all his actions.   The Protagorean sentence that "the man is
the measure of all things" became practically carried out only
too faithfully, and the influence of the orator in the assemblies of
the people and the courts, the corruptibility of the great masses
and their leaders, and the weak points which showed to the adroit
student of human nature the covetousness, vanity, and factious-
ness of others around him, offered only too many opportunities to
bring this rule into practice.   Custom had lost its weight; the

laws were regarded as only an agreement of the majority, the civil ordinance as an arbitrary restriction, the moral feeling as the effect of the policy of the state in education, the faith in the gods as a human invention to intimidate the free power of action, while piety was looked upon as a statute which some men have enacted and which every one else is justified in using all his eloquence to change. This degradation of a necessity, which is conformable to nature and reason, and which is of universal validity, —to an accidental human ordinance, is chiefly the point in which the Sophistic philosophy came in contact with the universal consciousness of the educated class of that period, and we cannot with certainty determine what share science and what share the life may have had in this connection,—whether the Sophistic philosophy found only the theoretical formula for the practical life and tendencies of the age, or whether the moral corruption was rather a consequence of that destructive influence which the principles of the Sophists exerted upon the whole course of cotemporaneous thought.

It would be, however, to mistake the spirit of history if we were only to bewail the epoch of the Sophists instead of admitting for it a relative justification. These phenomena were in part the necessary product of the collective development of the age. The faith in the popular religion fell so suddenly to the ground simply because it possessed in itself no inner, moral support. The grossest vices and acts of baseness could all be justified and ex cused from the examples of mythology. Even Plato himself, though otherwise an advocate of a devout faith in the traditional religion, accuses the poets of his nation with leading the very moral feeling astray, through the unworthy representations which they had spread abroad concerning the gods and the hero world. It was moreover unavoidable that the advancing science should clash with tradition. The physical philosophers had already long lived in open hostility to the popular religion, and the more convincingly they demonstrated by analogies and laws that many things which had hitherto been regarded as the immediate effect of Divine omnipotence, were only the results of natural causes so much the more easily would it happen that the educated classes would become perplexed in reference to all their previous convictions. It was no wonder then that the transformed consciousness of the time should penetrate all the provinces of art and poesy; that in sculpture, wholly analogous to the rhetoric art of the Sophistic philosophy, the emotive should occupy the place of the elevated style; that Euripides, the sophist among tragedians, should bring the whole philosophy of the time and its manner of moral reflection upon the stage; and that, instead of like the earlier poets, bringing forward his actors to represent an idea, he should use them only as means to excite a momentary emotion or some other stage effect.

3. TENDENCIES OF THE SOPHISTIC PHILOSOPHY.—To give a definite classification of the Sophistic philosophy, which should be derived from the conception of the general phenomena of the age, is exceedingly difficult, since, like the French "clearing up" of the last century, it entered into every department of knowledge. The Sophists directed the universal culture of the time. Protagoras was known as a teacher of virtue, Gorgias as a rhetorician and politician, Prodicus as a grammarian and teacher of synonyms, Hippias as a man of various attainments, who besides astronomical and mathematical studies busied himself with a theory of mnemonics; others took for their problem the art of education, and others still the explanation of the old poets; the brothers Euthydemus and Dionysidorus gave instruction in the bearing of arms and military tactics; many among them, as Gorgias, Prodicus, and Hippias, were intrusted with embassies: in short the Sophists, each one according to his individual tendency, took upon themselves every variety of calling and entered into every sphere of science; their method is the only thing common to all. Moreover the relation of the Sophists to the educated public, their striving after popularity, fame and money, disclose the fact that their studies and occupations were for the most part controlled, not by a subjective scientific interest, but by some external motive. With that roving spirit which was an essential peculiarity of the later Sophists, travelling from city to city, and

announcing themselves as thinkers by profession—and giving their instructions with prominent reference to a good recompense and the favor of the rich private classes, it was very natural that they should discourse upon the prominent questions of universal interest and of public culture, with occasional reference also to the favorite occupation of this or that rich man with whom they might be brought in contact. Hence their peculiar strength lay far more in a formal dexterity, in an acuteness of thought and a capacity of bringing it readily into exercise, in the art of discourse than in any positive knowledge; their instruction in virtue was given either in positive dogmatism or in empty bombast, and even where the Sophistic philosophy became really polymathic, the art of speech still remained as the great thing. So we find in Xenophon, Hippias boasting that he can speak repeatedly upon every subject and say something new each time, while we hear it expressly affirmed of others, that they had no need of positive knowledge in order to discourse satisfactorily upon every thing, and to answer every question extemporaneously; and when many Sophists make it a great point to hold a well-arranged discourse about something of the least possible significance (*c. g.* salt), so do we see that with them the thing was only a means while the word was the end, and we ought not to be surprised that in this respect the Sophistic philosophy sunk to that empty technicality which Plato in his Phædrus, on account of its want of character, subjects to so rigid a criticism.

4. THE SIGNIFICANCE OF THE SOPHISTIC PHILOSOPHY FROM ITS RELATION TO THE CULTURE OF THE AGE.—The scientific and moral defect of the Sophistic philosophy is at first view obvious; and, since certain modern writers of history with over-officious zeal have painted its dark sides in black, and raised an earnest accusation against its frivolity, immorality, and greediness for pleasure, its conceitedness and selfishness, and bare appearance of wisdom and art of dispute—it needs here no farther elucidation. But the point in it most apt to be overlooked is the merit of the Sophists in their effect upon the culture of the age. To say, as is done, that they had only the negative merit of calling out the opposi-

tion of Socrates and Plato, is to leave the immense influence and
the high fame of so many among them, as well as the revolution
which they brought about in the thinking of a whole nation, an
inexplicable phenomenon. It were inexplicable that e. g. Socrates
should attend the lectures of Prodicus, and direct to him other
students, if he did not acknowledge the worth of his grammatical
performances or recognize his merit for the soundness of his logic.
Moreover, it cannot be denied that Protagoras has hit upon many
correct principles of rhetoric, and has satisfactorily established
certain grammatical categories.   Generally may it be said of the
Sophists, that they threw among the people a fulness in every
department of knowledge; that they strewed about them a vast
number of fruitful germs of development; that they called out
investigations in the theory of knowledge, in logic and in language; that they laid the basis for the methodical treatment of
many branches of human knowledge, and that they partly founded
and partly called forth that wonderful intellectual activity which
characterized Athens at that time.   Their greatest merit is their
service in the department of language.   They may even be said
to have created and formed the Attic prose.   They are the first
who made style as such a separate object of attention and study,
and who set about rigid investigations respecting number and the
art of rhetorical representation.   With them Athenian eloquence,
which they first incited, begins.   Antiphon as well as Isocrates—
the latter the founder of the most flourishing school of Greek
rhetoric—are offshoots of the Sophistic philosophy.   In all this
there is ground enough to regard this whole phenomenon as not
barely a symptom of decay.

5. INDIVIDUAL SOPHISTS.—The first, who is said to have been
called, in the received sense, Sophist, is *Protagoras* of Abdera,
who flourished about 440 B. c.   He taught, and for wages, in
Sicily and in Athens, but was driven out of the latter place as a
reviler of the gods, and his book concerning the gods was burnt
by the herald in the public market-place.   It began with these
words: "I can know nothing concerning the gods, whether they
exist or not; for we are prevented from gaining such knowledge

not only by the obscurity of the thing itself, but by the shortness of the human life." In another writing he exhibits his doctrine concerning knowing or not-knowing. Starting from the Heraclitic position that every thing is in a constant flow, and applying this preëminently to the thinking subject, he taught that the man is the measure of all things, who determines in respect of being that it may be, and of not-being that it may not be, *i. e.* that is true for the perceiving subject which he, in the constant movement of things and of himself, at every moment perceives and is sensible of—and hence he has theoretically no other relation to the external world than the sensuous apprehension, and practically no other than the sensuous desire. But now, since perception and sensation are as diverse as the subjects themselves, and are in the highest degree variable in the very same subject, there follows the farther result that nothing has an objective validity and determination, that contradictory affirmations in reference to the same object must be received as alike true, and that error and contradiction cannot be. Protagoras does not seem to have made any efforts to give these frivolous propositions a practical and logical application. According to the testimony of the ancients, a personal character worthy of esteem, cannot be denied him; and even Plato, in the dialogue which bears his name, goes no farther than to object to his complete obscurity respecting the nature of morality, while, in his Gorgias and Philebus, he charges the later Sophists with affirming the principles of immorality and moral baseness.

Next to Protagoras, the most famous Sophist was *Gorgias*. During the Peloponnesian war (426 B. C.), he came from Leontini to Athens in order to gain assistance for his native city against the encroachments of Syracuse. After the successful accomplishment of his errand he still abode for some time in Athens, but resided the latter part of his life in Thessaly, where he died about the same time with Socrates. The pompous ostentation of his external appearance is often ridiculed by Plato, and the discourses through which he was wont to exhibit himself display the same character, attempting, through poetical ornament, and florid

3

metaphors, and uncommon words, and a mass of hitherto unheard of figures of speech, to dazzle and delude the mind. As a philosopher he adhered to the Eleatics, especially to Zeno, and attempts to prove upon the basis of their dialectic schematism, that universally nothing is, or if there could be a being, it would not be cognizable, or if cognizable it would not be communicable. Hence his writing bore characteristically enough the title—" *Concerning Not-being or Nature.*" The proof of the first proposition that universally nothing is, since it can be established neither as being nor as not-being, nor yet as at the same time both being and not-being, rests entirely upon the position that all existence is a space-filling existence (has place and body), and is in fact the final consequence which overturns itself, in other words the self-destruction of the hitherto physical method of philosophizing.

The later Sophists with reckless daring carried their conclusions far beyond Gorgias and Protagoras. They were for the most part free thinkers, who pulled to the ground the religion, laws, and customs of their birth. Among these should be named, prominently, the tyrant Critias, Polus, Callicles, and Thrasymachus. The two latter openly taught the right of the stronger as the law of nature, the unbridled satisfaction of desire as the natural right of the stronger, and the setting up of restraining laws as a crafty invention of the weaker; and Critias, the most talented but the most abandoned of the thirty tyrants, wrote a poem, in which he represented the faith in the gods as an invention of crafty statesmen. Hippias of Elis, a man of great knowledge, bore an honorable character, although he did not fall behind the rest in bombast and boasting; but before all, was Prodicus, in reference to whom it became a proverb to say—" as wise as Prodicus," and concerning whom Plato himself and even Aristophanes never spoke without veneration. Especially famous among the ancients were his parenetical (persuasive) lectures concerning the choice of a mode of life (Xenophon's Memorabilia, II. 1), concerning external good and its use, concerning life and death, &c., discourses in which he manifests a refined moral feeling, and his observation of life; although through the want of a higher ethical and scientific principle, he must be placed behind Socrates, whose forerunner he has been called. The later generations of Sophists, as they are shown in the Euthydemus of Plato, sink to a common level of buffoonery and disgraceful strife for gain, and comprise their whole dialectic art in certain formulæ for entangling fallacies.

6. TRANSITION TO SOCRATES AND CHARACTERISTIC OF THE FOL-LOWING PERIOD.—That which is true in the Sophistic philosophy is the truth of the subjectivity, of the self-consciousness, *i. e.* the demand that every thing which I am to admit must be shown as rational before my own consciousness—that which is false in it is its apprehension of this subjectivity as nothing farther than finite, empirical egoistic subjectivity, *i. e.* the demand that my accidental will and opinion should determine what is rational; its truth is that it set up the principle of freedom, of self-certainty; its untruth is that it established the accidental will and notion of the individual upon the throne. To carry out now the principle of freedom and self-consciousness to its truth, to gain a true world of objective thought with a real and distinct content, by the same means of reflection which the Sophists had only used to destroy it, to establish the objective will, the rational thinking, the absolute or ideal in the place of the empirical subjectivity was the problem of the next advent in philosophy, the problem which Socrates took up and solved. To make the absolute or ideal subjectivity instead of the empirical for a principle, is to affirm that the true measure of all things is not *my* (*i. e.* the individual person's) opinion, fancy and will; that what is true, right and good, does not depend upon my caprice and arbitrary determination, or upon that of any other empirical subject; but while it is *my* thinking, it is my *thinking*, the rational within me, which has to decide upon all these points. But my thinking, my reason, is not something specially belonging to me, but something common to every rational being; something universal, and in so far as I am a rational and thinking being, is my subjectivity a universal one. But every thinking individual has the consciousness that what he holds as right, as duty, as good or evil, does not appear as such to him alone but

to every rational being, and that consequently his thinking has
the character of universality, of universal validity, in a word—of
objectivity.   This then in opposition to the Sophistic philosophy
is the stand-point of Socrates, and therefore with him the *philosophy of objective thought* begins.   What Socrates could do in
opposition to the Sophists was to show that reflection led to the
same results as faith or obedience, hitherto without reflection,
had done, and that the thinking man guided by his free consciousness and his own conviction, would learn to form the same judgments and take the same course to which life and custom had
already and unconsciously induced the ordinary man.   The position, that while the man is the measure of all things, it is the
man as universal, as thinking, as rational, is the fundamental
thought of the Socratic philosophy, which is, by virtue of this
thought, the positive complement of the Sophistic principle.

With Socrates begins the second period of the Grecian philosophy.   This period contains three philosophical systems, whose
authors, standing to each other in the personal relation of teacher
and pupil, represent three successive generations,—SOCRATES,
PLATO, ARISTOTLE.

SECTION XII.

SOCRATES.[*]

1. HIS PERSONAL CHARACTER.—The new philosophical principle appears in the personal character of Socrates.   His philosophy
is his mode of acting as an individual ; his life and doctrine cannot be separated.   His biography, therefore, forms the only complete representation of his philosophy, and what the narrative of
Xenophon presents us as the definite doctrine of Socrates, is consequently nothing but an abstract of his inward character, as

---

[*] The article on Socrates, from page 52 to page 64, was translated by
Prof. N. G. Clark, of the University of Vermont.

it found expression from time to time in his conversation. Plato yet more regarded his master as such an archetypal personality, and a luminous exhibition of the historical Socrates is the special object of his later and maturer dialogues, and of these again, the Symposium is the most brilliant apotheosis of the Eros incarnated in the person of Socrates, of the philosophical impulse transformed into character.

Socrates was born in the year 469 B. C., the son of Sophroniscus, a sculptor, and Phænarete, a midwife. In his youth he was trained by his father to follow his own profession, and in this he is said not to have been without skill. Three draped figures of the Graces, called the work of Socrates, were seen by Pausanias, upon the Akropolis. Little farther is known of his education. He may have profited by the instruction of Prodicus and the musician, Damon, but he stood in no personal connection with the proper philosophers, who flourished before, or cotemporaneously with him. He became what he was by himself alone, and just for this reason does he form an era in the old philosophy. If the ancients call him a scholar of Anaxagoras, or of the natural philosopher, Archelaus, the first is demonstrably false, and the second, to say the least, is altogether improbable. He never sought other means of culture than those afforded in his native city. With the exception of one journey to a public festival, and the military campaigns which led him as far as Potidæa, Delion, and Amphipolis, he never left Athens.

The period when Socrates first began to devote himself to the education of youth, can be determined only approximately from the time of the first representation of the Clouds of Aristophanes, which was in the year 423. The date of the Delphic oracle, which pronounced him the wisest of men, is not known. But in the traditions of his followers, he is almost uniformly represented as an old, or as a gray-headed man. His mode of instruction, wholly different from the pedantry and boastful ostentation of the Sophists, was altogether unconstrained, conversational, popular, starting from objects lying nearest at hand and the most insignificant, and deriving the necessary illustrations and proofs from the most common matters of every day life; in fact, he was reproached by his cotemporaries for speaking ever only of drudges, smiths, cobblers and tanners. So we find him at the market, in the gymnasia, in the workshops, busy early and late, talking with youth, with young men, and with old men, on the proper aim and business of life, convincing them of their ignorance, and wakening up in them the slumbering desires after knowledge. In every human effort, whether directed to the interests of the commonwealth, or to the private individual and the gains of trade, to science or to art, this master of helps to spiritual births could find fit points of contact for the awakening of a true self-knowledge, and a moral and religious consciousness. However often his attempts failed, or were rejected with bitter scorn, or requited with hatred and unthankfulness, yet, led on by the clear conviction that a real improvement in the condition of the state could come only from a proper education of its youth, he remained to the last true to his chosen vocation. Purely Greek in these relations to the rising generation, he designated himself, by preference, as the most ardent lover; Greek too in this, that with him, notwithstanding these free relations of friendship, his own domestic life fell quite into the background. He nowhere shows much regard for his wife and children; the notorious, though altogether too much exaggerated ill-nature of Xantippe, leads us to suspect, however, that his domestic relations were not the most happy.

As a man, as a practical sage, Socrates is pictured in the brightest colors by all narrators. " He was," says Xenophon, "so pious, that he did nothing without the advice of the gods; so just, that he never injured any one even in the least; so completely master of himself, that he never chose the agreeable instead of the good; so discerning, that he never failed in distinguishing the better from the worse;" in short, he was " just the best and happiest man possible." (Xen. *Mem.* I. 1, 11. IV. 8, 11.) Still that which lends to his person such a peculiar charm, is the happy blending and harmonious connection of all its characteristic traits, the perfection of a beautiful, plastic nature. In all this universality of his genius, in this force of character, by which he combined the most contradictory and incongruous elements into a harmonious whole, in this lofty elevation above every human weakness,—in a word, as a perfect model, he is most strikingly depicted in the brilliant eulogy of Alcibiades, in the Symposium of Plato. In the scantier representation of Xenophon, also, we find everywhere a classic form, a man possessed of the finest social culture, full of Athenian politeness, infinitely removed from every thing like gloomy asceticism, a man as valiant upon the field of battle as in the festive hall, conducting himself with the most unconstrained freedom, and yet with entire sobriety and self-control, a perfect picture of the happiest Athenian time, without the acerbity, the one-sidedness, and contracted reserve of the later moralists, an ideal representation of the genuinely human virtues.

2. SOCRATES AND ARISTOPHANES.—Socrates seems early to have attained universal celebrity through the peculiarities attaching to his person and character. Nature had furnished him with a remarkable external physiognomy. His crooked, turned-up nose, his projecting eye, his bald pate, his corpulent body, gave his form a striking similarity to the Silenic, a comparison which is carried out in Xenophon's "Feast," in sprightly jest, and in Plato's Symposium, with as much ingenuity as profoundness. To this was added his miserable dress, his going barefoot, his posture, his often standing still, and rolling his eyes. After all this, one will hardly be surprised that the Athenian comedy took advantage of such a remarkable character. But there was another and peculiar motive, which influenced Aristophanes. He was a most ardent admirer of the good old times, an enthusiastic eulogist of the manners and the constitution, under which the fathers had been reared. As it was his great object to waken up anew in his people, and to stimulate a longing after those good old times, his passionate hatred broke out against all modern efforts in politics, art and philosophy, of that increasing mock-wisdom, which went hand in hand with a degenerating democracy. Hence comes his bitter railing at Cleon, the Demagogue (in the

Knights), at Euripides, the sentimental play-writer (in the *Frogs*)
and at Socrates, the Sophist (in the *Clouds*). The latter, as the
representative of a subtle, destructive philosophy, must have appeared to him just as corrupt and pernicious, as the party of progress in politics, who trampled without conscience upon every
thing which had come down from the past. It is, therefore, the
fundamental thought of the Clouds to expose Socrates to public
contempt, as the representative of the Sophistic philosophy, a
mere semblance of wisdom, at once vain, profitless, corrupting in
its influence upon the youth, and undermining all true discipline
and morality. Seen in this light, and from a moral stand-point,
the motives of Aristophanes may find some excuse, but they cannot be justified ; and his representation of Socrates, into whose
character all the characteristic features of the Sophistic philosophy are interwoven, even the most contemptible and hateful, yet
so that the most unmistakable likeness is still apparent, cannot be
admitted on the ground that Socrates did really have the greatest
formal resemblance to the Sophists. The Clouds can only be designated as a culpable misunderstanding, and as an act of gross
injustice brought about by blinded passion ; and Hegel, when he
attempts to defend the conduct of Aristophanes, forgets, that,
while the comic writer may caricature, he must do it without
having recourse to public calumniation. In fact all the political
and social tendencies of Aristophanes rest on a gross misunderstanding of historical development. The good old times, as he
fancies them, are a fiction. It lies just as little in the realm of
possibility, that a morality without reflection, and a homely in-
genuousness, such as mark a nation's childhood, should be forced
upon a time in which reflection has utterly eaten out all immediateness, and unconscious moral simplicity, as that a grown up
man should become a child again in the natural way. Aristophanes himself attests the impossibility of such a return, when in
a fit of humor, with cynic raillery, he gives up all divine and
human authority to ridicule, and thereby, however commendable
may have been the patriotic motive prompting him to this comic
extravagance, demonstrates, that he himself no longer stands

upon the basis of the old morality, that he too is the son of his time.

3. THE CONDEMNATION OF SOCRATES.—To this same confounding of his efforts with those of the Sophists, and the same tendency to restore by violent means the old discipline and morality, Socrates, twenty-four years later, fell a victim. After he had lived and labored at Athens for many years in his usual manner, after the storm of the Peloponnesian war had passed by, and this city had experienced the most varied political fortunes, in his seventieth year he was brought to trial and accused of neglecting the gods of the state, of introducing new deities, and also of corrupting the youth. His accusers were Melitus, a young poet, Anytus, a demagogue, and Lycon, an orator, men in every respect insignificant, and acting, as it seems, without motives of personal enmity. The trial resulted in his condemnation. After a fortunate accident had enabled him to spend thirty days more with his scholars in his confinement, spurning a flight from prison, he drank the poisoned cup in the year 399 B. C.

The first motive to his accusation, as already remarked, was his identification with the Sophists, the actual belief that his doctrines and activity were marked with the same character of hostility to the interests of the state, as those of the Sophists, which had already occasioned so much mischief. The three points in the accusation, though evidently resting on a misunderstanding, alike indicate this; they are precisely those by which Aristophanes had sought to characterize the Sophist in the person of Socrates. This " corruption of the youth," this bringing in of new customs, and a new mode of culture and education generally, was precisely the charge which was brought against the Sophists; moreover, in Plato's Menon, Anytus, one of the three accusers, is introduced as the bitter enemy of the Sophists and of their manner of instruction. So too in respect to the denial of the national gods : before this, Protagoras, accused of denying the gods, had been obliged to flee, and Prodicus, to drink hemlock, a victim to the same distrust. Even five years after the death of Socrates, Xenophon, who was not present at the trial, felt himself called upon

3*

to write his Memorabilia in defence of his teacher, so wide-spread
and deep-rooted was the prejudice against him.

Beside this there was also a second, probably a more decisive
reason.   As the Sophistic philosophy was, in its very nature,
eminently aristocratic, and Socrates, as a supposed Sophist, consequently passed for an aristocrat, his entire mode of life could
not fail to make him appear like a bad citizen in the eyes of the
restored democracy.   He had never concerned himself in the
affairs of the state, had never but once sustained an official character, and then, as chief of the Prytanes, had disagreed with the
will of the people and the rulers. (*Plat. Apol.* § 32. Xen. *Mem.*
I. 1, 18.)   In his seventieth year, he mounted the orator's stand
for the first time in his life, on the occasion of his own accusation.
His whole manner was somewhat cosmopolitan; he is even said
to have remarked, that he was not an Athenian, nor a Greek, but
a citizen of the world.   We must also take into account, that he
found fault with the Athenian democracy upon every occasion,
especially with the democratic institution of choice by lot, that he
decidedly preferred the Spartan state to the Athenian, and that
he excited the distrust of the democrats by his confidential relations with the former leaders of the oligarchic party. (Xen. *Mem.*
I. 2, 9, sq.)   Among others who were of the oligarchic interest,
and friendly to the Spartans, Critias in particular, one of the
thirty tyrants, had been his scholar; so too Alcibiades—two men,
who had been the cause of much evil to the Athenian people.   If
now we accept the uniform tradition, that two of his accusers were
men of fair standing in the democratic party, and farther, that
his judges were men who had fled before the thirty tyrants, and
later had overthrown the power of the oligarchy; we find it much
more easy to understand how they, in the case before them, should
have supposed they were acting wholly in the interest of the
democratic party, when they pronounced condemnation upon the
accused, especially as enough to all appearance could be brought
against him.   The hurried trial presents nothing very remarkable,
in a generation which had grown up during the Peloponnesian
war, and in a people that adopted and repented of their passion-

ate resolves with the like haste. Yea, more, if we consider that Socrates spurned to have recourse to the usual means and forms adopted by those accused of capital crime, and to gain the sympathy of the people by lamentations, or their favor by flattery, that he in proud consciousness of his innocence defied his judges, it becomes rather a matter of wonder, that his condemnation was carried by a majority of only three to six votes. And even now he might have escaped the sentence to death, had he been willing to bow to the will of the sovereign people for the sake of a commutation of his punishment. But as he spurned to set a value upon himself, by proposing another punishment, a fine, for example, instead of the one moved by his accuser, because this would be the same as to acknowledge himself guilty, his disdain could not fail to exasperate the easily excited Athenians, and no farther explanation is needed to show why eighty of his judges who had before voted for his innocence, now voted for his death. Such was the most lamentable result—a result, afterwards most deeply regretted by the Athenians themselves—of an accusation, which at the outset was probably only intended to humble the aristocratic philosopher, and to force him to an acknowledgment of the power and the majesty of the people.

Hegel's view of the fate of Socrates, that it was the result of the collision of equally just powers—the Tragedy of Athens as he calls it—and that guilt and innocence were shared alike on both sides, cannot be maintained on historical grounds, since Socrates can neither be regarded exclusively as the representative of the modern spirit, the principle of freedom, subjectivity, the concrete personality; nor his judges, as the representatives of the old Athenian unreflecting morality. The first cannot be, since Socrates, if his principle was at variance with the old Greek morality, rested nevertheless so far on the basis of tradition, that the accusations brought against him in this respect were false and groundless; and the last cannot be, since at that time, after the close of the Peloponnesian war, the old morality and piety had long been wanting to the mass of the people, and given place to the modern culture, and the whole process against Socrates must

be regarded rather as an attempt to restore by violence, in connection with the old constitution, the old defunct morality. The
fault is not therefore the same on both sides, and it must be held,
that Socrates fell a victim to a misunderstanding, and to an un-
justifiable reaction of public sentiment.

4. THE "GENIUS" (δαιμόνιον) OF SOCRATES.—Those traces
of the old religious sentiment, which have been handed down to
us from so many different sources, and are certainly not to be
explained from a bare accommodation to the popular belief, on
the part of the philosopher, and which distinguish him so decidedly
from the Sophists, show how little Socrates is really to be regarded
as an innovator in discipline and morals. He commends the art
of divination, believes in dreams, sacrifices with all proper care,
speaks of the gods, of their omniscience, omnipresence, goodness,
and complete sufficiency in themselves, even with the greatest
reverence, and, at the close of his defence, makes the most solemn
asseveration of his belief in their existence. In keeping with his
attaching himself in this way to the popular religion, his new
principle, though in its results hostile to all external authority,
nevertheless assumed the form of the popular belief in "Demonic"
signs and symbols. These suggestions of the "Demon" are a
knowledge, which is at the same time connected with unconscious-
ness. They occupy the middle ground between the bare external
of the Greek oracle, and the purely internal of the spirit. That
Socrates had the conception of a particular subject, a personal
"Demon," or "Genius," is altogether improbable. Just as little
can these "Demonic" signs, this inward oracle, whose voice
Socrates professed to hear, be regarded after the modern accep-
tation, simply as the personification of the conscience, or of the
practical instinct, or of the individual tact. The first article in
the form of accusation, which evidently refers to this very point,
shows that Socrates did not speak barely metaphorically of this
voice, to which he professed to owe his prophecies. And it was
not solely in reference to those higher questions of decided importance, that Socrates had these suggestions, but rather and pre-
eminently with respect to matters of mere accident and arbitrary

choice, as for example, whether, and when, his friends should set out on a journey. It is no longer possible to explain the "Demon" or "Genius" of Socrates on psychological grounds; there may have been something of a magnetic character about it. It is possible that there may be some connection between this and the many other ecstatic or cataleptic states, which are related of Socrates in the Symposium of Plato.

5. THE SOURCES OF THE PHILOSOPHY OF SOCRATES.—Well known is the old controversy, whether the picture of Socrates, drawn by Xenophon or by Plato, is the more complete and true to history, and which of the two men is to be considered as the more reliable source for obtaining a knowledge of his philosophy. This question is being decided more and more in favor of Xenophon. Great pains have been taken in former as in later times, to bring Xenophon's Memorabilia into disrepute, as a shallow and insufficient source, because their plain, and any thing other than speculative contents, seemed to furnish no satisfactory ground for such a revolution in the world of mind as is attributed to Socrates, or for the splendor which invests his name in history, or for the character which Plato assigns him; because again the Memorabilia of Xenophon have especially an apologetic aim, and their defence does not relate so much to the philosopher as to the man; and finally, because they have been supposed to have the appearance of carrying the philosophical over into the unphilosophical style of the common understanding. A distinction has therefore been made between an exoteric and an esoteric Socrates, obtaining the first from Xenophon, the latter from Plato. But the preference of Plato to Xenophon has in the first place no historical right in its favor, since Xenophon appears as a proper historian and claims historical credibility, while Plato on the other hand never professes to be an historical narrator, save in a few passages, and will by no means have all the rest which he puts in the mouth of Socrates understood as his authentic expressions and discourse. There is, therefore, no historical reason for preferring the representation of Socrates which is given by Plato. In the second place, the under-valuation of Xenophon

rests, for the most part, on the false notion, that Socrates had a
proper philosophy, *i. e.* a speculative system, and on an unhistorical
mistaking of the limits by which the philosophical character of
Socrates was conditioned and restricted.   There was no proper
Socratic doctrine, but a Socratic life; and, just on this ground,
are the different philosophical tendencies of his scholars to be
explained.

6. The Universal Character of the Philosophizing of
Socrates.—The philosophizing of Socrates was limited and restricted by his opposition, partly to the preceding, and partly to
the Sophistic philosophy.

Philosophy before the time of Socrates had been in its essential character investigation of nature.   But in Socrates, the
human mind, for the first time, turned itself in upon itself, upon
its own being, and that too in the most immediate manner, by
conceiving itself as active, moral spirit.   The positive philosophizing of Socrates, is exclusively of an ethical character, exclusively an inquiry into the nature of virtue, so exclusively, and
so onesidedly, that, as is wont to be the case upon the appearance
of a new principle, it even expressed a contempt for the striving
of the entire previous period, with its natural philosophy, and its
mathematics.   Setting every thing under the stand-point of immediate moral law, Socrates was so far from finding any object in
"irrational" nature worthy of study, that he rather, in a kind of general teleological manner, conceived it simply in the light of external
means for the attainment of external ends; yea, he would not even
go out to walk, as he says in the Phædrus of Plato, since one can
learn nothing from trees and districts of country.   Self-knowledge,
the Delphic (γνῶθι σαυτόν) appeared to him the only object
worthy of a man, as the starting-point of all philosophy.   Knowledge of every other kind, he pronounced so insignificant and
worthless, that he was wont to boast of his ignorance, and to declare that he excelled other men in wisdom only in this, that he
was conscious of his own ignorance.   (Plat. *Ap. S.* 21, 23.)

The other side of the Socratic philosophizing, is its opposition
to the philosophy of the time.   His object, as is well understood,

could have been only this, to place himself upon the same position as that occupied by the philosophy of the Sophists, and overcome it on its own ground, and by its own principles. That Socrates shared in the general position of the Sophists, and even had many features of external resemblance to them—the Socratic irony, for instance—has been remarked above. Many of his assertions, particularly these propositions, that no man knowingly does wrong, and if a man were knowingly to lie, or to do some other wrong act, still he would be better than he who should do the same unconsciously, at first sight bear a purely Sophistic stamp. The great fundamental thought of the Sophistic philosophy, that all moral acting must be a conscious act, was also his. But whilst the Sophists made it their object, through subjective reflection to confuse and to break up all stable convictions, to make all rules relating to outward conduct impossible, Socrates had recognized thinking as the activity of the universal principle, free, objective thought as the measure of all things, and, therefore, instead of referring moral duties, and all moral action to the fancy and caprice of the individual, had rather referred all to true knowledge, to the essence of spirit. It was this idea of knowledge that led him to seek, by the process of thought, to gain a conceivable objective ground, something real, abiding, absolute, independent of the arbitrary volitions of the subject, and to hold fast to unconditioned moral laws. Hegel expresses the same opinion, when he says that Socrates put morality from ethical grounds, in the place of the morality of custom and habit. Hegel distinguishes morality, as conscious right conduct, resting on reflection and moral principles, from the morality of unsophisticated, half-unconscious virtue, which rests on the compliance with prevailing custom. The logical condition of this ethical striving of Socrates, was the determining of conceptions, the method of their formation. To search out the "what" of every thing says Xenophon (*Mem.* IV. 6, 1.) was the uninterrupted care of Socrates, and Aristotle says expressly that a twofold merit must be ascribed to him, viz. : the forming of the method of induction and the giving of strictly logical definitions,—the two elements which constitute the basis of science. How these two elements stand connected with the principle of Socrates we shall at once see.

7. THE SOCRATIC METHOD.—We must not regard the Socratic method as we are accustomed to speak of method in our day, *i. e.* as something which, as such, was distinctly in his consciousness, and which he abstracted from every, concrete content, but it rather had its growth in the very mode of his philosophizing, which was not directed to the imparting of a system but to the education of the subject in philosophical thinking and life. It is only a subjective technicality for his mode of instruction, the peculiar manner of his philosophical, familiar life.

The Socratic method has a twofold side, a negative and a positive one. The negative side is the well known Socratic *irony*. The philosopher takes the attitude of ignorance, and would apparently let himself be instructed by those with whom he converses, but through the questions which he puts, the unexpected consequences which he deduces, and the contradictions in which he involves the opposite party, he soon leads them to see that their supposed knowledge would only entangle and confuse them. In the embarrassment in which they now find themselves placed, and seeing that they do not know what they supposed, this supposed knowledge completes its own destruction, and the subject who had pretended to wisdom learns to distrust his previous opinions and firmly held notions. "What we knew, has contradicted itself," is the refrain of the most of these conversations.

This result of the Socratic method was only to lead the subject to know that he knew nothing, and a great part of the dialogues of Xenophon and Plato go no farther than to represent ostensibly this negative result. But there is yet another element in his method in which the irony loses its negative appearance.

The positive side of the Socratic method is the so-called obstetrics or art of intellectual midwifery. Socrates compares himself with his mother Phœnarete, a midwife, because his position was rather to help others bring forth thoughts than to produce them himself, and because he took upon himself to distinguish the birth of an empty thought from one rich in its content. (Plato

Theatætus, p. 149.) Through this art of midwifery the philosopher, by his assiduous questioning, by his interrogatory dissection
of the notions of him with whom he might be conversing, knew
how to elicit from him a thought of which he had previously been
unconscious, and how to help him to the birth of a new thought.
A chief means in this operation was the method of *induction*, or
the leading of the representation to a conception. The philosopher, thus, starting from some individual, concrete case, and seiz-
ing hold of the most common notions concerning it, and finding
illustrations in the most ordinary and trivial occurrences, knew
how to remove by his comparisons that which was individual, and
by thus separating the accidental and contingent from the essential, could bring up to consciousness a universal truth and a universal determination,—in other words, could form conceptions.
In order *e. g.* to find the conception of justice or valor, he would
start from individual examples of them, and from these deduce
the universal character or conception of these virtues. From this
we see that the direction of the Socratic induction was to gain
logical *definitions.* I define a conception when I develope what
it is, its essence, its content. I define the conception of justice
when I set up the common property and logical unity of all its
different modes of manifestation. Socrates sought to go no farther than this. " To seek for the essence of virtue," says an
Aristotelian writing (*Eth.* I. 5), " Socrates regarded as the
problem of philosophy, and hence, since he regarded all virtue as
a knowing, he sought to determine in respect of justice or valor
what they might really be, *i. e.* he investigated their essence or
conception." From this it is very easy to see the connection
which his method of definitions or of forming conceptions had
with his practical strivings. He went back to the conception of
every individual virtue, *e. g.* justice, only because he was convinced that the knowledge of this conception, the knowledge of it
for every individual case, was the surest guide for every moral
relation. Every moral action, he believed, should start as a conscious action from the conception.

From this we might characterize the Socratic method as the

skill by which a certain sum of given, homogeneous and individual phenomena was taken, and their logical unity, the universal principle which lay at their base, inductively found. This method presupposes the recognition that the essence of the objects must be comprehended in the thought, that the conception is the true being of the thing. Hence we see that the Platonic doctrine of ideas is only the objectifying of this method which in Socrates appears no farther than a subjective dexterity. The Platonic ideas are the universal conceptions of Socrates posited as real individual beings. Hence Aristotle (*Metaph.* XIII. 4) most fittingly characterizes the relation between the Socratic method and the Platonic doctrine of ideas with the words, " Socrates posits the universal conceptions not as separate, individual substances, while Plato does this, and names them ideas."

8. THE SOCRATIC DOCTRINE CONCERNING VIRTUE.—The single, positive doctrinal sentence which has been transmitted us from Socrates is, that virtue is a knowing,—that, consequently, nothing is good which happens without discernment, and nothing bad which is done with discernment, or, what is the same thing, that no man is voluntarily vicious, that the base are such against their will, aye, even he who knowingly does wrong is better than he who does it ignorantly, because in the latter case, morality and true knowledge are both wanting, while in the former—if such a case could happen—morality alone is violated. Socrates could not conceive how a man should know the good and yet not do it; it was to him a logical contradiction that the man who sought his own well being should at the same time knowingly despise it. Therefore, with him the good action followed as necessarily from the knowledge of the good as a logical conclusion from its premise.

The sentence that virtue is a knowing, has for its logical consequence the unity of virtue and for its practical consequence the teachableness of it. With these three propositions, in which every thing is embraced which we can properly term the Socratic philosophy, Socrates has laid the first foundation stone for a scientific treatment of ethics, a treatment which must be dated first from him. But he laid only the foundation stone, for on the one side he attempted no carrying out of his principle into details, nor any setting up of a concrete doctrine of ethics, but only, after the ancient manner, referred to the laws of states and the unwritten laws of the universal human order, and on the other side, he has not seldom served himself with utilitarian motives to establish his ethical propositions, in other words he has referred to the external advantages and useful consequences of virtue, by which the purity of his ethical point of view became tarnished.

SECTION XIII.

THE PARTIAL DISCIPLES OF SOCRATES.

1. THEIR RELATION TO THE SOCRATIC PHILOSOPHY.—The death of Socrates gave to his life an ideal perfection, and this became an animating principle which had its working in many directions. The apprehension of him as an ideal type forms the common character of the immediate Socratic schools. The fundamental thought, that men should have one universal and essentially true aim, they all received from Socrates; but since their master left no complete and systematic doctrine, but only his many-sided life to determine the nature of this aim, every thing would depend upon the subjective apprehension of the personal character of Socrates, and of this we should at the outset naturally expect to find among his different disciples a different estimate. Socrates had numerous scholars, but no school. Among these, three views of his character have found a place in history. That of *Antisthenes*, or the Cynical, that of *Aristippus*, or the Cyrenian, and that of *Euclid*, or the Megarian—three modes of apprehending him, each of which contains a true element of the Socratic character, but all of which separate that which in the master was a harmonious unity, and affirm of the isolated

elements that which could be truly predicated only of the whole
They are therefore, one-sided, and give of Socrates a false pic
ture.   This, however, was not wholly their fault; but in that
Aristippus was forced to go back to the theory of knowledge of
Protagoras, and Euclid to the metaphysics of the Eleatics, they
rather testify to the subjective character and to the want of
method and system of the Socratic philosophy, and exhibit in
their defects and one-sidedness, in part, only the original weakness which belongs to the doctrine of their master.

2. ANTISTHENES AND THE CYNICS.—As a strictly literal adherent of the doctrine of Socrates, and zealously though grossly,
and often with caricature imitating his method, Antisthenes stands
nearest his master.   In early life a disciple of Gorgias, and himself a teacher of the Sophistic philosophy, he subsequently became
an inseparable attendant of Socrates, after whose death he founded
a school in the Cynosarges, whence his scholars and adherents
took the name of Cynics, though according to others this name
was derived from their mode of life.   The doctrine of Antisthenes is only an abstract expression for the Socratic ideal of
virtue.   Like Socrates he considered virtue the final cause of
men, regarding it also as knowledge or science, and thus as an
object of instruction; but the ideal of virtue as he had beheld it
in the person of Socrates was realized in his estimation only in
the absence of every need (in his appearance he imitated a beg-
gar with staff and scrip) and hence in the disregarding of all
former intellectual interests; virtue with him aims only to avoid
evil, and therefore has no need of dialectical demonstrations, but
only of Socratic vigor; the wise man, according to him, is self-
sufficient, independent of every thing, indifferent in respect of
marriage, family, and the public life of society, as also in respect
of wealth, honor, and enjoyment.   In this ideal of Antisthenes,
which is more negative than positive, we miss entirely the genial
humanity and the universal susceptibility of his master, and still
more a cultivation of those fruitful dialectic elements which the
Socratic philosophizing contained.   With a more decided contempt for all knowledge, and a still greater scorn of all the cus-

toms of society, the later Cynicism became frequently a repulsive and shameful caricature of the Socratic spirit. This was especially the case with Diogenes of Sinope, the only one of his disciples whom Antisthenes suffered to remain with him. In their high estimation of virtue and philosophy these Cynics, who have been suitably styled the Capuchins of the Grecian world, preserved a trace of the original Socratic philosophy, but they sought virtue "in the shortest way," in a life according to nature as they themselves expressed it, that is, in shutting out the outer world, in attaining a complete independence, and absence of every need, and in renouncing art and science as well as every determinate aim. To the wise man said they nothing should go amiss; he should be mighty over every need and desire, free from the restraints of civil law and of custom, and of equal privileges with the gods. An easy life, said Diogenes, is assigned by the gods to that man who limits himself to his necessities, and this true philosophy may be attained by every one, through perseverance and the power of self-denial. Philosophy and philosophical interest is there none in this school of beggars. All that is related of Diogenes are anecdotes and sarcasms.

We see here how the ethics of the Cynic school lost itself in entirely negative statements, a consequence naturally resulting from the fact that the original Socratic conception of virtue lacked a concrete positive content, and was not systematically carried out. Cynicism is the negative side of the Socratic doctrine.

3. ARISTIPPUS AND THE CYRENIANS.—Aristippus of Cyrene, numbered till the death of Socrates among his adherents, is represented by Aristotle as a Sophist, and this with propriety, since he received money for his instructions. He appears in Xenophon as a man devoted to pleasure. The adroitness with which he adapted himself to every circumstance, and the knowledge of human nature by which in every condition he knew how to provide means to satisfy his desire for good living and luxury, were well known among the ancients. Brought in contact with the government, he kept himself aloof from its cares lest he should become dependent; he spent most of his time abroad in order to free himself from

every restraint; he made it his rule that circumstances should be dependent upon him, while he should be independent of them. Though such a man seems little worthy of the name of a Socraticist, yet has he two points of contact with his master which should not be overlooked. Socrates had called virtue *and* happiness co-ordinately the highest end of man, *i. e.* he had indeed asserted most decidedly the idea of a moral action, but because he brought this forward only in an undeveloped and abstract form, he was only able in concrete cases to establish the obligation of the moral law in a utilitarian way, by appealing to the benefit resulting from the practice of virtue. This side of the Socratic principle Aristippus adopted for his own, affirming that pleasure is the ultimate end of life, and the highest good. Moreover, this pleasure, as Aristippus regards it, is not happiness as a condition embracing the whole life, nor pleasure reduced to a system, but is only the individual sensation of pleasure which the body receives, and in this all determinations of moral worth entirely disappear; but in that Aristippus recommends knowledge, self-government, temperance, and intellectual culture as means for acquiring and preserving enjoyment, and, therefore, makes a cultivated mind necessary to judge respecting a true satisfaction, he shows that the Socratic spirit was not yet wholly extinguished within him, and that the name of pseudo-Socraticist which Schleiermacher gives him, hardly belongs to him.

The other leaders of the Cyrenian school, *Hegesias, Theodorus, Anniceris,* we can here only name. The farther development of this school is wholly occupied in more closely defining the nature of pleasure, *i. e.* in determining whether it is to be apprehended as a momentary sensation, or as an enduring condition embracing the whole life; whether it belonged to the mind or the body, whether an isolated individual could possess it, or whether it is found alone in the social relations of life; whether we should regard it as positive or negative, (*i. e.* simply the absence of pain)

4. EUCLID AND THE MEGARIANS.—The union of the dialectical and the ethical is a common character in all the partial Socratic schools; the difference consists only in this, that in the

one the ethical is made to do service to the dialectical, and that in
the other, the dialectical stands in subjection to the ethical. The
former is especially true of the Megarian school, whose essential
peculiarity was pointed out by the ancients themselves as a combination of the Socratic and Eleatic principles. The idea of the
good is on the ethical side the same as the idea of being on the
physical; it was, therefore, only an application to ethics of the
Eleatic view and method when Euclid called the good pure being,
and the not-good, not-being. What is farther related of Euclid is
obscure, and may here be omitted. The Megarian school was
kept up under different leaders after his death, but without living
force, and without the independent activity of an organic development. As hedonism (the philosophical doctrine of the Cyreneans
that pleasure is the chief good) led the way to the doctrine of
Epicurus, and cynicism was the bridge toward the Stoic, so the
later Megaric development formed the transition point to scepticism. Directing its attention ever more exclusively towards the
culture of the formal and logical method of argument, it left
entirely out of view the moral thoughts of Socrates. Its sophis-
tries and quiddities which were, for the most part, only plays of
word and wit, were widely known and noted among the ancients.

5. PLATO, AS THE COMPLETE SOCRATICIST.—The attempts thus
far to build upon the foundation pillars of the Socratic doctrine,
started without a vigorous germinating principle, and ended fruit-
lessly. Plato was the only one of his scholars who has approached
and represented *the whole* Socrates. Starting from the Socratic
idea of knowledge he brought into one focus the scattered elements and rays of truth which could be collected from his master
or from the philosophers preceding him, and gave to philosophy a
systematic completeness. Socrates had affirmed the principle that
conception is the true being and the only actual, and had urged to
a knowledge according to the conception; but these positions were
no farther developed. His philosophy is not yet a system, but is
only the first impulse toward a philosophical development and
method. Plato is the first who has approached a systematic rep-

resentation and development of the ideal world of conceptions true in themselves.

The Platonic system is Socrates objectified, the blending and reconciling of preceding philosophy.

SECTION XIV.

PLATO.

I. PLATO'S LIFE. 1. His YOUTH.—Plato, the son of Aristo, of a noble Athenian family, was born in the year 429 B. C. It was the year of the death of Pericles, the second year of the Peloponnesian war, so fatal to Athens. Born in the centre of Grecian culture and industry, and descended from an old and noble family, he received a corresponding education, although no farther tidings of this have been transmitted to us, than the insignificant names of his teachers. That the youth growing up under such circumstances should choose the seclusion of a philosophic life rather than a political career may seem strange, since many and favorable opportunities for the latter course lay open before him. Critias, one of the thirty tyrants, was the cousin of his mother, and Charmides, who subsequently, under the oligarchic rule at Athens, met his death at the hands of Thrasybulus on the same day with Critias, was his uncle. Notwithstanding this, he is never known to have appeared a single time as a public speaker in the assembly of the people. In view of the rising degeneracy and increasing political corruption of his native land, he was too proud to court for himself the favor of the many-headed *Demos;* and more attached to Doricism than to the democracy and practice of the Attic public life, he chose to make science his chief pursuit, rather than as a patriot to struggle in vain against unavoidable disaster, and become a martyr to his political opinions. He regarded the Athenian state as lost, and to hinder its inevitable ruin he would not bring a useless offering.

2. HIS YEARS OF DISCIPLINE.—A youth of twenty, Plato came to Socrates, in whose intercourse he spent eight years. Besides a few doubtful anecdotes, nothing is known more particularly of this portion of his history. In Xenophon's Memorabilia (III. 6) Plato is only once cursorily mentioned, but this in a way that indicates an intimate relation between the scholar and his master. Plato himself in his dialogues has transmitted nothing concerning his personal relations to Socrates; only once (*Phæd.* p. 59) he names himself among the intimate friends of Socrates. But the influence which Socrates exerted upon him, how he recognized in him the complete representation of a wise man, how he found not only in his doctrine but also in his life and action the most fruitful philosophic germs, the significance which the personal character of his master as an ideal type had for him—all this we learn with sufficient accuracy from his writings, where he places his own incomparably more developed philosophical system in the mouth of his master, whom he makes the centre of his dialogues and the leader of his discourses

3. HIS YEARS OF TRAVEL.—After the death of Socrates 399 B. C., in the thirtieth year of his age, Plato, fearing lest he also should be met by the incoming reaction against philosophy, left, in company with other Socraticists, his native city, and betook himself to Euclid, his former fellow-scholar, the founder of the Megaric school (*cf.* § XIII. 4) at Megara. Up to this time a pure Socraticist, he became greatly animated and energized by his intercourse with the Megarians, among whom a peculiar philosophical direction, a modification of Socraticism, was already asserted. We shall see farther on the influence of this residence at Megara upon the foundation of his philosophy, and especially upon the elaboration and confirmation of his doctrine of Ideas. One whole period of his literary activity and an entire group of his dialogues, can only be satisfactorily explained by the intellectual stimulus gained at this place. From Megara, Plato visited Cyrene, Egypt, Magna-Grecia and Sicily. In Magna-Grecia he became acquainted with the Pythagorean philosophy, which was then in its highest bloom. His abode among the Pythagoreans had a marked effect

4.

upon him; as a man it made him more practical, and increased his zest for life and his interest in public life and social intercourse; as a philosopher it furnished him with a new incitement to science, and new motives to literary labor. The traces of the Pythagorean philosophy may be seen through all the last period of his literary life; especially his aversion to public and political life was greatly softened by his intercourse with the Pythagoreans. While in the Theatætus, he affirmed most positively the incompatibility of philosophy with public life, we find in his later dialogues, especially in the Republic and also in the Statesman— upon which Pythagoreanism seems already to have had an influence—a returning favor for the actual world, and the well-known sentence that the ruler must be a philosopher is an expression very characteristic of this change. His visit to Sicily gave him the acquaintance of the elder Dionysius and Dion his brother-in-law, but the philosopher and the tyrant had little in common. Plato is said to have incurred his displeasure to so high a degree, that his life was in danger. After about ten years spent in travel, he returned to Athens in the fortieth year of his age, (389 or 388 B. C.)

4. Plato as Head of the Academy; His Years of Instruction.—On his return, Plato surrounded himself with a circle of pupils. The place where he taught was known as the academy, a gymnasium outside of Athens where Plato had inherited a garden from his father. Of his school and of his later life, we have only the most meagre accounts. His life passed evenly along, interrupted only by a second and third visit to Sicily, where meanwhile the younger Dionysius had come to the throne. This second and third residence of Plato at the court of Syracuse abounds in vicissitudes, and shows us the philosopher in a great variety of conditions (cf. Plutarch's Life of Dion); but to us, in estimating his philosophical character, it is of interest only for the attempt, which, as seems probable from all accounts, he there made to realize his ideal of a moral state, and by the philosophical education of the new ruler to unite philosophy and the reins of government in one and the same hand, or at least in some way by means

of philosophy to achieve a healthy change in the Sicilian state constitution. His efforts were however fruitless; the circumstances were not propitious, and the character of the young Dionysius, who was one of those mediocre natures who strive after renown and distinction, but are capable of nothing profound and earnest, deceived the expectations concerning him which Plato, according to Dion's account, thought he had reason to entertain.

When we look at Plato's philosophical labors in the academy, we are struck with the different relations to public life which philosophy already assumes. Instead of carrying philosophy, like Socrates, into the streets and public places and making it there a subject of social conversation with any one who desired it, he lived and labored entirely withdrawn from the movements of the public, satisfied to influence the pupils who surrounded him. In precisely the measure in which philosophy becomes a system and the systematic form is seen to be essential, does it lose its popular character and begin to demand a scientific training, and to become a topic for the school, an esoteric affair. Yet such was the respect for the name of a philosopher, and especially for the name of Plato, that requests were made to him by different states to compose for them a book of laws, a work which in some instances it was said was actually performed. Attended by a retinue of devoted disciples, among whom were even women disguised as men, and receiving reiterated demonstrations of respect, he reached the age of eighty-one years, with his powers of mind unweakened to the latest moment.

The close of his life seems to have been clouded by disturbances and divisions which arose in his school under the lead of Aristotle. Engaged in writing, or as others state it at a marriage feast, death came upon him as a gentle sleep, 348 B. C. His remains were buried in the Ceramicus, not far from the academy.

II. The Inner Development of the Platonic Philosophy and Writings.—That the Platonic philosophy has a real development, that it should not be apprehended as a perfectly finished system to which the different writings stand related as constitu-

ent elements, but that these are rather steps of this inner development, as it were stages passed over in the philosophical
journeyings of the philosopher—is a view of the highest importance for the true estimate of Plato's literary labors.

Plato's philosophical and literary labors may be divided into
three periods, which we can characterize in different ways. Looking at them in a chronological or biographical respect, we might
call them respectively the periods of his years of discipline, of
travel, of instruction, or if we view them in reference to the prevailing external influence under which they were formed, they
might be termed the Socratic, Heraclitic-Eleatic, and the Pythagorean; or if we looked at the content alone, we might term them
the Anti-Sophistic-Ethic, the Dialectic or mediating, and the systematic or constructive periods.

THE FIRST PERIOD—the Socratic—is marked externally by
the predominance of the dramatic element, and in reference to its
philosophical stand-point, by an adherence to the method and
the fundamental principles of the Socratic doctrine. Not yet
accurately informed of the results of former inquiries, and rather
repelled from the study of the history of philosophy than attracted to it by the character of the Socratic philosophizing, Plato
confined himself to an analytical treatment of conceptions, particularly of the conception of virtue, and to a reproducing of his
master, which, though something more than a mere recital of ver-
bal recollections, had yet no philosophical independence. His
Socrates exhibits the same view of life and the same scientific
stand-point which the historical Socrates of Xenophon had had.
His efforts were thus, like those of his contemporary fellow disciples, directed prominently toward practical wisdom. His conflicts
however, like those of Socrates, had far more weight against the
prevailing want of science and the shallow sophisms of the day
than for the opposite scientific directions. The whole period
bears an eclectic and hortatory character. The highest point in
which the dialogues of this group culminate is the attempt which
at the same time is found in the Socratic doctrine to determine

the certainty of an absolute content (of an objective reality) to the good.

The history of the development of the Platonic philosophy would assume a very different form if the view of some modern scholars respecting the date of the Phædrus were correct. If, as they claim, the Phædrus were Plato's earliest work, this circumstance would betray from the outset an entirely different course of culture for him than we could suppose in a mere scholar of Socrates. The doctrine in this dialogue of the pre-existence of souls, and their periodical transmigrations, of the relation of earthly beauty with heavenly truth, of divine inspiration in contrast to human wisdom, the conception of love,—these and other Pythagorean ingredients are all so distinct from the original Socratic doctrine that we must transfer the most of that which Plato has creatively produced during his whole philosophical career, to the beginning of his philosophical development. The improbability of this, and numerous other grounds of objection, claim a far later composition for this dialogue. Setting aside for the present the Phædrus, the Platonic development assumes the following form :

Among the earliest works (if they are genuine) are the small dialogues which treat of Socratic questions and themes in a Socratic way. Of these e. g. the Charmides discusses temperance, the Lysis friendship, the Laches valor, the lesser Hippias knowing and wilful wrong-doing, the first Alcibiades, the moral and intellectual qualifications of a statesman, &c. The immaturity and the crudeness of these dialogues, the use of scenic means which have only an external relation to the content, the scantiness and want of independence in the content, the indirect manner of investigation which lacks a satisfactory and positive result, the formal and analytical treatment of the conceptions discussed —all these features indicate the early character of these minor dialogues.

The Protagoras may be taken as a proper type of the Socratic period. Since this dialogue, though directing its whole polemic against the Sophistic philosophy, confined itself almost exclusively to the outward manifestation of this system, to its influence on its age and its method of instruction in opposition to that of Socrates, without entering into the ground and philosophical character of the doctrine itself, and, still farther, since, when it comes in a strict sense to philosophize, it confines itself, in an indirect investigation, to the Socratic conception of virtue according to its different sides (virtue as knowing, its unity and its teachableness, *cf.* § XII. 8),—it represents in the clearest manner the tendency, character and want of the first period of Plato's literary life.

The Gorgias, written soon after the death of Socrates, represents the third and highest stage of this period. Directed against the Sophistical identification of pleasure and virtue, of the good and of the agreeable, *i. e.* against the affirmation of an absolute moral relativity, this dialogue maintains the proof that the good, far from owing its origin only to the right of the stronger, and thus to the arbitrariness of the subject, has in itself an independent reality and objective validity, and, consequently, alone is truly useful, and thus, therefore, the measure of pleasure must follow the higher measure of the good. In this direct and positive polemic against the Sophistic doctrine of pleasure, in its tendency to a view of the good as something firm and abiding, and secure against all subjective arbitrariness, consists prominently the advance which the Gorgias makes over the Protagoras.

In the first Socratic period the Platonic philosophizing became ripe and ready for the reception of Eleatic and Pythagorean categories. To grapple by means of these categories with the higher questions of philosophy, and so to free the Socratic philosophy from its so close connection with practical life, was the task of the second period.

THE SECOND PERIOD—the dialectic or the Megaric—is marked externally, by a less prominence of form and poetic contemplation, and not unfrequently indeed, by obscurity and difficulties of style, and internally, by the attempt to give a satisfactory mediation for the Eleatic doctrine and a dialectic foundation for the doctrine of ideas.

By his exile at Megara, and his journeys to Italy, Plato became acquainted with other and opposing philosophical directions, from which he must now separate himself in order to elevate the Socratic doctrine to its true significance. It was now that he first learned to know the philosophic theories of the earlier sages, for whose study the necessary means could not at that period, so wanting in literary publicity, be found at Athens. By his sepa-ration from these varying stand-points, as his older fellow pupils had already striven to do, he attempted striding over tue narrow limits of ethical philosophizing, to reach the final ground of know-ing, and to carry out the art of forming conceptions as brought forward by Socrates, to a science of conceptions, *i. e.* to the doc-trine of ideas. That all human acting depends upon knowing, and that all thinking depends upon the conception, were results to which Plato might already have attained through the scientific generalization of the Socratic doctrine itself, but now to bring this Socratic wisdom within the circle of speculative thinking, to establish dialectically that the conception in its simple unity is that which abides in the change of phenomena, to disclose the fundamental principles of knowledge which had been evaded by Socrates, to grasp the scientific theories of the opposers direct in their scientific grounds, and follow them out in all their ramifica-tions,—this is the problem which the Megaric family of dialogues attempts to solve. ·

The Theatætus stands at the head of this group. This is chiefly directed against the Protagorean theory of knowledge, against the identification of the thinking and the sensible percep-tion, or against the claim of an objective relativity of all knowl-edge. As the Gorgias before it had sought to establish the in-dependent being of the ethical, so does the Theatætus ascending from the ethical to the theoretical, endeavor to prove an indepen dent being and objective reality for the logical conceptions which lie at the ground of all representation and thinking, in a word, to prove the objectivity of truth, the fact that there lies a province of thought immanent in the thinking and independent of the per ceptions of the senses. These conceptions, whose objective reality is thus affirmed, are those of a species, likeness and unlikeness, sameness and difference, &c.

The Theatætus is followed by the trilogy of the Sophist, the Statesman, and the Philosopher, which completes the Megaric group of dialogues. The first of these dialogues examines the conception of appearance, that is of the not-being, the last (for which the Parmenides may be taken) the conception of being. Both dialogues are especially directed to the Eleatic doctrine. After Plato had recognized the conception in its simple unity as that which abides in the change of phenomena, his attention was naturally turned towards the Eleatics, who in an opposite way had attained the similar result that in unity consists all true substantiality, and to multiplicity as such no true being belongs. In order more easily on the one side to carry out this fundamental thought of the Eleatic to its legitimate result, in which the Megarians had already preceded him, he was obliged to give a metaphysical substance to his abstract conceptions of species, i. e. ideas. But on the other side, he could not agree with the inflexibility and exclusiveness of the Eleatic unity, unless he would wholly sacrifice the multiplicity of things; he was rather obliged to attempt to show by a dialectic development of the Eleatic principle that the one must be at the same time a totality, organically connected, and embracing multiplicity in itself. This double relation to the Eleatic principle is carried out by the Sophist and the Parmenides; by the former polemically against the Eleatic doctrine, in that it proves the being of the appearance or the not-being, and by the latter pacifically, in that it analyzes the Eleatic one by its own logical consequences into many. The inner progress of the doctrine of Ideas in the Megaric group of dialogues is therefore this, viz., that the Theatætus, in opposition to the Heraclitico-Protagorean theory of the absolute becoming, affirms the objective and independent reality of ideas, and the Sophist shows their reciprocal relation and combining qualities, while the Parmenides in fine exhibits their whole dialectic completeness with their relation to the phenomenal world.

THE THIRD PERIOD begins with the return of the philosopher

to his native city. It unites the completeness of form belonging to the first with the profounder characteristical content belonging to the second. The memories of his youthful years seem at this time to have risen anew before the soul of Plato, and to have imparted again to his literary activity the long lost freshness and fulness of that period, while at the same time his abode in foreign lands, and especially his acquaintance with the Pythagorean philosophy, had greatly enriched his mind with a store of images and ideals. This reviving of old memories is seen in the fact that the writings of this group return with fondness to the personality of Socrates, and represent in a certain degree the whole philosophy of Plato as the exaltation of the doctrine and the ideal embodiment of the historical character of his early master. In opposition to both of the first two periods, the third is marked externally by an excess of the mythical form connected with the growing influence of Pythagoreanism in this period, and internally by the application of the doctrine of ideas to the concrete spheres of psychology, ethics and natural science. That ideas possess objective reality, and are the foundation of all essentiality and truth, while the phenomena of the sensible world are only copies of these, was a theory whose vindication was no longer attempted, but which was presupposed as already proved, and as forming a dialectical basis for the pursuit of the different branches of science. With this was connected a tendency to unite the hitherto separate branches of science into a systematic whole, as well as to mould together the previous philosophical directions, and show the inner application of the Socratic philosophy for ethics, of the Eleatic for dialectics, and the Pythagorean for physics.

Upon this stand-point, the Phædrus, Plato's inaugural to his labors in the Academy, together with the Symposium, which is closely connected with it, attempts to subject the rhetorical theory and practice of their time to a thorough criticism, in order to show in opposition to this theory and practice, that the fixedness and stability of a true scientific principle could only be attained by grounding every thing on the idea. On the same stand-point the Phædon attempts to prove the immortality of the soul from the

4*

doctrine of ideas; the Philebus to bring out the conception ot pleasure and of the highest good; the Republic to develop the essence of the state, and the Timæus that of nature.

Having thus sketched the inner development of the Platonic philosophy, we now turn to a systematic statement of its principles.

III.—CLASSIFICATION OF THE PLATONIC SYSTEM.—The philosophy of Plato, as left by himself, is without a systematic statement, and has no comprehensive principle of classification. He has given us only the history of his thinking, the statement of his philosophical development; we are therefore limited in reference to his classification of philosophy to simple intimations. Accordingly, some have divided the Platonic system into theoretical and practical science, and others into a philosophy of the good, the beautiful and the true. Another classification, which has some support in old records, is more correct. Some of the ancients say that Plato was the first to unite in one whole the scattered philosophical elements of the earlier sages, and so to obtain for philosophy the three parts, logic, physics, and ethics. The more accurate statement is given by *Sextus Empiricus*, that Plato has laid the foundation for this threefold division of philosophy, but that it was first expressly recognized and affirmed by his scholars, Xenocrates and Aristotle. The Platonic system may, however, without difficulty, be divided into these three parts. True, there are many dialogues which mingle together in different proportions the logical, the ethical, and the physical element, and though even where Plato treats of some special discipline, the three are suffered constantly to interpenetrate each other, still there are some dialogues in which this fundamental scheme can be clearly recognized. It cannot be mistaken that the Timæus has predominantly a physical, and the Republic as decidedly an ethical element, and if the dialectic is expressly represented in no separate dialogue, yet does the whole Megaric group pursue the common end of bringing out the conception of science and its true object, being, and is, therefore, in its content decidedly dialectical. Plato must have been led to this threefold division by even the earlier de-

velopment of philosophy, and though Xenocrates does not clearly
see it, yet since Aristotle presupposes it as universally admitted,
we need not scruple to make it the basis on which to represent
he Platonic system.

The order which these different parts should take, Plato himself has not declared. Manifestly, however, dialectics should
have the first place as the ground of all philosophy, since Plato
uniformly directs that every philosophical investigation should
begin with accurately determining the *idea* (*Phæd.* p. 99. *Phædr.*
p. 237), while he subsequently examines all the concrete spheres
of science on the stand-point of the doctrine of ideas. The
relative position of the other two parts is not so clear. Since,
however, the physics culminates in the ethics, and the ethics,
on the other hand, has for its basis physical investigations into
the ensouling power in nature, we may assign to physics the
former place of the two.

The mathematical sciences Plato has expressly excluded from
philosophy. He considers them as helps to philosophical thinking (*Rep.* VII. 526), as necessary steps of knowledge, without which no one can come to philosophy (*Ib.* VI. 510); but
mathematics with him is not philosophy, for it assumes its principles or axioms, without at all accounting for them, as though
they were manifest to all, a procedure which is not permitted to
pure science; it also serves itself for its demonstrations, with illustrative figures, although it does not treat of these, but of that
which they represent to the understanding (*Ib.*). Plato thus
places mathematics midway between a correct opinion and science, clearer than the one, but more obscure than the other. (*Ib.*
VII. 533.)

IV. THE PLATONIC DIALECTICS. 1. CONCEPTION OF DIALEC-
TICS.—The conception of dialectics or of logic, is used by the
ancients for the most part in a very wide sense, while Plato employs it in repeated instances interchangeably with philosophy,
though on the other hand he treats it also as a separate branch
of philosophy. He divides it from physics as the science of the
eternal and unchangeable from the science of the changeable,

which never is, but is only ever becoming; he distinguishes also between it and ethics, so far as the latter treats of the good not absolutely, but in its concrete exhibition in morals and in the state; so that dialectics may be termed philosophy in a higher sense, while physics and ethics follow it as two less exact sciences, or as a not yet perfected philosophy. Plato himself defines dialectics, according to the ordinary signification of the word, as the art of evolving knowledge by way of dialogue in questions and answers. (*Rep.* VII. 534). But since the art of communicating correctly in dialogue is according to Plato, at the same time the art of thinking correctly, and as thus thinking and speaking could not be separated by the ancients, but every process of thought was a living dialogue, so Plato would more accurately define dialectics as the science which brings speech to a correct issue, and which combines or separates the species, *i. e.* the conceptions of things correctly with one another. (*Soph.* p. 253. *Phædr.* p. 266). Dialectics with him has two divisions, to know what can and what cannot be connected, and to know how division or combination can be. But as with Plato these conceptions of species or ideas are the only actual and true existence, so have we, in entire conformity with this, a third definition of dialectics (*Philebus* p. 57), as the science of being, the science of that which is true and unchangeable, the science of all other sciences. We may therefore briefly characterize it as the science of absolute being or of ideas.

2. WHAT IS SCIENCE? (1.) *As opposed to sensation and the sensuous representation.*—The Theatætus is devoted to the discussion of this question in opposition to the Protagorean sensualism. That all knowledge consists in perception, and that the two are one and the same thing, was the Protagorean proposition. From this it followed, as Protagoras himself had inferred, that things are, as they appear to me, that the perception or sensation is infallible. But since perception and sensation are infinitely diversified with different individuals, and even greatly vary in the same individual, it follows farther, that there are no objective determinations and predicates, that we can never affirm what a

thing is in itself, that all conceptions, great, small, light, heavy, to increase, to diminish, &c., have only a relative significance, and consequently, also, the conceptions of species, as combinations of the changeful many, are wholly wanting in constancy and stability. In opposition to this Protagorean thesis, Plato urges the following objections and contradictions. *First.* The Protagorean doctrine leads to the most startling consequences. If being and appearance, knowledge and perception are one and the same thing, then is the irrational brute, which is capable of perception, as fully entitled to be called the measure of all things, as man, and if the representation is infallible, as the expression of my subjective character at a given time, then need there be no more instruction, no more scientific conclusion, no more strife, and no more refutation. *Second.* The Protagorean doctrine is a logical contradiction; for according to it Protagoras must yield the question to every one who disputes with him, since, as he himself affirms, no one is incorrect, but every one judges only according to truth; the pretended truth of Protagoras is therefore true for no man, not even for himself. *Third.* Protagoras destroys the knowledge of future events. That which I may regard as profitable may not therefore certainly prove itself as such in the result. To determine that which is really profitable implies a calculation of the future, but since the ability of men to form such a calculation is very diverse, it follows from this that not man as such, but only the wise man can be the measure of things. *Fourth.* The theory of Protagoras destroys perception. Perception, according to him, rests upon a distinction of the perceived object and the perceiving subject, and is the common product of the two. But in his view the objects are in such an uninterrupted flow, that they can neither become fixed in seeing nor in hearing. This condition of constant change renders all knowledge from sense, and hence (the identity of the two being assumed), all knowledge impossible. *Fifth.* Protagoras overlooks the apriori element in knowledge. It is seen in an analysis of the sense-perception itself, that all knowledge cannot be traced to the activity of the senses, but that there must also be presupposed besides these, intellectual functions, and hence an independent province of supersensible knowledge. We see with the eyes, and hear with the ears, but to group together the perceptions attained through these different organs, and to hold them fast in the unity of self-consciousness, is beyond the power of the activity of the senses. Again, we compare the different sense-perceptions with one another, a function which cannot belong to the senses, since each sense can only furnish its own distinctive perception. Still farther, we bring forward determinations respecting the perceptions which we manifestly cannot owe to the senses, in that we predicate of these perceptions, being and not-being, likeness and unlikeness, &c. These determinations, to which also belong the beautiful and the odious, good and evil, constitute a peculiar province of knowledge, which the soul, independently of every sense-perception, brings forward through its own independent activity. The ethical element of this, Plato exhibits in his attack upon sensualism, and also in other dialogues. He maintains (*in the Sophist*), that men holding such opinions must be improved before they can be instructed, and that when made morally better, they will readily recognize the truth of the soul and its moral and rational capacities, and affirm that these are real things, though objects of neither sight nor of feeling.

(2.) *The Relation of Knowing to Opinion.*—Opinion is just as little identical with knowing as is the sense-perception. An incorrect opinion is certainly different from knowing, and a correct one is not the same, for it can be engendered by the art of speech without therefore attaining the validity of true knowledge. The correct opinion, so far as it is true in matter though imperfect in form, stands rather midway between knowing and not-knowing, and participates in both.

(3.) *The Relation of Science to Thinking.*—In opposition to the Protagorean sensualism, we have already referred to an energy of the soul independent of the sensuous perception and sensation, competent in itself to examine the universal, and grasp true being in thought. There is, therefore, a double source of knowledge, sensation and rational thinking. Sensation refers to that which is conceived in the constant becoming and perpetual change, to the pure momentary, which is in an incessant transition from the was, through the now, into the shall be (*Parm.* p. 152); it is, therefore, the source of dim, impure, and uncertain knowledge; thinking on the other hand refers to the abiding, which neither becomes nor departs, but remains ever the same. (*Tim.* p. 51.) Existence, says the Timæus (p. 27) is of two kinds, "that which ever is but has no becoming, and that which ever becomes but never is. The one kind, which is always in the same state, is comprehended through reflection by the reason, the other, which becomes and departs, but never properly is, may be apprehended by the sensuous perception without the reason." True science, therefore, flows alone from that pure and thoroughly internal activity of the soul which is free from all corporeal qualities and every sensuous disturbance. (*Phæd.* p. 65.) In this state the soul looks upon things purely as they are (*Phæd.* p. 66) in their eternal being and their unchangeable condition. Hence the true state of the philosopher is announced in the Phædon (p. 64) to be a willingness to die, a longing to fly from the body, as from a hinderance to true knowledge, and become pure spirit. According to all this, science is the thinking of true being or of ideas; the means to discover and to know these ideas, or the organ for their apprehension is the dialectic, as the art of separating and combining conceptions; the true objects of dialectics are ideas.

3. THE DOCTRINE OF IDEAS IN ITS GENESIS.—The Platonic doctrine of ideas is the common product of the Socratic method of forming conceptions, the Heraclitic doctrine of absolute becoming, and the Eleatic doctrine of absolute being. To the first of these Plato owes the idea of a knowing through conceptions, to the second the recognition of the becoming in the field of the sensuous, to the third the positing of a field of absolute reality. Elsewhere (*in the Philebus*) Plato connects the doctrine of ideas with the Pythagorean thought that every thing may be formed from unity and multiplicity, from the limit and the unlimited. The aim of the Theatætus, the Sophist, and the Parmenides is to refute the principles of the Eleatics and Heraclitics; this refuta-

tion is effected in the Theatætus by combating directly the principle of an absolute becoming, in the Sophist by combating
directly the principle of abstract being, and in the Parmenides by
taking up the Eleatic one and showing its true relations. We
have already spoken of the Theatætus; we will now look for the
development of the doctrine of ideas in the Sophist and Parmenides.

The ostensible end of the former of these dialogues is to show
that the Sophist is really but a caricature of the philosopher, but
its true end is to fix the reality of the appearance, i. e. of the not-
being, and to discuss speculatively the relation of being and not-
being. The doctrine of the Eleatics ended with the rejection of
all sensuous knowledge, declaring that what we receive as the
perception of a multiplicity of things or of a becoming is only an
appearance. In this the contradiction was clear, the not-being
was absolutely denied, and yet its existence was admitted in the
notion of men. Plato at once draws attention to this contradiction, showing that a delusive opinion, which gives rise to a false
image or representation, is not possible upon this theory which
rests upon the assumption that the false, the not-true, i. e. not-
being cannot even be thought. This, Plato continues, is the great
difficulty in thinking of not-being, that both he who denies and
he who affirms its reality is driven to contradict himself. For
though it is inexpressible and inconceivable either as one or as
many, still, when speaking of it, we must attribute to it both being
and multiplicity. If we admit that there is such a thing as a
false opinion, we assume in this very fact the notion of not-being,
for only that opinion can be said to be false which supposes either
the not-being to be, or makes that, which is, not to be. In short,
if there actually exists a false notion, so does there actually and
truly exist a not-being. After Plato had thus fixed the reality of
not-being, he discusses the relation of being and not-being, i. e.
the relation of conceptions generally in their combinations and
differences. If not-being has no less reality than being, and being
no more than not-being, if, therefore, e. g. the not-great is as truly
real as the great, then every conception may be apprehended ac

cording to its opposite sides as being and not-being at the same time : it is a being in reference to itself, as something identical with itself, but it is not-being in reference to every one of the numberless other conceptions which can be referred to it, and with which, on account of its difference from them, it can have nothing in common. The conception of the same (ταὐτὸν) and the different (θάτερον) represent the general form of an antithesis. These are the universal formulæ of combination for all conceptions. This reciprocal relation of conceptions as at the same time being and not-being, by virtue of which they can be arranged among themselves, forms now the basis for the art of dialectics, which has to judge what conceptions can and what cannot be joined together. Plato illustrates here by taking the conceptions of being, motion (becoming), and rest (existence), and showing what are the results of the combinations of these ideas. The conceptions of motion and rest cannot well be joined together, though both of them may be joined with that of being, since both are ; the conception of rest is therefore in reference to itself a being, but in reference to the conception of motion a not-being or different. Thus the Platonic doctrine of ideas, after having in the Theatætus attained its general foundation in fixing the objective reality of conceptions, becomes now still farther developed in the Sophist to a doctrine of the agreement and disagreement of conceptions. The category which conditions these reciprocal relations is that of not-being or difference. This fundamental thought of the Sophist, that being is not without not-being and not-being is not without being, may be expressed in modern phraseology thus : negation is not not-being but determinateness, and on the other hand all determinateness and concreteness of conceptions, or every thing affirmative can be only through negation ; in other words the conception of contradiction is the soul of a philosophical method.

The doctrine of ideas appears in the Parmenides as the positive consequence and progressive development of the Eleatic principle. Indeed in this dialogue, in that Plato makes Parmenides the chief speaker, he seems willing to allow that his doctrine is in substance that of the Eleatic sage. True, the fundamental thought of the dialogue—that the one is not conceivable in its complete singleness without the many, nor the many without the one, that each necessarily presupposes and reciprocally conditions the other—stands in the most direct contradiction to Eleaticism. Yet Parmenides himself, by dividing his poem into two parts, and treating in the first of the one and in the second of the many, postulates an inner mediation between these two externally so disjointed parts of his philosophy, and in this respect the Platonic theory of ideas might give itself out as the farther elimination, and the true sense of the Parmenidean philosophizing. This dialectical mediation between the one and the not-one or the many Plato now attempts in four antinomies, which have ostensibly only a negative result in so far as they show that contradictions arise both whether the one be adopted or rejected. The positive sense of these antinomies, though it can be gained only through inferences which Plato himself does not expressly utter, but leaves to be drawn by the reader—is as follows. The first antinomy shows that the one is inconceivable as such since it is only apprehended in its abstract opposition to the many; the second, that in this case also the reality of the many is inconceivable; the third, that the one or the idea cannot be conceived as not-being, since there can be neither conception nor predicate of the absolute not-being, and since, if not-being is excluded from all fellowship with being, all becoming and departing, all similarity and difference, every representation and explanation concerning it must also be denied; and lastly, the fourth affirms that the not-one or the many cannot be conceived without the one or the idea. What now is Plato's aim in this discussion of the dialectic relations between the conceptions of the one and the many? Would he use the conception of the one only as an example to explain his dialectic method with conceptions, or is the discussion of this conception itself the very object before him? Manifestly the latter, or the dialogue ends without result and without any inner connection of its two parts. But how came Plato to make such a special investigation of this conception of the one? If we bear in mind that the

Eleatics had already perceived the antithesis of the actual and the phenomenal world in the antithesis of the one and the many, and that Plato himself had also regarded his ideas as the unity of the manifold, as the one and the same in the many—since he repeatedly uses "idea" and "the one" in the same sense, and places (*Rep.* VII. 537) dialectics in the same rank with the faculty of bringing many to unity—then is it clear that the one which is made an object of investigation in the Parmenides is the idea in its general sense, *i. e.* in its logical form, and that Plato consequently in the dialectic of the one and the many would repre-sent the dialectic of the idea and the phenomenal world, or in other words would dialectically determine and establish the correct view of the idea as the unity in the manifoldness of the phenomenal. In that it is shown in the Parmenides, on the one side, that the many cannot be conceived without the one, and on the other side, that the one must be something which embraces in itself mani-foldness, so have we the ready inference on the one side, that the phenomenal world, or the many, has a true being only in so far as it has the one or the conception within it, and on the other side, that since the conception is not an abstract one but mani-foldness in unity, it must actually have manifoldness in unity in order to be able to be in the phenomenal world. The indirect result of the Parmenides is that matter as the infinitely divisible and undetermined mass has no actuality, but is in relation to the ideal world a not-being, and though the ideas as the true being gain their appearance in it, yet the idea itself is all that is actual in the appearance or phenomenon ; the phenomenal world derives its whole existence from the ideal world which appears in it, and has a being only so far as it has a conception or idea for its con-tent.

4. Positive Exposition of the Doctrine of Ideas.—Ideas may be defined according to the different sides of their historical connection, as the common in the manifold, the universal in the particular, the one in the many, or the constant and abiding in the changing. Subjectively they are principles of knowing which cy·not be derived from experience they are the intuitively cer-

tain and innate regulators of our knowledge. Objectively they are the immutable principles of being and of the phenomenal world, incorporeal and simple unities which have no relation to space, and which may be predicated of every independent thing. The doctrine of ideas grew originally out of the desire to give a definite conception to the inner essence of things, and make the real world conceivable as a harmoniously connected intellectual world. This desire of scientific knowledge Aristotle cites expressly as the motive to the Platonic doctrine of ideas. " Plato," he says (*Metaph.* XIII. 4), " came to the doctrine of ideas because he was convinced of the truth of the Heraclitic view which regarded the sensible world as a ceaseless flowing and changing. His conclusion from this was, that if there be a science of any thing there must be, besides the sensible, other substances which have a permanence, for there can be no science of the fleeting." It is, therefore, the idea of science which demands the reality of ideas, a demand which cannot be granted unless an idea or conception is also the ground of all being. This is the case with Plato. According to him there can be neither a true knowing nor a true being without ideas and conceptions which have an independent reality.

What now does Plato mean by idea? From what has already been said it is clear that he means something more than ideal conceptions of the beautiful and the good. An idea is found, as the name itself (εἶδο.) indicates, wherever a universal conception of a species or kind is found. Hence Plato speaks of the idea of a bed, table, strength, health, voice, color, ideas of simple relations and properties, ideas of mathematical figures, and even ideas of not-being, and of that, which in its essence only contradicts the idea, baseness and vice. In a word, we may put an idea wherever many things may be characterized by a common name (*Rep.* X. 596): or as Aristotle expresses it (*Met.* XII. 3). Plato places an idea to every class of being. In this sense Plato himself speaks in the beginning of the Parmenides. Parmenides asks the young Socrates what he calls ideas. Socrates answers by naming unconditionally the moral ideas, the ideas of the true, the beautiful, the good, and then after a little delay he mentions some physical ones, as the ideas of man, of fire, of water; he will not allow ideas to be predicated of that which is only a formless mass, or which is a part of something else, as hair, mud and clay, but in this he is answered by Parmenides, that if he would be fully imbued with philosophy, he must not consider such things as these to be wholly despicable, but should look upon them as truly though remotely participating in the idea. Here at least the claim is asserted that no province of being is excluded from the idea, that even that which appears most accidental and irrational is yet a part of rational knowledge, in fact that every thing existing may be brought within a rational conception.

5. THE RELATION OF IDEAS TO THE PHENOMENAL WORLD. Analogous to the different definitions of idea are the different names which Plato gives to the sensible and phenomenal world. He calls it the many, the divisible, the unbounded, the undetermined and measureless, the becoming, the relative, great and small, not-being. The relation now in which these two worlds of sense and of ideas stand to each other is a question which Plato has answered neither fully nor consistently with himself. His most common way is to characterize the relation of things to conceptions as a participant, or to call things the copies and adumbrations, while ideas are the archetypes. Yet this is so indefinite that Aristotle properly says that to talk in this way is only to use poetical metaphors. The great difficulty of the doctrine of ideas is not solved but only increased by these figurative representations. The difficulty lies in the contradiction which grows out of the fact that while Plato admits the reality of the becoming and of the province of the becoming, he still affirms that ideas which are substances ever at rest and ever the same are the only actual. Now in this Plato is formally consistent with himself, while he characterizes the *matériel* of matter not as a positive substratum but as not-being, and guards himself with the express affirmation that he does not consider the sensible as being, but only as something similar to being. (*Rep.* X. 597.) The position laid down in the Parmenides is also consistent with this, that a

perfect philosophy should look upon the idea as the cognizable in the phenomenal world, and should follow it out in the smallest particulars until every part of being should be known and all dualism removed. In fine, Plato in many of his expressions seems to regard the world of sensation only as a subjective appearance, as a product of the subjective notion, as the result of a confused way of representing ideas. In this sense the phenomena are entirely dependent on ideas; they are nothing but the ideas themselves in the form of not being; the phenomenal world derives its whole existence from the ideal world which appears in it. But yet when Plato calls the sensible a mingling of the same with the different or the not-being (*Tim.* p. 35), when he characterizes the ideas as vowels which go through every thing like a chain (*Soph.* p. 253), when he himself conceives the possibility that matter might offer opposition to the formative energy of ideas (*Tim.* p. 56), when he speaks of an evil soul of the world (*de Leg.* X. 896), and gives intimations of the presence in the world of a principle in nature hostile to God (*Polit.* p. 268), when he in the Phædon treats of the relation between body and soul as one wholly discordant and malignant,—in all this there is evidence enough, even after allowing for the mythical form of the Timæus, and the rhetorical composition which prevails in the Phædon, to substantiate the contradiction mentioned above. This is most clear in the Timæus. Plato in this dialogue makes the sensible world to be formed by a Creator after the pattern of an idea, but in this he lays down as a condition that this Demiurge or Creator should find at hand a something which should be apt to receive and exhibit this ideal image. This something Plato compares to the matter which is fashioned by the artisan (whence the later name *hyle*). He characterizes it as wholly undetermined and formless, but possessing in itself an aptitude for every variety of forms, an invisible and shapeless thing, a something which it is difficult to characterize, and which Plato even does not seem inclined very closely to describe. In this the actuality of matter is denied; while Plato makes it equivalent to space it is only the place, the negative condition of the sensible while it possesses a being only as it receives in itself the ideal form. Still matter remains the objective and phenomenal form of the idea: the visible world arises only through the mingling of ideas with this substratum, and if matter be metaphysically expressed as " the different," then does it follow with logical necessity in a dialectical discussion that it is just as truly being as not-being. Plato does not conceal from himself this difficulty, and therefore attempts to represent with comparisons and images this presupposition of a *hyle* which he finds it as impossible to do without as to express in a conceivable form. If he would do without it he must rise to the conception of an absolute creation, or consider matter as an ultimate emanation from the absolute spirit, or else explain it as appearance only. Thus the Platonic system is only a fruitless struggle against dualism.

6. THE IDEA OF THE GOOD AND THE DEITY. If the true and the real is exhibited in general conceptions which are so related to each other that every higher conception embraces and combines under it several lower, so that any one starting from a single idea may eventually discover all (*Meno.* p. 81), then must the sum of ideas form a connected organism and succession in which the lower idea appears as a stepping-stone and presupposition to a higher. This succession must have its end in an idea which needs no higher idea or presupposition to sustain it. This highest idea, the ultimate limit of all knowledge, and itself the independent ground of all other ideas, Plato calls the idea of the good, *i. e.* not of the moral but of the metaphysical good. (*Rep.* VII. 517.)

What this good is in itself, Plato undertakes to show only in images. " In the same manner as the sun," he says in the Republic (VI. 506), " is the cause of sight, and the cause not merely that objects are visible but also that they grow and are produced, so the good is of such power and beauty, that it is not merely the cause of science to the soul, but is also the cause of being and reality to whatever is the object of science, and as the sun is not itself sight or the object of sight but presides over both, so the good is not science and truth but is superior to both, they being not the good itself but of a goodly nature." The good has unconditioned worth, and gives to every other thing all the value it possesses. The idea of the good excludes all presupposition. It is the ultimate ground at the same time of knowing and of being, of the perceiver and the perceived, of the subjective and the objective, of the ideal and the real, though exalted itself above such a division. (*Rep.* VI. 508–517.) Plato, however, has not attempted a derivation of the remaining ideas from the idea of the good; his course here is wholly an empirical one; a certain class of objects are taken, and having referred these to their common essence this is given out as their idea. He has treated the individual conceptions so independently, and has made each one so complete in itself, that it is impossible to find a proper division or establish an immanent continuation of one into another.

It is difficult to say precisely what relation this idea of the good bore to the Deity in the Platonic view. Taking every thing together it seems clear that Plato regarded the two as identical, but whether he conceived this highest cause to be a personal being or not is a question which hardly admits of a definite answer. The logical result of his system would exclude the personality of God. If only the universal (the idea) is the true being, then can the only absolute idea, the Deity, be only the absolute universal; but that Plato was himself conscious of this logical conclusion we can hardly affirm, any more than we can say on the other hand that he was clearly a theist. For whenever in a mythical or popular statement he speaks of innumerable gods, this only indicates that he is speaking in the language of the popular religion, and when he speaks in an accurate philosophical sense, he only makes the relation of the personal deity with the idea a very uncertain one. Most probable, therefore, is it that this whole question concerning the personality of God was not yet definitely before him, that he took up the religious idea of God and defended it in ethical interest against the anthropomorphism of the mythic poets, that he sought to establish it by arguments drawn from the evidences of design in nature, and the universal prevalence of a belief in a God, while as a philosopher he made no use of it.

V. The Platonic Physics. 1. Nature.—The connection

ctween the Physics and the Dialectics of Plato lies principally in two points—the conception of becoming, which forms the chief property of nature, and that of real being, which is at once the all sufficient and good, and the true end of all becoming. Because nature belongs to the province of irrational sensation we cannot look for the same accuracy in the treatment of it, as is furnished in dialectics. Plato therefore applied himself with much less zest to physical investigations than to those of an ethical or dialectical character, and indeed only attended to them in his later years. Only in one dialogue, the Timæus, do we find any extended evolution of physical doctrines, and even here Plato seems to have gone to his work with much less independence than his wont, this dialogue being more strongly tinctured with Pythagoreanism than any other of his writings. The difficulty of the Timæus is increased by the mythical form on which the old commentators themselves have stumbled. If we take the first impression that it gives us, we have, before the creation of the world, a Creator as a moving and a reflecting principle, with on the one side the ideal world existing immovable as the eternal archetype, and on the other side, a chaotic, formless, irregular, fluctuating mass, which holds in itself the germ of the material world, but has no determined character nor substance. With these two elements the Creator now blends the world-soul which he distributes according to the relation of numbers, and sets it in definite and harmonious motion. In this way the material world, which has become actual through the arrangement of the chaotic mass into the four elements, finds its external frame, and the process thus begun is completed in its external structure by the formation of the organic world.

It is difficult to separate the mythical and the philosophical elements in this cosmogony of the Timæus, especially difficult to determine how far the historical construction, which gives a succession in time to the acts of creation, is only a formal one, and also how far the affirmation that matter is absolutely a not-being can be harmonized with the general tenor of Plato's statements. The significance of the world-soul is clearer. Since the soul in the Platonic system is the mean between spirit and body, and as in the same way mathematical relations, in their most universal expression as numbers, are the mean between mere sensuous existence and the pure idea (between the one and the many as Plato expresses it), it would seem clear that the world-soul, construed according to the relation of numbers, must express the relation of the world of ideas to that of sense, in other words, that it denotes the sensible world as a thought represented in the form of material existence. The Platonic view of nature, in opposition to the mechanical attempts to explain it of the earlier philosophers, is entirely teleological, and based upon the conception of the good, or, on the moral idea. Plato conceives the world as the image of the good, as the work of the divine munificence. As it is the image of the perfect it is therefore only one, corresponding to the idea of the single all-embracing substance, for an infinite number of worlds is not to be conceived as actual. For the same reason the world is spherical, after the most perfect and uniform structure, which embraces in itself all other forms; its movement is in a circle, because this, by returning into itself, is most like the movement of reason. The particular points of the Timæus, the derivation of the four elements, the separation of the seven planets according to the musical scale, the opinion that the stars were immortal and heavenly substances, the affirmation that the earth holds an abiding position in the middle of the world, a view which subsequently became elaborated to the Ptolemaic system, the reference of all material figures to the triangle as the simplest plane figure, the division of inanimate nature, according to the four elements, into creatures of earth, water, and air, his discussions respecting organic nature, and especially respecting the construction of the human body—all these we need here only mention. Their philosophical worth consists not so much in their material content, but rather in their fundamental idea, that the world should be conceived as the image and the work of reason, as an organism of order, harmony, and beauty, as the good actualizing itself.

2. The Soul.—The doctrine of the soul, considering it simply as the basis of a moral action, and leaving out of view all ques-

tions of concrete ethics, forms a constituent element in the Platonic physics. Since the soul is united to the body, it participates in the motions and changes of the body, and is, in this respect, related to the perishable. But in so far as it participates in the knowledge of the eternal, *i. e.* in so far as it knows ideas, does there live within it a divine principle—reason. Accordingly, Plato distinguishes two components of the soul—the divine and the mortal, the rational and the irrational. These two are united by an intermediate link, which Plato calls θυμὸς or spirit, and which, though allied to reason is not reason itself, since it is often exhibited in children and also in brutes, and since even men are often carried away by it without reflection. This threefoldness, here exhibited psychologically, is found, in different applications, through all the last general period of Plato's literary life. Based upon the anthropological triplicate of reason, soul and body, it corresponds also to the division of theoretical knowledge into science (or thinking), correct opinions (or sense-perception), and ignorance, to the triple ladder of eroticism in the Symposium and the mythological representation connected with this of Poros, Eros, and Penia; to the metaphysical triplicate of the ideal world, mathematical relations and the sensible world; and furnishes ground for deriving the ethical division of virtue and the political division of ranks.

So far as the soul is a mean between the spiritual and corporeal, may we connect the Phædon's proofs of its immortality with the psychological view now before us. The common thought of these arguments is that the soul, in its capacity for thinking, participates in the reason, and being thus of an opposite nature to, and uncontrolled by the corporeal, it may have an independent existence. The arguments are wholly analytical, and possess no valid and universal proof; they proceed entirely upon a *petitio principii*, they are derived partly from mythical philosophemes, and manifest not only an obscure conception of the soul, but of its relations to the body and the reason, and, so far as the relation of the soul to the ideal world is in view, they furnish in the best case only some proof for the immortality of him who has raised his soul to a pure spirit, *i. e.* the immortality of the philosopher. Plato

was not himself deceived as to the theoretical insufficiency of his
arguments. Their number would show this, and, besides, he expressly calls them proofs which amount to only human probability,
and furnish practical postulates alone. With this view he introduces at the close of his arguments the myth of the lower world,
and the state of departed souls, in order, by complying with the
religious notions, and traditions of his countrymen, to gain a positive support for belief in the soul's immortality. Elsewhere
Plato also speaks of the lower world, and of the future rewards
and punishments of the good and the evil, in accordance with the.
popular notions, as though he saw the elements of a divine revelation therein ; he tells of purifying punishment in Hades, analogous to a purgatory ; he avails himself of the common notion to
affirm that shades still subject to the corporeal principle will
hover after death over their graves, seeking to recover their lifeless bodies, and at times he dilates upon the migration of the soul
to various human and brute forms. On the whole, we find in
Plato's proofs of immortality, as in his psychology generally, that
dualism, which here expresses itself as hatred to the corporeal,
and is connected with the tendency to seek the ultimate ground
of evil in the nature of the " different " and the sensible world.

VI. The Platonic Ethics.—The ground idea of the good,
which in physics served only as an inventive conception, finds
now, in the ethics, its true exhibition. Plato has developed it
prominently according to three sides, as good, as individual virtue,
and as ethical world in the state. The conception of duty remains in the background with him as with the older philosophers.

1. Good and Pleasure.—That the highest good can be nothing other than the idea of the good itself, has already been shown
in the dialectics, where this idea was suffered to appear as the ultimate end of all our striving. But since the dialectics represent
the supreme good as unattainable by human reason, and only cog
nizable in its different modes of manifestation, we can, therefore
only follow these different manifestations of the highest good,
which represent not the good itself, but the good in becoming,
where it appears as science, truth, beauty, virtue, &c. We are

thus not required to be equal to God, but only like him (*Theæt.*)
It is this point of view which lies at the basis of the graduated
table of good, given in the Philebus. .

In seeking the highest good, the conception of pleasure must
be investigated. The Platonic stand-point here is the attempt to
strike a balance between Hedonism, (the Cyrenian theory that
pleasure is the highest good, *cf.* § XIII. 3), and Cynicism. While
he will not admit with Aristippus that pleasure is the true good,
neither will he find it as the Cynics maintain, simply in the negation of its contrary, pain, and thus deny that it belongs to the
good things of human life. He finds his refutation of Hedonism
in the indeterminateness and relativity of all pleasure, since that
which at one time may seem as pleasure, under other circumstances may appear as pain; and since he who chooses pleasure
without distinction, will find impure pleasures always combined
in his life with more or less of pain; his refutation of Cynicism
he establishes by showing the necessary connection between virtue
and true pleasure, showing that there is a true and enduring pleasure, the pleasure of reason, found in the possession of truth and
of goodness, while a rational condition separate from all pleasure,
cannot be the highest good of a finite being. It is most prominently by this distinction of a true and false, of a pure and impure pleasure, that Plato adjusts the controversy of the two
Socratic schools.—A detailed exhibition of the Philebus we must
here omit.—On the whole, in the Platonic apprehension of pleasure, we cannot but notice that same vacillation with which Plato
every where treats of the relation between the corporeal and the
spiritual, at one time considering the former as a hindrance to the
latter, and at another as its serving instrument; now, regarding it
as a concurring cause to the good, and then, as the ground of all
evil; here, as something purely negative, and there, as a positive
substratum which supports all the higher intellectual developments; and in conformity with this, pleasure is also considered at
one time as something equivalent to a moral act, and to knowledge, and at another as the means and accidental consequence of
the good.

2. VIRTUE.—In his theory of virtue, Plato is wholly Socratic. He holds fast to the opinion that it is science (*Protagoras*), and therefore, teachable (*Meno*), and as to its unity, it follows from the dialectical principle that the one can be manifold, or the manifold one, that, therefore, virtue must both be regarded as one, and also in a different respect, as many. Plato thus brings out prominently the union and connection of all virtues, and is fond of painting, especially in the introductory dialogues, some single virtue as comprising in itself the sum of all the rest. Plato follows for the most part the fourfold division of virtues, as popularly made; and first, in the Republic (IV. 441), he attempts a scientific derivation of them, by referring to each of the three parts of the soul its appropriate virtue   The virtue of the reason he calls prudence or wisdom, the directing or measuring virtue, without whose activity valor would sink to brute impulse, and calm endurance to stupid indifference; the virtue of spirit is valor, the help-meet of reason, or spirit ($\vartheta\nu\mu\delta\varsigma$) penetrated by science, which in the struggle against pleasure and pain, desire and fear, preserves the rational intelligence against the alarms with which sensuous desires, would seek to sway the soul; the virtue of the sensuous desires, and which has to reduce these within true and proper grounds, is temperance, and that virtue in fine to which belong the due regulation and mutual adjustment of the several powers of the soul, and which, therefore, constitutes the bond and the unity of the three other virtues, is justice.

In this last conception, that of justice, all the elements of moral culture meet together and centre, exhibiting the moral life of the individual as a perfect whole, and then, by requiring an application of the same principle to communities, the moral consideration is advanced beyond the narrow circle of individual life. Thus is established the whole of the moral world—Justice " in great letters," the moral life in its complete totality, is the state. In this is first actualized the demand for the complete harmony of the human life. In and through the state comes the complete formation of matter for the reason.

3. THE STATE.—The Platonic state is generally regarded as

an ideal or chimera, which it is impracticable to realize among men. This view of the case has even been ascribed to Plato, and it has been said that in his *Republic* he attempted to sketch only a fine ideal of a state constitution, while in the *Laws* he traced out a practicable philosophy of the state from the stand-point of the common consciousness. But in the first place, this was not Plato's true meaning. Although he acknowledges that the state he describes cannot be found on earth, and has its archetype only in heaven, by which the philosopher ought to form himself (IX. 592), still he demands that efforts should be made to realize it here, and he even attempts to show the conditions and means under which such a state could be made actual, not overlooking in all this the defects arising from the different characters and temperaments of men. A composition, dissociated from the idea, could only appear untrue to a philosopher like Plato, who saw the actual and the true only in the idea; and the common view which supposes that he wrote his Republic in the full consciousness of its impracticability, mistakes entirely the stand-point of the Platonic philosophy. Still farther the question whether such a state as the Platonic is attainable and the best, is generally perverted. The Platonic state is the Grecian state-idea given in a narrative form. It is no vain and powerless ideal to picture the idea as a rational principle in every moment of the world's history, since the idea itself is that which is absolutely actual, that which is essential and necessary in existing things. The truly ideal *ought* not to be actual, but *is* actual, and the only actual; if an idea were too good for existence, or the empirical actuality too bad for it, then were this a fault of the ideal itself. Plato has not given himself up merely to abstract theories; the philosopher cannot leap beyond his age, but can only see and grasp it in its true content. This Plato has done. His stand-point is his own age. He looks upon the political life of the Greeks as then existing, and it is this life, exalted to its idea, which forms the real content of the Platonic Republic. Plato has here represented the Grecian morality in its substantial condition. If the Platonic Republic seems prominently an ideal which can never be realized

this is owing much less to its ideality than to the defects of
the old political life.   The most prominent characteristic of the
Hellenic conception of the state, before the Greeks began to fall
into unbridled licentiousness, was the constraint thrown upon
personal subjective freedom, in the sacrifice of every individual
interest to the absolute sovereignty of the state.   With Plato
also, the state is every thing.   His political institutions, so loudly
ridiculed by the ancients, are only the undeniable consequences
following from the very idea of the Grecian state, which allowed
neither to the individual citizen nor to a corporation, any lawful
sphere of action independent of itself.

The grand feature of the Platonic state is, as has been said,
the exclusive sacrifice of the individual to the state, the reference
of moral to political virtue.   Since man cannot reach his complete
development in isolation but only as a member of an organic society (the state), Plato therefore concludes that the individual purpose should wholly conform to the general aim, and that the state
must represent a perfect and harmonious unity, and be a counterpart
of the moral life of the individual.   In a perfect state all things,
joy and sorrow, and even eyes, ears and hands, must be common
to all, so that the social life would be as it were the life of one
man.   This perfect universality and unity, can only be actualized
when every thing individual and particular falls away, and hence
the difficulty of the Platonic Republic.   Private property and
domestic life (in place of which comes a community of goods and
of wives), the duty of education, the choice of rank and profession,
the arts and sciences, all these must be subjected and placed under the exclusive and absolute control of the state. The individual may lay claim only to that happiness which belongs to him as
a constituent element of the state.   From this point Plato goes
down into the minutest particulars, and gives the closest directions
respecting gymnastics and music, which form the two means of
culture of the higher ranks; respecting the study of mathematics,
and philosophy, the choice of stringed instruments, and the proper
measure of verse; respecting bodily exercise and the service of
women in war; respecting marriage settlements, and the age at

which any one should study dialectics, marry, and beget children. The state with him is only a great educational establishment, a family in the mass.—Lyric poetry he would allow only under the inspection of competent judges. Epic and dramatic poetry, even Homer and Hesiod, should be banished from the state, since they rouse and lead astray the passions, and give unworthy representations of the gods. Exhibitions of physical degeneracy or weakness should not be tolerated in the Platonic state; deformed and sickly infants should be abandoned, and food and attention should be denied to the sick.—In all this we find the chief antithesis of the ancient to the modern state. Plato did not recognize the will and choice of the individual, and yet the individual has a right to demand this. The problem of the modern state has been to unite these two sides, to bring the universal end and the particular end of the individual into harmony, to reconcile the highest possible freedom of the conscious individual will, with the highest possible supremacy of the state.

The political institutions of the Platonic state are decidedly aristocratic. Grown up in opposition to the extravagances of the Athenian democracy, Plato prefers an absolute monarchy to every other constitution, though this should have as its absolute ruler only the perfect philosopher. It is a well-known expression of his, that the state can only attain its end when philosophers become its rulers, or when its present rulers have carried their studies so far and so accurately, that they can unite philosophy with a superintendence of public affairs (V. 473). His reason for claiming that the sovereign power should be vested only in one, is the fact that very few are endowed with political wisdom. This ideal of an absolute ruler who should be able to lead the state perfectly, Plato abandons in the *Laws*, in which work he shows his preference for a mixed constitution, embracing both a monarchical and an aristocratic element. From the aristocratic tendency of the Platonic ideal of a state, follows farther the sharp division of ranks, and the total exclusion of the third rank from a proper political life. In reality Plato makes but two classes in his state, the subjects and the sovereign, analogous to his twofold psychological division of sensible and intellectual, mortal and immortal, but as in psychology he had introduced a middle step, spirit, to stand between his two divisions there, so in the state he brings in the military class between the ruler and those intended to supply the bodily wants of the community. We have thus three ranks, that of the ruler, corresponding to the reason, that of the watcher or warrior, answering to spirit, and that of the craftsman, which is made parallel to the appetites or sensuous desires. To these three ranks belong three separate functions: to the first, that of making the law and caring for the general good; to the second, that of defending the public welfare from attacks of external foes; and to the third, the care of separate interests and wants, as agriculture, mechanics, &c. From each of these three ranks and its functions the state derives a peculiar virtue—wisdom from the ruler, bravery from the warrior, and temperance from the craftsman, so far as he lives in obedience to his rulers. In the proper union of these three virtues is found the justice of the state, a virtue which is thus the sum of all other virtues. Plato pays little attention to the lowest rank, that of the craftsman, who exists in the state only as means. He held that it was not necessary to give laws and care for the rights of this portion of the community. The separation between the ruler and the warrior is not so broad. Plato suffers these two ranks to interpenetrate each other, and analogous to his original psychological division, as though the reason were but spirit in the highest step of its development, he makes the oldest and the best of the warriors rise to the dignity and power of the rulers. The education of its warriors should therefore be a chief care of the state, in order that their spirit, though losing none of its peculiar energy, may yet be penetrated by reason. The best endowed by nature and culture among the warriors, may be selected at the age of thirty, and put upon a course of careful training. When he has reached the age of fifty and looked upon the idea of the good, he may be bound to actualize this archetype in the state, provided always that every one wait his turn, and spend his remaining time in philosophy. Only thus can the state be raised to the unconditioned rule of reason under the supremacy of the good.

SECTION XV.

THE OLD ACADEMY.

In the old Academy, we lose the presence of inventive genius; with few exceptions we find here no movements of progress, but rather a gradual retrogression of the Platonic philosophizing. After the death of Plato, Speusippus, his nephew and disciple, held the chair of his master in the Academy during eight years. He was succeeded by Xenocrates, after whom we meet with Polemo, Crates, and Crantor. It was a time in which schools for high culture were established, and the older teacher yielded to his younger successor the post of instruction. The general characteristics of the old Academy, so far as can be gathered from the scanty accounts, were great attention to learning, the prevalence of Pythagorean elements, especially the doctrine of numbers, and lastly, the reception of fantastic and demonological notions, among which the worship of the stars played a part. The prevalence of the Pythagorean doctrine of numbers in the later instructions of the Academy, gave to mathematical sciences, particularly arithmetic and astronomy, a high place, and at the same time assigned to the docrine of ideas a much lower position than Plato had given it. Subsequently, the attempt was made to get back to the unadulterated doctrine of Plato. Crantor is said to be the first editor of the Platonic writings.

As Plato was the only true Socraticist, so was Aristotle the only genuine disciple of Plato, though often abused by his fellow-disciples as unfaithful to his master's principles.

We pass on at once to him, without stopping now to inquire into his relation to Plato, or the advance which he made beyond his predecessor, since these points will come up before us in the exhibition of the Aristotelian philosophy. (*See* § XVI : III. 1.)

SECTION XVI.

ARISTOTLE.

I. LIFE AND WRITINGS OF ARISTOTLE.—Aristotle was born 384 B. C. at Stagira, a Greek colony in Thrace. His father, Nicomachus, was a physician, and the friend of Amyntas, king of Macedonia. The former fact may have had its influence in determining the scientific direction of the son, and the latter may have procured his subsequent summons to the Macedonian court. Aristotle at a very early age lost both his parents. In his seventeenth year he came to Plato at Athens, and continued with him twenty years. On account of his indomitable zeal for study, Plato named him " the Reader," and said, upon comparing him with Xenocrates, that the latter required the spur, the former the bit. Among the many charges made against his character, most prominent are those of jealousy and ingratitude towards his master, but most of the anecdotes in which these charges are embodied merit little credence. It is certain that Aristotle, after the death of Plato, stood in friendly relations with Xenocrates; still, as a writer, he can hardly be absolved from a certain want of friendship and regard towards Plato and his philosophy, though all this can be explained on psychological grounds. After Plato's death, Aristotle went with Xenocrates to Hermeas, tyrant of Atarneus, whose sister Pythias he married after Hermeas had fallen a prey to Persian violence. After the death of Pythias he is said to have married his concubine, Herpyllis, who was the mother of his son Nicomachus. In the year 343 he was called by Philip of Macedon, to take the charge of the education of his son Alexander, then thirteen years old. Both father and son honored him highly, and the latter, with royal munificence, subsequently supported him in his studies. When Alexander went to Persia, Aristotle betook himself to Athens, and taught in the Lyceum, the only gymnasium then vacant, since Xenocrates had possession of the Academy, and the Cynics of the Cynosaerges. From the shady walks (περίπατοι) of the Lyceum, in which Aristotle was accustomed to walk and expound his philosophy, his school received the name of the Peripatetic. Aristotle is said to have spent his mornings with his more mature disciples, exercising them in the profoundest questions of philosophy, while his evenings were occupied with a greater number of pupils in a more general and preparatory instruction. The former investigations were called acroamatic, the latter exoteric. He abode at Athens, and taught thirteen years, and then, after the death of Alexander, whose displeasure he had incurred, he is said to have been accused by the Athenians of impiety towards the gods, and to have fled to Chalcis, in order to escape a fate similar to that of Socrates. He died in the year 322 at Chalcis, in Eubœa.

Aristotle left a vast number of writings, of which the smaller (perhaps a fourth), but unquestionably the more important portion have come down to us, though in a form which cannot be received without some scruples. The story of Strabo about the fate of the Aristotelian writings, and the injury which they suffered in a cellar at Scepsis, is confessedly a fable, or at least limited to the original manuscripts; but the fragmentary and descriptive form which many among them, and even the most important (e. g. the metaphysics) possess, the fact that scattered portions of one and the same work (e. g. the ethics) are repeatedly found in different treatises, the irregularities and striking contradictions in one and the same writing, the disagreement found in other particulars among different works, and the distinction made by Aristotle himself between acroamatic and exoterical writings, all this gives reason to believe that we have, for the most part, before us only his oral lectures written down, and subsequently edited by his scholars.

II. Universal Character and Division of the Aristotelian Philosophy.—With Plato, philosophy had been national in both its form and content, but with Aristotle, it loses its Hellenic peculiarity, and becomes universal in scope and meaning; the Platonic dialogue changes into barren prose; a rigid, artistic language takes the place of the mythical and poetical dress; the thinking which had been with Plato intuitive, is with Aristotle discursive; the immediate beholding of reason in the former, becomes reflection and conception in the latter. Turning away from the Platonic unity of all being, Aristotle prefers to direct his attention to the manifoldness of the phenomenal; he seeks the idea only in its concrete actualization, and consequently grasps the particular far more prominently in its peculiar determinateness and reciprocal differences, than in its connection with the idea. He embraces with equal interest the facts given in nature, in history, and in the inner life of man. But he ever tends toward the individual, he must ever have a fact given in order to develope his thought upon it; it is always the empirical, the actual, which solicits and guides his speculation; his whole course is a description of the facts given, and only merits the name of a philosophy because it comprehends the empirical in its totality and synthesis; because it has carried out its induction to the farthest extent. Only because he is the absolute empiricist may Aristotle be called the truly philosopher.

This character of the Aristotelian philosophy explains at the outset its encyclopedian tendency, inasmuch as every thing given in experience is equally worthy of regard and investigation. Aristotle is thus the founder of many courses of study unknown before him; he is not only the father of logic, but also of natural history, empirical psychology, and the science of natural rights.

This devotion of Aristotle to that which is given will also explain his predominant inclination towards physics, for nature is the most immediate and actual. Connected also with this is the fact that Aristotle is the first among philosophers who has given to history and its tendencies an accurate attention. The first book of the *Metaphysics* is also the first attempt at a history of philosophy, as his politics is the first critical history of the different states and constitutions. In both these cases he brings out his own theory only as the consequence of that which has been historically given, basing it in the former case upon the works of his predecessors, and in the latter case upon the constitutions which lie before him.

It is clear that according to this, the method of Aristotle must be a different one from that of Plato. Instead of proceeding like the latter, synthetically and dialectically, he pursues for the most part an analytic and regressive course, that is, going backward from the concrete to its ultimate ground and determination. While Plato would take his stand-point in the idea, in order to explain from this position and set in a clearer light that which is given and empirical, Aristotle on the other hand, starts with that which is given, in order to find and exhibit the idea in it. His method is, hence, induction; that is, the derivation of certain principles and maxims from a sum of given facts and phenomena; his mode of procedure is, usually, argument, a barren balancing of facts, phenomena, circumstances and possibilities. He stands out for the most part only as the thoughtful observer. Renouncing all claim to universality and necessity in his results, he is content to have brought out that which has an approximative truth, and the highest degree of probability. He often affirms that science does not simply relate to the changeless and necessary, but also to that which ordinarily takes place, that being alone excluded from its province, which is strictly accidental. Philosophy, consequently, has with him the character and worth of a reckoning of probabilities, and his mode of exhibition assumes not unfrequently only the form of a doubtful deliberation. Hence there is no trace of the Platonic ideals, hence, also, his repugnance to a glowing and poetic style in philosophy, a repugnance which, while indeed it induces in him a fixed, philosophical terminology, also frequently leads him to mistake and misrepresent the opinions of his predecessors. Hence, also, in whatever he treated, his thorough adherence to that which is actually given.

Connected in fine with the empirical character of the Aristotelian philosophizing, is the fragmentary form of his writings, and their want of a systematic division and arrangement. Proceeding always in the line of that which is given, from individual to individual, he considers every province of the actual by itself, and makes it the subject of a separate treatise; but he, for the most part, fails to indicate the lines by which the different parts

hang together, and are comprehended in a systematic whole.
Thus he holds up a number of co-ordinate sciences, each one of
which has an independent basis, but he fails to give us the highest
science which embraces them all.   The principle is sometimes
affirmed that all the writings follow the idea of a whole; but in
their procedure there is such a want of all systematic connection,
and every one of his writings is a monograph so thoroughly independent and complete in itself, that we are sometimes puzzled to
know what Aristotle himself received as a part of philosophy, and
what he excluded.   We are never furnished with an independent
scheme or outline, we rarely find definite results or summary explanations, and even the different divisions of philosophy which
he gives, vary essentially from one another.   At one time he
divides science into theoretical and practical, at another, he adds
to these two a poetical creative science, while still again he speaks
of the three parts of science, ethics, physics, and logic.   At one
time he divides the theoretical philosophy into logic and physics,
and at another into theology, mathematics, and physics.   But no
one of these divisions has he expressly given as the basis on which
to represent his system; he himself places no value upon this
method of division, and, indeed, openly declares himself opposed
to it.   It is, therefore, only for the sake of uniformity that we
can give the preference here to the threefold division of philosophy as already adopted by Plato.

III. Logic and Metaphysics.   1. Conception and Relation of the Two.—The word metaphysics was first furnished by
the Aristotelian commentators.   Plato had used the term dialectics, and Aristotle had characterized the same thing as "first philosophy," while he calls physics the "second philosophy."   The
relation of this first philosophy to the other sciences Aristotle determines in the following way.   Every science, he says, must have
for investigation a determined province and separate form of being,
but none of these sciences reaches the conception of being itself.
Hence there is needed a science which should investigate that
which the other sciences take up hypothetically, or through experience.   This is done by the first philosophy which has to do

with being as such, while the other sciences relate only to determined and concrete being. The metaphysics, which is this science of being and its primitive grounds, is the *first* philosophy, since it is presupposed by every other discipline. Thus, says Aristotle, if there were only a physical substance, then would physics be the first and the only philosophy, but if there be an immaterial and unmoved essence which is the ground of all being, then must there also be an antecedent, and because it is antecedent, a universal philosophy. The first ground of all being is God, whence Aristotle occasionally gives to the first philosophy the name of theology.

It is difficult to determine the relation between this first philosophy as the science of the ultimate ground of things, and that science which is ordinarily termed the logic of Aristotle, and which is exhibited in the writings bearing the name of the *Organon*. Aristotle himself has not accurately examined the relations of these two sciences, the reason of which is doubtless to be found in the incomplete form of the metaphysics. But since he has embraced them both under the same name of logic, since the investigation of the essence of things (VII. 17), and the doctrine of ideas (XIII. 5), are expressly called logical, since he repeatedly attempts in the Metaphysics (*Book* IV.), to establish the logical principle of contradiction as an absolute presupposition for all thinking and speaking and philosophizing, and employs the method of argument belonging to that science which has to do with the essence of things (III. 2. IV. 3), and since, in fine, the categories to which he had already dedicated a separate book in the Organon are also discussed again in the Metaphysics (*Book* V.), it follows that this much at least may be affirmed with certainty, that he would not absolutely separate the investigations of the Organon from those of the Metaphysics, and that he would not counsel the ordinary division of formal logic and metaphysics, although he has omitted to show more clearly their inner connection.

2. LOGIC.—The great problem both of the logical faculty and also of logic both as science and art, consists in this, viz., to form

and judge of conclusions, and through conclusions to be able to establish a proof. The conclusions, however, arise from propositions, and the propositions from conceptions. According to this natural point of view, which lies in the very nature of the case, Aristotle has divided the content of the logical and dialectical doctrine contained in the different treatises of the Organon. The first treatise in the Organon is that containing the *categories*, a work which treats of the universal determinations of being, and gives the first attempt at an ontology. Of these categories Aristotle enumerates ten; essence, magnitude, quality, relation, the where, the when, position, habit, action, and passion. The second treatise (*de interpretatione*) investigates speech as the expression of thought, and discusses the doctrine of the parts of speech, propositions and judgments. The third are the analytic books, which show how conclusions may be referred back to their principles and arranged in order of their antecedence. The first Analytic contains in two books the universal doctrine of the Syllogism. Conclusions are according to their content and end either apodictic, which possess a certain and incontrovertible truth, or dialectic, which are directed toward that which may be disputed and is probable, or, finally, sophistic, which are announced deceptively as correct conclusions while they are not. The doctrine of apodictic conclusions and thus of proofs is given in the two books of the second Analytic, that of dialectic, is furnished in the eight books of the Topic, and that of sophistic in the treatise concerning "Sophistical Convictions."

A closer statement of the Aristotelian logic would be familiar to every one, since the formal representations of this science ordinarily given, employ for the most part only the material furnished by Aristotle. Kant has remarked, that since the time of the Grecian sage, logic has made neither progress nor retrogression. Only in two points has the formal logic of our time advanced beyond that of Aristotle; first, in adding to the categorical conclusion which was the only one Aristotle had in mind, the hypothetical and disjunctive, and second, in adding the fourth to the first three figures of conclusion. But the incompleteness of the Aristotelian logic, which might be pardoned in the founder of this science, yet abides, and its thoroughly empirical method not only still continues, but has even been exalted to a principle by making the antithesis, which Aristotle did not, between the form of a thought and the content. Aristotle, in reality, only attempted to collect the logical facts in reference to the formation of propositions, and the method of conclusions; he has given in his logic only the natural history of finite thinking. However highly now we may rate the correctness of his abstraction, and the clearness with which he brings into consciousness the logical operation of the understanding, we must make equally conspicuous with this the want of all scientific derivation and foundation. The ten categories which he, as already remarked, has discussed in a separate treatise, he simply mentions, without furnishing any ground or principle for this enumeration; that there are this number of categories is only a matter of fact to him, and he even cites them differently in different writings. In the same way also he takes up the figures of the conclusion empirically; he considers them only as forms and determinations of relation of the formal thinking, and continues thus, although he allows the conclusion to stand for the only form of science within the province of the logic of the understanding. Neither in his Metaphysics nor in his Physics does he cite the rules of the formal methods of conclusion which he develops in the Organon, clearly proving that he has nowhere in his system properly elaborated either his categories or his analytic: his logical investigations do not influence generally the development of his philosophical thought, but have for the most part only the value of a preliminary scrutiny.

3. METAPHYSICS.—Among all the Aristotelian writings, the Metaphysics is least entitled to be called a connected whole; it is only a connection of sketches, which, though they follow a certain fundamental idea, utterly fail of an inner mediation and a perfect development. We may distinguish in it seven distinct groups. (1) Criticism of the previous philosophic systems viewed in the light of the four Aristotelian principles, *Book* I. (2) Positing of the apories or the philosophical preliminary questions,

III. (3) The principle of contradiction, IV. (4) Definitions,
V. (5) Examination of the conception of essence (οὐσία) and
conceivable being (the τί ἦν εἶναι) or the conception of matter
(ὕλη), form (εἶδος), and that which arises from the connection
of these two (σύνολον), VII. VIII. (6) Potentiality and actuality, IX. (7) The Divine Spirit moving all, but itself unmoved, XII. (8) To these we may add the polemic against the
Platonic doctrine of ideas and numbers, which runs through the
whole Metaphysics, but is especially carried out in *Books* XIII.
and XIV.

(1) *The Aristotelian Criticism of the Platonic Doctrine of
Ideas.*—In Aristotle's antagonism to the Platonic doctrine of
ideas, we must seek for the specific difference between the two
systems, a difference of which Aristotle avails himself of every
opportunity (especially *Metaph.* I. and XIII.) to express. Plato
had beheld every thing actual in the idea, but the idea was to him
a rigid truth, which had not yet become interwoven with the life
and the movement of existence. Such a view, however, had this
difficulty, the idea, however little Plato would have it so, found
standing over against it in independent being the phenomenal
world, while it furnished no principle on which the being of the
phenomenal world could be affirmed. This Aristotle recognizes
and charges upon Plato, that his ideas were only "immortalized
things of sense," out of which the being and becoming of the
sensible could not be explained. In order to avoid this consequence, he himself makes out an original reference of mind to
phenomenon, affirming that the relation of the two is, that of the
actual to the possible, or that of form to matter, and considering
also mind as the absolute actuality of matter, and matter, as the
potentially mind. His argument against the Platonic doctrine
of ideas, Aristotle makes out in the following way.

Passing by now the fact that Plato has furnished no satisfactory proof for the objective and independent reality of ideas, and
that his theory is without vindication, we may affirm in the first
place that it is wholly unfruitful, since it possesses no ground of
explanation for being. The ideas have no proper and independent

content. To see this we need only refer to the manner in which Plato introduced them. In order to make science possible he had posited certain substances independent of the sensible, and uninfluenced by its changes. But to serve such a purpose, there was offered to him nothing other than this individual thing of sense. Hence he gave to this individual a universal form, which was with him the idea. From this it resulted, that his ideas can hardly be separated from the sensible and individual objects which participate in them. The ideal duality and the empirical duality is one and the same content. The truth of this we can readily see, whenever we gain from the adherents to the doctrine of ideas a definite statement respecting the peculiar character of their unchangeable substances, in comparison with the sensible and individual things which participate in them. The only difference between the two consists in appending *per se* to the names expressing the respective ideas ; thus, while the individual things are *e. g.* man, horse, etc., the ideas are man *per se*, horse *per se*, etc. There is only this formal change for the doctrine of ideas to rest upon; the finite content is not removed, but is only *characterized* as perpetual. This objection, that in the doctrine of ideas we have in reality only the sensible posited as a not-sensible, and endowed with the predicate of immutability, Aristotle urges as above remarked when he calls the ideas " immortalized things of sense," not as though they were actually something sensible and spacial, but because in them the sensible individual loses at once its individuality, and becomes a universal. He compares them in this respect with the gods of the popular and anthropomorphical religion ; as these are nothing but deified men, so the ideas are only things of nature endowed with a supernatural potency, a sensible exalted to a not-sensible. This identity between the ideas and their respective individual things amounts moreover to this, that the introduction of ideas doubles the objects to be known in a burdensome manner, and without any good results. Why set up the same thing over again? Why besides the sensible twofold-ness and threefoldness, affirm a twofoldness and threefoldness in the idea ? The adherents of the doctrine of ideas, when they posit an idea for every class of natural things, and through this theory set up two equivalent theories of sensible and not-sensible substances, seem therefore to Aristotle like men who think they can reckon better with many numbers than with few, and who therefore go to multiplying their numbers before they begin their reckoning. Therefore again the doctrine of ideas is a tautology, and wholly unfruitful of the explanation of being. "The ideas give no aid to the knowledge of the individual things participating in them, since the ideas are not immanent in these things, but separate from them." Equally unfruitful are the ideas when considered in reference to the arising and departing of the things of sense. They contain no principle of becoming, of movement. There is in them no causality which might bring out the event, or explain the event when it had actually happened. Themselves without motion and process, if they had any effect, it could only be that of perfect repose. True, Plato affirms in his Phædon that the ideas are causes both of being and becoming, but in spite of the ideas, nothing ever *becomes* without a moving; the ideas, by their separation from the becoming, have no such capacity to move. This indifferent relation of ideas to the actual becoming, Aristotle brings under the categories, potentiality and actuality, and farther says that the ideas are only potential, they are only bare possibility and essentiality because they are wanting in actuality.—The inner contradiction of the doctrine of ideas is in brief this, viz., that it posits an individual immediately as a universal, and at the same time pronounces the universal, the species, as numerically an individual, and also that the ideas are set up on the one side as separate individual substances, and on the other side as participant, and therefore as universal. Although the ideas as the original conceptions of species are a universal, which arise when being is fixed in existence, and the one brought out in the many, and the abiding is given a place in the changeable, yet can they not be defined as they should be according to the Platonic notion, that they are individual substances, for there can be neither definition nor derivation of an absolute individual, since even the word (and only in words is a definition possible) is in its nature a universal, and belongs also to other objects, consequently, every predicate in which I attempt to determine an individual thing cannot belong exclusively to that thing. The adherents of the doctrine of ideas, are therefore not at all in a condition to give an idea a conceivable termination ; their ideas are indefinable.—In general, Plato has left the relation of the individual objects to ideas very obscure. He calls the ideas archetypes, and allows that the objects may participate in them ; yet are these only poetical metaphors. How shall we represent to ourselves this " participation," this copying of the original archetype ? We seek in vain for more accurate explanations of this in Plato. It is impossible to conceive how and why matter participates in the ideas. In order to explain this, we must add to the ideas a still higher and wider principle, which contains the cause for this " participation " of objects, for without a moving principle we find no ground for " participation." Alike above the idea (e. g. the idea of man), and the phenomenon (e. g. the individual man), there must stand a third common to both, and in which the two were united, i. e. as Aristotle was in the habit of expressing this objection, the doctrine of ideas leads to the adoption of a " third man." The result of this Aristotelian criticism is the immanence of the universal in the individual. The method of Socrates in trying to find the universal as the essence of the individual, and to give definitions according to conception, was as correct (for no science is possible without the universal) as the theory of Plato in exalting these universal conceptions to an independent subsistence as real individual substances, was erroneous. Nothing universal, nothing which is a kind or a species, exists besides and separate from the individual ; a thing and its conception cannot be separated from each other. With these principles Aristotle hardly deviated from Plato's fundamental idea that the universal is the only true being, and the essence of individual things ; it may rather be said that he has freed this idea from its original abstraction, and given it a more profound mediation with the phenomenal world. Notwithstanding his apparent contradiction to Plato, the fundamental position of Aristotle is the same as that of his master, viz., that the essence of a thing (τὸ τί ἐστιν, τὸ τί ἦν εἶναι) is known and represented in the conception; Aristotle however recognizes the universal, the conception to be as little separated from the determined phenomenon as form from matter, and essence or substance (οὐσία) in its most proper sense is, according to him, only that which cannot be predicated of another, though of this other every remaining thing may be predicated; it is that which is a this (τόδε τι), the individual thing and not a universal.

(2.) *The four Aristotelian principles or causes, and the relation of form and matter.*—From the criticism of the Platonic doctrine of ideas arose directly the groundwork of the Aristotelian system, the determinations of matter (ὕλη), and form (εἶδος). Aristotle enumerates four metaphysical principles or causes: matter, form, moving cause, and end. In a house, for instance, the matter is the wood, the form is the conception of the house, the moving cause is the builder, and the end is the actual house. These four determinations of all being resolve themselves upon a closer scrutiny into the fundamental antithesis of matter and form. The conception of the moving cause is involved with the two other ideal principles of form and of end. The moving cause is that which has secured the transition of the incomplete actuality or potentiality to the complete actuality, or induces the becoming of matter to form. But in every movement of the incomplete to the complete, the latter antedates in conception this movement, and is its motive. The moving cause of matter is therefore form. So is man the moving and producing cause of man; the form of the statue in the understanding of the artist is the cause of the movement by which the statue is produced; health must be in the thought of the physician before it can become the moving cause of convalescence; so in a certain degree is medicine, health, and the art of building the form of the house. But in the same way, the moving or first cause is also identical with the final cause or end, for the end is the motive for all becoming and movement. The moving cause of the house is the builder, but the moving cause of the builder is the end to be attained, *i. e.* the house.

From such examples as these it is seen that the determinations of form and end may be considered under one, in so far as both are united in the conception of actuality (ἐνέργεια), for the end of every thing is its completed being, its conception or its form, the bringing out into complete actuality that which was potentially contained in it. The end of the hand is its conception, the end of the seed is the tree. which is at the same time the essence of the seed. The only fundamental determinations, therefore, which cannot be wholly resolved into each other, are matter and form.

Matter when abstracted from form in thought, Aristotle regarded as that which was entirely without predicate, determination and distinction. It is that abiding thing which lies at the basis of all becoming; but which in its own being is different from every thing which has become. It is capable of the widest diversity of forms, but is itself without determinate form; it is every thing in possibility, but nothing in actuality. There is a first matter which lies at the basis of every determinate thing, precisely as the wood is related to the bench and the marble to the statue. With this conception of matter Aristotle prides himself upon having conquered the difficulty so frequently urged of explaining the possibility that any thing can become, since being can neither come out of being nor out of not-being. For it is not out of not-being absolutely, but only out of that which as to actuality is not-being, but which potentially is being, that any thing becomes. Possible or potential being is no more not-being than actuality. Every existing object of nature is hence but a potential thing which has become actualized. Matter is thus a far more positive substratum with Aristotle than with Plato, who had treated it as absolutely not-being. From this is clearly seen how Aristotle could apprehend matter in opposition to form as something positively negative and antithetic to the form, and as its positive denial (στέρησις).

As matter coalesces with potentiality, so does form coincide with actuality. It is that which makes a distinguishable and actual object, a this (τόδε τι) out of the undistinguished and in-

6

determinate matter; it is the peculiar virtue, the completed activity, the soul of every thing. That which Aristotle calls form,
therefore, is not to be confounded with what we perhaps may call
shape; a hand severed from the arm, for instance, has still the
outward shape of a hand, but according to the Aristotelian apprehension, it is only a hand now as to matter and not as to form : an
actual hand, a hand as to form, is only that which can do the
proper work of a hand. Pure form is that which, in truth, is
without matter (τὸ τί ἦν εἶναι); or, in other words, the conception
of being, the pure conception. But such pure form does not
exist in the realm of determined being; every determined being,
every individual substance (οὐσία), every thing which is a this, is
rather a totality of matter and form, a (σύνολον). It is, therefore, owing to matter, that being is not pure form and pure conception; matter is the ground of the becoming, the manifold, and
the accidental; and it is this, also, which gives to science its
limits. For in precisely the measure in which the individual
thing bears in itself a material element is it uncognizable. From
what has been said, it follows that the opposition between matter
and form is a variable one, that being matter in one respect
which in another is form; building-wood, e. g. is matter in relation to the completed house, but in relation to the unhewn tree it
is form; the soul in respect to the body is form, but in respect to
the reason, which is the form of form (εἶδος εἴδους) is it matter.
On this stand-point the totality of all existence may be represented as a ladder, whose lowest step is a prime matter (πρώτη
ὕλη), which is not at all form, and whose highest step is an ultimate
form which is not at all matter, but is pure form (the absolute,
divine spirit). That which stands between these two points is in
one respect matter, and in another respect form, i. e. the former
is ever translating itself into the latter. This position, which
lies at the basis of the Aristotelian view of nature, is attained
analytically through the observation that all nature exhibits the
perpetual and progressive transition of matter into form, and
shows the exhaustless and original ground of things as it comes
to view in ever ascending ideal formations. That all matter

should become form, and all that is potential should be actual, and all that is should be known, is doubtless the demand of the reason and the end of all becoming; yet is this actually impracticable, since Aristotle expressly affirms that matter as the antithesis, or denial of form, can never become wholly actualized, and therefore can never be perfectly known. The Aristotelian system ends thus like its predecessors, in the unsubdued dualism of matter and form.

(3.) *Potentiality and Actuality* (δύναμις and ενέργεια).—The relation of matter to form, logically apprehended, is but the relation of potentiality to actuality. These terms, which Aristotle first employed according to their philosophical significance, are very characteristic for his system. We have in the movement of potential being to actual being the explicit conception of becoming, and in the four principles we have a distribution of this conception in its parts. The Aristotelian system is consequently a system of the becoming, in which the Heraclitic principle appears again in a richer and profounder apprehension, as that of the Eleatics had done with Plato. Aristotle in this has made no insignificant step towards the subjection of the Platonic dualism. If matter is the possibility of form, or reason becoming, then is the opposition between the idea and the phenomenal world potentially overcome, at least in principle, since there is one being which appears both in matter and form only in different stages of development. The relation of the potential to the actual Aristotle exhibits by the relation of the unfinished to the finished work, of the unemployed carpenter to the one at work upon his building, of the individual asleep to him awake. Potentially the seed-corn is the tree, but the grown up tree is it actually; the potential philosopher is he who is not at this moment in a philosophizing condition; even before the battle the better general is the potential conqueror; potentially is space infinitely divisible; in fact every thing is potentially which possesses a principle of motion, of development, or of change, and which, if unhindered by any thing external, will be of itself. Actuality or entelechy on the other hand indicates the perfect act, the end as

gained, the completely actual (the grown-up tree e. g. is the entelechy of the seed-corn), that activity in which the act and the
completeness of the act fall together, e. g. to see, to think where
he sees and he has seen, he thinks and he has thought (the acting
and the completeness of the act) are one and the same, while in
those activities which involve a becoming, e. g. to learn, to go, to
become well, the two are separated. In this apprehension of form
(or idea) as actuality or entelechy, i. e. in joining it with the
movement of the becoming, is found the chief antagonism of the
Aristotelian and Platonic systems. Plato considers the idea as
being at rest, and consisting for itself, in opposition to the becoming and to motion; but with Aristotle the idea is the eternal
product of the becoming, it is an eternal energy, i. e. an activity
in complete actuality, it is not perfect being, but is being produced
in every moment and eternally, through the movement of the
potential to its actual end.

(4.) *The Absolute, Divine Spirit.*—Aristotle has sought to
establish from a number of sides, the conception of the absolute
spirit, or as he calls it, the first mover, and especially by joining it
to the relation of potentiality and actuality.

(a.) *The Cosmological Form.*—The actual is ever antecedent
to the potential not only in conception (for I can speak of potentiality only in reference to some activity) but also in time, for the
acting becomes actual only through an acting; the uneducated
becomes educated through the educated, and this leads to the
claim of a first mover which shall be pure activity. Or, again,
it is only possible that there should be motion, becoming, or a
chain of causes, except as a principle of motion, a mover exists.
But this principle of motion must be one whose essence is actuality, since that which only exists in possibility cannot alone become
actual, and therefore cannot be a principle of motion. All becoming postulates with itself that which is eternal and which has not
become, that which itself unmoved is a principle of motion, a first
mover.

(b.) *The Ontological Form.*—In the same way it follows from
the conception of potentiality, that the eternal and necessary

being cannot be potential. For that which potentially is, may just as well either be or not be; but that which possibly is not, is temporal and not eternal. Nothing therefore which is absolutely permanent, is potential, but only actual. Or, again, if potentiality be the first, then can there be no possible existence, but this contradicts the conception of the absolute or that which it is impossible should not be.

(*c.*) *The Moral Form.*—Potentiality always involves a possibility to the most opposite. He who has the capacity to be well, has also the capacity to be sick, but actually no man is at the same time both sick and well. Therefore actuality is better than potentiality, and only it can belong to the eternal.

(*d.*) So far as the relation of potentiality and actuality is identical with the relation of matter and form, we may apprehend in the following way these arguments for the existence of a being which is pure actuality. The supposition of an absolute matter without form (the πρώτη ὕλη) involves also the supposition of an absolute form without matter (a πρῶτον εἶδος). And since the conception of form resolves itself into the three determinations, of the moving, the conceivable, and the final cause, so is the eternal one the absolute principle of motion (the first mover πρῶτον χινοῦν), the absolute conception or pure intelligible (the pure τί ἦν εἶναι), and the absolute end.

All the other predicates of the first mover or the highest principle of the world, follow from these premises with logical necessity. Unity belongs to him, since the ground of the manifoldness of being lies in the matter and he has no participation in matter; he is immovable and abiding ever the same, since otherwise he could not be the absolute mover and the cause of all becoming; he is life as active self-end and actuality; he is at the same time intelligible and intelligence, because he is absolutely immaterial and free from nature; he is active, *i. e.* thinking intelligence, because his essence is pure actuality; he is self-contemplating intelligence, because the divine thought cannot attain its actuality in any thing extrinsic, and because if it were the thought of any thing other than itself, this would make it depend upon some potential existence for its actualization. Hence the famed Aristotelian definition of the absolute that it is the thought of thought (νόησις νοήσεως), the personal unity of the thinking and the thought, of the knowing and the known, the absolute subject-object. In the Metaphysics (XII. 1.) we have a statement in order of these attributes of the Divine Spirit, and an almost devout sketch of the eternally blessed Deity, knowing himself in his eternal tranquillity as the absolute truth, satisfied with himself, and wanting neither in activity nor in any virtue.

As would appear from this statement, Aristotle has never fully developed the idea of his absolute spirit, and still less has he harmonized it with the fundamental principles and demands of his philosophy, although many consequences of his system would seem to drive him to this, and numerous principles which he has laid down would seem to prepare the way for it. This idea is unexpectedly introduced in the twelfth book of the Metaphysics simply as an assertion, without being farther and inductively substantiated. It is at once attended with important difficulties. We do not see why the ultimate ground of motion or the absolute spirit must be conceived as a personal being; we do not see how any thing can be a moving cause and yet itself unmoved; how it can be the origin of all becoming, that is of the departing and arising, and itself remain a changeless energy, a principle of motion with no potentiality to be moved, for the moving thing must stand in a relation of passive and active with the thing moved. Moreover, Aristotle, as would follow from these contradictory determinations, has never thoroughly and consistently determined the relation between God and the world. He has considered the absolute spirit only as contemplative and theoretical reason, from whom all action must be excluded because he is perfect end in himself, but every action presupposes an end not yet perfected; we have thus no true motive for his activity in reference to the world. He cannot be truly called the first mover in his theoretical relation alone, and since he is in his essence extra-mundane and unmoved, he cannot once permeate the life of the world with his activity; and since also matter on one side never rises wholly to form, we have, therefore, here again the unreconciled dualism between the Divine spirit and the unmistakable reality of matter. Many of the arguments which Aristotle brings against the gods of Anaxagoras may be urged against his own theory.

IV. THE ARISTOTELIAN PHYSICS.—The Aristotelian Physics, which embraces the greater portion of his writings, follows the becoming and the building up of matter into form, the course through which nature as a living being progresses in order to become individual soul. All becoming has an end; but end is form, and the absolute form is spirit. With perfect consistency, therefore, Aristotle regards the human individual of the male sex as the end and the centre of earthly nature in its realized form. All else beneath the moon is, as it were, an unsuccessful attempt of nature to produce the male human, a superfluity which arises from the impotence of nature to subdue the whole of matter and bring it into form. Every thing which does not gain the universal end of nature must be regarded as incomplete, and is properly an exception or abortion. For instance, he calls it an abortion when a child does not resemble its father; and the female child he looks upon as an abortion in a less degree, which he accounts for by the insufficient energy of the male as the forming principle. In general, Aristotle regards the female as imperfect in comparison with the male, an imperfection which belongs in a higher degree to all animals except man. If nature did her work with perfect consciousness, then were all these mistakes, these incomplete and improper formations inexplicable, but she is an artist working only after an unconscious impulse, and does not complete her work with a clear and rational insight.

1. The universal conditions of all natural existence, *motion*, *matter*, *space* and *time*, Aristotle investigates in the books of Physics. These physical conceptions may, moreover, be reduced to the metaphysical notions of potentiality and actuality; motion is accordingly defined as the activity of being potentially, and is therefore a mean between the merely potential entity and the

perfectly realized activity;—space is the possibility of motion
and possesses, therefore, potentially, though not actively, the property of infinite divisibility; time is in the same way the infinitely divisible, expressing the measure of motion in number,
and is the number of motion according to before and after.   All
three are infinite, but the infinite which is represented in them is
only potentially but not actually a whole : it comprehends nothing,
but is itself comprehended,—a fact mistaken by those who are
accustomed to extol the infinite as though it comprehended and
held every thing in itself, because it had some similarity with the
whole.

2. From his conception of motion Aristotle derives his view
of the *collective universe*, as brought out in his books *De Cœlo*
The most perfect motion is the circular, because this is constant,
uniform, and ever returning into itself.   The world as a whole is
therefore conditioned by the circular motion, and being a whole
complete in itself, it has a spherical form.   But because the motion which returns into itself is better than every other, it follows, from the same ground, that in this spherical universe the
better sphere will be in the circumference where the circular
motion is most perfect, and the inferior one will arrange itself
around the centre of the universal sphere.   The former is heaven,
the latter is earth, and between the two stand the planetary
spheres.   Heaven, as the place of circular motion, and the scene
of unchangeable order, stands nearest the first moving cause, and
is under its immediate influence ; it is the place where the ancients, guided by the correct tradition of a lost wisdom, have
placed the Divine abode.   Its parts, the fixed stars, are passionless and eternal essences, which have attained the best end, which
must be eternally conceived in a tireless activity, and which,
though not clearly cognizable, are yet much more divine than
man.   A lower sphere, next to that of the fixed stars, is the
sphere of the planets, among which, besides the five known to the
ancients, he reckons the sun and the moon.   This sphere stands
a little removed from the greatest perfection : instead of moving
directly from right to left, as do the fixed stars, the planets move

in contrary directions and in oblique orbits; they serve the fixed stars, and are ruled by their motion. Lastly, the earth is in the centre of the universe, farthest removed from the first mover, and hence partaking in the smallest degree of the Divine. There are thus three kinds of being, exhibiting three stages of perfection, and necessary for the explanation of nature; first, the absolute spirit or God, an immaterial being, who, himself unmoved, produces motion; second, the super-terrestrial region of the heavens, a being which is moved and which moves, and which, though not without matter, is eternal and unchangeable, and possesses ever a circular motion; and, lastly, in the lowest course this earth, a changeful being, which has only to play the passive part of being moved.

3. *Nature in a strict sense*, the scene of elemental working represents to us a constant and progressive transition of the elementary to the vegetative, and of the vegetative to the animal world. The lowest step is occupied by the inanimate bodies of nature, which are simple products of the elements mingling themselves together, and have their entelechy only in the determinate combinations of these elements, but whose energy consists only in striving after a fitting place in the universe, and in resting there so far as they reach it unhindered. But now such a mere external entelechy is not possessed by the living bodies; within them dwells a motion as organizing principle by which they attain to actuality, and which as a preserving activity develops in them towards a perfected organization,—in a word they have a soul, for a soul is the entelechy of an organic body. In plants we find the soul working only as persevering and nourishing energy : the plant has no other function than to nourish itself and to propagate its kind ; among animals—where we find a progress according to the mode of their reproduction—the soul appears as sensitive ; animals have sense, and are capable of locomotion ; lastly, the human soul is at the same time nutritive, sensitive, and cognitive.

4. *Man*, as the end of all nature, embraces in himself the different steps of development in which the life of nature is ex-

6*

hibited.   The division of the faculties of the soul must therefore
be necessarily regulated, according to the division of living creatures.   As the nutritive faculty is alone the property of vegeta-
bles, and sensation, of animals, while to the more perfect animals
locomotion also belongs, so are these three activities also development steps of the human soul, the antecedent being the necessary condition of, and presupposed in time by, the subsequent,
while the soul itself is nothing other than the union of these different activities of an organic body in one common end, as the
entelechy of the organic body.   The fourth step, thought or reason, which, added to the three others, constitutes the peculiarity
of the human soul, forms alone an exception from the general
law.   It is not a simple product of the lower faculties of the soul,
it does not stand related to them simply as a higher stage of development, nor simply as the soul to the body, as the end to the
instrument, as actuality to possibility, as form to matter.   But as
pure intellectual activity, it completes itself without any mediation of a bodily organ ; as the reason comes into the body from
without, so is it separable from the body, and therefore has it no
inner connection with the bodily functions, but is something
wholly foreign in nature.   True, there exists a connection between thought and sensation, for while the sensations are outwardly divided, according to the different objects of sense, yet
internally they meet in one centre, as a common sense.   Here
they become changed into images and representations, which
again become transmuted into thoughts, and so it might seem as
if thought were only the result of the sensation, as if intelligence
were passively determined; (here we might notice the proposition
falsely ascribed to Aristotle : *nihil est in intellectu quod non
fuerit in sensu,* and also the well-known though often misunderstood comparison of the soul with an unwritten tablet, which
only implies this much, viz., that as the unwritten tablet is potentially but not actually a book, so does knowledge belong potentially though not actually to the human reason ; fundamentally
and radically the thought may have in itself universal conceptions, so far as it has the capacity to form them, but not actually,

nor in a determined or developed form). But this passivity pre-supposes rather an activity; for if the thought in its actuality, in that it appears as knowledge, *becomes* all forms and therefore all things, then must the thought *constitute itself* that which it becomes, and therefore all passively determined human intelligence rests on an originally active intelligence, which exists as self-actualizing possibility and pure actuality, and which, as such, is wholly independent of the human body, and has not its entelechy in it but in itself, and is not therefore participant in the death of the body, but lives on as universal reason, eternal and immortal. The Aristotelian dualism here again appears. Manifestly this active intelligence stands related to the soul as God to nature. The two sides possess no essential relation to each other. As the Divine spirit could not enter the life of the world, so is the human spirit unable to permeate the life of sense; although it is determined as something passionless and immaterial, still must it as soul be connected with matter, and although it is pure and self-contemplative form, still it should be distinguished from the Divine spirit which is its counterpart; the want of a satisfactory mediation on the side of the human and on that of the Divine, is in these respects unmistakable.

V. THE ARISTOTELIAN ETHICS. 1. RELATION OF ETHICS TO PHYSICS.—Aristotle, guided by his tendency towards the natural, has more closely connected ethics and physics than either of his predecessors, Socrates or Plato, had done. While Plato found it impossible to speak of the good in man's moral condition, disconnected from the idea of the good in itself, Aristotle's principal object is to determine what is good for man solely; and he supposes that the good in itself, the idea of the good, in no way facilitates the knowledge of that good, which alone is attainable in practical life. It is only the latter, the moral element in the life of men, and not the good in the great affairs of the universe, with which ethics has to do. Aristotle therefore considers the good especially in its relation to the natural condition of men, and affirms that it is the end towards which nature herself tends. Instead of viewing the moral element as something purely intel-

lectual, he rather apprehends it as only the bloom of the physical, which here becomes spiritualized and ethical; instead of
making virtue to be knowledge, he treats it as the normal perfection of the natural instinct. That man is *by nature* a political
animal, is his fundamental proposition for the doctrine of the
state.

From this connection of the ethical and the physical, arose the
objections which Aristotle urged against the Socratic conception
of virtue. Socrates had looked to the dialectical exclusively for
the ground of all morality, and had accordingly made virtue and
knowledge one. But in this, said Aristotle, the pathological element which is associated by nature with every moral act, is
destroyed. It is not reason, but the circumstances and natural
bias of the soul which are the first ground of virtue. There is an
instinct in the soul which at first strives unconsciously after the
good, which is only subsequently sought with the full moral insight. Moral virtue arises first from that which is natural. It
is on this ground, also, that Aristotle combats the notion that
virtue may be learned. It is not through the perfection of
knowledge, but by exercise that we become acquainted with the
good. It is by a practice of moral acts that we become virtuous,
just as by a practice of building and of music we become archi-
tects and musicians; for the habit which is the ground of moral
constancy, is only a fruit of the abundant repetition of a moral
action. Hence it is that originally we have our virtuous or our
vicious dispositions in our power, but as soon as they are formed
either to virtue or to vice, we are no longer able to control them.
It is by three things, therefore, nature, habit, and reason, that man
becomes good. The stand-point of Aristotle is in these respects
directly opposed to that of Socrates. While Socrates regarded
the moral and the natural as two opposites, and made the moral
conduct to be the consequent of a rational enlightenment, Aristotle treated both as different steps of development, and reversing
the order of Socrates, made the rational enlightenment in moral
things consequent upon the moral conduct.

2. THE HIGHEST GOOD.—Every action has an end; but since

every end is only itself a means to some other, we need therefore something after which we can strive for its own sake, and which is a good absolutely, or a best. What now is this highest good and supreme object of human pursuit? In name, at least, all men are agreed upon it, and call it happiness, but what happiness is, is a much disputed point. If asked in what human happiness consists, the first characteristic given would be that it belongs alone to the peculiar being of man. But sensation is not peculiar to man, for he shares this with the brute. A sensation of pleasure, therefore, which arises when some desire is gratified, may be the happiness of the brute, but certainly does not constitute the essential of human happiness. Human happiness must express the completeness of intelligent existence, and because intelligence is essentially activity, therefore the happiness of man cannot consist in any merely passive condition, but must express a completeness of human action. Happiness therefore is a well-being, which is at the same time a well-doing, and it is a well-doing which satisfies all the conditions of nature, and which finds the highest contentment or well-being in an unrestrained energy. Activity and pleasure are thus inseparably bound together by a natural bond, and happiness is the result of their union when they are sustained through a perfect life. Hence the Aristotelian definition of happiness. It is a perfect practical activity in a perfect life.

Although it might seem from this as though Aristotle placed the happiness of man in the natural activity of the soul, and regarded this as self-sufficient, still he is not blind to the fact that perfect happiness is dependent on other kinds of good whose possession is not absolutely within our power. It is true he expresses an opinion that outward things in moderation are sufficient, and that only great success or signal reverses materially influence the happiness of life; still he holds that wealth, the possession of friends and children, noble birth, beauty of body, etc., are more or less necessary conditions of happiness, though these are partly dependent on accidental circumstances. These wavering and inconsistent views of Aristotle respecting the nature of happiness, naturally rise from his empirical method of investigation. Careful in noting every thing which our limited experience seems to utter, he expressly avoids making either virtue or pleasure his principle, because actual experience shows the separation of the two. Although therefore he gives directions in general to strive after that pleasure in which the good man delights, or which is connected with a virtuous activity, yet is pleasure with him an end for its own sake, and not merely an accident of virtue, an empiricist, Aristotle is here also a dualist, while the Stoics and Epicureans have respectively taken and held fast to each of the two sides.

3. CONCEPTION OF VIRTUE.—As has already been seen in the Aristotelian Polemic against Socrates, virtue is the product of an oft-repeated moral action, a condition acquired through practice, a moral dexterity of the soul. The nature of this dexterity is seen in the following way : every action completes something as its work; but now if a work is imperfect when it has either a want or a superfluity, so also is every action imperfect in so far as there is in it either too little or too much; its perfection, therefore, is only found as it contains the right degree, the true mean between the too much and too little. Accordingly, virtue in general may be explained as the observation of the right mean in action, by which is meant not the arithmetical or absolute mean, but the one relative to ourselves. For what is enough for one individual is insufficient for another. The virtue of a man, of a woman, of a child, and of a slave is respectively different. Thus, virtue depends upon time, circumstance, and relation. The determination of this correct mean will always waver. In the impossibility of an active and exhaustive formula, we can only say respecting it that it is the correct mean as determined by a correct practical insight which is seen to be such by the intelligent man.

It follows from this general conception of virtue, that there will be as many separate virtues as there are circumstances of life, and as men are ever entering into new relations, in which it becomes difficult practically to determine the correct method of action, Aristotle, in opposition to Plato, would limit the field of separate virtues by no definite number. Only certain fundamental virtues can be named according as there are certain fixed and fundamental relations among men. For instance, man has a fixed relation to pleasure and pain. In relation to pain, the true moral mean is found in neither fearing nor courting it, and this is valor. In relation to pleasure, the true mean standing between greediness and indifference is temperance. In social life, the moral mean is between doing and suffering wrong, which is justice. In a similar way many other virtues might be characterized, each one of them standing as a mean between two vices, the one of which expresses a want and the other a superfluity. A closer exhibition of the Aristotelian doctrine of virtue would have much psychological and linguistic interest, though but little philosophical worth. Aristotle takes the conception of his virtues more from the use of language than from a thoroughly applied principle of classification. His classification of virtues is, therefore, without any stable ground, and is differently given in different places. The conception of the correct mean which Aristotle makes the measure of a moral act is obviously unworthy of a systematic representation, for as it cannot be determined how the intelligent man would act in every case, there could never be given any specific directions how others should act. In fine, the criterion of virtue as the correct mean between two vices cannot be always applied for in the virtue of wisdom, *e. g.* which Aristotle describes as the mean between simplicity and cunning, there is no such thing as too much.

4. THE STATE.—Aristotle, like Plato, makes the highest condition of moral virtue attainable only through political life. The state exists before the individual, as the whole is prior to its parts. The rationality and morality of the state is thus antecedent to that of the individual. Hence in the best state, moral and political virtue, the virtue of the man and the virtue of the citizen are one and the same thing, although in states as they are, the good citizen is not necessarily also the good man. But though this principle harmonized with Plato, yet Aristotle, at whose time the old aboriginal states had already begun their process of dis-

solution, cherished a very different view concerning the relation of the individual and the family to the state. He allows to both these an incomparably greater consideration, and yields to them a far wider field of independent action. Hence he combats Plato's community of wives and goods, not simply on the ground of its practicability, but also on the ground of its principle, since the state cannot be conceived as a strict unit, or as possessing any such centralization as would weaken or destroy individual activity. With Plato the state is but the product of the philosophical reflection, while with Aristotle it results from given circumstances, from history and experience, and he therefore wholly omits to sketch a model state or a normal constitution, but carefully confines his attention to those which actually exist. Although the ideal of a state constitution in the form of a limited monarchy is unmistakably in his mind, still he contents himself with portraying the different kinds of polities in their peculiarities, their origin, and their reciprocal transitions. He does not undertake to declare which is the best state absolutely, since this depends upon circumstances, and one constitution is not adapted for every state. He simply attempts to show what form of the state is relatively the best and the most advisable under certain historical circumstances, and under given natural, climatic, geographic, economic, and intellectual conditions. In this he is faithful to the character of his whole philosophy. Standing on the basis of the empirical, he advances here as elsewhere, critically and reflectively, and in despair of attaining the absolutely true and good, he seeks for these relatively, with his eye fixed only on the probable and the practicable.

VI.—The Peripatetic School.—The school of Aristotle, called the Peripatetic, can here only be mentioned; the want of independence in its philosophizing, and the absence of any great and universal influence, rendering it unworthy an extended notice. Theophrastus, Eudemus, and Strato are its most famous leaders. Like most philosophical schools, it confines itself chiefly to a more thorough elaboration and explanation of the system of its master. In some empirical provinces, especially the physical, the attempt was made to carry out still further the system, while at the same time its speculative basis was set aside and neglected.

VII.—TRANSITION TO THE POST-ARISTOTELIAN PHILOSOPHY.— The productive energy of Grecian philosophy expends itself with Aristotle, contemporaneously and in connection with the universal decay of Grecian life and spirit. Instead of the great and universal systems of a Plato and an Aristotle, we have now systems of a partial and one-sided character, corresponding to that universal breach between the subject and the objective world which characterized the civil, religious, and social life of this last epoch of Greece, the time succeeding Alexander the Great. That subjectivity, which had been first propounded by the Sophists, was at length, after numerous struggles, victorious, though its triumph was gained upon the ruins of the Grecian civil and artistic life; the individual has become emancipated, the subject is no longer to be given up to the objective world, the liberated subjectivity must now be perfected and satisfied. This process of development is seen in the post-Aristotelian philosophy, though it finds its conditioning cause in the character of the preceding philosophical strivings. The dualism which formed the chief want of the systems both of Plato and Aristotle, has forced itself upon our attention at every step. The attempt which had been made, with the greatest expenditure of which the Grecian mind was capable, to refer back to one ultimate ground both subject and object, mind and matter, had produced no satisfactory result; and these two oppositions, around which all previous philosophy had struggled in vain, still remained disconnected. Wearied with the fruitless attempts at mediation, the subject now breaks with the objective world. Its attention is directed towards itself in its own self-consciousness. The result of this gives us either STOICISM, where the moral subject appears in the self-sufficiency of the sage to whom every external good and every objective work is indifferent, and who finds a good only in a moral activity; or EPICUREANISM, where the subject delights himself in the inner feeling of pleasure and the calm repose of a satisfied heart, enjoying the present and the past, and never fearing the future while it sees in the objective world only a means by which it can utter itself; or, again, SCEPTICISM, where the subject, doubting and rejecting all objective truth and science, appears in the apathy of the Sceptic, who has broken both theoretically and practically with the objective world. In fine, NEW-PLATONISM, the last of the ancient philosophical systems, bears this same character of sub-jectivity, for this whole system turns upon the exaltation of the subject to the absolute, and wherever it speculates respecting God and his relation to man, it is alone in order to establish the pro-gressive transition from the absolute object to the human person-ality. The ruling principle in it all is the interest of the subjec-tivity, and the fact that in this system there are numerous objective determinations, is only because the subject has become absolute.

SECTION XVII.

STOICISM.

Zeno, of Cittium, a city of Cyprus, an elder contemporary of Antigonus Gonatas, king of Macedon, is generally given as the founder of the Stoical school. Deprived of his property by shipwreck, he took refuge in philosophy, incited also by an inner bias to such pursuits. He at first became a disciple of the Cynic Crateas, then of Stilpo, one of the Megarians, and lastly he be-took himself to the Academy, where he heard the lessons of Xenocrates and Polemo. Hence the eclectic character of his teaching. It has in fact been charged against him, that differing but little if at all from the earlier schools, he attempted to form a school of his own, with a system wherein he had changed noth-ing but names. He opened a school at Athens, in the "varie-gated porch," so called from the paintings of Polygnotus, with which it was adorned, whence his adherents received the name of "philosophers of the porch" (Stoics). Zeno is said to have presi-ded over his school for fifty-eight years, and at a very advanced age to have put an end to his existence. He is praised for the temperance and the austerity of his habits, while his abstemiousness is proverbial. The monument in his honor, erected after his death by the Athenians, at the instance of Antigonus, bore the high but simple eulogium that his life had been in unison with his philosophy. *Cleanthes* was the successor of Zeno in the Stoic school, and faithfully carried out the method of his master. Cleanthes was succeeded by *Chrysippus*, who died about 208 B. C. He has been regarded as the chief prop of this school, in which respect it was said of him, that without a Chrysippus there would never have been a Porch. At all events, as Chrysippus was an object of the greatest veneration, and of almost undisputed authority with the later Stoics, he ought to be considered as the principal founder of the school. He was a writer so voluminous, that his works have been said to amount to seven hundred and five, among which, however, were repeated treatises upon the same propositions, and citations without measure from poets and historians, given to prove and illustrate his opinions. Not one of all his writings has come down to us. Chrysippus closes the series of the philosophers who founded the Porch. The later heads of the school, as *Panætius*, the friend of the younger Scipio (his famous work De Officiis, Cicero has elaborated in his treatise of the same name), and *Posidonius*, may be classed with Cicero, Pompeius, and others, and were eclectic in their teachings. The Stoics have connected philosophy most intimately with the duties of practical life. Philosophy is with them the practice of wisdom, the exercise of virtue. Virtue and science are with them one, in so far at least that they divide virtue in reference to philosophy into physical, ethical, and logical. But though they go on according to this threefold division, and treat of logic and physics, and though they even rank physics higher than either of the other sciences, regarding it as the mother of the ethical and the science of the Divine, yet do we find their characteristic stand-point most prominently in their theory of morals.

1. Logic.—We have already said that it is the breach be-

tween subject and object, which forms the basis of all post-Aristotelian philosophy. The beginning of this philosophy of subjectivity is found with the Stoics. The feature most worthy of notice in their logic, is the striving after a subjective criterion of the truth, by which they might distinguish the true representation from the false. Since they limited all scientific knowledge to the knowledge of the senses, they found this criterion in that which was evident in the sensuous impression. They conceived that they had answered the whole problem, in affirming that the true or conceivable representation reveals not only itself, but also its object: it, they said, is nothing else than a representation which is produced by a present object in a manner like itself.

2. PHYSICS.—In their physics, where they follow for the most part Heraclitus, the Stoics are distinguished from their predecessors, especially from Plato and Aristotle, by their thoroughly carried out proposition that nothing uncorporeal exists, that every thing essential is corporeal (just as in their logic they had sought to derive all knowledge from the sensuous perception). This sensualism or materialism of the Stoics which, as we have seen in their logic, lies at the basis of their theory of knowledge, might seem foreign to all their moral and idealistic tendencies, but is clearly explained from their subjective stand-point, for, when the thought has become so intensely engrossed in the subject, the objective world can only be regarded as a corporeal and material existence. The most immediate consequence of such a view is their pantheism. Aristotle before them had separated the Divine Being from the world, as the pure and eternal form from the eternal matter; but so far as this separation implied a distinction which was not simply logical, but actual and real, the Stoics would not admit it. It seemed to them impossible to dissever God from matter, and they therefore considered God and the world as power and its manifestation, and thus as one. Matter is the passive ground of things, the original substratum for the divine activity: God is the active and formative energy of matter dwelling within it, and essentially united to it: the world is the body of God, and God is the soul of the world. The Stoics, therefore, considered

God and matter as one identical substance, which, on the side of its passive and changeable capacity they call matter, and on the side of its active and changeless energy, God. But since they, as already remarked, considered the world as ensouled by God in the light of a living and rational being, they were obliged to treat the conception of God not only in a physical but also in its ethical aspect. God is not only in the world as the ruling and living energy of this great ζῷον (animal), but he is also the universal reason which rules the whole world and penetrates all matter; he is the gracious Providence which cares for the individual and the whole; he is wise, and is the ground of that natural law which commands the good and forbids the evil; he punishes and rewards; he possesses a perfect and blessed life. But accustomed to regard every thing spiritual only in a sensuous way, the Stoics were obliged to clothe this ideal conception of God in a material form, apprehending it as the vital warmth or an original fire, analogous to the view of the earlier natural philosophers, who held that the soul, and even reason itself, consisted in the vital warmth. The Stoics express this thought in different ways. At one time they call God the rational breath which passes through all nature; at another, the artistic fire which fashions or begets the universe; and still again the ether; which, however, they hardly distinguish from the artistic fire. From these varying views, we see that it did not belong to the Stoics to represent the conception of God in any determinate kind of existence. They availed themselves of these expressions only to indicate that God, as the universal animating energy in the world, could not be disconnected from a corporeal agency. This identification of God and the world, according to which the Stoics regarded the whole formation of the universe as but a period in the development of God, renders their remaining doctrine concerning the world very simple. Every thing in the world seemed to them to be permeated by the divine life, and was regarded as but the flowing out of this most perfect life through certain channels, until it returned in a necessary circle back again to itself. It is not necessary here to speak more closely of the physics of this school.

3. THE ETHICS.—The ethics of the Stoics is most closely connected with their physics. In the physics we saw the rational
order of the universe as it existed through the divine thought.
In the ethics, the highest law of human action, and thus the whole
moral legality of life is dependent upon this rational order and
conformity to law in universal nature, and the highest good or the
highest end of our strivings is to shape our life according to this
universal law, to live in conformity with the harmony of the world
or with nature. "Follow nature," or "live in harmony with nature," is the moral maxim of the Stoics. More accurately: live
in harmony with thy rational nature so far as this has not been
distorted nor refined by art, but is held in its natural simplicity.

From this moral principle, in which we have also the Stoic
conception of virtue, the peculiarities of their theory of morals
follow with logical necessity.

(1.) *Respecting the Relation of Virtue to Pleasure.*—When
the demand is made that the life should be in conformity with
nature, the individual becomes wholly subjected to the universal,
and every personal end is excluded. Hence pleasure, which of
all ends is the most individual, must be disregarded. In pleasure
that activity in which blessedness consists is abated, and this could
only appear to the Stoics as a restraint of life, and thus as an evil.
Pleasure is not in conformity with nature, and is no end of nature,
says Cleanthes; and though other Stoics relax a little from the
strictness of this opinion, and admit that pleasure may be according to nature, and is to be considered in a certain degree as a good,
yet they all held fast to the doctrine, that it has no moral worth
and is no end of nature, but is only something which is accidentally connected with the free and fitting activity of nature, while
itself is not an activity, but a passive condition of the soul. In
this lies the whole severity of the Stoic doctrine of morals;
every thing personal is cast aside, every external end of action is
foreign to the moral man, the action in wisdom is the only good.
From this follows directly:

(2.) *The View of the Stoics Concerning External Good.*—If
virtue, as the activity in conformity to nature, is exclusively a

good, and if it alone can lead to happiness, then external good of every kind is something morally indifferent, and can neither be the object of our striving nor the end of any moral action. The action itself and not that towards which it tends is good. Hence such special ends as health, wealth, &c., are in themselves worthless and indifferent. They may result either in good or evil, and when deprived of them the happiness of the virtuous man is not destroyed. The Stoics yield from the rigor of their fundamental principle only in a single instance. They admit that there may be a distinction among indifferent things ; that while none of these can be called a moral good, yet some may be preferable to others, and that the preferable, so far as it contributes to a life in conformity to nature, should enter into the account of a moral life. So the sage will prefer health and wealth when these are balanced in the choice with sickness and poverty, but though these objects have been rationally chosen, he does not esteem them as really good, for they are not the highest, they are inferior to the virtuous acting, in comparison with which every thing else sinks to insignificance. In making this distinction between the good and the preferable, we see how the Stoics exclude from the good every thing relative, and hold fast to it alone in its highest significance.

(3.) This abstract apprehension of the conception of virtue is still farther verified in the rigid antagonism which the Stoics affirmed between virtue and not-virtue, reason and sense. Either, they conclude, reason is awakened in the life of man and holds the mastery over him, or it is not awakened, and he serves his irrational instincts. In the former case we have a good and in the latter a bad man, while between these two cases as between virtue and vice, there is no mean. And since virtue cannot be partially possessed, but the man must be wholly virtuous or not at all, it follows that virtue as such is without degree, just as truth is, and hence also all good acts are equally good, because they spring from the full freedom of the reason, and all vicious ones equally bad because they are impelled by the irrational instinct.

(4.) But this abstractedness of the moral stand-point, this rigid opposition of reason and irrationality, of the highest good and the

individual good, of virtue and pleasure, has no power to furnish
a system of concrete moral duties. The universal moral principle of
the Stoics fails in its applicability to the individual instance. The
Stoic morals has no concrete principle of moral self-determination.
How must we act in every individual instance, in every moral
relation, so as to act according to nature? To this inquiry Stoicism can give no answer. Its system of particular duties is thus
wholly without a scientific form, and is only held together by
some universal conceptions which it contains. For the most part
they satisfy themselves with describing in general terms the action
according to nature, and with portraying their ideal of the wise
man. The characteristics which they give this ideal are partly
paradoxical. The wise man is free even in chains, for he acts
from himself unmoved by fear or desire; the wise man alone is
king, for he alone is not bound by laws and owes fealty to no one;
he is the true rich man, the true priest, prophet, and poet. He
is exalted above all law and every custom; even that which is
most despicable and base—deception, suicide, murder—he may
commit at a proper time and in a virtuous character. In a word
the Stoics describe their wise man as a god, and yield it to him
to be proud and to boast of his life like Zeus. But where shall we
find such a sage? Certainly not among the living. In the time
long ago there may have been a perfect sage of such a pattern;
but now, and for a long time back, are men at best only fools
who strive after wisdom and virtue. The conception of the wise
man represented, therefore, to the Stoics only an ideal, the actualization of which we should strive after, though without ever
hoping to reach it; and yet their system of particular duties is
almost wholly occupied in portraying this unreal and abstract
ideal—a contradiction in which it is seen most clearly that their
whole stand-point is one of abstract subjectivity.

SECTION XVIII.

EPICUREANISM.

The Epicurean school arose at Athens, almost contemporaneously with the Porch, though perhaps a little earlier than this. Epicurus, its founder, was born 342 B.C., six years after the death of Plato. Of his youth and education little is known. In his thirty-sixth year he opened a philosophical school at Athens, over which he presided till his death, 271 B.C. His disciples and adherents formed a social league, in which they were united by the closest band of friendship, illustrating the general condition of things in Greece after the time of Alexander, when the social took the place of the decaying poetical life. Epicurus himself compared his society to the Pythagorean fraternity, although the community of goods, which forms an element in the latter, Epicurus excludes, affirming that true friends can confide in one another. The moral conduct of Epicurus has been repeatedly assailed but, according to the testimony of the most reliable witnesses, his life was blameless in every respect, and his personal character was estimable and amiable. Moreover, it cannot be doubted that much of that, which is told by some, of the offensive voluptuousness of the Epicurean band, should be regarded as calumny. Epicurus was a voluminous writer, surpassing, in this respect, even Aristotle, and exceeded by Chrysippus alone. To the loss of his greater works he has himself contributed, by his practice of composing summaries of his system, which he recommended his disciples to commit to memory. These summaries have been for the most part preserved.

The end which Epicurus proposed to himself in science is distinctly revealed in his definition of philosophy. He calls it an activity which, by means of conceptions and arguments, procures the happiness of life. Its end is, therefore, with him essentially a practical one, and on this account the object of his whole system

7

is to produce a scheme of morals which should teach us how we might inevitably attain a happy life. It is true that the Epicureans adopted the usual division of philosophy into logic, which they called canonics, physics, and ethics; but they confined logic to the doctrine of the criterion of truth, and considered it only as an instrument and introduction to physics, while they only treated of physics as existing wholly for ethics, and being necessary in order to free men from superstitious fear, and deliver them from the power of fables and mythical fancies concerning nature, which might hinder the attainment of happiness. We have therefore in Epicureanism the three old parts of philosophy, but in a reversed order, since logic and physics here stand as the handmaids of ethics. We shall confine ourselves in our exposition to the latter, since the Epicurean canonics and physics offer little scientific interest, and since the physics especially is not only very incomplete and without any internal connection, but rests entirely upon the atomic theory of Democritus.

Epicurus, like Aristotle and the other philosophers of his day, placed the highest good in happiness, or a happy life. More closely he makes pleasure to be the principal constituent of happiness, and even calls it the highest good. But Epicurus goes on to give a more accurate determination of pleasure, and in this he differs essentially from his predecessors, the Cyrenians. (*cf.* §XIII. 3.)

1. While with Aristippus the pleasure of the moment is made the end of human efforts, Epicurus directs men to strive after a system of pleasures which should insure an abiding course of happiness for the whole life. *True* pleasure is thus the object to be considered and weighed. Many a pleasure should be despised because it will result in pain, and many a pain should be rejoiced in because it would lead to a greater pleasure.

2. Since the sage will seek after the highest good, not simply for the present but for his whole life, he will hold the pleasures and pains of the soul, which like memory and hope stretch over the past and the future, in greater esteem than those of the body, which relate only to the present moment. The pleasure of the soul consists in the untroubled tranquillity of the sage, who rests

secure in the feeling of his inner worth and his exaltation above the strokes of destiny. Thus Epicurus, would say that it is better to be miserable but rational than to be happy and irrational, and that the wise man might be happy though in torture. He would even affirm, like a true follower of Aristotle, that pleasure and happiness were most closely connected with virtue, that virtue is in fact inseparable from true pleasure, and that there can be no agreeable life without virtue, and no virtue without an agreeable life.

3. While other Hedonists would regard the most positive and intense feeling of pleasure as the highest good, Epicurus, on the other hand, fixed his eye on a happiness which should be abiding and for the whole life. He would not seek the most exquisite enjoyments in order to attain to a happy life, but he rather recommends one to be satisfied with little, and to practise sobriety and temperance of life. He guards himself against such a false application of his doctrine as would imply that the pleasure of the debauchee were the highest good, and boasts that with a little barley-bread and water he would rival Zeus in happiness. He even expresses an aversion for all costly pleasures, not, however, in themselves, but because of the evil consequences which they entail. True, the Epicurean sage need not therefore live as a Cynic. He will enjoy himself where he can without harm, and will even seek to acquire means to live with dignity and ease. But though all these enjoyments of life may properly belong to the sage, yet he *can* deprive himself of them without misery—though he *ought* not to do so—since he enjoys the truest and most essential pleasure in the calmness of his soul and the tranquillity of his heart. In opposition to the positive pleasure of some Hedonists, the theory of Epicurus expends itself in negative conceptions, representing that freedom from pain is pleasure, and that hence the activity of the sage should be prominently directed to avoid that which is disagreeable. All that man does, says Epicurus, is that he may neither suffer nor apprehend pain, and in another place he remarks, that not to live is far from being an evil. Hence death, for which men have the greatest terror, the wise man does

not fear. For while we live, death is not, and when death is, we are not; when it is present we feel it not, for it is the end of all feeling, and that, which by its presence cannot affect our happiness, ought not, when thought of as a future, to trouble us. Here Epicurus must bear the censure urged against him by the ancients, that he does not recognize any positive end of life, and that the object after which his sage should strive is a mere passionless state.

The crown of Epicurus's view of the universe is his doctrine of the gods, where he has carried over his ideal of happiness. To the gods belong a human form, though without any fixed body or human wants. In the void space they lead an undisturbed and changeless life, whose happiness is incapable of increase. From the blessedness of the gods he inferred that they had nothing to do with the management of our affairs, for blessedness is repose, and on this account the gods neither take trouble to themselves nor cause it to others. It may indeed be said that these inactive gods of Epicurus, these indestructible and yet not fixed forms, these bodies which are not bodies, have but an ill connection with his general system, in which there is in fact no point to which his doctrine of the gods can be fitly joined—but a strict scientific connection is hardly the merit of this whole philosophy.

SECTION XIX.

SCEPTICISM AND THE NEW ACADEMY.

This subjective direction already noticed was carried out to its farthest extent by the Sceptics, who broke down completely the bridge between subject and object, denying all objective truth, knowledge and science, and wholly withdrawing the philosopher from every thing but himself and his own subjective estimates. In this direction we may distinguish between the old Scepticism, the new Academy, and the later Scepticism.

1. THE OLD SCEPTICISM.—*Pyrrho* of Elis, who was perhaps a cotemporary of Aristotle, was the head of the old Sceptics. He left no writings behind him, and we are dependent for a knowledge of his opinions upon his scholar and follower, Timon of Phlius. The tendency of these sceptical philosophers, like that of the Stoics and Epicureans, was a practical one, for philosophy, said they, ought to lead us to happiness. But in order to live happily we must know how things are, and, therefore, in what kind of a relation we stand to them. The first of these questions the Sceptics answered by attempting to show that all things, without exception, are indifferent as to truth and falsehood, uncertain, and in nowise subject to man's judgment. Neither our senses nor our opinions concerning any thing teach us any truth; to every precept and to every position a contrary may be advanced, and hence the contradictory views of men, and especially of the philosophies of the schools respecting one and the same thing. All objective knowledge and science being thus impossible, the true relation of the philosopher to things consists in the entire suspension of judgment, and the withholding of every positive assertion. In order to avoid every thing like a positive assertion, the Sceptics had recourse to a variety of artifices, and availed themselves of doubtful modes of expression, such as *it is possible; it may be so; perhaps; I assert nothing,*—cautiously subjoining to this last—*not even that I assert nothing.* By this suspension of judgment the Sceptics thought they could attain their practical end, happiness; for the abstinence from all positive opinion is followed by a freedom from all mental disturbance, as a substance is by a shadow. He who has embraced Scepticism lives thenceforward tranquilly, without inquietude, without agitation, with an equable state of mind, and, in fact, divested of his humanity. Pyrrho is said to have originated the doctrine which lies at the basis of sceptical apathy, that no difference exists between sickness and health, or between life and death. The Sceptics, for the most part, derived the material for their views from the previous investigations in the dogmatic schools. But the grounds on which they rested were far from being profound, and were for the

most part either dialectic errors which could easily be refuted, or mere subtleties. The use of the following ten tropes is ascribed to the old Sceptics, though these were perhaps not definitely brought out by either Pyrrho or Timon, but were probably first collected by Ænesidemus, soon after the time of Cicero. The withholding of all decisive judgment may rest; (1) upon the distinction generally existing between individual living objects; (2) upon the difference among men; (3) the different functions of the organs of sense; (4) the circumstances under which objects appear; (5) the relative positions, intervals, and places; (6) intermixtures; (7) the quantities and modifications of the objects we perceive; (8) relations; (9) the frequent or rare occurrence; (10) the different ways of life, the varieties of customs and laws, the mythical representations and dogmatic opinions of men.

2. THE NEW ACADEMY.—Scepticism, in its conflict with the Stoics, as it appeared in the Platonic school established by *Arcesilaus* (316–241), has a far greater significance than belongs to the performances of the Pyrrhonists. In this school Scepticism sought its support by its great respect for the writings and its transmission of the oral teachings of Plato. Arcesilaus could neither have assumed nor maintained the chair of instruction in the Academy, had he not carefully cherished and imparted to his disciples the impression that his own view, respecting the withholding of a decisive judgment, coincided essentially with that of Socrates and of Plato, and if he had not also taught that he only restored the genuine and original significance of Platonism, when he set aside the dogmatic method of teaching. An immediate incitement to the efforts of Arcesilaus is found in his opposition to the rigid dogmatic system which had lately arisen in the Porch, and which claimed to be in every respect an improvement upon Platonism. Hence, as Cicero remarks, Arcesilaus directed all his sceptical and polemic attacks against Zeno, the founder of Stoicism. He granted with his opponent that no representation should form a part of undoubted knowledge, if it could possibly have arisen through any other object than that from which it actually sprung, but he would not admit that there might be a notion which ex-

pressed so truly and accurately its own object, that it could not nave arisen from any other. Accordingly, Arcesilaus denied the existence of a criterion which could certify to us the truth of our knowledge. If there be any truth in our affirmations, said he, we cannot be certain of it. In this sense he taught that one can know nothing, not even that he does know nothing. But in moral matters, in choosing the good and rejecting the evil, he taught that we should follow that which is probable.

Of the subsequent leaders in the new Academy, *Carneades* (214-129) alone need here be mentioned, whose whole philosophy, however, consists almost exclusively in a polemic against Stoicism and in the attempt to set up a criterion of truth. His positive performance is the attempt to bring out a philosophical theory of probabilities. The later Academicians fell back to an eclectic dogmaticism.

3. THE LATER SCEPTICISM.—Once more we meet with a peculiar Scepticism at the time when Grecian philosophy had wholly fallen to decay. To this time belong *Ænesidemus*, who probably —though this cannot be affirmed with certainty—lived but a little after Cicero ; *Agrippa*, whose date is also uncertain, though subsequent to Ænesidemus, and *Sextus Empiricus*—i. e. a Grecian physician of the empiric sect, who probably flourished in the first half of the third century of the Christian era. These are the most significant names. Of these the last has the greatest interest for us, from two writings which he left behind him (the hypotyposes of Pyrrho in three books, and a treatise against the mathematicians in nine books), which are sources of much historical information. In these he has profusely collected every thing which the Scepticism of the ancients knew how to advance against the certainty of knowledge.

SECTION XX.

THE ROMANS.

The Romans have taken no independent part in the progress of philosophy. After Grecian philosophy and literature had begun to gain a foothold among them, and especially after three distinguished representatives of Attic culture and eloquence—Carneades the Academician, Critolaus the Peripatetic, and Diogenes the Stoic—had appeared in Rome as envoys from Athens; and after Greece, a few years later, had become a Roman province, and thus outwardly in a close connection with Rome, almost all the more significant systems of Grecian philosophy, especially the Epicurean (Lucretius), and the Stoic (Seneca), flourished and found adherents in Rome, though without gaining any real philosophical progress. The Romish philosophizing is wholly eclectic, as is seen in Cicero, the most important and influential philosophic writer among the Romans. But the popular philosophy of this man and of the minds akin to him cannot be strongly assailed, for, notwithstanding its want of originality and logical sequence, it gave philosophy a broad dissemination, and made it a means of universal culture.

———•◆•———

SECTION XXI.

NEW PLATONISM.

In New Platonism, the ancient mind made its last and almost despairing attempt at a philosophy which should resolve the dualism between the subjective and the objective. The attempt was made by taking on the one side a subjective stand-point, like the other philosophies of the post-Aristotelian time (cf. § XVI 7);

and on the other with the design to bring out objective determinations concerning the highest conceptions of metaphysics, and concerning the absolute ; in other words, to sketch a system of absolute philosophy. In this respect the effort was made to copy the Platonic and Aristotelian philosophy, and the claim was set up by the new system to be a revival of the original Platonism. On both sides the new attempt formed the closing period of an ancient philosophy. It represents the last struggle, but at the same time the exhaustion of the ancient thinking and the dissolution of the old philosophy.

The first, and also the most important, representative of New Platonism, is *Plotinus*. He was a pupil of Ammonius Saccas, who taught the Platonic philosophy at Alexandria in the beginning of the third century, though he left no writings behind him. Plotinus (A. D. 205—270) from his fortieth year taught philosophy at Rome. His opinions are contained in a course of hastily written and not closely connected treatises, which, after his death, were collected and published in six enneads by *Porphyry* (who was born A. D. 233, and taught both philosophy and eloquence at Rome), his most noted disciple. From Rome and Alexandria, the New Platonism of Plotinus passed over in the fourth century to Athens, where it established itself in the Academy. In the fourth century, *Jamblichus*, a scholar of Porphyry, and in the fifth, *Proclus*, (412—485), were prominently distinguished among the New Platonists. With the triumph of Christianity and the consequent fall of heathenism, in the course of the sixth century, even this last bloom of Grecian philosophy faded away.

The common characteristic of all the New Platonists is a tendency to mysticism, theosophy, and theurgy. The majority of them gave themselves up to magic and sorcery, and the most distinguished boasted that they were the subjects of divine inspiration and illumination, able to look into the future, and to work miracles. They professed to be hierophants as much as philosophers, and exhibited the unmistakable tendency to represent a Pagan copy of Christianity, which should be at the same time a

7*

philosophy and a universal religion. In the following sketch of
New Platonism we follow mainly the track of Plotinus.

1. ECSTASY AS A SUBJECTIVE STATE.—The result of the philo
sophical strivings antecedent to New Platonism had been Scepticism ; which, seeing the impracticability of both the Stoic and
Epicurean wisdom, had assumed a totally negative relation to
every positive and theoretical content. But the end which Scepticism had actually gained was the opposite of that for which it
had striven. It had striven for the perfect apathy of the sage,
but it had gained only the necessity of incessantly opposing every
positive affirmation. Instead of the rest which they had sought,
they found rather an absolute unrest. This absolute unrest of
the consciousness striving after an absolute rest, begat immediately a longing to be freed from this unrest, a longing after some
content which should be absolutely satisfying, and stripped of
every sceptical objection. This longing after an absolutely true,
found its historical expression in New Platonism. The subject
sought to master and comprehend the absolute ; and this, neither
by objective knowledge nor dialectic mediation, but immediately,
by an inner and mystical mounting up of the subject in the form
of an immediate beholding, or ecstasy. The knowledge of the
true, says Plotinus, is not gained by proof nor by any mediation ;
it cannot be found when the objects known remain separate from
the subject knowing, but only when the distinction between know-
er and known disappears ; it is a beholding of the reason in itself,
not in the sense that we see the reason, but the reason beholds
itself ; in no other way can knowledge come. If any one has attained to such a beholding, to such a true unison with the divine,
he will despise the pure thinking which he otherwise loved, for
this thinking was only a movement which presupposed a difference
between the perceiver and the perceived. This mystical absorp-
tion into the Deity, or, the One, this resolving the self into the
absolute, is that which gives to New Platonism a character so peculiarly distinct from the genuine Grecian systems of philosophy.

2. THE COSMICAL PRINCIPLES.—The doctrine of the three
cosmical principles is most closely connected with the theory just

named. To the two cosmical principles already received, viz., the world-soul and the world-reason, a third and higher one was added by the New Platonists. For if the reason apprehends the true by means of thinking, and not within itself alone; if, in order to grasp the absolute and behold the divine, it must lose its own self-consciousness, and go out beyond itself, then reason cannot be the highest principle, but there stands above it that primal essence, with which it must be united if it will behold the true. To this primal essence Plotinus gives different names, as " the first," " the one," " the good," and " that which stands above being " (being is with him but a conception, which, like the reason, may be resolved into a higher ground, and which, united with the reason, forms but the second step in the series of highest conceptions). In all these names, Plotinus does not profess to have satisfactorily expressed the essence of this primal one, but only to have given a representation of it. In characterizing it still farther, he denies it all thinking and willing, because it needs nothing and can desire nothing; it is not energy, but above energy; life does not belong to it; neither being nor essence nor any of the most general categories of being can be ascribed to it; in short, it is that which can neither be expressed nor thought. Plotinus has thoroughly striven to think of this first principle not as first principle, i. e. not in its relation to that of which it is the ground, but only in itself, as being wholly without reference either to us or to any thing else. This pure abstraction, however, he could not carry out. He sets himself to show how every thing else, and especially the two other cosmical principles, could emanate from this first; but in order to have a principle for his emanation theory, he was obliged to consider the first in its relation to the second and as its producer

3. THE EMANATION THEORY OF THE NEW PLATONISTS.—Every emanation theory, and hence also that of the New Platonists, considers the world as the effluence of God, and gives to the emanation a greater or less degree of perfection, according as it is nearer or more remote from its source. They all have for their principle the totality of being, and represent a progressively

ascending relation in its several parts. Fire, says Plotinus, emits heat, snow cold, fragrant bodies odors, and every organic thing so far as it is perfect begets something like itself. In the same way the all-perfect and the eternal, in the overflowing of his perfection sends out from himself that which is also eternal, and after him, the best, viz., the reason or world-intelligence, which is the immediate reflection and image of the primal one. Plotinus abounds in figures to show how the primal one need lose nothing or become weakened by this emanation of reason. Next to the original one, reason is the most perfect. It contains in itself the ideal world, and the whole of true and changeless being. Some notion may be formed of its exaltation and glory by carefully beholding the sensible world in its greatness, its beauty, and the order of its ceaseless motion, and then by rising to contemplate its archetype in the pure and changeless being of the intelligible world, and then by recognizing in intelligence the author and finisher of all. In it there is neither past nor future, but only an over abiding present. It is, moreover, as incapable of division in space as of change in time. It is the true eternity, which is only copied by time. As reason flows from the primal one, so does the world-soul eternally emanate from reason, though the latter incurs no change thereby. The world-soul is the copy of reason, permeated by it, and actualizing it in an outer world. It gives ideas externally to sensible matter, which is the last and lowest step in the series of emanations and in itself is undetermined, and has neither quality nor being. In this way the visible universe is but the transcript of the world-soul, which forms it out of matter, permeates and animates it, and carries it forward in a circle. Here closes the series of emanations, and, as was the aim of the theory, we have been carried in a constant current from the highest to the lowest, from God to the mere image of true being, or the sensible world.

Individual souls, like the world-soul, are linked both to the higher and the lower, to reason and the sensible; now bound with the latter and sharing its destiny, and anon rising to their source in reason. Their original and proper home was in the rational world, from whence they have come down, each one in its proper time, into the corporeal; not, however, wholly forsaking their ideal abode, but as a sunbeam touches at the same time the sun and the earth, so are they found alike in the world of reason and the world of sense.   Our calling, therefore—and here we come back to the point from which we started in our exhibition of New Platonism—can only be to direct our senses and aspirations towards our proper home, in the ideal world, and by asceticism and crucifying of the flesh, to free our better self from its participation with the body.   But when our soul has once mounted up to the ideal world, that image of the originally good and beautiful, it then attains the final goal of all its longings and efforts, the immediate union with God, through the enraptured beholding of the primal one in which it loses its consciousness and becomes buried and absorbed.

According to all this, the New Platonic philosophy would seem to be a monism, and thus the most perfect development of ancient philosophy, in so far as this had striven to carry back the sum of all being to one ultimate ground.   But as it attained its highest principle from which all the rest was derived, by means of ecstasy, by a mystical self-destruction of the individual person (*Ichheit*), by asceticism and theurgy, and not by means of self-conscious thinking, nor by any natural or rational way, it is seen that ancient philosophy, instead of becoming perfected in New Platonism, only makes a despairing leap beyond itself to its own self-destruction.

----••----

SECTION XXII.

CHRISTIANITY AND SCHOLASTICISM.

1. THE CHRISTIAN IDEA.—The Grecian intellectual life at the time of its fairest bloom, was characterized by the immediate sacrifice of the subject to the object (nature, the state, &c.): the full breach between the two, between spirit and nature, had not

yet arrived; the subject had not yet so far reflected upon him-self that he could apprehend his own absolute worth. This breach came in, with the decay of Grecian life, in the time after Alexan-der the Great. As the objective world lost its influence, the thinking consciousness turned back upon itself; but even in this very process, the bridge between subject and object was broken down. The self-consciousness had not yet become sufficiently absorbed in itself to look upon the true, the divine, in any other light than as separate from itself, and belonging to an opposite world; while a feeling of pain, of unsatisfied desire, took the place of that fair unity between spirit and nature which had been pecu-liar to the better periods of the Grecian civil and artistic life. New Platonism, by its overleaping speculation, and, practically, by its mortification of the sense, made a last and despairing at-tempt to overcome this separation, or to bury itself within it, by bringing the two sides forcibly together. The attempt was in vain, and the old philosophy, totally exhausted, came to its end. Dualism is therefore the rock on which it split. This problem, thus left without a solution, Christianity took up. It assumed for its principle the idea which the ancient thinking had not known how to carry out, affirming that the separation between God and man might be overcome, and that the human and the divine could be united in one. The speculative fundamental idea of Chris-tianity is, that God has become incarnate, and this had its practi-cal exhibition (for Christianity was a practical religion) in the idea of the atonement and the demand of the new birth, *i. e.* the posi-tive purifying of the sense from its corruptions, instead of hold-ing it, as asceticism, in a merely negative relation.

From the introduction of Christianity, monism has been the character and the fundamental tendency of the whole modern philosophy. In fact, the new philosophy started from the very point at which the old had stood still. The turning of the self-con-sciousness upon itself, which was the stand-point of the post-Aris-totelian speculations, forms in Descartes the starting-point of the new philosophy, whose whole course has been the reconciling of that opposition beyond which the old could not pass.

2. SCHOLASTICISM.—It very early resulted that Christianity came in contact with the cotemporaneous philosophy, especially with Platonism. This arose first with the apologists of the second century, and the fathers of the Alexandrian church. Subsequently, in the ninth century, Scotus Erigena made an attempt to combine Christianity with New Platonism, though it was not till the second half of the Middle Ages, from the eleventh century, that there was developed any thing that might be properly termed a Christian philosophy. This was the so-called Scholasticism.

The effort of Scholasticism was to mediate between the dogma of religion and the reflecting self-consciousness; to reconcile faith and knowledge. When the dogma passed over into the schools from the Church which had given it utterance, and theology became a science of the universities, the scientific interest asserted its rights, and undertook to bring the dogma which had hitherto stood over against the self-consciousness as an external power, into a closer relation to the thinking subject. A series of attempts was now made to bring out the doctrines of the Church in the form of scientific systems (the first complete dogmatic system was given by *Peter Lombard*, who died 1164, in his four books of sentences, and was voluminously commented upon by the later Scholastics), all starting from the indisputable premise (beyond which scholastic thinking never reached), that the faith of the church is absolute truth; but all guided likewise by the interest to make this revealed truth intelligible, and to show it to be rational. " *Credo ut intelligam*"—this expression of *Anselm*, the beginner and founder of Scholasticism (he was born about 1034, and made Archbishop of Canterbury in 1093), was the watchword of this whole direction. Scholasticism applied to the solution of its problem the most remarkable logical acumen, and brought out systems of doctrine like the Gothic cathedrals in their architecture. The extended study of Aristotle, called *par eminence* " the philosopher," whom many of the most distinguished Scholastics wrote commentaries upon, and who was greatly studied at the same period among the Arabians (*Avicenna* and *Averroes*), furnished their terminology and most of their points of view. At the summit of Scholasticism we must place the two incontestably greatest masters of the Scholastic art and method, *Thomas Aquinas* (Dominican, who died 1274) and *Duns Scotus* (Franciscan, who died 1308), the founders of two schools, in which since their time the whole Scholastic theology divides itself—the former exalting the understanding (*intellectus*), and the latter the will (*voluntas*), as their highest principle, both being driven into essentially differing directions by this opposition of a theoretical and a practical principle. Even with this began the downfall of Scholasticism; its highest point was also the turning-point to its self-destruction. The rationality of the dogma, the oneness of faith and knowledge, had been constantly their fundamental premise; but this premise fell away, and the whole basis of their metaphysics was given up in principle, the moment Duns Scotus placed the problem of theology in the practical. When the practical and the theoretical became divided, and still more when thought and being were separated by Nominalism (*cf.* 3), philosophy broke loose from theology and knowledge from faith; knowledge assumed its position above faith and above authority (modern philosophy), and the religious consciousness broke with the traditional dogma (the Reformation).

3. NOMINALISM AND REALISM.—Hand in hand with the whole development of Scholasticism, there was developed the opposition between Nominalism and Realism, an opposition whose origin is to be found in the relation of Scholasticism to the Platonic and Aristotelian philosophy. The Nominalists were those who held that the conceptions of the universal (the *universalia*) were simple names, *flatus vocis*, representations without content and without reality. According to them there are no universal conceptions, no species, no class; every thing which is, exists only as separate in its pure individuality; there is, therefore, no pure thinking, but only a representation and sensuous perception. The Realists, on the other hand, taking pattern from Plato, held fast to the objective reality of the universals (*universalia ante rem*). These opposite directions appeared first between *Roscellinus*, who took the side of Nominalism, and *Anselm*, who advocated the

Realistic theory, and it is seen from this time through the whole period of Scholasticism, though from the age of *Abelard* (born 1079) a middle view, which was both Nominalistic and Realistic, held with some slight modifications the prominent place (*universalia in re*). According to this view the universal is only something thought and represented, though as such it is not simply a product of the representing consciousness, but has also its objective reality in objects themselves, from which it was argued we could not abstract it if it were not essentially contained in them. This identity of thought and being, is the fundamental premise on which the whole dialectic course of the Scholastics rests. All their arguments are founded on the claim, that that which has been syllogistically proved is in reality the same as in logical thinking. If this premise is overthrown, so falls with it the whole basis of Scholasticism; and there remains nothing more for the thinker to do, who has gone astray in his objectivity, but to fall back upon himself. This self-dissolution of Scholasticism actually appears with *William of Occam* (died 1347), the most influential reviver of that Nominalism which had been so mighty in the beginning of Scholasticism, but which now, more victorious against a decaying than then against a rising form of culture, plucked away its foundation from the framework of Scholastic dogmatism, and brought the whole structure into inevitable ruin.

SECTION XXIII.

TRANSITION TO THE MODERN PHILOSOPHY.

The emancipation of modern philosophy from the bondage of Scholasticism was a gradual process. It first showed itself in a series of preparative movements during the fifteenth century, and became perfected, negatively, in the course of the sixteenth, and positively in the first half of the seventeenth century.

1. FALL OF SCHOLASTICISM.—The immediate ground of this

changed direction of the time, we have already seen in the inner decay of Scholasticism itself. Just so soon as the fundamental premise on which the Scholastic theology and method rested, the rationality of the dogma, was abandoned, the whole structure, as already remarked, fell to inevitable ruin. The conviction, directly opposed to the principle of Scholasticism, that what might be true dogmatically, might be false, or, at least, incapable of proof in the eye of the reason—a point of view from which *e. g.* the Aristotelian *Pomponatius* (1462-1530) treated the doctrines of the future state, and in whose light *Vanini* subsequently went over the chief problems of philosophy—kept gaining ground, not-withstanding the opposition of the Church, and even associated with itself the opinion that reason and revelation could not be harmonized. The feeling became prevalent that philosophy must be freed from its previous condition of minority and servitude ; a struggle after a greater independence of philosophic investigation was awakened, and though no one yet ventured to attack directly the doctrine of the Church, the effort was made to shatter the confidence in the chief bulwark of Scholasticism, the Aristotelian philosophy, or what at that period was regarded as such ; (especially in this connection *Peter Ramus*, (1515-1572) should be men-tioned, who fell in the massacre of St. Bartholomew). The authority of the Church became more and more weakened in the faith of the people, and the great principles of Scholasticism came to an end.

2. The Results of Scholasticism.—Notwithstanding all, Scholasticism was not without its positively good results. Though standing wholly in the service of the Church, it had, nevertheless, grown out of a scientific impulse, and so naturally awakened a free spirit of inquiry and a sense for knowledge. It made the objects of faith the objects of thought, it raised men from the sphere of unconditional faith to the sphere of doubt, of investigation and of knowledge, and by its very effort to demonstrate the principles of theology it established, though against its knowledge and de-sign, the authority of reason. It thus introduced to the world another principle than that of the old Church, the principle of the

thinking spirit, the self-consciousness of the reason, or at least prepared the way for the victory of this principle. Even the deformities and unfavorable side of Scholasticism, the many absurd questions upon which the Scholastics divided, even their thousand-fold unnecessary and accidental distinctions, their inquisitiveness and subtleties, all sprang from a rational principle, and grew out of a spirit of investigation, which could only utter itself in this way under the all powerful ecclesiastical spirit of the time. Only when it was surpassed by the advancing spirit of the age, did Scholasticism, falsifying its original meaning, make common cause and interest with the old ecclesiasticism, and turned itself as the most violent opposer against the improvements of the new period.

3. THE REVIVAL OF LETTERS.—The revival of classic literature contributed prominently to that change in the spirit of the age which marks the beginning of the new epoch of philosophy. The study of the ancients, especially of the Greeks, had almost wholly ceased in the course of the Middle Ages; even the philosophy of Plato and Aristotle was known, for the most part, only through Latin translations or secondary sources; no one realized the spirit of classic life, and all sense for beauty of form and elegant composition had passed away. The change was chiefly brought about by means of the Greek scholars who fled from Constantinople to Italy; the study of the ancients in the original sources came up again; the newly discovered art of printing allowed the classics to be widely circulated; the Medicis drew classic scholars to their court; all this working for a far better understanding of the ancient philosophy. *Besarion* (died 1472) and *Ficinus* (died 1499) were prominent in this movement. The result was presently seen. The new scholars contended against the stiff and uncouth manner in which the sciences had hitherto been treated, new ideas began to circulate, and there arose again the free, universal, thinking spirit of antiquity. In Germany, also, classic studies found a fruitful soil. *Reuchlin* (born 1454), *Melancthon* and *Erasmus*, labored in this sense, and the classic movement, hostile as it was to the Scholastic impulse, favored most decidedly the growing tendencies to the Reformation.

4. THE GERMAN REFORMATION.—All the elements of the new age, the struggle against Scholasticism, the revival of letters and the more enlarged culture thus secured, the striving after national independence, the attempts of the state to free itself from the Church and the hierarchy, and above all, the desire of the thinking self-consciousness for autonomy, for freedom from the fetters of authority—all these elements found their focus and point of union in the German Reformation. Though having its root at first in practical, and religious, and national interests, and expending itself mainly upon the Christian doctrine and Church, yet was the Reformation in principle and in its true consequences a rupture of the thinking spirit with authority, a protesting against the fetters of the positive, a return of the mind from its self-estrangement to itself. From that which was without, the mind now came back to that which is within, and the purely human as such, the individual heart and conscience, the subjective conviction, in a word, the rights of the subject now began to be of worth. While marriage had formerly been regarded, though not immoral, as yet inferior to continence and celibacy, it appeared now as a divine institution, a natural law ordained of God. While poverty had formerly been esteemed higher than wealth, and the contemplative life of the monk was superior to the manual labor of the layman supporting himself by his own toil, yet now poverty ceased to be desirable in itself, and labor was no longer despised. Ecclesiastical freedom took the place of spiritual bondage; monasticism and the priesthood lost their power. In the same way, on the side of knowledge the individual man came back to himself, and threw off the restraints of authority. He was impressed with the conviction that the whole process of redemption must be experienced within himself, that his reconciliation to God and salvation was his own concern, for which he needed no mediation of priests, and that he stood in an immediate relation to God. He found his whole being in his faith, in the depth of his feelings and convictions.

Since thus Protestantism sprang from the essence of the same spirit in which modern philosophy had its birth, the two have the closest relation to each other, though of course there is a specific difference between the religious and the scientific principle. Yet in their origin, both kinds of Protestantism, that of religion and that of thought, are one and the same, and in their progress they have also gone hand in hand together. For religion, reduced to its simple elements, will be found to have its source, like philosophy, in the self-knowledge of the reason.

5. THE ADVANCEMENT OF THE NATURAL SCIENCES.—To all these phenomena, which should be regarded both as causes and as symptoms of the intellectual revolution of this period, we must add yet another, which essentially facilitated and gave a positive assistance to the freedom of the mind from the fetters of authority —the starting up of the natural sciences and the inductive method of examining nature. This epoch was a period of the most fruitful and influential discoveries in nature. The discovery of America and the passage to the East Indies had already widened the circle of view, but still greater revolutions are connected with the name of a *Copernicus* (died 1543), *Kepler* (died 1630), and *Galileo* (died 1642), revolutions which could not remain, without an influence upon the whole mode of thinking of that age, and which contributed prominently to break the faith in the prevailing ecclesiastical authority. Scholasticism had turned away from nature and the phenomenal world, and, blind towards that which lay before the very eyes, had spent itself in a dreamy intellectuality; but now nature rose again in honor; her glory and exaltation, her infinite diversity and fulness of life became again the immediate objects of observation; to investigate nature became an essential object of philosophy, and scientific empiricism was thus regarded as a universal and essential concern of the thinking man. From this time the natural sciences date their historical importance, for only from this time have they had an uninterrupted history. The results of this new intellectual movement can be readily estimated. Such a scientific investigation of nature not only destroyed a series of traditional errors and prejudices, but, what was of greater importance, it directed the intellectual interest towards that which is real and actual, it nourished and protected the self-thinking and feeling of self-dependence, the spirit of inquiry and

proof. The stand-point of observation and experiment presupposes an independent self-consciousness of the individual, a breaking loose from authority—in a word, scepticism, with which, in fact, the founders of modern philosophy, *Bacon* and *Descartes*, began; the former by conditioning the knowledge of nature upon the removal of all prejudice and every preconceived opinion, and the latter by demanding that philosophy should be begun with universal doubt. No wonder that a bitter struggle should soon break out between the natural sciences and ecclesiastical orthodoxy, which could only result in breaking the power of the latter.

6. BACON OF VERULAM.—Francis of Verulam was born in 1561, and was Lord High Chancellor of England and keeper of the king's seal under James I. From these offices he was subsequently expelled, and died in 1626, with a character which has not been without reproach. He took as his principle the inductive method, which he directed expressly against Scholasticism and the ruling scientific method. On this account he is frequently placed at the head of modern philosophy.

The sciences, says Bacon, have hitherto been in a most sad condition. Philosophy, wasted in empty and fruitless logomachies, has failed during so many centuries to bring out a single work or experiment of actual benefit to human life. Logic hitherto has served more to the establishment of error than to the investigation of truth. Whence all this? Why this penury of the sciences? Simply because they have broken away from their root in nature and experience. The blame of this is chargeable to many sources; first, the old and rooted prejudice that the human mind loses somewhat of its dignity when it busies itself much and continuously with experiments and material things; next, superstition and a blind religious zeal, which has been the most irreconcilable opposer to natural philosophy; again, the exclusive attention paid to morals and politics by the Romans, and since the Christain era to theology by every acute mind; still farther, the great authority which certain philosophers have professed, and the great reverence given, to antiquity; and in fine, a want of courage and a despair of overcoming the many and great difficulties which lie in the way of the investigation of nature. All these causes have contributed to keep down the sciences. Hence they must now be renewed, and regenerated, and reformed in their most fundamental principles; there must now be found a new basis of knowledge and new principles of science. This radical reformation of the sciences depends upon two conditions, objectively upon the referring of science to experience and the philosophy of nature, and subjectively upon the purifying of the sense and the intellect from all abstract theories and traditional prejudices. Both conditions furnish the correct method of natural science, which is nothing other than the method of induction. Upon a true induction depends all the soundness of the sciences.

In these propositions the Baconian philosophy is contained. The historical significance of its founder is, therefore, in general this,—that he directed the attention and reflection of his cotemporaries again upon the given actuality, upon nature; that he affirmed the necessity of experience, which had been formerly only a matter of accident, and made it as in and for itself an object of thought. His merit consists in having brought up the principle of scientific empiricism, and only in this. Strictly speaking, we can allow no *content* to the Baconian philosophy, although (in his treatise *de augmentis scientiarum*) he has attempted a systematic encyclopedia of the sciences according to a new principle of classification, through which he has scattered an abundance of fine and fruitful observations, which are still used as apothegms.

7. The Italian Philosophers of the Transition Epoch.— Besides Bacon, other phenomena must be noticed which have prepared and introduced the new age of philosophy. First among these is a list of Italian philosophers, from the second half of the sixteenth and the first half of the seventeenth century. These philosophers are connected in a twofold manner with the movements already sketched of this transition period, first by an enthusiasm for nature which among them all partook in a greater or less degree of pantheism (Vanini *e. g.* gave to one of his writings the title "concerning the wonderful secrets of nature, the queen and goddess of mortals"), and second, by their connection with the systems of

ancient philosophy. The best known of these philosophers are
the following: *Cardanus* (1501–1575), *Campanella* (1568–1639),
Giordano Bruno (— 1600), *Vanini* (1586–1619.) They were all
men of a passionate, enthusiastic and impetuous nature, unsteady
and wild in character, restless and adventurous in life, men who
were inspired by an eager impulse towards knowledge, but who
were carried away by great fantasy, wildness of imagination, and
a seeking after secret astrological and geomantic knowledge. For
these reasons they also passed away, leaving no fruitful result
behind. They were all persecuted by the hierarchy, and two of
them (Bruno and Vanini) ended their lives at the stake. In their
whole historical appearance they are like the eruption of a volcano,
and are to be regarded more as forerunners and announcers than as
beginners and founders of the new age of philosophy. The most
important among them is *Giordano Bruno*. He revived the old
idea of the Stoics, that the world is a living being, and that a
world-soul penetrates it all. The content of his general thought
is the profoundest enthusiasm for nature, and the plastic reason
which is present in it. The reason is, according to him, the inner
artist who shapes the matter and manifests himself in the forms
of the universe. From the heart of the root or the germ he sends
out the lobes, and from these again he evolves the shoots, and
from the shoots the branches, until bud, and leaf, and blossom are
brought forth. Every thing is arranged, adjusted, and perfected
within. Thus the universal reason calls back from within the
sap out of the fruits and flowers to the branches again, &c. The
universe thus is an infinite living thing, in which every thing lives
and moves after the most manifold way.

The relation of the reason to matter, Bruno determines wholly
in the Aristotelian manner; both stand related to each other as
form and matter, as actuality and potentiality, neither is without
the other; the form is the inner impelling might of matter, and
matter, as the unlimited possibility, as the capability for an infinite diversity of form, is the mother of all forms. The other side
of Bruno's philosophizing, his elaboration of the topics of Lullus,

which occupies the greater part of his writings, has little philosophic interest, and we therefore pass it by.

8. JACOB BOEHME.—As Bacon among the English and Bruno among the Italians, so *Jacob Boehme* is the index among the Germans of this transition period.   Each one of these three indicates it in a way peculiar to his own nationality; Bacon as the herald of empiricism, Bruno as the representative of a poetic pantheism, and Boehme as the father of the theosophic mysticism. If we regarded alone the profoundness of his principle, Boehme should hold a much later place in the history of philosophy, but if we looked chiefly at the imperfect form of his philosophizing, his rank would be assigned to the mystics of the Middle Ages, while chronologically we must associate him with the German Reformation and the protestant elements that were nourished at that time.   His true position is among the forerunners and prophets of the new age.

Jacob Boehme was born in 1575, in old Seidenburg, a village of upper Lusace, not far from Goerlitz.   His parents were poor peasants.   In his boyhood he took care of the cattle, and in his youth, after he had acquired the rudiments of reading and writing in a village school, he was sent to Goerlitz to learn the shoemaker's art.   He finished his apprenticeship and settled down at Goerlitz in 1594 as master of his trade.   Even in his youth he had received illuminations or mysterious revealings, which were subsequently repeated when his soul, striving for the truth, had become profoundly agitated by the religious conflicts of the age. Besides the Bible, the only books which Boehme read were some mystical writings of a theosophic and alchymistic content, *e. g.* those of Paracelsus.   His entire want of culture is seen as soon as he undertakes to write down his thoughts, or, as he calls them, his illuminations.   Hence the imperious struggle of the thought with the expression, which, however, not unfrequently rises to a dialectical acuteness and a poetic beauty.   His first treatise, Aurora, composed in the year 1612, brought Boehme into trouble with the chief pastor in Goerlitz, Gregorious Richter, who publicly condemned the book from the pulpit, and even ridiculed the

8

person of its author. The writing of books was prohibited him by a magistrate, a prohibition which Boehme observed for many years, till at length the command of the spirit was too mighty within him, and he took up again his literary labors. Boehme was a plain, quiet, modest and gentle man. He died in 1624.

To give an exhibition of his theosophy in a few words is very difficult, since Boehme, instead of clothing his thoughts in a logical form, dressed them only in pictures of the sense and obscure analogies, and often availed himself of the most arbitrary and singular modes of expression. A twilight reigns in his writings, as in a Gothic cathedral where the light falls through variegated windows. Hence the magic effect which he has made upon many hearts. The chief thought of his philosophizing is this, viz., that the distinguishing of the self from the not-self is the essential determination of spirit, and hence of God so far as God is to be apprehended as spirit. God, according to Boehme, is living spirit only at the time and in the degree in which he conceives the distinction within himself from himself, and is in this distinction object and consciousness. The distinction of God in himself is the only source of his and of all actuosity and spontaneity, the spring and fountain of that self-active life which produces consciousness out of itself. Boehme is inexhaustible in images by which this negativity in God, his self-distinguishing and self-renunciation to the world, may be made conceivable. The great expansion without end, he says, needs limitation and a compass in which it may manifest itself, for in expansion without limit there could be no manifestation, there must be a contraction and an enclosing, in order that a manifestation may arise. See, he says in another place, if the will were only of one kind, then would the soul have only one quality, and were an immovable thing, which would always lie still and never do any thing farther than one thing; in this there could be no joy, as also no art nor science of other things, and no wisdom; every thing would be a nothing, and there would be neither heart nor will for any thing, for there would be only the single. Hence it cannot be said that the whole God is in one will and essence, there is a distinction. Nothing can ever become manifest to itself without resistance, for if it has nothing resisting, it expends itself and never comes to itself again; but if it does not come to itself again except in that from which it has originally sprung, it thus knows nothing of its original condition. The above thought Boehme expresses when he says in his *Questionibus Theosophicis ;* the reader should know that in yea and nay all things consist, whether divine, devilish, earthly, or whatever may be named. The one as the yea, is simple energy and love, and is the truth of God and God himself. But this were inconceivable, and there were neither delight, nor importance, nor sensibility, without the nay. The nay is thrown in the way of the yea, or of truth, in order that the truth may be manifest and something, in which there may be a contrarium, where eternal love may work and become sensitive and willing. There is nothing in the one which is an occasion for willing until the one becomes duplicated, and so there can be no sensation in unity, but only in duality. In brief, according to Boehme, neither knowledge nor consciousness is possible, without distinction, without opposition, without duplication; a thing becomes clear and an object of consciousness only through something else, through its own opposition identical with its own being. It was very natural to connect this thought of a unity distinguishing itself in itself, with the Christian doctrine of the Trinity, as Boehme has, in fact, repeatedly done when treating of the Divine life and its process of duplication. Schelling afterwards took up these ideas of Boehme and philosophically elaborated them.

If we should assign to the theosophy of Boehme a position in the development of later philosophy corresponding to the inner content of its principle, it would most properly be placed as a complement to the system of *Spinoza*. If Spinoza taught the flowing back of all the finite into the eternal one, Boehme, on the other hand, shows the procession of the finite from the eternal one, and the inner necessity of this procession, since the being of this one would be rather a not-being without such a self-duplication. Compared with Descartes, Boehme has at least more profoundly apprehended the conception of self consciousness and the relation

of the finite to God.   But his historical position in other respects
is far too isolated and exceptional, and his mode of statement far
too impure, to warrant us in incorporating him anywhere in a
series of systems developed continuously and in a genetic connection.

———•••———

SECTION XXIV.

DESCARTES.

The beginner and founder of modern philosophy is *Descartes*.
While he, like the men of the transition epoch just noticed, broke
loose entirely from the previous philosophizing, and began his
work wholly *de novo*, yet he did not content himself, like Bacon,
with merely bringing out a new method, or like Boehme and his
cotemporaries among the Italians, with affirming philosophical
views without a methodical ground.   He went further than any
of these, and making his stand-point one of universal doubt, he
affirms a new, positive, and pregnant philosophical principle, from
which he attempted logically to deduce the chief points of his
system.   The character and novelty of his principle makes him
the beginner, and its inner fruitfulness the founder, of modern
philosophy.

Rene Descartes (*Renatus Cartesius*) was born in 1596, at La
Haye in Torraine.   Possessing an independent property, he volun-
teered as a soldier in his twenty-first year, and served in the wars
with the Dutch, the Bavarians, and the Imperialists.   After this
he travelled a good deal, and then abode a considerable time in
Paris.   In 1629 he left his native land, and betook himself to
Holland, that he might there, undisturbed and unknown, devote
himself to philosophy, and elaborate his scientific ideas.   He spent
twenty years in Holland, enduring much vexatious treatment from
fanatical theologians, till in 1649 he accepted an invitation from
Queen Christina of Sweden, to visit Stockholm, where he died in
the following year.

The chief content of the Cartesian system may be seen condensed in the following epitome.

1. If science would have any thing fixed and abiding, it must begin with the primal ground of things; every presupposition which we may have cherished from infancy must be abandoned; in a word, we must doubt at every point to which the least uncertainty is attached. We must therefore doubt not only the existence of the objects of sense, since the senses so frequently deceive, but also the truths of mathematics and geometry—for, however evident the proposition may appear that two and three make five, or that the square has four sides, yet we cannot know but what God may have designedly formed us for erroneous judgments. It is therefore advisable to doubt every thing, in fact to deny every thing, to posit every thing as false.

2. But though we posit every thing as false to which the slightest doubt may be attached, yet we cannot deny one thing, viz., the truth that we, who so think, do exist. But rather from the very fact that I posit every thing as false, that I doubt every thing, is it manifest that I, the doubter, exist. Hence the proposition: I think, therefore I am (*cogito ergo sum*), is the first and most certain position which offers itself to every one attempting to philosophize. Upon this the most certain of all propositions, the certainty of all other knowledge depends. The objection of *Gassendi* that the truth of existence follows from any other activity of man as well as from thinking, that I might just as well say : I go to walk, therefore I exist,—has no weight; for, of all my actions, I can be absolutely certain only of my thinking.

3. From the proposition I think, therefore, I am, the whole nature of the mind may be determined. When we examine who we are who hold every thing to be false that is distinct from ourselves, we see clearly that neither extension nor figure, nor any thing which can be predicated of body, but only thought, belongs to our nature. I am therefore only a thinking being, *i. e.* mind, soul, intelligence, reason. Thought is my substance. Mind can therefore be apprehended clearly and completely for itself alone, without any of those attributes which belong to body. Its con-

ception contains nothing of that which belongs to the conception of body. It is therefore impossible to apprehend it through any sensuous representation, or to make an image of it : it apprehends itself only through the pure intelligence.

4. From the proposition *cogito ergo sum*, follows still farther the universal rule of all certainty. I am certain that I am a thinking being, what now is involved in the fact that I am certain of any thing? Whence comes this certainty? From no other source than the knowledge that this first proposition contains a clear conception of that which I affirm. I know of a certainty that I am, and I know any thing else only when I know it as certainly as I know that I am. Hence I may regard it as a universal rule, that every thing is true which I know clearly and determinately.

5. This rule, however, is only a principle of certainty, not of knowledge and of truth. We apply it therefore to our thoughts or ideas, in order to discover what is objectively true. But our ideas are partly innate, partly acquired, and partly self-originated. Among those of the first class we find the idea of a God. The question arises, whence have we this idea? Manifestly not from ourselves; this idea could only be implanted within us by a being who has the fulness of all perfection in himself, *i. e.* only by an actually existing God. If I ask now the question, whence have I the faculty to conceive of a nature more perfect than my own? the answer must ever come, that I have it only from him whose nature is actually more perfect. All the attributes of God, the more I contemplate them, show that their idea could not have originated with myself alone. For though there might be in me the idea of substance because I am a substance, yet I could not of myself have the idea of an infinite substance, since I am finite; such an idea could only be given me through a substance actually infinite. Moreover, we must not think that the conception of the infinite is to be gained through abstraction and negation, as we might gain darkness through the negation of light; but I perceive, rather, that the infinite contains more reality than the finite, and that, therefore, the conception of the infinite must be correspondingly antecedent in me to that of the finite. Since then I have a clear

and determined idea of the infinite substance, and since this has a greater objective reality than every other, so is there no other which I have so little reason to doubt. But now since I am certain that the idea of God has come to me from God himself, it only remains for me to examine the way in which I have received it from God. I have never derived it directly nor indirectly from the sense, for ideas through the sense arise only by affecting the external organs of sense; neither have I devised it, for I can neither add to it nor diminish it in any respect,—it must, therefore, be innate as the idea of myself is innate. Hence the first proof we can assign for the being of a God is the fact that we find the idea of a God within us, and that we must have a cause for its being. Again, the being of a God may be concluded from my own imperfection, and especially from the knowledge of my imperfection. For since I know that there is a perfection which is wanting in me, it follows that there must exist a being who is more perfect than I, on whom I depend and from whom I receive all I possess.—But the best and most evident proof for the being of a God is, in fine, that which is gained from the conception of a God. The mind among all its different ideas singles out the chiefest of all, that of the most perfect being, and perceives that this has not only the possibility of existence, *i. e.* accidental existence like all other ideas, but that it possesses necessary existence in itself. And as the mind knows that in every triangle its three angles are equal to two right angles, because this is involved in the very idea of a triangle, so does the mind necessarily infer that necessary existence belongs to the conception of the most perfect being, and that, therefore, the most perfect being actually exists. No other idea which the mind finds within itself contains necessary existence, but from the idea of the highest being existence cannot be separated without contradiction. It is only our prejudices which keep us from seeing this. Since we are accustomed in every thing to separate its conception from its existence, and since we often make ideas arbitrarily, it readily happens, that when we contemplate the highest being we are in doubt whether its idea may not be one also arbitrarily devised, or at least one in whose conception existence does not lie.—This proof is essentially different from that of Thomas (Anselm of Canterbury). His argument was as follows: " If we understand what is indicated by the word God, it is all that can be conceived of greatness ; but now there is actually and in thought more belonging to him than the word represents, and therefore God exists not only in word (or representation), but in fact." Here the defect in the syllogism is manifest, for from the premise it could only be concluded that God must therefore be *represented* as existing in fact, while his actual existence would not follow. My proof on the other hand is this,—we may predicate of a thing what we clearly see belongs to its true and changeless nature, or to its essence, or to its form. But now after we had examined what God is, we found existence to belong to his true and changeless nature, and therefore may we properly predicate existence of God. Necessary existence is contained in the idea of the most perfect being, not by a fiction of our understanding but because existence belongs to his eternal and changeless nature.

6. The result just found—the existence of God—is of the highest consequence. Before attaining this we were obliged to doubt every thing, and give up even every certainty, for we did not know but that it belonged to the nature of the human mind to err, but that God had created us for error. But so soon as we look at the necessary attributes of God in the innate idea of him, so soon as we know that he is true, it would be a contradiction to suppose that he would deceive us, or that he could have made us to err ; for though an ability to deceive might prove his skill, a willingness to deceive would only demonstrate his frailty. Our reason, therefore, can never apprehend an object which would not be true so far as the reason apprehended it, *i. e.* so far as it is clearly known. For God might justly be styled a deceiver if he had given us a reason so perverted as to hold the false for the true. And thus every absolute doubt with which we began is dispelled. From the being of God we derive every certainty. For every sure knowledge it is only necessary that we have clearly known a

thing, and are also certain of the existence of a God, who would not deceive.

7. From the true idea of God follow the principles of a philosophy of nature or the doctrine of the two substances. Substance is that which so exists that it needs nothing else for its existence. In this (highest) sense God is the only substance. God, as the infinite substance, has his ground in himself, is the cause of himself. The two created substances, on the other hand, the thinking and the corporeal substance, mind and matter, are substances only in a broader sense of the word; they may be apprehended under the common conception that they are things which need only the co-operation of God for their existence. Each of these two substances has an attribute which constitutes its nature and its essence, and to which all its other determinations may be referred. The attribute and essence of matter is extension, that of mind, thought. For every thing else which can be predicated of body presupposes extension, and is only a mode of extension, as every thing we can find in mind is only a modification of thought. A substance to which thought immediately belongs is called mind, and a substance, whose immediate substratum is extension, is called body. Since thought and extension are distinct from each other, and since mind can not only be known without the attributes of the body, but is in itself the negation of those attributes, we may say that the essence of these substances is in their reciprocal negation. Mind and body are wholly distinct, and have nothing in common.

8. We pass by the physics of Descartes, which has only a subordinate philosophical interest, and notice next his views of anthropology. From this dualistic relation between mind and matter there follows a dualistic relation between soul and body. If matter is essentially extension, and mind essentially thought, and if the two have nothing in common, then the union of soul and body can be conceived only as a mechanical one. The body is to be regarded as an artistic automaton, which God has made, as a statue or machine formed by God from the earth. Within this body the soul dwells, closely but not internally connected with it

8*

The union of the two is only a powerful bringing of the two together, since each is not only an independent factor, but is essentially distinct from and even opposed to the other. The body by
itself is a machine fully prepared, in which nothing is changed by
the entrance of the thinking soul, except that through it certain
motions are secured : the wheel-work of the machine remains as
it was. It is only thought which distinguishes this machine from
every other; hence, therefore, brutes which are not self-conscious
nor thinking, must be ranked with all other machines. From this
stand-point arose especially the question concerning the seat of
the soul. If body and soul are independent substances, each essentially opposed to the other, they cannot interpenetrate each other,
but can touch only at one point when they are powerfully brought
together. This point where the soul has its seat, is, according to
Descartes, not the whole brain but the pineal gland, a little kernel
in the middle of the brain. The proof for this claim, that the
pineal gland is the only place where the soul immediately exhibits
its energy, is found in the circumstance that all other parts of the
brain are twofold, which should not be in an organ where the soul
has its seat, else objects would appear double. There is, therefore, no other place in the body where impressions can be so well
united as in this gland. The pineal gland is, therefore, the chief
seat of the soul, and the place where all our thoughts are formed.

We have thus developed the fundamental thoughts of the Cartesian system, and will now recapitulate in a few words the features characteristic of its stand-point and historic position.
Descartes was the founder of a new epoch in philosophy, *first*,
from his postulate of universal freedom from all preconceptions.
His protesting against every thing which is not posited by the
thought, against taking any thing for granted in respect of the
truth, has remained from that time onward the fundamental principle of the new age. *Secondly.* Descartes has brought out the
principle of self-consciousness (the mind or the thinking substance
is regarded by him as an individual self, a particular Ego)—a new
principle, unknown in this view to the ancients. *Thirdly.* Descartes has shown the opposition between being and thought, exist-

ence and consciousness, and the mediation of this opposition, which has been the problem of the whole modern philosophy, he first affirmed as the true philosophical problem. But with these ideas, which make an epoch in the history of philosophy, there are at the same time connected the defects of the Cartesian philosophizing. *First.* Descartes gained the content of his system, namely his three substances, empirically. True, the system which begins with a protestation against all existence would seem to take nothing for granted, but to derive every thing from the thinking. But in fact this protesting is not thoroughly carried out. That which seems to be cast aside is afterwards, when the principle of certainty is gained, taken up again unchanged. And so it happens that Descartes finds at hand not only the idea of God, but his two substances as something *immediately given.* True, in order to reach them, he abstracts every thing which lies immediately before him, but in the end the two substances are seen as that which remains when all else is abstracted. They are received *empirically.* The *second* defect is, that Descartes separates so wholly from each other the two sides of the opposition between thought and being. He posits both as "substances," *i. e.* as powers, which reciprocally exclude and negate each other. The essence of matter according to him consists *only* in extension, *i. e.* in the pure being *extra se* (*Aussersichsein*), and that of mind *only* in thought, *i. e.* in the pure being *in se* (*Insichsein.*) The two stand over against each other as centrifugal and centripetal. But with this apprehension of mind and matter, an inner mediation of the two is an impossibility; there must be a powerful act of creation, there must be the divine assistance in order that the two sides may ever come together, and be united as they are in man. Nevertheless Descartes demands and attempts such a mediation of the two sides. But the impossibility of truly overcoming the dualism of his stand-point is the *third,* and the chief defect of his system. In the proposition "I think, therefore I am," or "I am thinking," the two sides, being and thought, are indeed connected together, but only that they may become fixed independently in respect of each other. If the question is asked, how does the Ego stand related to the extended ? the answer can only be : by thinking, *i. e.* negatively, by excluding it.   The idea of God, therefore, is all that remains for the mediation of these two sides.   The two substances are created by God, and through the divine will may be bound together; through the idea of God, the Ego attains the certainty that the extended exists.   God is therefore in a certain degree a *Deus ex machina,* necessary in order to mediate the conflict of the Ego with the extended.   It is obvious how external such a mediation is.

This defect of the Cartesian system operated as an impelling motive to those which succeeded.

SECTION XXV.

GEULINCX AND MALEBRANCHE.

1. Mind and matter, consciousness and existence, Descartes had fixed in the farthest separation from each other.   Both, with him, are substances, independent powers, reciprocally excluding oppositions.   Mind (*i. e.* in his view the simple self, the Ego) he regarded as essentially the abstraction from the sensuous, the distinguishing itself from matter and the separating of matter from itself; matter was essentially the complete opposition to thought.   If the relation of these two powers be as has been given, then the question arises, how can there ever be a filiation (*Rapport*) between them ?   How, on the one hand, can the affections of the body work upon the soul, and on the other hand, how can the volition of the soul direct the body, if the two are absolutely distinct and opposed to each other ?   At this point, *Arnold Geulincx* (a disciple of Descartes, born at Antwerp 1625, and died as professor of philosophy at Leyden 1669) took up the Cartesian system, and endeavored to give it a greater logical perfection.   According to Geulincx neither the soul works immediately

upon the body, nor the body immediately upon the soul. Certainly not the former : for though *I* can determine and move my body in many respects arbitrarily, yet *I* am not the cause of this movement; for I know not how it happens, I know not in what manner motion is communicated from my brain to the different parts of my body, and it is impossible that I should do that in respect of which I cannot see how it is done. But if I cannot produce motion in my body, much less can I do this outside of my body. I am therefore simply a contemplator of the world ; the only act which is peculiarly mine is contemplation. But even this contemplation arises in a singular manner. For if we ask how we obtain our observations of the external world, we find it impossible that the external world should directly give them to us. For however much we may say that, *e. g.* in the act of seeing, the external objects produce an image in my eye or an impression in my brain as in wax, yet this impression or picture is after all only something corporeal or material, and cannot therefore come into my mind, which is absolutely distinct from every thing material. There remains, therefore, only that we seek the mediation of the two sides in God. It is God alone who can unite the outer with the inner, and the inner with the outer ; who can make the outer phenomena to become inner representations or notions of the mind ; who can thus bring the world within the mind's observation, and the inner determinations of the will outward into deed. Hence every working, every act which unites the outer and inner, which brings the mind and the world into connection, is neither a working of the mind nor of the world, but only an immediate working of God. The movement of my limbs does not follow from my will, but only because it is the will of God that these movements should follow when I will. My will is an *occasion* by which God moves my body—an affection of my body is an *occasion* by which God brings within me a representation of the external world : the one is only the occasional cause of the other (hence the name occasionalism). My will, however, does not move God to move my limbs, but he who has imparted motion to matter and given it its laws, created also my will, and has so connected together the most diverse things, the movement of matter and the arbitrium of my will, that when my will puts forth a volition, such a motion follows as it wills, and the motion follows the volition without any interaction or physical influence exerted by the one upon the other. But just as it is with two clocks which go exactly alike, the one striking precisely as the other, their harmony is not the result of any reciprocal interacting, but follows because both have been fashioned and directed alike,—so is it with the movements of the body and the will, they harmonize only through that exalted artist who has in this ineffable way connected them together. We see from this that Geulincx has carried to its limit the dualistic basis of Descartes. While Descartes called the union of mind and matter a conjunction through power, Geulincx named it a miracle. There is consequently in this view no immanent, but only a transcendent mediation possible.

2. Closely connected with this view of Geulincx, and at the same time a real consequence and a wider development of the Cartesian philosophizing, is the philosophic stand-point of *Nicolas Malebranche*. He was born at Paris in 1638, chosen a member of the " *Congrégation de l'oratoire* " in his twenty-second year, won over to philosophy through the writings of Descartes, and died, after numerous feuds with theological opposers, in 1715.

Malebranche started with the Cartesian view of the relation between mind and matter. Both are strictly distinct from each other, and in their essence opposed. How now does the mind, (*i. e.* the Ego) gain a knowledge of the external world and have ideas of corporeal things? For it comes to know things only by means of ideas,—not through itself, not immediately. Now the mind can neither gain these ideas from itself, nor from the things themselves. Not from itself, for it is absolutely opposed to the bodily world, and hence has no capacity to idealize, to spiritualize material things, though they must become spiritualized before they can be introduced to the mind; in a word, the mind, which in relation to the material world is only an opposition, has no power to destroy this opposition. Just as little has the mind derived these ideas from things: for matter is not visible through itself, but rather as antithetic to mind is it that which is absolutely unintelligible, and which cannot be idealized, that which is absolutely without light and clearness.—It only remains, therefore, that the mind beholds things in a third that stands above the opposition of the two, viz., God. God, as the absolute substance, is the absolute ideality, the infinite power to spiritualize all things. Material things have no real opposition for God, to him they are no impenetrable darkness, but an ideal existence; all things are in him spiritually and ideally; the whole world, as intellectual or ideal, is God. God is, therefore, the higher mean between the Ego and the external world. In him we behold ideas, we being so strictly united with him, that he may properly be called the place of minds.

The philosophy of Malebranche, whose simple thought is this, that we know and see all things in God,—shows itself, like the occasionalism of Geulincx, to be a peculiar attempt to stand upon the basis of the Cartesian philosophy, and with its fundamental thought to overcome its dualism.

3. Two defects or inner contradictions have manifested themselves in the philosophy of Descartes. He had considered mind and matter as substances, each one of which excluded the other from itself, and had sought a mediation of the two. But with such conditions no mediation other than an external one is possible. If thought and existence are each one substance, then can they only negate and exclude each other. Unnatural theories, like those which have been mentioned, are the inevitable result of this. The simplest way out of the difficulty is to give up the principle first assumed, to strip off their independence from the two opposites, and instead of regarding them as substances, view them as accidents of one substance. This way of escape is moreover indicated by a particular circumstance. According to Descartes, God is the infinite substance, the peculiar substance in the proper sense of the word. Mind and matter are indeed substances, but only in relation to each other; in relation to God they are dependent, and not substances. This is, strictly taken, a contradiction. The true consequence were rather to say that neither the Ego (*i. e.* the

individual thinking) nor the material things are independent, but that this can be predicated only of the one substance, God; this substance alone has a real being, and all the being which belongs to individual essences these latter possess not as a substantial being, but only as accidents of the one only true and real substance. Malebranche approached this consequence. With him the bodily world is ideally at least resolved and made to sink in God, in whom are the eternal archetypes of all things. But *Spinoza* has most decidedly and logically adopted this consequence, and affirmed the accidence of all individual being and the exclusive substantiality of God alone. His system is the perfection and the truth of the Cartesian.

SECTION XXVI.

SPINOZA.

Baruch or Benedict Spinoza was born at Amsterdam, Nov. 24, 1632. His parents were Jews of Portuguese descent, and being merchants of opulence, they gave him a finished education. He studied with great diligence the Bible and the Talmud, but soon exchanged the pursuit of theology for the study of physics and the works of Descartes. He early became dissatisfied with Judaism, and presently came to an open rupture with it, though without going over formally to Christianity. In order to escape the persecutions of the Jews, who had excommunicated him, and who even went so far as to make an attempt upon his life, he left Amsterdam and betook himself to Rhynsberg, near Leyden. He finally settled down at the Hague, where he spent his life in the greatest seclusion, devoted wholly to scientific pursuits. He supported himself by grinding optic glasses, which his friends sold for him. The Elector Palatine, Charles Louis, offered him a Professorship of Philosophy at Heidelberg, with the full permission to teach as he chose, but Spinoza declined the post. Naturally of a weak constitution, which consumption had for many years been undermining, Spinoza died at the age of 44, on the 21st of February, 1677. In his life there was mirrored the unclouded clearness and exalted serenity of the perfected sage. Abstemious in his habits, satisfied with little, the master of his passions, never intemperately sad nor joyous, gentle and benevolent, with a character of singular excellence and purity, he faithfully illustrated in his life, the doctrines of his philosophy. His chief work, the *Ethica*, appeared the year of his death. His design was probably to have published it during his life, but the odious report that he was an atheist restrained him. The friend he most trusted, Louis Mayer, a physician, attended to its publication after the author's death and according to his will.

The system of Spinoza rests upon three fundamental conceptions, from which all the rest may be derived with mathematical necessity. These conceptions are that of substance, of attribute, and of mode.

1. Spinoza starts from the Cartesian conception of substance : substance is that which needs nothing other for its existence. But with such a conception there can exist only one single substance. A number of substances like that of Descartes is necessarily a contradiction. There can be nothing which has a substantial being besides the one substance of all things. This one substance Spinoza calls God. Of course, with such a view, the Christian idea of God, the notion of a spiritual and personal being, must be laid aside. Spinoza expressly declares, that his notion of God is entirely different from that of the Christian ; he denied that understanding and will could be predicated of God ; he ridiculed those who supposed that God worked for an end, and even scorned the view which regarded the world as a product of the Divine willing or thinking. God is, with him, only substance, and nothing more. The propositions that there is only one God, and that the substance of all things is only one, are with him identical.

What now peculiarly is this substance ? What is positive being ? This question it is very difficult to answer directly from the stand-point of Spinoza, partly because a definition, according to him, must contain (*i. e.* must be genetically) the immediate cause of that which is to be explained, but substance is uncreated and can have no cause besides itself; but prominently because Spinoza held that every determination is a negation, since it must indicate a want of existence, a relative not-being. (*Omnis determinatio est negatio* is an expression which, though he uses it only occasionally, expresses the fundamental idea of his whole system.) Hence, by setting up any positive determinations of being, we only take away from substance its infinity and make it finite. When we therefore affirm any thing concerning it, we can only speak negatively, *e. g.* that it has no foreign cause, that it has no plurality, that it cannot be divided, etc. It is even reluctantly that Spinoza declares concerning it that it is one, for this predicate might readily be taken numerically, as implying that others, the many, stood over against it. Thus there can remain only such positive affirmations respecting it as express its absolute reference to itself. In this sense Spinoza says that substance is the cause of itself, *i. e.* its being concludes existence in itself. When Spinoza calls it eternal, it is only another expression for the same thought; for by eternity he understands existence itself, so far as it is conceived to follow from the definition of the thing, in a sense similar to that in which geometricians speak of the eternal properties of figures. Still farther he calls substance infinite, because the conception of infinity expressed to him the conception of true being, the absolute affirmation of existence. So also the expression, God is free, affirms nothing more than those already mentioned, viz., negatively, that every foreign restraint is excluded from him, and positively, that God is in harmony with himself, that his being corresponds to the laws of his essence.

The comprehensive statement for the above is, that there is only one infinite substance that excludes from itself all determination and negation, and is named God, or nature.

2. Besides the infinite substance or God, Descartes had assumed two other substances created by God, viz., mind (thought).

and matter (extension). These two Spinoza considers in the light
of attributes, though, like Descartes, he receives them empirically
What, now, is the relation of these attributes to the infinite substance? This is the severe question, the tendon-Achilles of Spinoza's system. They cannot be essential forms in which the substance may manifest itself or appear, for this would make them
determine the essence of the substance, which would contradict its
conception as already given. Substance, as such, is neither understanding nor extension. If, then, the two attributes do not
flow out of the essence of the substance, and do not constitute
the substance, there remains only one other supposition, viz., that
they are externally attached to the substance; and this is, in
fact, Spinoza's view. Attribute, according to him, is that which
the understanding perceives in the substance as constituting its
essence. But understanding, as Spinoza expressly says, does not
belong to substance as such. Attributes, therefore, are those determinations which express the essence of the substance only for
the perceiving understanding; since they express the essence of
the substance in a determinate way, while substance itself has no
determinate way of being, they can only fall outside the substance,
viz., in the reflective understanding. To the substance itself it is
indifferent whether the understanding contemplate it under these
two attributes or not; the substance in itself has an infinity of
attributes, *i. e.* every possible attribute which is not a limitation,
may be predicated of it; it is only the human understanding
which attaches these two attributes to the substance, and it affixes
no more than these, because, among all the conceptions it can
form, these alone are actually positive, or express a reality. God,
or the substance, is therefore thinking, in so far as the understanding contemplates him under the attribute of thought, and is
extended in so far as the understanding contemplates him under
the attribute of extension. It is, says Spinoza—using a figure to
express this relation of substance to attribute—it is, like a surface
reflecting the light, which (objectively taken) may be hot, though,
in reference to the man looking upon it, it is white. More accurately substance is a surface, standing opposite to a beholder who

can see only through yellow and blue glasses; to whom, therefore the surface must appear either yellow or blue, though it is neither the one nor the other.

In relation to substance, therefore, the attributes must be apprehended as entirely independent: they must be conceived through themselves: their conception is not dependent upon that of substance. This is necessarily true; for since the substance can have no determinateness, then the attribute which is its determinate being, cannot be explained from the substance, but only through itself. Only by apprehending the attribute independently can the unity of the substance be maintained.

In relation to each other, the attributes are to be taken as opposites strictly and determinately diverse. Between the bodily and the ideal world there is no reciprocal influence nor interaction: a body can only spring from a body, and an idea can only have an idea for its source. Hence, therefore, neither the mind can work upon the body nor the body upon the mind. Nevertheless there exists between the two worlds a perfect harmony and an entire parallelism. It is one and the same substance which is conceived under each of the two attributes, and under which one of the two we may contemplate it is indifferent to the substance itself, for each mode of contemplation is equally correct. From this follows at once the proposition of Spinoza, that the connection of ideas and of things is the same. Hence the solution to the problem of the relation of body and soul, so difficult to find from the Cartesian stand-point, is readily seen from that of Spinoza. Body and soul are one and the same thing, only viewed under different attributes. Mind is nothing but the idea of body, *i. e.* it is the same thing as body, only that it is viewed under the attribute of thought. In the same way is explained the apparent but not real influence of the body upon the mind, and the mind upon the body. That which, in one point of view is bodily motion, in another is an act of thought. In short, the most perfect parallelism reigns between the world of bodily things and that of ideas.

3. Individual beings, which considered under the attribute of

thought are ideas, and under the attribute of extension are bodies, Spinoza comprehends under the conception of accidence, or, as he calls it, mode. By modes we are therefore to understand the changing forms of substance. The modes stand related to the substance as the rippling waves of the sea to the water of the sea, as forms constantly disappearing and never having a real being. In fact this example goes too far, for the waves of the sea are at least a part of the water of the sea, while the modes, instead of being parts of the substance, are essentially nothing and without being. The finite has no existence as finite; only the infinite substance has actual existence. Substance, therefore, could not be regarded more falsely than if it should be viewed as made up of modes. That would be, Spinoza remarks, as if one should say that the line is made up out of points. It is just as false to affirm that Spinoza identifies God and the world. He identifies them so little that he would rather say that the world, as world, *i. e.* as an aggregate of individuals, does not at all exist; we might rather say with Hegel that he denies the world (his system is an acosmism), than with Bayle, that he makes every thing God, or that he ascribes divinity to every thing.

Whence do finite things or individuals arise, if they can have no existence by the side of substance ? They are only the product of our deceptive apprehension. There are two chief ways of knowledge—the intuitive, through the reason, and the imaginative. To the latter belong the knowledge of experience, and all that is abstract, superficial, and confused ; to the former, the collection of all fitting (adequate) ideas. It is only the fault of the imagination that we should look upon the world as a manifoldness of individuals ; the manifoldness is only a form of representation. The imagination isolates and individualizes what the reason sees together in its unity. Hence it is only as considered through the imagination (experience or opinion) that modes are *things;* the reason looks upon them as necessary, or, what is the same thing, as eternal.

Such are the fundamental thoughts and features of Spinoza's system. His *practical philosophy* yet remains to be characterized

and in a few words. Its chief propositions follow necessarily
from the metaphysical grounds already cited. First, it follows
from these, that what is called free will cannot be admitted. For
since man is only a mode, he, like every other mode, stands in an
endless series of conditioning causes, and no free will can therefore be predicated of him. The will must thus, like the body
(and the resolution of the will is only a modification of the body),
be determined by something other than itself. Men regard themselves as free only because they are conscious of their actions and
not of the determining causes. Just so the notions which one
commonly connects with the words good and evil, rest on an error
as follows at once from the conception of the absolute divine
causality. Good and evil are not something actually in the things
themselves, but only express relative conceptions which we have
formed from a comparison of things with one another. Thus, by
observing certain things we form a certain universal conception,
which we thereupon treat as though it were the rule for the being
and acting of all individuals, and if any individual varies from
this conception we fancy that it does not correspond to its nature,
and is incomplete. Evil or sin is therefore only something relative, for nothing happens against God's will. It is only a simple
negation or deprivation, which only seems to be a reality in our
representation. With God there is no idea of the evil. What is
therefore good and what evil? That is good which is useful to
us, and that evil which hinders us from partaking of a good.
That, moreover, is useful to us which brings us to a greater reality,
which preserves and exalts our being. But our true being is
knowledge, and hence that only is useful to us which aids us in
knowing; the highest good is the knowledge of God; the highest
virtue of the mind is to know and love God. From the knowledge of God we gain the highest gladness and joy of the mind,
the highest blessedness. Blessedness, hence, is not the reward of
virtue, but virtue itself.

The grand feature of Spinoza's philosophy is that it buries
every thing individual and particular, as a finite, in the abyss of
the divine substance. With its view unalterably fixed upon the

eternal one, it loses sight of every thing which seems actual in the ordinary notions of men. But its defect consists in its inability to transform this negative abyss of substance into the positive ground of all-being and becoming. The substance of Spinoza has been justly compared to the lair of a lion, which many footsteps enter, but from which none emerge. The existence of the phenomenal world, though it be only the apparent and deceptive reality of the finite, Spinoza does not explain. With his abstract conception of substance he cannot explain it. And yet the means to help him out of the difficulty lay near at hand. He failed to apply universally his fundamental principle that all determination is negation; he applied it only to the finite, but the abstract infinite, in so far as it stands over against the finite, is also a determinate; this infinite must be denied by its negation, which is the case when a finite world is posited. Jacob Boehme rightly apprehended this, when he affirmed, that without a self-duplication, without an ingress into the limited, the finite, the original ground of things is an empty nothing (*cf.* § XXIII. 8). So the original ground of Spinoza is a nothing, a purely indeterminate, because with him substance was only a principle of unity and not also a principle of distinction, because its attributes, instead of being an expression of an actual difference and a positive distinction to itself, are rather wholly indifferent to itself. The system of Spinoza is the most abstract Monotheism that can be thought. It is not accidental that its author, a Jew, should have brought out again this view of the world, this view of absolute identity, for it is in a certain degree with him only a consequence of his national religion—an echo of the Orient.

SECTION XXVII.

IDEALISM AND REALISM.

We have now reached a point of divergence in the development of philosophy. Descartes had affirmed and attempted to
mediate the opposition, between thought and being, mind and
matter. This mediation, however, was hardly successful, for the
two sides of the opposition he had fixed in their widest separation, when he posited them as two substances or powers, which
reciprocally negated each other. The followers of Descartes
sought a more satisfactory mediation, but the theories to which
they saw themselves driven, only indicated the more clearly that
the whole premise from which they started must be given up.
At length Spinoza abandoned the false notion, and took away its
substantiality from each of the two opposed principles. Mind
and matter, thought and extension, are now one in the infinite
substance. Yet they are not one *in themselves*, which would be
the only true unity of the two. That they are one in the substance is of little avail, since they are indifferent to the substance,
and are not immanent distinctions in it. Thus even with Spinoza
the two remain strictly separate. The ground of this isolation
we find in the fact that Spinoza himself did not sufficiently re-
nounce the Cartesian notion, and thus could not escape the Cartesian dualism. With him, as with Descartes, thought is *only*
thought, and extension *only* extension, and in such an apprehension of the two, the one necessarily excludes the other. If we
would find an inner mediation for the two, we must cease to abstract every thing essential from each. The opposite sides must
be mediated even in their strictest opposition. To do this, two
ways alone were possible. A position could be taken either on
the material or on the ideal side, and the attempt made to explain
the ideal under the material, or the material under the ideal,
comprehending one through the other. Both these attempts were

in fact made, and at about the same time. The two parallel courses of a one-sided *idealism*, and a one-sided *realism* (Empiricism, Sensualism, Materialism), now begin their development.

SECTION XXVIII.

LOCKE.

The founder of the realistic course and the father of modern Empiricism and Materialism, is *John Locke*, an Englishman. *Thomas Hobbes* (1588-1679) was his predecessor and countryman, whose name we need here only mention, as it has no importance except for the history of natural rights.

John Locke was born at Wrington, 1632. His student years he devoted to philosophy and prominently to medicine, though his weak health prevented him from practising as a physician. Few cares of business interrupted his leisure, and he devoted his time mostly to literary pursuits. His friendly relations with Lord Anthony Ashley, afterwards Earl of Shaftesbury, exerted a weighty influence upon his course in life. At the house of this distinguished statesman and author he always found the most cordial reception, and an intercourse with the most important men of England. In the year 1670 he sketched for a number of friends the first plan of his famous *Essay on the Human Understanding*, though the completed work did not appear till 1689. Locke died aged 72 in the year 1704. His writings are characterized by clearness and precision, openness and determinateness. More acute than profound in his philosophizing, he does not in this respect belie the characteristic of his nation. The fundamental thoughts and results of his philosophy have now become common property, especially among the English, though it should not therefore be forgotten that he is the first who has scientifically established them, and is, on this account, entitled to a true place

in the history of philosophy, even though his principle was wanting in an inner capacity for development.

Locke's Philosophy (*i. e.* his theory of knowledge, for his
whole philosophizing expends itself in investigating the faculty of
knowing) rests upon two thoughts, to which he never ceases to revert : first (negatively). there are no innate ideas; second (positively), all our knowledge arises from experience.

Many, says Locke, suppose that there are innate ideas which
the soul receives coetaneous with its origin, and brings with it into
the world.   In order to prove that these ideas are innate, it is
said that they universally exist, and are universally valid with
all men.   But admitting that this were so, such a fact would
prove nothing if this universal harmony could be explained in
any other way.   But men mistake when they claim such a fact.
There is, in reality, no fundamental proposition, theoretical or
practical, which would be universally admitted.   Certainly there
is no such practical principle, for the example of different people
as well as of different ages shows that there is no moral rule uni
versally admitted as valid.   Neither is there a theoretical one
for even those propositions which might lay the strongest claim
to be universally valid, *e. g.* the proposition,—" what is, is," or—
" it is imposible that one and the same thing should be and
not be at the same time,"—receive by no means a universal assent.
Children and idiots have no notion of these principles, and even
uncultivated men know nothing of these abstract propositions.
They cannot therefore have been imprinted on all men by nature.
If ideas were innate, then they must be known by all from earliest
childhood.   For " to be in the understanding," and " to become
known," is one and the same thing.   The assertion therefore that
these ideas are imprinted on the understanding while it does not
know it, is hence a manifest·contradiction.   Just as little is gained
by the subterfuge, that these principles come into the consciousness *so soon* as men use their reason.   This affirmation is directly false, for these maxims which are called universal come into the
consciousness much later than a great deal of other knowledge,
and children, *e. g.* give many proofs of their use of reason before

they know that it is impossible that a thing should be and at the same time not be. It is only correct to say that no one becomes conscious of these propositions without reasoning,—but to say that they are all known with the first reasoning is false. Moreover, that which is first known is not universal propositions, but relates to individual impressions. The child knows that sweet is not bitter long before he understands the logical proposition of contradiction. He who carefully bethinks himself, will hesitate before he affirms that particular dicta as " sweet is not bitter," are derived from universal ones. If the universal propositions were innate, then must they be the first in the consciousness of the child; for that which nature has stamped upon the human soul must come into consciousness antecedently to any thing which she has not written there. Consequently, if there are no innate ideas, either theoretical or practical, there can be just as truly no innate art nor science. The understanding (or the soul) is essentially a *tabula rasa*,—a blank and void space, a white paper on which nothing is written.

How now does the understanding become possessed of ideas? Only through experience, upon which all knowledge rests, and on which as its principle all knowledge depends. Experience itself is twofold; either it arises through the perception of external objects by means of the sense, in which case we call it sensation; or it is a perception of the activities of our own understanding, in which case it is named the inner sense, or, better, reflection. Sensation and reflection give to the understanding all its ideas; they are the windows through which alone the light of ideas falls upon the naturally dark space of the mind; external objects furnish us with the ideas of sensible qualities, and the inner object, which is the understanding itself, offers us the ideas of its own activities. To show the derivation and to give an explanation of all the ideas derived from both is the problem of the Lockian philosophy. For this end Locke divides ideas (representations or notions) into *simple* and *compound*. *Simple ideas*, he names those which are impressed from without upon the understanding while it remains wholly passive, just as the images of certain objects are represented in a mirror. These simple ideas are *partly* such as come to the understanding through an individual sense, *e. g.* the ideas of color, which are furnished to the mind through the eye, or those of sound, which come to it through the ear, or those of solidity or impenetrability, which we receive through the touch; *partly* such as a number of senses have combined to give us, as those of space and of motion, of which we become conscious by means of the sense both of touch and of sight; *partly* such as we receive through reflection, as the idea of thought and of will; and *partly*, in fine, such as arise from both sensation and reflection combined, *e. g.* power, unity, &c. These simple ideas form the material, as it were the letters of all our knowledge. But now as language arises from a manifold combination of letters, syllables and words, so the understanding forms complex ideas by the manifold combination of simple ideas with each other. The complex ideas may be referred to three classes, viz.: the ideas of mode, of substance, and of relation. Under the ideas of mode, Locke considers the modifications of space (as distance, measurement, immensity, surface, figure, &c.), of time (as succession, duration, eternity), of thought (perception, memory, abstraction, &c.), of number, power, &c. Special attention is given by Locke to the conception of substance. He explains the origin of this conception in this way, viz.: we find both in sensation and reflection, that a certain number of simple ideas seem often to be connected together. But as we cannot divest ourselves of the impression that these simple ideas have not been produced through themselves, we are accustomed to furnish them with a ground in some existing substratum, which we indicate with the word substance. Substance is something unknown, and is conceived of as possessing those qualities which are necessary to furnish us with simple ideas. But from the fact that substance is a product of our subjective thinking, it does not follow that it has no existence outside of ourselves. On the contrary, this is distinguished from all other complex ideas in the fact that this is an idea which has its archetype distinct from ourselves, and possesses objective reality, while other complex ideas are formed by the mind at pleasure, and have no reality corresponding to them external to the mind. We do not know what is the archetype of substance, and of the substance itself we are acquainted only with its attributes. From consider-ing the conception of substance, Locke next passes over to the idea of *relation*. A relation arises when the understanding has con-nected two things with each other, in such a way, that in consider-ing them it passes over from the one to the other. Every thing is capable of being brought by the understanding into relation, or what is the same thing, to be transformed into something relative. It is consequently impossible to enumerate the sum of every pos-sible relation. Hence Locke treats only of some of the more weighty conceptions of relation, among others, that of identity and difference, but especially that of cause and effect. The idea of cause and effect arises when our understanding perceives that any thing whatsoever, be it substance or quality, begins to exist through the activity of another. So much concerning ideas. The combination of ideas among themselves gives the conception of knowing. Hence knowledge stands in the same relation to the simple and complex ideas as a proposition does to the letters, syl-lables and words which compose it. From this it follows that our knowledge does not pass beyond the compass of our ideas, and hence that it is bounded by experience.

These are the prominent thoughts in the Lockian philosophy. Its empiricism is clear as day. The mind, according to it, is in itself bare, and only a mirror of the outer world,—a dark space which passively receives the images of external objects; its whole content is made by the impressions furnished it by material things. *Nihil est in intellectu, quod non fuerit in sensu*—is the watch-word of this standpoint. While Locke, by this proposition, ex-presses the undoubted preponderance of the material over the intellectual, he does so still more decisively when he declares that it is possible and even probable that the mind is a material essence. He does not admit the reverse possibility, that material things may be classed under the intellectual as a special kind. Hence with him mind is the secondary to matter, and hence he is seen to take the characteristic standpoint of realism (*cf.* § XXVII).

It is true that Locke was not always logically consistent, and in
many points did not thoroughly carry out his empiricism : but we
can clearly see that the road which will be taken in the farther
development of this direction, will result in a thorough denial of
the ideal factor.

The empiricism of Locke, wholly national as it is, soon became the ruling philosophy in England. Standing on its basis
we find *Isaac Newton*, the great mathematician (1642–1727),
Samuel Clarke, a disciple of Newton, whose chief attention was
given to moral philosophy (1675–1729), the English moralists of
this period, *William Wollaston* (1659–1724), the Earl of *Shaftesbury* (1671–1713), *Francis Hutcheson* (1694–1746), and even
some opponents of Locke, as *Peter Brown*, who died 1735.

———————

SECTION XXIX.

HUME.

As already remarked, Locke had not been wholly consistent
with the standpoint of empiricism. Though conceding to material objects a decided superiority above the thinking subject,
there was yet one point, viz., the recognition of substance, where
he claimed for the thinking a power above the objective world.
Among all the complex ideas which are formed by the subjective
thinking, the idea of substance is, according to Locke, the only
one which has objective reality ; all the rest being purely subjective, with nothing actually corresponding to them in the objective world.   But in the very fact that the subjective thinking
places the conception of substance, which it has formed, in the
objective world, it affirms an objective relation of things, an objective connection of them among each other, and an existing
rationality.   The reason of the subject in this respect stands in a
certain degree above the objective world, for the relation of substance is not derived immediately from the world of sense, and is

no product of sensation nor of perception through the sense. On a pure empirical standpoint—and such was Locke's—it was therefore illogical to allow the conception of substance to remain possessed of objective being. If the understanding is essentially a bare and empty space, a white unwritten paper, if its whole content of objective knowledge consists in the impressions made upon it by material things, then must the conception of substance also be explained as a mere subjective notion, a union of ideas joined together at the mind's pleasure, and the subject itself, thus fully deprived of every thing to which it could lay claim, .nust become wholly subordinated to the material world. This stride to a logical empiricism Hume has made in his criticism on the conception of causality.

David Hume was born at Edinburgh 1711. Devoted in youth to the study of law, then for some time a merchant, he afterwards gave his attention exclusively to philosophy and history. His first literary attempt was hardly noticed. A more favorable reception was, however, given to his "*Essays*,"—of which he published different collections from 1742 to 1757, making in all five volumes. In these Hume has treated philosophical themes as a thoughtful and cultivated man of the world, but without any strict systematic connection. In 1752 he was elected to the care of a public library in Edinburgh, and began in this same year his famous history of England. Afterwards he became secretary of legation at Paris, where he became acquainted with Rousseau. In 1767 he became under secretary of state, an office, however, which he filled for only a brief period. His last years were spent in Edinburgh, in a quiet and contented seclusion. He died 1776.

The centre of Hume's philosophizing is his criticism of the conception of cause. Locke had already expressed the thought that we attain the conception of substance only by the *habit* of always seeing certain modes together. Hume takes up this thought with earnestness. Whence do we know, he asks, that two things stand to each other in the relation of cause and effect? We do not know it apriori, for since the effect is something other

than the cause, while knowledge apriori embraces only that which
is identical, the effect cannot thus be discovered in the cause;
neither do we know it through experience, for experience reveals
to us only the succession in time of two facts. All our conclusions from experience, therefore, rest simply upon habit. Because we are in the habit of seeing that one thing is followed in
time by another, do we form the notion that the latter *must* follow out of the former: we make the relation of causality out of
the relation of succession; but a connection in time is naturally
something other than a causal connection. Hence, with the conception of causality, we transcend that which is given in perception and form for ourselves, notions to which we are properly not
entitled.—That which belongs to causality belongs to every necessary relation. We find within us conceptions, as those of power
and expression, and in general that of necessary connection; but
let us note how we attain these: not through sensation, for
though external objects seem to us to have coetaneousness of
being, they show us no necessary connection. Do they then come
through reflection? True, it seems as if we might get the idea
of power by seeing that the organs of our body move in consequence of the dictate of our mind. But since we do not know
the means through which the mind works, and since all the organs of the body cannot be moved by the will, it follows, that we
are indeed pointed to experience in reference to this activity; but
since experience can show us only a frequent conjunction, but no
real connection, it follows also that we come to the conception of
power as of every necessary connection, only because we are *accustomed* to a transcending process in our notions. All conceptions which express a relation of necessity, all knowledge pre-
sumptive of a real objective connection of things, rests therefore
ultimately only upon the association of ideas. Having denied
the conception of substance, Hume was led also to deny that of
the Ego or self. If the Ego or self really exists, it must be a
substance possessing inherent qualities. But since our conception of substance is purely subjective, without objective reality,
it follows that there is no correspondent reality to our conception

of the self or the Ego. The self or the Ego is, in fact, nothing other than a compound of many notions following rapidly upon each other; and under this compound we lay a conceived substratum, which we call soul, self, Ego (I). The self, or the Ego, rests wholly on an illusion. Of course, with such premises, nothing can be said of the immortality of the soul. If the soul is only the compound of our notions, it necessarily ceases with the notions—that which is compounded of the movements of the body dies with those movements.

There needs no further proof, than simply to utter these chief thoughts of Hume, to show that his scepticism is only a logical carrying out of Locke's empiricism. Every determination of universality and necessity must fall away, if we derive our knowledge only from perceptions through the sense; these determinations cannot be comprised in sensation.

----- •♦• -----

SECTION XXX.

CONDILLAC.

The French took up the problem of carrying out the empiricism of Locke, to its ultimate consequences in sensualism and materialism. Although this empiricism had sprung up on English soil, and had soon become universally prevalent there, it was reserved for France to push it to the last extreme, and show that it overthrew all the foundations of moral and religious life. This final consequence of empiricism did not correspond to the English national character. But on the contrary, both the empiricism of Locke, and the scepticism of Hume, found themselves opposed in the latter half of the eighteenth century, by a reaction in the Scotch philosophy (*Reid* 1710–1796, *Beattie*, *Oswald*, *Dugald Stewart*, 1753–1828). The attempt was here made to establish certain principles of truth as innate and immanent in the subject, which should avail both against the *tabula rasa* of Locke,

9*

and the scepticism of Hume. These principles were taken in a
thoroughly English way, as those of common sense, as facts of
experience, as facts of the moral instinct and sound human understanding; as something empirically given, and found in the
common consciousness by self-contemplation and reflection. But
in France, on the other hand, there was such a public and social
condition of things during the eighteenth century, that we can
only regard the systems of materialism and egoistic moralism
which here appeared, as the last practical consequences of the
empirical standpoint,—to be the natural result of the universal
desolation. The expression of a lady respecting the system of
Helvetius is well known, that it uttered only the secret of all the
world.

Most closely connected with the empiricism of Locke, is the
sensualism of the Abbé *Condillac*. Condillac was born at Gre-
noble, 1715. In his first writings he adhered to Locke, but subsequently passed beyond him, and sought to ground a philosophical standpoint of his own. He was elected a member of the
French Academy in 1768, and died in 1780. His writings fill
twenty-three volumes, and have their origin in a moral and religious interest.

Condillac, like Locke, started with the proposition that all
our knowledge comes from experience. While, however, Locke
had indicated two sources for this knowledge, sensation and reflection, the outer and the inner sense, Condillac referred reflection to sensation, and reduced the two sources to one. Reflection
is, with him, only sensation ; all intellectual occurrences, even the
combination of ideas and volition, are to be regarded only as
modified sensations. It is the chief problem and content of Condillac's philosophizing to carry out this thought, and derive the
different functions of the soul out of the sensations of the outer
sense. He illustrates this thought by a statue, which has been
made with a perfect internal organization like a man, but which
possesses no ideas, and in which only gradually one sense after
another awakens and fills the soul with impressions. In such a
view man stands on the same footing as the brute, for all his

knowledge and all his incentives to action he receives from sensation. Condillac consequently names men perfect animals, and brutes imperfect men. Still he revolts from affirming the materiality of the soul, and denying the existence of God. These ultimate consequences of sensualism were first drawn by others after him, as would naturally enough follow. As sensualism affirmed that truth or being could only be perceived through the sense, so we have only to reverse this proposition, and have the thesis of materialism, viz. : the sensible alone is, there is no other being but material being.

SECTION XXXI.

HELVETIUS.

Helvetius has exhibited the moral consequences of the sensualistic standpoint. While theoretical sensualism affirms that all our knowledge is determined by sensation, practical sensualism adds to this the analogous proposition that all our volition springs from the same source, and is regulated by the sensuous desire. Helvetius adopted it as the principle of morals to satisfy this sensuous desire.

Helvetius was born at Paris in 1715. Gaining a position in his twenty-third year as farmer-general, he found himself early in the possession of a rich income, but after a few years he found this office so vexatious that he abandoned it. The study of Locke decided his philosophic direction. Helvetius wrote his famed work, *de l'Esprit*, after he had given up his office and withdrawn himself in seclusion. It appeared in 1758, and attracted a great attention at home and abroad, though it drew upon him a violent persecution, especially from the clergy. It was fortunate for him that the persecution satisfied itself with suppressing his book. The repose in which he spent his later years was interrupted only by two journeys which he made to

Germany and England. He died in 1771. His personal character was wholly estimable, full of kindness and generosity. Especially in his place as farmer-general he showed himself benevolent towards the poor, and resolute against the encroachments of his subalterns. The style of his writings is easy and elegant.

Self-love or interest, says Helvetius, is the lever of all our mental activities. Even that activity which is purely intellectual, our instinct towards knowledge, our forming of ideas, rests upon this. Since now all self-love refers essentially only to bodily pleasure, it follows that every mental occurrence within us has its peculiar source only in the striving after this pleasure; but in saying this, we have only affirmed where the principle of all morality is to be sought. It is an absurdity to require a man to do the good simply for its own sake. This is just as impracticable as that he should do the evil simply for the sake of the evil. Hence if morality would not be wholly fruitless, it must return to its empirical basis, and venture to adopt the true principle of all acting, viz., sensuous pleasure and pain, or, in other words, selfishness as an actual moral principle. Hence, as a correct legislation is that which secures obedience to its laws through reward and punishment, i. e. through selfishness, so will a correct system of morals be that which derives the duties of men from self-love, which shows that that which is forbidden is something which is followed by disagreeable consequences. A system of ethics which does not involve the self-interest of men, or which wars against this, necessarily remains fruitless.

SECTION XXXII.

THE FRENCH CLEARING UP (*Aufklaerung*) AND MATERIALISM.

1. It has already been remarked (§ XXX.) that the carrying out of empiricism to its extremes, as was attempted in France, was most intimately connected with the general condition of the French people and state, in the period before the revolution. The contradictory element in the character of the Middle Ages, the external and dualistic relation to the spiritual world, had developed itself in Catholic France till it had corrupted and destroyed every condition. Morality, mainly through the influence of a licentious court, had become wholly corrupted; the state had sunk to an unbridled despotism, and the church to a hierarchy as hypocritical as it was powerful. Thus, as every intellectual edifice was threatened with ruin, nature, as matter without intellect, as the object of sensation and desire, alone remained. Yet it is not the materialistic extreme which constitutes the peculiar character and tendency of the period now before us. The common character of the philosophers of the eighteenth century is rather, and most prominently, the opposition against every ruling restraint, and perversion in morals, religion, and the state. Their criticism and polemics, which were much more ingenious and eloquent than strictly scientific, were directed against the whole realm of traditional and given and positive notions. They sought to show the contradiction between the existing elements in the state and the church, and the incontrovertible demands of the reason. They sought to overthrow in the faith of the world every fixed opinion which had not been established in the eye of reason, and to give the thinking man the full consciousness of his pure freedom. In order that we may correctly estimate the merit of these men, we must bring before us the French world of that age against which their attacks were directed; the dissoluteness of a pitiful court,

the slavish obedience exacted by a corrupt priesthood, a church
sunken into decay yet seeking worldly honor, a state constitution,
a condition of rights and of society, which must be profoundly
revolting to every thinking man and every moral feeling. It is
the immortal merit of these men that they gave over to scorn and
hatred the abjectness and hypocrisy which then reigned; that
they brought the minds of men to look with indifference upon the
idols of the world, and awakened within them a consciousness of
their own autonomy.

2. The most famous and influential actor in this period of the
French clearing up, is *Voltaire* (1694-1778). Though a writer
of great versatility, rather than a philosopher, there was yet no
philosopher of that time who exerted so powerful an influence
upon the whole thinking of his country and his age. Voltaire
was no atheist. On the contrary, he regarded the belief in a
Supreme Being to be so necessary, that he once said that if there
were no God we should be under the necessity of inventing one.
He was just as little disposed to deny the immortality of the soul,
though he often expressed his doubts upon it. He regarded the
atheistic materialism of a La Mettrie as nothing but nonsense. In
these respects, therefore, he is far removed from the standpoint of
the philosophers who followed him. His whole hatred was expended against Christianity as a positive religion. To destroy this
system he considered as his peculiar mission, and he left no means
untried to attain this anxiously longed-for end. His unwearied
warfare against every positive religion prepared the way and gave
weapons for the attacks against spiritualism which followed.

3. The Encyclopedists had a more decidedly sceptical relation
to the principles and the basis of spiritualism. The philosophical
Encyclopedia established by *Diderot* (1713-1784), and published by
him in connection with d'Alembert, is a memorable monument of
the ruling spirit in France in the time before the revolution. It
was the pride of France at that age, because it expressed in a
splendid and universally accessible form the inner consciousness
of the French people. With the keenest wit it reasoned away
law from the state, and freedom from morality, and spirit and

God from nature, though all this was done only in scattered, and, for the most part, timorous intimations. In Diderot's independent writings we find talent of much philosophic importance united with great earnestness. But it is very difficult to fix and accurately to limit his philosophic views, since they were very gradually formed, and Diderot expressed them always with some reserve and accommodation. In general, however, it may be remarked, that in the progress of his speculations he constantly approached nearer the extreme of the philosophical direction of his age. In his earlier writings a Deist, he afterwards avowed the opinion that every thing is God. At first defending the immateriality and immortality of the soul, he expressed himself at a later period decidedly against these doctrines, affirming that the species alone has an abiding being while the individual passes away, and that immortality is nothing other than to live in the thoughts of coming generations. But Diderot did not venture to the real extreme of logical materialism; his moral earnestness restrained him from this.

4. The last word of materialism was spoken with reckless audacity by *La Mettrie* (1709—1751), a cotemporary of Diderot: every thing spiritual is a delusion, and physical enjoyment is the highest end of men. Faith in the existence of a God, says La Mettrie, is just as groundless as it is fruitless. The world will not be happy till atheism becomes universally established. Then alone will there be no more religious strife, then alone will theologians, the most odious of combatants, disappear, and nature, poisoned at present by their influence, will come again to its rights. In reference to the human soul, there can be no philosophy but materialism. All the observation and experience of the greatest philosophers and physicians declare this. Soul is nothing but a mere name, which has a rational signification only when we understand by it that part of our body which thinks. This is the brain, which has its muscles of thought, just as the limbs have their muscles of motion. That which gives man his advantage over the brutes is, first, the organization of his brain, and second, its capacity for receiving instruction. Otherwise, is man

a brute like the beasts around him, though in many respects surpassed by these. Immortality is an absurdity. The soul per-
ishes with the body of which it forms a part. With death every
thing is over, *la farce est jouée!* The practical and selfish application of all this is—let us enjoy ourselves as long as we exist,
and not throw away any satisfaction we can attain.

5. The *Systéme de la Nature* afterwards attempted to
elaborate with greater earnestness and scientific precision, that
which had been uttered so superficially and so superciliously by
La Mettrie, viz., the doctrine that matter alone exists, while
mind is nothing other than matter refined.

The *Systéme de la Nature* appeared in London under a ficti-
tious name in 1770. It was then published as a posthumous
work of Mirabaud, late secretary of the Academy. It doubtless
had its origin in the circle which was wont to assemble with
Baron Holbach, and of which Diderot, Grimm, and others formed
a part. Whether the Baron Holbach himself, or his tutor La-
grange is the author of this work, or whether it is the joint production of a number, cannot now be determined. The *Systéme de la Nature* is hardly a French book : the style is too
heavy and tedious.

There is, in fact, nothing but matter and motion, says this
work. Both are inseparably connected. If matter is at rest, it
is only because hindered in motion, for in its essence it is not a
dead mass. Motion is twofold, attraction and repulsion. The
different motions which we see are the product of these two, and
through these different motions arise the different connections
and the whole manifoldness of things. The laws which direct in
all this are eternal and unchangeable.—The most weighty consequences of such a doctrine are :

(1.) *The materiality of man.* Man is no twofold being compounded of mind and matter, as is erroneously believed. If the
inquiry is closely made what the mind is, we are answered, that
the most accurate philosophical investigations have shown, that
the principle of activity in man is a substance whose peculiar nature cannot be known, but of which we can affirm that it is in

divisible, unextended, invisible, &c. But now, who should conceive any thing determinate in a substance which is only the negation of that which gives knowledge, an idea which is peculiarly only the absence of all ideas? Still farther, how can it be explained upon such a hypothesis, that a substance which itself is not material can work upon material things; and how can it set these in motion, since there is no point of contact between the two? In fact, those who distinguish their soul from their body, have only to make a distinction between their brain and their body. Thought is only a modification of our brain, just as volition is another modification of the same bodily organ.

(2.) Another chimera, the belief in the being of a God, is connected with the twofold division of man into body and soul. This belief arises like the hypothesis of a soul-substance, because mind is falsely divided from matter, and nature is thus made twofold. The evil which men experienced, and whose natural cause they could not discover, they assigned to a deity which they imagined for the purpose. The first notions of a God have their source therefore in sorrow, fear, and uncertainty. We tremble because our forefathers for thousands of years have done the same. This circumstance awakens no auspicious prepossession. But not only the rude, but also the theological idea of God is worthless, for it explains no phenomenon of nature. It is, moreover, full of absurdities, for, since it ascribes moral attributes to God, it renders him human; while on the other hand, by a mass of negative attributes, it seeks to distinguish him absolutely from every other being. The true system, the system of nature, is hence atheistic. But such a doctrine requires a culture and a courage which neither all men nor most men possess. If we understand by the word atheist one who considers only *dead* matter, or who designates the *moving power* in nature with the name God, then is there no atheist, or whoever would be one is a fool. But if the word means one who denies the existence of a spiritual being, a being whose attributes can only be a source of annoyance to men, then are there indeed atheists, and there would be more of them, if a correct knowledge of nature and a sound reason

were more widely diffused. But if atheism is true, then should
it be diffused. There are, indeed, many who have cast off the
yoke of religion, who nevertheless think it is necessary for the
common people in order to keep them within proper limits. But
this is just as if we should determine to give a man poison lest
he should abuse his strength. Every kind of Deism leads necessarily to superstition, since it is not possible to continue on the
stand-point of pure deism.

(3.) With such premises the freedom and immortality of the
soul both disappear. Man, like every other substance in nature,
is a link in the chain of necessary connection, a blind instrument
in the hands of necessity. If any thing should be endowed with
self-motion, that is, with a capacity to produce motion without any
other cause, then would it have the power to destroy motion in
the universe; but this is contrary to the conception of the universe, which is only an endless series of necessary motions spread-
ing out into wider circles continually. The claim of an individual
immortality is absurd. For to affirm that the soul exists after
the destruction of the body, is to affirm that a modification of a
substance can exist after the substance itself has disappeared.
There is no other immortality than to live in the remembrance of
posterity.

(4.) The practical consequences of these principles are in the
highest degree favorable for the system of nature, the utility of
any doctrine being ever the first criterion of its truth. While the
ideas of theologians are productive only of disquiet and anxiety
to man, the system of nature frees him from all such unrest,
teaches him to enjoy the present moment, and to quietly yield to
his destiny, while it gives him that kind of apathy which every
one must regard as a blessing. If morality would be active, it
can rest only upon self-love and self-interest; it must show man
whither his well-considered interest would lead him. He is a
good man who gains his own interest in such a way that others
will find it for their interest to assist him. The system of self-
interest, therefore, demands the union of men among each other,
and hence we have true morality.

The logical dogmatic materialism of the *Système de la Nature* is the farthest limit of an empirical direction in philosophy, and consequently closes that course of the development of a one-sided realism which had begun with Locke. The attempt first made by Locke to explain and derive the ideal world from the material, ended in materialism with the total reduction of every thing spiritual to the material, with the total denial of the spiritual. We must now, before proceeding farther, according to the classification made § XXVII., consider the idealistic course of development which ran parallel with the systems of a partial realism. At the head of this course stands *Leibnitz*.

———••———

SECTION XXXIII.

LEIBNITZ.

As empiricism sprang from the striving to subject the intellectual to the material, to materialize the spiritual, so on the other hand, idealism had its source in the effort to spiritualize the material, or so to apprehend the conception of mind that matter could be subsumed under it. To the empiric-sensualistic direction, mind was nothing but refined matter, while to the idealistic direction matter was only degenerated (*vergröbert*) mind ("a confused notion," as Leibnitz expresses it). The former, in its logical development, was driven to the principle that only material things exist, the latter (as with Leibnitz and Berkeley) comes to the opposite principle, that there are only souls and their ideas. For the partial realistic stand-point, material things were the truly substantial. But for the idealistic stand-point, the substantial belongs alone to the intellectual world, to the Egos. Mind, to the partial realism, was essentially void, a *tabula rasa*, its whole content came to it from the external world. But a partial idealism sought to carry out the principle that nothing can come into the mind which had not at least been preformed within it, that all its knowledge is furnished it by itself. According to the former view knowledge was a passive relation, according to the latter was it wholly active. While, in fine, a partial realism had attempted to explain the becoming in nature for the most part through real, *i. e.* through mechanical motives (*l'homme machine* is the title of one of la Mettrie's writings), idealism had sought an explanation of the same through ideal motives, *i. e.* teleologically. While the former had made its prominent inquiry for moving causes, and had, indeed, often ridiculed the search for a final cause; it is final causes toward which the latter directs its chief aim. The mediation between mind and matter, between thought and being, will now be sought in the final cause, in the teleological harmony of all things (*pre-established harmony*). The stand-point of Leibnitz may thus be characterized in a word.

Gottfried Wilhelm Leibnitz was born in 1646, at Leipsic, where his father was professor. Having chosen the law as his profession, he entered the university in 1661, and in 1663 he defended for his degree of doctor in philosophy, his dissertation *de principio individui*, a theme well characteristic of the direction of his later philosophizing. He afterwards went to Jena, and subsequently to Altdorf, where he became doctor of laws. At Altdorf he was offered a professorship of jurisprudence, which he refused. The rest of his life was unsettled and desultory, spent for the most part in courts, where, as a versatile courtier, he was employed in the most varied duties of diplomacy. In the year 1672 he went to Paris, in order to induce Louis XIV. to undertake the conquest of Egypt. He subsequently visited London, whence he was afterwards called to Hanover, as councillor of the Duke of Brunswick. He received later a post as librarian at Wolfenbüttel, between which place and Hanover he spent the most of his subsequent life, though interrupted with numerous journeys to Vienna, Berlin, etc. He was intimately associated with the Prussian Electress, Maria Charlotte, a highly talented woman, who surrounded herself with a circle of the most distinguished scholars of the time, and for whom Leibnitz wrote, at her own request, his *Theodicée*. In 1701, after Prussia had be-

come a kingdom, an academy was established at Berlin, through
his efforts, and he became its first president. Similar, but fruitless attempts were made by him to establish academies in Dres-
den and Vienna. In 1711 the title of imperial court councillor,
and a baronage, was bestowed upon him by the emperor Charles VI.
Soon after, he betook himself to Vienna, where he remained a
considerable period, and wrote his Monadology, at the solicitation
of Prince Eugene. He died in 1716. Next to Aristotle, Leibnitz was the most highly gifted scholar that had ever lived; with
the richest and most extensive learning, he united the highest and
most penetrating powers of mind. Germany has reason to be
proud of him, since, after Jacob Boehme, he is the first philosopher of any note among the Germans. With him philosophy
found a home in Germany. It is to be regretted that the great
variety of his efforts and literary undertakings, together with his
roving manner of life, prevented him from giving any connected
exhibition of his philosophy. His views are for the most part
developed only in brief and occasional writings and letters, composed frequently in the French language. It is hence not easy
to state his philosophy in its internal connection, though none of
his views are isolated, but all stand strictly connected with each
other. The following are the chief points :

1. THE DOCTRINE OF MONADS.—The fundamental peculiarity
of Leibnitz's theory is its opposition to Spinozism. Substance,
as the indeterminate universal, was with Spinoza the only positive.
With Leibnitz also the conception of substance lay at the basis of
his philosophy, but his definition of it was entirely different.
While Spinoza had sought to exclude from his substance every
positive determination, and especially all acting, and had apprehended it simply as pure being, Leibnitz viewed it as living
activity and active energy, an example for which might be found
in a stretched bow, which moved and straightened itself through
its own energy as soon as the external hindrance was removed.
That this active energy forms the essence of substance is a principle to which Leibnitz ever returns, and from which, in fact, all
the other chief points in his philosophy may be derived. From

this there follow at the outset two determinations of substance directly opposed to Spinozism; first, that it is a single being, a monad; and second, that there are a multiplicity of monads. The first follows because substance, in so far as it exercises an activity similar to an elastic body, is essentially an excluding activity, or repulsion; the conception of an individual or a monad being that which excludes another from itself. The second follows because the existence of one monad involves the existence of many. The conception of one individual postulates other individuals, which stand over against the one as excluded from it. Hence the fundamental thesis of the Leibnitz philosophy in opposition to Spinozism is this, viz., there is a multiplicity of individual substances or monads.

2. THE MONADS MORE ACCURATELY DETERMINED.—The monads of Leibnitz are similar to atoms in their general features. Like these they are corpuscular units, independent of any external influence, and indestructible by any external power. But notwithstanding this similarity, there is an important and characteristic difference between the two. First, the atoms are not distinguished from each other, they are all qualitatively alike; but each one of the monads is different in quality from every other, every one is a peculiar world for itself, every one is different from every other. According to Leibnitz, there are no two things in the world which are exactly alike. Secondly, atoms can be considered as extended and divisible, but the monads are metaphysical points, and actually indivisible. Here, lest we should stumble at this proposition (for an aggregate of unextended monads can never give an extended world), we must take into consideration Leibnitz's view of space, which, according to him, is not something real, but only confused, subjective representation. Thirdly, the monad is a representative being. With the atomists such a determination would amount to nothing, but with Leibnitz it has a very important part to play. According to him, in every monad, every other is reflected; every monad is a living mirror of the universe, and ideally contains the whole within itself as in a germ. In thus mirroring the world, however, the monad is not passive but spon-

tancously self-active : it does not receive the images which it mirrors, but produces them spontaneously itself, as the soul does a dream. In every monad, therefore, the all-seeing and all-knowing one might read every thing, even the future, since this is potentially contained in the present. Every monad is a kind of God. (*Parvus in suo genere Deus.*)

3. THE PRE-ESTABLISHED HARMONY.—The universe is thus the sum of all the monads. Every thing, every composite, is an aggregate of monads. Thus every bodily organism is not one substance, but many, it is a multiplicity of monads, like a machine which is made up of a number of distinct pieces of mechanism. Leibnitz compared bodies to a fish-pond, which might be full of living elements, though dead itself. The ordinary view of things is thus wholly set aside; the truly substantial does not belong to bodies, *i. e.* to the aggregates, but to their original elements. Matter in the vulgar sense, as something conceived to be without mind, does not at all exist. How now must the inner connection of the universe be conceived? In the following way. Every monad is a representative being, and at the same time, each one is different from every other. This difference, therefore, depends alone upon the difference of representation : there are just as many different degrees of representation as there are monads, and these degrees may be fixed according to some of their prominent stages. The representations may be classified according to the distinction between confused and distinct knowledge. Hence a monad of the lowest rank (a monad *toute nue*) will be one which *simply* represents, *i. e.* which stands on the stage of most confused knowledge. Leibnitz compares this state with a swoon, or with our condition in a dreamy sleep, in which we are not without representations, (notions)—for otherwise we could have none when awaking—but in which the representations are so numerous that they neutralize each other and do not come into the consciousness. This is the stage of inorganic nature. In a higher rank are those monads in which the representation is active as a formative vital force, though still without consciousness. This is the stage of the vegetable world. Still higher ascends the life of the monad when

it attains to sensation and memory, as is the case in the animal kingdom. The lower monads may be said to sleep, and the brute monads to dream. When still farther the soul rises to reason or reflection, we call it mind, spirit.—The distinction of the monads from each other is, therefore, this, that each one, though mirroring the whole and the same universe in itself, does it from a different point of view, and, therefore, differently, the one more, and the rest less perfectly. Each one is a different centre of the world which it mirrors. Each one contains the whole universe, the whole infinity within itself, and in this respect is like God, the only difference being that God knows every thing with perfect distinctness, while the monad represents it confusedly, though one monad may represent it more confusedly than another. The limitation of a monad does not, therefore, consist in its containing less than another or than God, but only in its containing more imperfectly or in its representing less distinctly.—Upon this standpoint the universe, in so far as every monad mirrors one and the same universe, though each in a different way, represents a drama of the greatest possible difference, as well as of the greatest possible unity and order, i. e. of the greatest possible perfection, or the *absolute harmony*. For distinction in unity is harmony.— But in still another respect the universe is a system of harmony. Since the monads do not work upon each other, but each one follows only the law of its own being, there is danger lest the inner harmony of the universe may be disturbed. How is this danger removed ? Thus, viz., every monad mirrors the whole and the same universe. The changes of the collected monads, therefore, run parallel with each other, and in this consists the harmony of all as pre-established by God.

4. THE RELATION OF THE DEITY TO THE MONADS.—What part does the conception of God play in the system of Leibnitz ? An almost idle one. Following the strict consequences of his system, Leibnitz should have held to no proper theism, but the harmony of the universe should have taken the place of the Deity. Ordinarily he considers God as the sufficient cause of all monads. But he was also accustomed to consider the final cause of a thing

as its sufficient cause. In this respect, therefore, he almost identifies God and the absolute final cause. Elsewhere he considers
the Deity as a simple primitive substance, or as the individual
primitive unity. Again, he speaks of God as a pure immaterial
actuality, *actus purus*, while to the monads belongs matter, *i. e.*
restrained actuality, striving, *appetitio*. Once he calls him a
monad, though this is in manifest contradiction with the determinations otherwise assigned him. It was for Leibnitz a very
difficult problem to bring his monadology and his theism into harmony with each other, without giving up the premises of both.
If he held fast to the substantiality of the monads, he was in danger of making them independent of the Deity, and if he did not,
he could hardly escape falling back into Spinozism.

5. THE RELATION OF SOUL AND BODY is clearly explained on
the standpoint of the pre-established harmony. This relation, taking the premises of the monadology, might seem enigmatical. If
no monad can work upon any other, how can the soul work upon
the body to lead and move it? The enigma is solved by the pre-
established harmony. While the body and soul, each one independently of the other, follows the laws of its being, the body
working mechanically, and the soul pursuing ends, yet God has
established such a concordant harmony of the two activities, such
a parallelism of the two functions, that there is in fact a perfect
unity for body and soul. There are, says Leibnitz, three views
respecting the relation of body and soul. The first and most
common supposes a reciprocal influence between the two, but such
a view is untenable, because there can be no interchange between
mind and matter. The second and occasional one (*cf.* § XXV. 1),
brings about this interchange through the constant assistance of
God, which is nothing more nor less than to make God a *Deus ex
machina*. Hence the only solution for the problem is the hypothesis of a pre-established harmony. Leibnitz illustrates these three
views in the following example. Let one conceive of two watches,
whose hands ever accurately point to the same time. This
agreement may be explained, first (the common view), by sup-
posing an actual connection between the hands of each, so that

10

the hand of the one watch might draw the hand of the other after it, or second (the occasional view), by conceiving of a watch-maker who continually keeps the hands alike, or in fine (the pre-established harmony), by ascribing to each a mechanism so ex-quisitely wrought that each one goes in perfect independence of the other, and at the same time in entire agreement with it.—That the soul is immortal (indestructible), follows at once from the doctrine of monads. There is no proper death. That which is called death is only the soul losing a part of the monads which compose the mechanism of its body, while the living element goes back to a condition similar to that in which it was before it came upon the theatre of the world.

6. The monadology has very important consequences in refer-ence to THE THEORY OF KNOWLEDGE. As the philosophy of Leibnitz, by its opposition to Spinozism, had to do with the doctrine of be-ing, so by its opposition to the empiricism of Locke must it expound the theory of knowledge. Locke's Essay on the Human Under-standing had attracted Leibnitz without satisfying him, and he therefore attempted a new investigation in his *Nouveaux Essais*, in which he defended the doctrine of innate ideas. But this hypothesis of innate ideas Leibnitz now freed from that defective view which had justified the objections of Locke. The innateness of the ideas must not be held as though they were explicitly and consciously contained in the mind, but rather the mind possesses them potentially and only virtually, though with the capacity to produce them out of itself. All thoughts are properly innate, *i. e.* they do not come into the mind from without, but are rather pro-duced by it from itself. Any external influence upon the mind is inconceivable, it even needs nothing external for its sensations. While Locke had compared the mind to an unwritten piece of paper, Leibnitz likened it to a block of marble, in which the veins prefigure the form of the statue. Hence the common antithesis between rational and empirical knowledge disappears with Leib-nitz in the degrees of greater or less distinctness.—Among these theoretically innate ideas, Leibnitz recognizes two of special prominence, which take the first rank as principles of all knowl-

edge and all ratiocination,—the principle of contradiction (*principium contradictionis*), and the principle of sufficient cause (*principium rationis sufficientis*). To these, as a principle of the second rank, must be added the *principium indiscernibilium*, or the principle that there are in nature no two things wholly alike.

7. The most elaborate exhibition of Leibnitz's theological views is given in his *Théodicée*. The Théodicée, is, however, his weakest work, and has but a loose connection with the rest of his philosophy. Written at the instigation of a woman, it belies this origin neither in its form nor in its content—not in its form, for in its effort to be popular it becomes diffuse and unscientific, and not in its content, for it accommodates itself to the positive dogmas and the premises of theology farther than the scientific basis of the system of Leibnitz would permit. In this work, Leibnitz investigates the relation of God to the world in order to show a conformity in this relation to a final cause, and to free God from the charge of acting without or contrary to an aim. Why is the world as it is ? God might have created it very differently. True, answers Leibnitz, God saw an infinite number of worlds as possible before him, but out of all these he chose the one which actually is as the best. This is the famous doctrine of the best world, according to which no more perfect world is possible than the one which is.—But how so ? Is not the existence of evil at variance with this ? Leibnitz answers this objection by distinguishing three kinds of evil, the metaphysical, the physical, and the moral. The metaphysical evil, *i. e.* the finiteness and incompleteness of things, is necessary because inseparable from finite existence, and is thus independent of the will of God. Physical evil (pain, &c.), though not independent of the will of God, is often a good conditionally, *i. e.* as a punishment or means of improvement. Moral evil or wickedness can in no way be charged to the will of God. Leibnitz took various ways to account for its existence, and obviate the contradiction lying between it and the conception of God. At one time he says that wickedness is only permitted by God as a *conditio sine qua non*, because without wickedness there were no

freedom, and without freedom no virtue. Again, he reduces the moral evil to the metaphysical, and makes wickedness nothing but a want of perfection, a negation, a limitation, playing the same part as do the shadows in a painted picture, or the discords in a piece of music, which do not diminish the beauty, but only increase it through contrast. Again, he distinguishes between the material and the formal element in a wicked act. The material of sin, the power to act, is from God, but the formal element, the wickedness of the act, belongs wholly to man, and is the result of his limitation, or, as Leibnitz here and there expresses it, of his eternal self-predestination. In no case can the harmony of the universe be destroyed through such a cause.

These are the chief points of Leibnitz's philosophy. The general characteristic of it as given in the beginning of the present section, will be found to have its sanction in the specific exhibition that has now been furnished.

SECTION XXXIV.

BERKELEY.

Leibnitz had not carried out the standpoint of idealism to its extreme. He had indeed, on the one side, explained space and motion and bodily things as phenomena which had their existence only in a confused representation, but on the other side, he had not wholly denied the existence of the bodily world, but had recognized as a reality lying at its basis, the world of monads. The phenomenal or bodily world had its fixed and substantial foundation in the monads. Thus Leibnitz, though an idealist, did not wholly break with realism. The ultimate consequence of a subjective idealism would have been to wholly deny the reality of the objective, sensible world, and explain corporeal objects as *simply* phenomena, as nothing but subjective notions without any objective reality as a basis. This consequence the idealistic counterpart to the ultimate realistic result of materialism—appears in *George Berkeley*, who was born in Ireland, 1684, made bishop of the Anglican Church in 1734, and died in 1753. Hence, though he followed the empiricism of Locke, and sustained no outward connection with Leibnitz, we must place him in immediate succession to the latter as the perfecter of a subjective idealism.

Our sensations, says Berkeley, are entirely subjective. We are wholly in error if we believe that we have a sensation of external objects or perceive them   That which we have and perceive is only our sensations.   It is *e. g.* clear, that by the sense of sight we can *see* neither the distance, the size, nor the form of objects, but that we only *conclude* that these exist, because our experience has taught us that a certain sensation of sight is always attended by certain sensations of touch.   That which we see is only colors, clearness, obscurity, &c., and it is therefore false to say that we see and feel the same thing.   So also we never go out of ourselves for those sensations to which we ascribe most decidedly an objective character.   The peculiar objects of our understanding are only our own affections; all ideas are hence only our own sensations.   But just as there can be no sensations outside of the sensitive subject, so no idea can have existence outside of him who possesses it.   The so-called objects exist only in our notion, and have a being only as they are perceived.   It is the great error of most philosophers that they ascribe to corporeal objects a being outside the conceiving mind, and do not see that they are only mental.   It is not possible that material things should produce any thing so wholly distinct from themselves as sensations and notions.   There is no such thing as a material external world ; *mind alone exists* as thinking being, whose nature consists in thinking and willing.   But whence then arise all our sensations which come to us like the images of fancy, without our agency, and which are thus no products of our will ?   They arise from a spirit superior to ourselves—for only a spirit can produce within us notions—even from God.   God gives us ideas ; but as it would be contradictory to assert that a being could give what it does not possess, so ideas exist *in God*, and we derive them from him. These ideas in God may be called archetypes, and those in us ectypes.—In consequence of this view, says Berkeley, we do not deny an independent reality of things, we only deny that they can exist elsewhere than in an understanding. Instead therefore of speaking of a nature in which, *e. g.* the sun is the cause of warmth, &c., the accurate expression would be this: God announces to us through the sense of sight that we should soon perceive a sensation of warmth. Hence by nature we are only to understand the succession or the connection of ideas, and by natural laws the constant order in which they proceed, *i. e.* the laws of the association of ideas. This thorough-going subjective idealism, this complete denial of matter, Berkeley considered as the surest way to oppose materialism and atheism.

SECTION XXXV.

WOLFF.

The idealism of Berkeley, as was to be expected from the nature of the case, remained without any farther development, but the philosophy of Leibnitz was taken up and subjected to a farther revision by *Christian Wolff.* He was born in Breslau in 1679. He was chosen professor at Halle, where he became obnoxious to the charge of teaching a doctrine at variance with the Scriptures, and drew upon himself such a violent opposition from the theologians of the university, that a cabinet order was issued for his dismissal on the 8th of November, 1723, and he was enjoined to leave Prussia within forty-eight hours on pain of being hung. He then became professor in Marburg, but was afterwards recalled to Prussia by Frederic II. immediately upon his accession to the throne. He was subsequently made baron, and died 1754. In his chief thoughts he followed Leibnitz, a connection which he himself admitted, though he protested against the identification of his philosophy with that of Leibnitz, and objected to the name, *Philosophia Leibnitio-Wolffiana*, which was taken by his disciple Bilfinger. The historical merit of Wolff is threefold. First, and most important, he laid claim again to the whole domain of knowledge in the name of philosophy, and sought again to build up a systematic framework, and make an encyclopedia of philosophy in the highest sense of the word. Though he did not himself furnish much new material for this purpose, yet he carefully elaborated and arranged that which he found at hand. Secondly, he made again the philosophical method as such, an object of attention. His own method is, indeed, an external one as to its content, namely, the mathematical or the mathematico-syllogistical, recommended by Leibnitz, and by the application of this his whole philosophizing sinks to a level formalism. (For instance, in his principles of architecture, the eighth proposition is—" a window must be wide enough for two persons to recline together conveniently,"—a proposition which is thus proved : " we are more frequently accustomed to recline and look out at a window in company with another person than alone, and hence, since the builder of the house should satisfy the owner in every respect (§ 1), he must make a window wide enough for two persons conveniently to recline within it at the same time ". Still this formalism is not without its advantage, for it subjects the philosophical content to a logical treatment. Thirdly, Wolff has taught philosophy to speak German, an art which it has not since forgotten. Next to Leibnitz, he is entitled to the merit of having made the German language for ever the organ of philosophy.

The following remarks will suffice for the content and the scientific classification of Wolff's philosophy. He defines philosophy to be the science of the possible as such. But that is possible which contains no contradiction. Wolff defends this definition against the charge of presuming too much. It is not affirmed, he says, with this definition that either he or any other philosopher knows every thing which is possible. The definition only claims for philosophy the whole province of human knowledge, and it is certainly proper that philosophy should be described according to the highest perfection which it can attain, even though it has not yet actually reached it.—In what parts now does this science of the possible consist? Resting on the perception that there are within the soul two faculties, one of knowing and one of willing, Wolff divides philosophy into two great parts, theoretical philosophy (an expression, however, which first appears among his followers), or metaphysics, and practical philosophy. Logic precedes both as a preliminary training for philosophical study. Metaphysics are still farther divided by Wolff into ontology, cosmology, psychology, and natural theology; practical philosophy he divides into ethics, whose object is man as man; economics, whose object is man as a member of the family; and politics, whose object is man as a citizen of the state.

1. ONTOLOGY is the first part of Wolff's metaphysics. Ontology treats of what are now called categories, or those fundamental conceptions which are applied to every object, and must therefore at the outset be investigated. Aristotle had already furnished a table of categories, but he had derived them wholly empirically. It is not much better with the ontology of Wolff; it is laid out like a philosophical dictionary. At its head he places the principle of contradiction, viz.: it is not possible for any thing to be, and at the same time not to be. The conception of the possible at once follows from this principle. That is possible which contains no contradiction. That is necessary, the opposite of which contradicts itself, and that is accidental, the opposite of which is possible. Every thing which is possible is a thing, though only an imaginary one; that which neither is, nor is possible, is nothing. When many things together compose a thing, this is a whole, and the individual things comprehended by it are its parts. The greatness of a thing consists in the multitude of its parts. If A contains that by which we can understand the being of B, then that in A by which B becomes understood is the ground of B, and the whole A which contains the ground of B is its cause. That which contains the ground of its properties is the essence of a thing. Space is the arrangement of things which

exist conjointly. Place is the determinate way in which a thing
exists in conjunction with others. Movement is change of place.
Time is the arrangement of that which exists successively, etc.

2. Cosmology.—Wolff defines the world to be a series of changing objects, which exist conjointly and successively, but which are
so connected together that one ever contains the ground of the
other. Things are connected in space and in time. By virtue of
this universal connection, the world is one united whole; the
essence of the world consists in the manner of its connection.
But this manner cannot be changed. It can neither receive any
new ingredients nor lose any of those it possesses. From the
essence of the world spring all its changes. In this respect the
world is a machine. Events in the world are only hypothetically
necessary in so far as previous events have had a certain character;
they are accidental in so far as the world might have been directed
otherwise. In respect to the question whether the world had a
beginning in time, Wolff does not express himself explicitly.
Since God is independent of time, but the world has been from
eternity in time, the world therefore is in no case eternal in any
sense like God. But according to Wolff, neither space nor time
has any substantial being. Body is a connected thing composed
of matter, and possessing a moving power within itself. The
powers of a body taken together are called its nature, and the
comprehension of all being is called nature in general. That
which has its ground in the essence of the world is called natural,
and that which has not, is supernatural, or a wonder. At the
close of his cosmology, Wolff treats of the perfection and imperfection of the world. The perfection of a world consists in the
harmony with each other of every thing which exists conjointly
and successively. But since every thing has its separate rules,
the individual must give up so much from its perfection as is
necessary for the symmetry of the whole.

3. Rational Psychology.—The soul is that within us which
is self-conscious. In the self-consciousness of the soul are itself and
other objects. Consciousness is either clear or indistinct. Clear
consciousness is thought. The soul is a simple incorporeal sub-

10*

stance. There dwells within it a power to represent to itself a
world. In this sense brutes also may have a soul, but a soul
which possesses understanding and will is mind, and mind belongs
alone to men. The soul of man is a mind joined to a body, and
this is the distinction between men and superior spirits. The
movements of the soul and of the body harmonize with each other
by virtue of the preëstablished harmony. The freedom of the
human soul is the power according to its own arbitrament, to
choose of two possible things that which pleases it best. But the
soul does not decide without motives, it ever chooses that which
it holds to be the best. Thus the soul would seem impelled to its
action by its representations, but the understanding is not constrained to its representations of that which is good and bad, and
hence also the will is not constrained, but free. As a simple
being the soul is indivisible, and hence incorruptible; the souls
of brutes, however, have no understanding, and hence enjoy no
conscious existence after death. This belongs alone to the human
soul, and hence the human soul alone is immortal.

4. NATURAL THEOLOGY.—Wolff uses here the cosmological
argument to demonstrate the existence of a God. God might
have made different worlds, but has preferred the present one as
the best. This world has been called into being by the will of
God. His aim in its creation was the manifestation of his own
perfection. Evil in the world does not spring from the Divine
will, but from the limited being of human things. God permits
it only as a means of good.

This brief aphoristic exposition of Wolff's metaphysics, shows
how greatly it is related to the doctrine of Leibnitz. The latter,
however, loses much of its speculative profoundness by the abstract
and logical treatment it receives in the hands of Wolff. For the
most part, the specific elements of the monadology remain in the
background; with Wolff, his simple beings are not representative
like the Monads, but more like the Atoms. Hence there is with
him much that is illogical and contradictory. His peculiar merit in
metaphysics is ontology, which he has elaborated far more strictly
than his predecessors. A multitude of philosophical terminations

owe to him their origin, and their introduction into philosophical language.

The philosophy of Wolff, comprehensible and distinct as it was, and by its composition in the German language more accessible than that of Leibnitz, soon became the popular philosophy, and gained an extensive influence. Among the names which deserve credit for their scientific treatment of it, we may mention *Thümming*, 1697–1728; *Bilfinger*, 1693–1750; *Baumeister*, 1708–1785; *Baumgarten* the esthetic, 1714–1762; and his scholar *Meier*, 1718–1777.

SECTION XXXVI.

THE GERMAN CLEARING UP.

Under the influence of the philosophy of Leibnitz and Wolff, though without any immediate connection with it, there arose in Germany during the latter half of the eighteenth century, an eclectic popular philosophy, whose different phases may be embraced under the name of the German clearing up. It has but little significance for the history of philosophy, though not without importance in other respects. Its great aim was to secure a higher culture, and hence a cultivated and polished style of reasoning is the form in which it philosophized. It is the *German* counterpart of the *French* clearing up. As the latter closed the realistic period of development by drawing the ultimate consequence of materialism, so the former closed the idealistic series by its tendency to an extreme subjectivism. To the men of this direction, the empirical, individual Ego becomes the absolute; they forget every thing else for it, or rather every thing else has a value in their eyes only in proportion as it refers and ministers to the subject by contributing to its demands and satisfying its inner cravings. Hence the question of immortality becomes now the great problem of philosophy (in which respect we may mention *Mendelssohn*, 1727–1786, the most important man in this direction); the eternal duration of the individual soul is the chief point of interest; objective ideas or truths of faith, *e. g.* the personality of God, though not denied, cease to have an interest; it is held as a standing article of belief that we can know nothing of God. In another current of this direction, it is moral philosophy and esthetics (*Garvey*, 1742–1798; *Engel*, 1741–1802; *Abbt*, 1738–1766; *Sulzer*, 1720–1779) which find a scientific treatment, because both these preserve a subjective interest. In general, every thing is viewed in its useful relations; the useful becomes the peculiar criterion of truth; that which is not useful to the subject, or which does not minister to his subjective ends, is set aside. In connection with this turn of mind stands the prevailing teleological direction which the investigations of nature assumed (*Reimarus*, 1694–1765), and the utilitarian character given to ethics. The happiness of the individual was considered as the highest principle and the supreme end (*Basedow*, 1723–1790). Even religion is contemplated from this point of view. Reimarus wrote a treatise upon the "*advantages*" of religion, in which he attempted to prove that religion was not subversive of earthly pleasure, but rather increased it; and *Steinbart* (1738–1809) elaborated, in a number of treatises, the theme that all wisdom consists alone in attaining happiness, *i. e.* enduring satisfaction, and that the Christian religion, instead of forbidding this, was rather itself the true doctrine of happiness. In other particulars Christianity received only a temperate respect; wherever it laid claim to any authority disagreeable to the subject (as in individual doctrines like that of future punishment), it was opposed, and in general the effort was made to counteract, as far as possible, the positive dogma by natural religion. Reimarus, for example, the most zealous defender of theism and of the teleological investigation of nature, is at the same time the author of the Wolfenbüttel fragments. By criticizing the Gospel history, and every thing positive and transmitted, and by rationalizing the supernatural in religion, the subject displayed its new-found independence. In fine, the subjective standpoint of this period exhibits itself in the numerous autobiographies and self-confessions then so prevalent; the isolated self is the object of admiring contemplation (*Rousseau*, 1712–1778, and his confessions); it beholds itself mirrored in its particular conditions, sensations, and views—a sort of flirtation with itself, which often rises to sickly sentimentality. According to all this, it is seen to be the extreme consequence of subjective idealism which constitutes the character of the German clearing up period, which thus closes the series of an idealistic development.

----•••----

SECTION XXXVII.

TRANSITION TO KANT.

The idealistic and the realistic stage of development to which we have now been attending, each ended with a one-sided result. Instead of actually and internally reconciling the opposition between thought and being, they both issued in denying the one or the other of these factors. Realism, on its side, had made matter absolute; and idealism, on its side, had endowed the empirical Ego with the same attribute—extremes in which philosophy was threatened with total destruction. It had, in fact, in Germany as in France, become merged in the most superficial popular philosophy. Then *Kant* arose, and brought again into one channel the two streams which, when separate from each other, threatened to lose themselves amid the sands. Kant is the great renovator of philosophy, who brought back to their point of divergence the one-sided efforts which had preceded him, and embraced them in their unity and totality. He stands in some special and fitting relation either antagonistic or harmonious to all others—to Locke no less than to Hume, to the Scottish philosophers no less than to the English and French moralists, to the philosophy of Leibnitz and of Wolff, as well as to the materialism of the French and the utilitarianism of the German clearing up period. His relation to the development of a partial idealism and a one-sided realism is thus stated : Empiricism had made the Ego purely passive and subordinate to the sensible external world—idealism had made it purely active, and given it a sovereignty over the sensible world ; Kant attempted to strike a balance between these two claims, by affirming that the Ego as practical is free and autonomic, an unconditioned lawgiver for itself, while as theoretical it is receptive and conditioned by the phenomenal world ; but at the same time the theoretical Ego contains the two sides within itself, for if, on the one side, empiricism may be justified upon the ground that the material and only field of all our knowledge is furnished by experience, so on the other side, rationalism may be justified on the ground that there is an apriori factor and basis to our knowledge, for in experience itself we make use of conceptions which are not furnished by experience, but are contained apriori in our understanding.

In order, now, that we may bring the very elaborate framework of the Kantian philosophy into a clearer outline, let us briefly glance at its fundamental conceptions, and notice its chief principles and results. Kant subjected the activity of the human mind in knowing, and the origin of our experience, to his critical investigation. Hence his philosophy is called critical philosophy, or criticism, because it aims to be essentially an examination of our faculty of knowledge ; it is also called transcendental philosophy, since Kant calls the reflection of the reason upon its relation to the objective world, a transcendental reflection (transcendental must not be confounded with transcendent), or, in other words, a transcendental knowledge is one " which does not relate so much to objects of knowledge, as to our way of knowing them, so far as this is apriori possible." The examination of the faculty of knowledge, which Kant attempts in his " *Critick of Pure Reason*," shows the following results. All knowledge is a product of two factors, the knowing subject and the external world. Of these two factors, the latter furnishes our knowledge with experience, as the matter, and the former with the conceptions of the understanding, as the form, through which a connected knowledge, or a synthesis of our perceptions in a whole of experience first becomes possible. If there were no external world, then would there be no phenomena; if there were no understanding, then these phenomena, or perceptions, which are infinitely manifold, would never be brought into the unity of a notion, and thus no experience were possible. Thus, while intuitions without conceptions are blind, and conceptions without intuitions are empty, knowledge is a union of the two, since it requires that the form of conception should be filled with the matter of experience, and that the matter of experience should be apprehended in the net of the understanding's conceptions. Nevertheless, we do not know things as they are in themselves. *First*, because the categories, or the forms of our understanding prevent. By bringing that which is given as the material of knowledge into our own conceptions as the form, there is manifestly a change in respect of the objects, which become thought of not as they are, but only as we apprehend them; they appear to us only as they are transmuted into categories. But besides this subjective addition, there is yet another. *Secondly*, we do not know things as they are in themselves, because even the intuitions which we bring within the form of the understanding's conceptions, are not pure and uncolored, but are already penetrated by a subjective medium, namely, by the universal form of all objects of sense, space and time. Space and time are also subjective additions, forms of sensuous intuition, which are just as originally present in our minds as the fundamental conceptions or categories of our understanding. That which we would represent intuitively to ourselves we must place in space and time, for without these no intuition is possible. From this it follows that it is only phenomena which we know, and not things in themselves separate from space and time.

A superficial apprehension of these Kantian principles might lead one to suppose that Kant's criticism did not essentially go beyond the standpoint of Locke's empiricism. But such a supposition disappears upon a careful scrutiny. Kant was obliged to recognize with Hume that the conceptions, cause and effect, substance and attribute, and the other conceptions which the human understanding sees itself necessitated to think in the phenomena, and in which every one of its thoughts must be found, do not arise from any experience of the sense. For instance, when we become affected through different senses, and perceive a white color, a sweet taste, a rough surface, &c., and predicate all these of one thing, as a piece of sugar, there come from without only the plurality of sensations, while the conception of unity cannot come through sensation, but is a category or conception borne over to the sensations from the mind itself. But instead of denying, for this reason, the reality of these conceptions of the understanding, Kant took a step in advance, assigning a peculiar province to this activity of the understanding, and showing that these forms of thought thus furnished to the matter of experience are immanent laws of the human faculty of knowledge, the peculiar laws of the understanding's operations, which may be obtained by a perfect analysis of our thinking activity. (Of these laws or conceptions there are twelve, viz., unity, plurality, totality; reality, negation, limitation; substantiality, causality, reciprocal action; possibility, actuality, and necessity.)

From what has been said we can see the three chief principles of the Kantian theory of knowledge:

1. WE KNOW ONLY PHENOMENA AND NOT THINGS IN THEMSELVES.—The experience furnished us by the external world becomes so adjusted and altered in its relations (for we apprehend it at first in the subjective framework of space and time, and then in the equally subjective forms of our understanding's conceptions), that it no longer represents the thing itself in its original condition, pure and unmixed.

2. NEVERTHELESS EXPERIENCE IS THE ONLY PROVINCE OF OUR KNOWLEDGE, AND THERE IS NO SCIENCE OF THE UNCONDITIONED.—This follows of course, for since every knowledge is the product of the matter of experience, and the form of the understanding, and depends thus upon the co-working of the sensory and the understanding, then no knowledge is possible of objects for which one of these factors, experience, fails us; a knowledge alone from the un-

derstanding's conceptions of the unconditioned is illusory since the sensory can show no unconditioned object corresponding to the conception. Hence the questions which Kant places at the head of his whole Critick; how are synthetical judgments apriori possible? *i. e.* can we widen our knowledge apriori, by thought alone, beyond the sensuous experience? is a knowledge of the supersensible possible? must be answered with an unconditional negative.

3. Still, if the human knowledge will make an effort to stride beyond the narrow limits of experience, *i. e.* to become transcendent, it involves itself in the greatest contradictions. The three ideas of the reason, the psychological, the cosmological, and the theological, viz. (*a*) the idea of an absolute subject, *i. e.* of the soul, or of immortality, (*b*) the idea of the world as a totality of all conditions and phenomena, (*c*) the idea of a most perfect being—are so wholly without application to the empirical actuality, are so truly regulative, and not constitutive principles, which are only the pure products of the reason, and are so entirely without a correspondent object in experience, that when ever they are applied to experience, *i. e.* become conceived of as actually existing objects, they lead to pure logical errors, to the most obvious paralogisms and sophisms. These errors, which are partly false conclusions and paralogisms, and partly unavoidable contradictions of the reason with itself, Kant undertook to show in reference to all the ideas of the reason. Take, *e. g.* the cosmological idea. Whenever the reason posits any transcendental expressions in reference to the universe, *i. e.* attempts to apply the forms of the finite to the infinite, it is at once evident that the antithesis of these expressions can be proved just as well as the thesis. The affirmation that the world has a beginning in time, and limits in space, can be proved as well as, and no better than its opposite, that the world has no beginning in time, and no spacial limits. Whence it follows that all speculative cosmology is an assumption by the reason. So also with the theological idea; it rests on bare logical paralogisms, and false conclusions, as Kant, with great acuteness, shows in reference to each

of the proofs for the being of a God, which previous dogmatic philosophies had attempted. It is therefore impossible to prove and to conceive of the existence of a God as a Supreme Being, or of the soul as a real subject, or of a comprehending universe. The peculiar problems of metaphysics lie outside the province of philosophical knowledge.

Such is the negative part of the Kantian philosophy; its positive complement is found in the "*Critick of the Practical Reason.*" While the mind as theoretical and cognitive is wholly conditioned, and ruled by the objective and sensible world, and thus knowledge is only possible through intuition, yet as practical does it go wholly beyond the given (the sense impulse), and is determined only through the categorical imperative, and the moral law, which is itself, and is therefore free and autonomic; the ends which it pursues are those which itself, as moral spirit, places before itself; objects are no more its masters and lawgivers, to which it must yield if it would know the truth, but its servants, which it may use for its own ends in actualizing its moral law. While the theoretical mind is united to a world of sense and phenomena, a world obedient to necessary laws, the practical mind, by virtue of the freedom essential to it, by virtue of its direction towards an absolute aim, belongs to a purely intelligible and supersensible world. This is the practical idealism of Kant, from which he derives the three practical postulates of the immortality of the soul, moral freedom, and the being of a God, which, as theoretical truths, had been before denied.

With this brief sketch for our guidance, let us now pass on to a more extended exposition of the Kantian Philosophy.

SECTION XXXVIII.

KANT.

Immanuel Kant was born at Königsberg in Prussia, April 22, 1724. His father an honest saddlemaker, and his mother a prudent and pious woman, exerted a good influence upon him in his earliest youth. In the year 1740 he entered the university, where he connected himself with the theological department, but devoted the most of his time to philosophy, mathematics, and physics. He commenced his literary career in his twenty-third year, in 1747, with a treatise entitled "*Thoughts concerning the true estimate of Living Forces.*" He was obliged by his pecuniary circumstances to spend some years as a private tutor in different families in the neighborhood of Königsberg. In 1755 he took a place in the university as "*privat-docent,*" which position he held for fifteen years, during which time he gave lectures upon logic, metaphysics, physics, mathematics, and also, during the latter part of the time, upon ethics, anthropology, and physical geography. At this period he adhered for the most part to the school of Wolff, though early expressing his doubts in respect of dogmatism. From the publication of his first treatise he applied himself to writing with unwearied activity, though his great work, the "*Critick of pure Reason,*" did not appear till his fifty-seventh year, 1781. His "*Critick of the practical Reason,*" was issued in 1787, and his "*Religion within the bounds of pure Reason,*" in 1793. In 1770, in his forty-sixth year, he was chosen ordinary professor of logic and metaphysics, a chair which he continued to fill uninterruptedly till 1794, when the weakness of age obliged him to leave it. Invitations to professorships at Jena, Erlangen, and Halle, were given him and rejected. As soon as he became known, the noblest and most active minds flocked from all parts of Germany to Königsberg, to sit at the feet of the sage who was master there. One of his worshippers, Reuss, professor of philosophy at Würzburg, who abode but a brief time at Königsberg, entered his chamber, declaring that he had come one hundred and sixty miles[*] in order to see Kant and to speak with him.—During the last seventeen years of his life he occupied a little house with a garden, in a quiet quarter of the city, where his calm and regular mode of life might be undisturbed. His habits of life were very simple. He never left his native province even to go as far as Dantzic. His longest journeys were to visit some country-seats in the environs of Königsberg. Nevertheless, as his lectures upon physical geography testify, he acquired by reading the most accurate knowledge of the earth. He knew all of Rousseau's works, of which *Emile* at its first appearance detained him for a number of days from his customary walks. Kant died February 12, 1804, in the eightieth year of his life. He was of medium stature, finely built, with blue eyes, and always enjoyed sound health till in his latter years, when he became childish. He was never married. His character was marked by an earnest love of truth, great candor, and simple modesty.

Though Kant's great work, the " Critick of pure Reason," which created an epoch in the history of philosophy, did not appear till 1781; yet had he previously shown an approach towards the same standpoint in several smaller treatises, and particularly in his inaugural dissertation which appeared in 1770, " *Concerning the form and the principles of the Sense-World and that of the Understanding.*" Kant himself refers the inner genesis of his critical standpoint to Hume. " I freely confess," he says, " that it was David Hume who first roused me from my dogmatic slumber, and gave a different direction to my investigations in the field of speculative philosophy." The critical view therefore first became developed in Kant as he left the dogmatic metaphysical school, the Wolffian philosophy in which he had grown up, and went over to the study of a sceptical empiricism in Hume. " Hitherto," says Kant at the close of his Critick of pure Reason, " men have been obliged to choose either a dogmati·

---

[*] A German mile is about four and a half English miles.—Tr.

cal direction, like Wolff, or a sceptical one, like Hume. The critical road alone is yet open. If the reader has had pleasure and patience in travelling along this in my company, let him now contribute his aid in making this by-path into a highway, in order that that which many centuries could not effect may now be attained before the expiration of the present, and the reason become perfectly content in respect of that which has hitherto, but in vain, engaged its curiosity." Kant had the clearest consciousness respecting the relation of his criticism to the previous philosophy. He compares the revolution which he himself had brought about in philosophy with that wrought by Copernicus in astronomy. " Hitherto it has been assumed that all our knowledge must regulate itself according to the objects; but all attempts to make any thing out of them apriori, through notions whereby our knowledge might be enlarged, proved, under this supposition, abortive. Let us, then, try for once whether we do not succeed better with the problems of metaphysics, by assuming that the objects must regulate themselves according to our knowledge, a mode of viewing the subject which accords so much better with the desired possibility of a knowledge of them apriori, which must decide something concerning objects before they are given us. The circumstances are in this case precisely the same as with the first thoughts of Copernicus, who, finding that his attempt to explain the motions of the heavenly bodies did not succeed, when he assumed the whole starry host to revolve around the spectator, tried whether he should not succeed better, if he left the spectator himself to turn, and the stars on the contrary at rest." In these words we have the principle of a subjective idealism, most clearly and decidedly expressed.

In the succeeding exposition of the Kantian philosophy we shall most suitably follow the classification adopted by Kant himself. His principle of classification is a psychological one. All the faculties of the soul, he says, may be referred to three, which are incapable of any farther reduction; knowing, feeling, and desire. The first faculty contains the principles, the governing laws for all the three. So far as the faculty of knowledge contains the principles of knowledge itself, is it theoretical reason, and so far as it contains the principles of desire and action, is it practical reason, while, so far as it contains the principles which regulate the feelings of pleasure and pain, is it a faculty of judgment. Thus the Kantian philosophy (on its critical side) divides itself into three criticks, (1) Critick of pure i. e. theoretical reason, (2) Critick of practical reason, (3) Critick of the judgment.

I. CRITICK OF PURE. REASON.—The critick of pure reason, says Kant, is the inventory in which all our possessions through pure reason are systematically arranged. What are these possessions? When we have a cognition, what is it that we bring thereto? To answer these questions, Kant explores the two chief fields of our theoretical consciousness, the two chief factors of all knowledge, the sensory and the understanding. Firstly: what does our sensory or our faculty of intuition possess apriori? Secondly; what is the apriori possession of our understanding? The first of these questions is discussed in the transcendental Æsthetics (a title which we must take not in the sense now commonly attached to the word, but in its etymological signification as the "science of the apriori principles of the sensory"); and the second in the transcendental Logic or Analytics. Sense and understanding are thus the two factors of all knowledge, the two stalks—as Kant expresses it—of our -knowledge, which may spring from a common root, though this is unknown to us: the sensory is the receptivity, and the understanding the spontaneity of our cognitive faculty; by the sensory, which can only furnish intuitions, objects become given to us; by the understanding, which forms conceptions, these objects become thought. Conceptions without intuitions are empty; intuitions without conceptions are blind. Intuitions and conceptions constitute the reciprocally complemental elements of our intellectual activity. What now are the apriori principles respectively of our knowledge, through the sense and through the thought? The first of these questions, as already said, is answered by

1. THE TRANSCENDENTAL ÆSTHETICS.—To anticipate at once

the answer, we may say that the apriori principles of our knowledge through the sense, the original forms of sensuous intuition, are space and time. Space is the form of the external sense, by means of which objects are given to us as existing outside of ourselves separately and conjointly; time is the form of the inner sense, by means of which the circumstances of our own soul-life become objects to our consciousness. If we abstract every thing belonging to the matter of our sensations, space remains as the universal form in which all the materials of the external sense must be arranged. If we abstract every thing which belongs to the matter of our inner sense, time remains as the form which the movement of the mind had filled. Space and time are the highest forms of the outer and inner sense. That these forms lie apriori in the human mind, Kant proves, first, directly from the nature of these conceptions themselves; and, secondly, indirectly by showing that without apriori presupposing these conceptions, it were not possible to have any certain science of undoubted validity. The first of these he calls the *metaphysical*, and the second the *transcendental discussion*.

(1.) In the *metaphysical discussion* it is to be shown, (*a*) that space and time are apriori given, (*b*) that these notions belong to the sensory (æsthetics) and not to the understanding (logic), *i. e.* that they are intuitions and not conceptions. (*a*) That space and time are apriori is clear from the fact that every experience, before it can be, must presuppose already a space and time. I perceive something as external to me; but this external presupposes space. Again, I have two sensations at the same time and successively; this presupposes time. (*b*) Space and time, however, are by no means conceptions, but forms of intuition, or intuitions themselves. For in every universal conception the individual is comprehended under it, and is not a part of it; but in space and time, all individual spaces and times are parts of and contained within the universal space and the universal time.

(2.) In the *transcendental discussion* Kant draws his proof indirectly by showing that certain sciences, universally recognized as such, can only be conceived upon the supposition that space and time are apriori. A pure mathematics is only possible on the ground that space and time are pure and not empirical intuitions. Kant comprises the whole problem of the Transcendental Æsthetics in the question—how are pure mathematical sciences possible? The ground, says Kant, upon which pure mathematics moves, is space and time. But now mathematics utters its principles as universal and necessary. Universal and necessary principles, however, can never come from experience; they must have an apriori ground; consequently it is impossible that space and time, out of which mathematics receives its principles, should be first given aposteriori; they must be given apriori as pure intuitions. Hence we have a knowledge apriori, and a science which rests upon apriori grounds; and the matter simply resolves itself into this, viz. : whosoever should deny that apriori knowledge can be, must also at the same time deny the possibility of mathematics. But if the fundamental truths of mathematics are intuitions apriori, we might conclude that there may be also apriori conceptions, out of which, in connection with these pure intuitions, a metaphysics could be formed. This is the positive result of the Transcendental Æsthetics, though with this positive side the negative is closely connected. Intuition or immediate knowledge can be attained by man only through the sensory, whose universal intuitions are only space and time. But since these intuitions of space and time are no objective relations, but only subjective forms, there is therefore something subjective mingled with all our intuitions, and we can know things not as they are in themselves, but only as they appear to us through this subjective medium of space and time. This is the meaning of the Kantian principle, that we do not know things in themselves, but only phenomena. But if on this account we should affirm that all things are in space and time, this would be too much; they are in space and time only for us,—all phenomena of the external sense appearing both in space and in time, and all phenomena of the inner sense appearing only in time. Notwithstanding this, Kant would in no ways have admitted that the world of sense is mere appearance. He affirmed, that while he contended for a transcendental ideality, there was, nevertheless, an empirical reality of space and time : things external to ourselves exist just as certainly as do we and the circumstances within us, only they are not represented to us as they are in themselves and in their independence of space and of time. As to the question, whether there is any thing in the thing itself back of the phenomena, Kant intimates in the first edition of his Critick, that it is not impossible that the Ego and the thing-in-itself are one and the same thinking substance. This thought, which Kant threw out as a mere conjecture, was the source of all the wider developments of the latest philosophy. It was afterwards the fundamental idea of the Fichtian system, that the Ego does not become affected through a thing essentially foreign to it, but purely through itself. In the second edition of his Critick, however, Kant omitted this sentence.

The Transcendental Æsthetics closes with the discussion of space and time, *i. e.* with finding out what is in the sensory apriori. But the human mind cannot be satisfied merely with the receptive relation of the sensory ; it does not simply receive objects, but it applies to these its own spontaneity, and attempts to think these through its conceptions, and embrace them in the forms of its understanding. It is the object of the *Transcendental Analytic* (which forms the first part of the *Transcendental Logic*), to examine these apriori conceptions or forms of thought which lie originally in the understanding, as the forms of space and time do in the intuitive faculty.

2. THE TRANSCENDENTAL ANALYTIC.—It is the first problem of the Analytic to attain the pure conceptions of the understanding. Aristotle had already attempted to form a table of these conceptions or categories, but he had collected them empirically instead of deriving them from a common principle, and had numbered among them space and time, though these are no pure conceptions of the understanding, but only forms of intuition. But if we would have a perfect, pure, and regularly arranged table of all the conceptions of the understanding, or all the apriori forms of thought, we must look for a principle out of which we may

11

derive them. This principle is the judgment. The general fundamental conceptions of the understanding may be perfectly attained
if we look at all the different modes or forms of the judgment.
For this end Kant considers the different kinds of judgment as
ordinarily pointed out to us by the science of logic. Now logic
shows that there are four kinds of judgment, viz., judgments of

Quantity.	*Quality.*	*Relation.*	*Modality.*
Universal,	Affirmative,	Categorical,	Problematical,
Plurative,	Negative,	Hypothetical,	Assertive,
Singular.	Illimitable.	Disjunctive.	Apodictic.

From these judgments result the same number of fundamental
conceptions or categories of the understanding, viz. :

Quantity.	*Quality.*	*Relation.*	*Modality.*
Totality,	Reality,	Substance and in-	Possibility and im-
Multiplicity,	Negation,	herence,	possibility,
Unity.	Limitation.	Cause and depend-	Being and not-be-
		ence,	ing,
		Reciprocal action.	Necessity and acci-
			dence.

From these twelve categories all the rest may be derived by
combination. From the fact that these categories are shown to
belong apriori to the understanding, it follows, (1) that these
conceptions are apriori, and hence have a necessary and universal
validity, (2) that by themselves they are empty forms, and attain
a content only through intuitions. But since our intuition is
wholly through the sense, these categories have their validity only
in their application to the sensuous intuition, which becomes a
proper experience only when apprehended in the conceptions of
the understanding.—Here we meet a second question ; how does
this happen ? How do objects become subsumed under these
forms of the understanding, which for themselves are so empty ?

There would be no difficulty with this subsumption if the objects and the conceptions of the understanding were the same in
kind. But they are not. Because the objects come to the understanding from the sensory, they are of the nature of the sense.

Hence the question arises : how can these sensible objects be subsumed under pure conceptions of the understanding, and fundamental principles (judgments apriori), be formed from them ? This
cannot result immediately, but there must come in between the
two, a third, which must have some thing in common with each,
i. e. which is in one respect pure and apriori, and in another sensible. The two pure intuitions of the Transcendental Æsthetics,
space and time, especially the latter, are of such a nature. A
transcendental time determination, as the determination of coetaneousness, corresponds on the one side to the categories, because it
is apriori, and on the other side to the phenomenal objects, because every thing phenomenal can be represented only in time.
The transcendental time determination, Kant calls in this respect
the transcendental *schema*, and the use which the understanding
makes of it, he calls the transcendental *schematism* of the pure
understanding. The schema is a product of the imaginative
faculty, which self-actively determines the inner sense to this,
though the schema is something other than a mere image. An
image is always merely an individual and determinate intuition,
but the schema merely represents the universal process of the
imagination, by which it furnishes for a conception a proper image.
Hence the schema can only exist in the conception, and never suffers itself to be brought within the sensuous intuition. If, now,
we consider more closely the schematism of the understanding,
and seek the transcendental time determination for every category,
we find that :

(1) *Quantity* has for a universal schema *the series of time* or
number, which represents the successive addition of one and one
of the same kind. I can only represent to myself the pure understanding conception of greatness, except as I bring into the
imagination a number of units one after another. If I stop this
process at its first beginning, the result is unity ; if I let it go on
farther I have plurality ; and if I suffer it to continue without
limit, there is totality. Whenever I meet with objects in the
phenomenal world, which I can only apprehend successively, I

am directed to apply the conception of greatness, which would not be possible without the schema of *the series of time*.

(2) *Quality* has for its schema *the content of time*. If I wish to represent to myself the understanding conception of reality, which belongs to quality, I bring before me in thought a time filled up, or a content of time. That is real which fills a time. If also I would represent to myself the pure understanding conception of negation, I bring into thought a void time.

(3) The categories of *relation* take their schemata from *the order of time ;* for if I would represent to myself a determinate relation, I always bring into thought a determinate order of things in time. Substance appears as the persistence of the real in time ; causality as regular succession in time ; reciprocal action as the regular coetaneousness of the determinations in the one substance, with the determinations in the other.

(4) The categories of *modality* take their schema from *the whole of time, i. e.* from whether, and how, an object belongs to time. The schema of possibility is the general harmony of a representation with the conditions of time ; the schema of actuality is the existence of an object in a determined time ; that of necessity is the existence of an object for all time.

We are thus furnished with all the means for forming metaphysical fundamental principles (judgments apriori); we have, *firstly*, conceptions apriori, and *secondly*, schemata through which we can apply these conceptions to objects; for since every object which we can perceive, falls in time, so must it also fall under one of these schemata, which have been borrowed from time, and must consequently permit the corresponding category to be applied to it. The judgments which we here attain are synthetical. They are, corresponding to the four classes of categories, the following : (1) All phenomena are, according to intuition, extensive greatness, since they cannot be apprehended otherwise than through space and time. On this principle the axioms of intuition rely. (2) All phenomena are, according to sensation, intensive greatness, since every sensation has a determined degree, and is capable of increase and diminution. On this principle the anticipations of perception rest. (3) The phenomena stand under necessary time-determinations. They contain the substantial, which abides, and the accidental, which changes. In reference to the change of accidence, they are subject to the law of the following connection, through the relation of cause and effect: as substances they are, in respect of their accidences, in a constant reciprocal action. From this principle spring the analogies of experience. (4) The postulates of empirical thinking are contained in the principles: (a) that which coincides with the formal conditions of experience, is possible, and can become phenomenon; (b) that which agrees with the material conditions of experience is actual, and is phenomenon; (c) that, whose connection with the actual is determined according to the universal conditions of experience, is necessary, and must be phenomenon. Such are the possible and authorized synthetical judgments apriori. But it must not be forgotten that we are entitled to make only an empirical use of all these conceptions and principles, and that we must ever apply them only to things as objects of a possible experience, and never to things in themselves; for the conception without an object is an empty form, but the object cannot be given to the conception except in intuition, and the pure intuition of space and time needs to be filled by experience. Hence, without reference to human experience, these apriori conceptions and principles are nothing but a sporting of the imagination and the understanding, with their representations. Their peculiar determination is only to enable us to spell perceptions, that we may read them as experiences. But here one is apt to fall into a delusion, which can hardly be avoided. Since the categories are not grounded upon the sensory, but have an apriori origin, it would seem as though their application would reach far beyond the sense; but such a view is a delusion; our conceptions are not able to lead us to a knowledge of things in themselves (*noumena*), since our intuition gives us only phenomena for the content of our conceptions, and the thing in itself can never be given in a possible experience; our knowledge remains limited to the phenomena. The source of all the confusions and errors and strife

in previous metaphysics, was in confounding the phenomenal with
the noumenal world.

Besides the categories or conceptions of the understanding,
which have been considered, and which are especially important for
experience, though often applied erroneously beyond the province
of experience, there are other conceptions whose peculiar province
is only to deceive; conceptions whose express determination is to
pass beyond the province of experience, and which may consequently be called transcendent. These are the fundamental conceptions and principles of the previous metaphysics. To examine
these conceptions, and destroy the appearance of objective science
and knowledge, which they falsely exhibit, is the problem of the
Transcendental Dialectics (the second part of the transcendental
logic).

3. THE TRANSCENDENTAL DIALECTICS.—In a strict sense,
the reason is distinguished from the understanding. As the understanding has its categories, the reason has its ideas; as the
understanding forms fundamental maxims from conceptions, the
reason forms principles from ideas, in which the maxims of the
understanding have their highest confirmation. The peculiar
work of the reason is, in general, to find the unconditioned for the
conditioned knowledge of the understanding, and to unify it.
Hence the reason is the faculty of the unconditioned, or of principles; but since it has no immediate reference to objects, but
only to the understanding and its judgments, its activity must remain an immanent one. If it would take the highest unity of
the reason not simply in a transcendental sense, but exalt it to an
actual object of knowledge, then it would become transcendent in
that it applied the conceptions of the understanding to the
knowledge of the unconditioned. From this transcending and
false use of the categories, arises the transcendental appearance
which decoys us beyond experience, by the delusive pretext of
widening the domain of the pure understanding. It is the problem of the transcendental logic to discover this transcendental
appearance.

The speculative ideas of the reason, derived from the three

kinds of logical conclusion, the categorical, the hypothetical, and the disjunctive, are threefold.

(1.) The psychological idea, the idea of the soul, as a thinking substance (the object hitherto of rational psychology).

(2.) The cosmological idea, the idea of the world as including all phenomena (the object hitherto of cosmology).

(3.) The theological idea, the idea of God as the highest condition of the possibility of all things (the object hitherto of rational theology).

But with these ideas, in which the reason attempts to apply the categories of the understanding to the unconditioned, the reason becomes unavoidably entangled in a semblance and an illusion. This transcendental semblance, or this optical illusion of the reason, exhibits itself differently in each of the different ideas. With the psychological ideas the reason perpetrates a simple paralogism, while with the cosmological it finds itself driven to contradictory affirmations or antinomies, and, with the theological, it wanders about in an empty ideal.

(1.) *The psychological ideas, or the paralogisms of the pure reason.*

Kant has attempted, under this rubric, to overthrow all rational psychology as this had been previously apprehended. Rational psychology has considered the soul as a thing called by that name with the attribute of immateriality, as a simple substance with the attribute of incorruptibility, as a numerically identical, intellectual substance with the predicate of personality, as an unextended and thinking being with the predicate of immortality. All these principles of rational psychology, says Kant, are surreptitious; they are all derived from the one premise, " I think ; " but this premise is neither intuition nor conception, but a simple consciousness, an act of the mind which attends, connects, and bears in itself all representations and conceptions. This thinking is now falsely taken as a real thing; the being of the Ego as object is connected with the Ego as subject, and that which is affirmed analytically of the latter is predicated synthetically of the former. But in order to treat the Ego also as object, and to be able to apply to it categories, it must be given empirically, in an intuition, which is not the case. From all this it follows that the proofs for immortality rest upon false conclusions. I can, indeed, separate my pure thinking *ideally* from the body; but obviously, it does not follow from this that my thinking can exist *really* when separate from the body. The result which Kant derives from his critick of rational psychology is this, viz., there is no rational psychology as a *doctrine* which can furnish us with any addition to our self-knowledge, but only as a *discipline*, which places impassable limits to the speculative reason in this field, in order that it may neither throw itself into the bosom of a soulless materialism, nor lose itself in the delusion of a groundless spiritualism. In this respect rational psychology would rather remind us, that this refusal of our reason to give a satisfactory answer to the questions which stretch beyond this life, should be regarded as an intimation of the reason for us to leave this fruitless and superfluous speculation, and apply our self-knowledge to some fruitful and practical use.

(2.) *The Antinomies of Cosmology.*

The cosmological ideas cannot be fully attained without the aid of the categories. (1) So far as the quantity of the world is concerned, space and time are the original *quanta* of all intuition. In a quantitative respect, therefore, the cosmological idea must hold fast to something concerning the totality of the times and spaces of the world. (2) In respect of quality, the divisibility of matter must be regarded. (3) In respect of relation, the complete series of causes must be sought for the existing effects in the world. (4) In respect of modality, the accidental acording to its conditions, or the complete dependence of the accidental in the phenomenon must be conceived. When, now, the reason attempts to establish determinations respecting these problems, it finds itself at once entangled in a contradiction with itself. Directly contrary affirmations can be made with equal validity in reference to each of these four points. We can show, upon grounds equally valid, (1) the *thesis*, the world has a beginning in time and limits in space; and the *antithesis*, the world has neither beginning in time nor limit in space. (2) The thesis: every compound substance in the world consists of simple parts, and there exists nothing else than the simple and that which it composes; and the antithesis: no compound thing consists of simple parts, and there exists nothing simple in the world. (3) The thesis: causality according to the laws of nature, is not the only one from which the phenomena of the world may be deduced, but these may be explained through a causality in freedom; and the antithesis: there is no freedom, but every thing in the world happens only according to natural laws. Lastly, (4) the thesis: something belongs to the world either as its part or its cause, which is an absolutely necessary being; and the antithesis: there exists no absolutely necessary being as cause of the world, either in the world or without it. From this dialectic conflict of the cosmological ideas, there follows at once the worthlessness of the whole struggle.

(3.) *The ideal of the pure Reason or the idea of God.*

Kant shows at first how the reason comes to the idea of a most real being, and then turns himself against the efforts of previous metaphysics to prove its valid existence. His critick of the arguments employed to prove the existence of a God, is essentially the following.

(a.) *The Ontological proof.*—The argument here is as follows : it is possible that there is a most real being; now existence is implied in the conception of all reality, and hence, existence necessarily belongs to the conception of the most real being. But, answers Kant, existence is not at all a reality, or real predicate which can be added to the conception of a thing, but it is the position of a thing with all its properties. The conception of a thing loses property, though the existence of the thing be wanting. Hence if it have any property, it does not at all follow that it possesses existence. Being is nothing but the logical copula, which does not in the least enlarge the content of the subject. A hundred actual dollars, *e. g.* contain no more than a hundred possible ones ; there is only a difference between them in reference to my own wealth. Thus the most real being may with perfect

11*

propriety be conceived of as the most real, while at the same time it should only be conceived of as possible, and not as actual. It was therefore wholly unnatural, and a simple play of school wit, to take an idea which had been arbitrarily formed, and deduce from it the existence of its corresponding object. Any effort and toil which might be spent upon this famous proof is thus only thrown away, and a man would become no richer in knowledge out of simple ideas than a merchant would increase his property by adding a number of ciphers to the balance of his accounts.

(*b.*) *The Cosmological proof.*—This, like the ontological, infers the existence of an absolute being from the necessity of existence. If any thing exist there must also exist an absolutely necessary being as its cause. But now there exists at least I myself, and there must hence also exist an absolutely necessary being as my cause. The last cosmological antinomy is here brought in to criticise the argument at this stage. The conclusion is erroneous, because from the phenomenal and the accidental a necessary being above experience is inferred. Moreover, if we allow the conclusion to be valid, it is still no God which it gives us. Hence the farther inference is made : that being can alone be necessary which includes all reality within itself. If now this proposition should be reversed, and the affirmation made that that being which includes all reality is absolutely necessary, then have we again the ontological proof, and the cosmological falls with this. In the cosmological proof, the reason uses the trick of bringing forth as a new argument an old one with a changed dress, that it might seem to have the power of summoning two witnesses.

(*c.*) *The Physico-theological proof.*—If thus neither conception nor experience can furnish a proof for the divine existence, there still remains a third attempt, viz., to start from a determinate experienc, and endeavor to see whether the existence of a supreme being can not be inferred from the arrangement and condition of things in the world. Such is the physico-theological proof, which starts from the evidences of design in nature, and directs its argument as follows : there is evidently design in the universe ; this is extraneous to the things of the world, and ad-

heres to them only contingently; there exists therefore a necessary cause of this design which works with wisdom and intelligence; this necessary cause must be the most real being; the most
real being has therefore necessary existence.—To this Kant
answers: The physico-theological proof is the oldest, clearest, and
most conformable to the common reason. But it is not demonstration (apodictic). It infers, from the form of the world, a pro-
portionate and sufficient cause of this form; but in this way we only
attain an originator of the form of the world, and not an originator
of its matter, a world-builder, and not a world-creator. To help
out with this difficulty the cosmological proof is brought in, and
the originator of the form becomes conceived as the necessary
being lying at the ground of the content. Thus we have an absolute being whose perfection corresponds to that of the world.
But in the world there is no absolute perfection; we have therefore only a very perfect being; to get the most perfect, we must
revert again to the ontological proof. Thus the teleological proof
rests upon the cosmological, while this in turn has its basis in
the ontological, and from this circle the metaphysical modes of
proof cannot escape.

From these considerations, it would follow that the ideal of a
supreme being is nothing other than a regulative principle of the
reason, by which it looks upon every connection in the world *as
if* it sprang from an all-sufficient and necessary cause; in order
that, in explaining this connection, it may establish the rule of a
systematic and necessary unity, it being also true that in this process the reason through a transcendental subreption cannot avoid
representing to itself this formal principle as constitutive, and
this unity as personal. But in truth this supreme being remains
for the simply speculative use of the reason, a mere but faultless
ideal, a conception which is the summit and the crown of the
whole human knowledge, whose objective reality, though it cannot
be proved with apodictic certainty, can just as little be dis-
proved.

With this critick of the ideas of the reason there is still another question. If these ideas have no objective significance, why

are they found within us? Since they are necessary, they will
doubtless have some good purpose to subserve. What this purpose is, has already been indicated in speaking of the theological
idea. Though not constitutive, yet are they regulative principles.
We cannot better order the faculties of our soul, than by acting
"*as if*" there were a soul. The cosmological idea leads us to
consider the world "*as if*" the series of causes were infinite,
without, however, excluding an intelligent cause. The theological idea enables us to look upon the world in all its complexity,
as a regulated unity. Thus, while these ideas of the reason are
not constitutive principles, by means of which our knowledge
could be widened beyond experience, they are regulative principles, by means of which our experience may be ordered, and
brought under certain hypothetical unities. These three ideas,
therefore, the psychological, the cosmological, and the theological,
do not form an organon for the discovery of truth, but only a ca-
non for the simplification and systematizing of our experiences.

Besides their regulative significance, these ideas of the reason
have also a practical importance. There is a sufficient certainty,
not objective, but subjective, which is especially of a practical
nature, and is called belief or confidence. If the freedom of the
will, the immortality of the soul, and the existence of a God, are
three cardinal principles, which, though not in any way contributing to our knowledge, are yet pressed continually upon us by the
reason, this difficulty is removed in the practical field where these
ideas have their peculiar significance for the moral confidence.
This confidence is not logical, but moral certainty. Since it rests
wholly upon subjective grounds, upon the moral character, I cannot say it is morally certain that there is a God, but only I am
morally certain, &c. That is, the belief in a God and in another
world is so interwoven with my moral character, that I am in just
as much danger of losing this character as of being deprived of
this belief. We are thus brought to the basis of the PRACTICAL
REASON.

II. CRITICK OF THE PRACTICAL REASON.—With the Critick of
the Practical Reason, we enter a wholly different world, where

the reason richly recovers that of which it was deprived in the theoretical province. The essential problem of the Critick of the Practical Reason is almost diametrically different from that of the critick of the theorctical reason. The object of investigation in the critick of the speculative reason, was,—how can the pure reason know objects apriori; in the practical reason it is,—how can the pure reason determine apriori the will in respect of objects. The critick of the speculative reason inquired after the cognizableness of objects apriori: the practical reason has nothing to do with the cognizableness of objects, but only with the determination of the will. Hence, in the latter critick, we have an order directly the reverse of that which we find in the former. As the original determinations of our theoretical knowledge are intuitions, so the original determinations of our will are principles and conceptions. The critick of the practical reason must, therefore, start from moral principles, and only after these are firmly fixed, may we inquire concerning the relation in which the practical reason stands to the sensory.

Freedom, says Kant, is given to us apriori as an inner fact, it is a fact of the inner experience. While, therefore, the reason in the theoretical field had only a negative result, because, when it would attain to a true thing in itself it became transcendent, yet now in the practical province it becomes positive through the idea of freedom, because with the fact of freedom we have no need to go out beyond ourselves, but possess a principle immanent to the reason. But why then give a critick of practical reason ? In order to determine the relation of freedom to the sensory. Since the free will works through its acts upon the sensory, there must be a point of contact between the two. This is found in the sensuous motives of the will, which exist implanted in it by nature, in the impulses and inclinations which, as the principle of the empiric in opposition to the free or pure will, bear in themselves the character of a want of freedom. Since, then, freedom cannot be touched, a critick of the practical reason can only relate to these empirical motives, in the sense of divesting these from the claim of being exclusively the motives by which the will is determined

While, therefore, in the theoretical reason the empirical element was immanent, and the intelligible transcendent, the reverse is the case in the practical reason, since here the empirical is transcendent, and the intelligible immanent. It is the object of the Analytic to show the relation of these two momenta of the will, and the highest moral principle which springs therefrom, while it belongs to the Dialectic to solve the antinomies which result from the contradiction of the pure and empiric will.

(1.) *The Analytic.*—Freedom, as the one constituent element which shows itself in the activity of our will, is the simple *form* of our actions. The universal law binding the will, is that it should determine itself purely from itself, independently of every external incitement. This capacity of self-lawgiving, or self-determining, Kant calls the *autonomy of the will.* The free autonomic will says to man : thou oughtest ! and since this moral ought commands to an unconditioned obedience, the moral imperative is a *categorical imperative.* What is it now which is categorically commanded by the practical reason ? To answer this question, we must first consider the empirical will, *i. e.* the nature-side of man.

The empirical, as the other constituent element of our will, first produces a definite deed when it has filled the empty *form* of action with the *matter* of action. The matter of the will is furnished by the sensory in the desire of pleasure and the dread of pain. Since this second principle of our actions does not find its seat in the freedom of the will as the higher faculty of desire, but in the sensory, as the lower faculty of desire, and a foreign law is thus laid upon the will,—Kant calls it, in opposition to the autonomy of the reason, the *heteronomy of the will.*

The categorical imperative is the necessary law of freedom binding upon all men, and is distinguished from material motives, in that the latter have no fixed character. For men are at variance in respect of pleasure and pain, since that which is disagreeable to one may seem pleasant to another, and if they ever agree, this is simply accidental. Consequently, these material motives can never act the part of laws binding upon every being, but each subject may find his end in a different motive. Such rules of acting, Kant calls *maxims* of the will. He also censures those moralists who have exalted such maxims as universal principles of morality.

Nevertheless, these maxims, though not the highest principles of morality, are yet necessary to the autonomy of the will, because they alone furnish for it a content. It is only by uniting the two sides, that we gain the true principle of morality. To this end the maxims of acting must be freed from their limitation, and widened to the form of universal laws of the reason. Only those maxims should be chosen as motives of action which are capable of becoming universal laws of the reason. *The highest principle of morality* will therefore be this: act so that the maxims of thy will can at the same time be valid as the principle of a universal lawgiving, *i. e.* that no contradiction shall arise in the attempt to conceive the maxims of thy acting as a law universally obeyed. Through this formal moral principle all material moral principles which can only be of a heteronomic nature, are excluded.

The question next arises—what impels the will to act conformably to this highest moral law? Kant answers: the moral law itself, apprehended and revered, must be the only moving spring of the human will. If an act which in itself might be conformable to the moral law, be done only through some impulse to happiness arising simply from an inclination of the sense, if it be not done purely for the sake of the law, then have we simply *legality* and not *morality*. That which is included in every inclination of the sense is self-love and self-conceit, and of these the former is restricted by the moral law, and the latter wholly stricken down. But that which strikes down our self-conceit and humbles us must appear to us in the highest degree worthy of esteem. But this is done by the moral law. Consequently the positive feeling which we shall cherish in respect of the moral law will be reverence. This reverence, though a feeling, is neither sensuous nor pathological, for it stands opposed to these; but is rather an intellectual feeling, since it arises from the notion

of the practical law of the reason.   On the one side as subor-
dination to law, the reverence includes pain; on the other side, since
the coercion can only be exercised through the proper reason, it
includes pleasure.   Reverence is the single sensation befitting
man in reference to the moral law.   Man, as creature of sense,
cannot rest on any inner inclination to the moral law, for he has
ever inclinations within him which resist the law ; love to the law
can only be considered as something ideal.—Thus the moral
purism of Kant, or his effort to separate every impulse of the
sense from the motives to action, merges into rigorism, or the dark
view that duty can never be done except with resistance.   A
similar exaggeration belongs to the well-known epigram of
Schiller, who answers the following scruple of conscience—

> The friends whom I love I gladly would serve,
>   But to this inclination incites me ;
> And so I am forced from virtue to swerve
>   Since my act, through affection, delights me—

with the following decision :

> The friends whom thou lov'st, thou must first seek to scorn,
>   For to no other way can I guide thee :
> 'Tis alone with disgust thou canst rightly perform
>   The acts to which duty would lead thee.

(2.) *The Dialectic.*—The pure reason has always its dialectics,
since it belongs to the nature of the reason to demand the unconditioned for the given conditioned.   Hence also the practical reason seeks an unconditioned highest good for that conditioned good
after which man strives.   What is this highest good ?   If we
understand by the highest good the fundamental condition of all
other goods, then it is virtue.   But virtue is not the perfect good,
since the finite reason as sensitive stands in need also of happiness.   Hence the highest good is only perfect when the highest
happiness is joined to the highest virtue.   The question now
arises : what is the relation of these two elements of the highest
good to each other ?   Are they analytically or synthetically con-

nected together ? The former would be affirmed by most of the ancients, especially by the Greek moral philosophers. We might allow with the Stoics, that happiness is contained as an accidental element in virtue, or, with the Epicureans, that virtue is contained as an accidental element in happiness. The Stoics said : to be conscious of one's virtue is happiness ; the Epicureans said : to be conscious of the maxims leading one to happiness is virtue. But, says Kant, an analytic connection between these two conceptions is not possible, since they are wholly different in kind. Consequently there can be between them only a synthetic unity, and this unity more closely scanned is seen to be a causal one, so that the one element is cause, and the other effect. Such a relation must be regarded as its highest good by the practical reason, whose thesis must therefore be : virtue and happiness must be bound together in a correspondent degree as cause and effect. But this thesis is all thwarted by the actual fact. Neither of the two is the direct cause of the other. Neither is the striving after happiness a moving spring to virtue, nor is virtue the efficient cause of happiness. Hence the antithesis : virtue and happiness do not necessarily correspond, and are not universally connected as cause and effect. The critical solution of this antinomy Kant finds in distinguishing between the sensible and the intelligible world. In the world of sense, virtue and happiness do not, it is true, correspond ; but the reason as *noumenon* is also a citizen of a supersensible world, where the counter-strife between virtue and happiness has no place. In this supersensible world virtue is always adequate to happiness, and when man passes over into this he may look for the actualization of the highest good. But the highest good has, as already remarked, two elements, (1) highest virtue, (2) highest happiness. The actualization demanded for the first of these elements postulates the *immortality of the soul*, and for the second, the *existence of God*.

(*a.*) To the highest good belongs in the first place perfect virtue or holiness. But no creature of sense can be holy : reason united to sense can only approximate holiness as an ideal in an endless progression. But such an endless progress is only possible in an endless continuance of personal existence. If, therefore, the highest good shall ever be actualized, the immortality of the soul must be presupposed.

(b.) To the highest good belongs, in the second place, perfect happiness. Happiness is that condition of a rational creature in the world, to whom every thing goes according to his desire and will. This can only occur when all nature is in accord with his ends. But this is not the case; as acting beings we are not the cause of nature, and there is not the slightest ground in the moral law for connecting morality and happiness. Notwithstanding this, we *ought* to endeavor to secure the highest good. It must therefore be possible. There is thus postulated the necessary connection of these two elements, *i. e.* the existence of a cause of nature distinct from nature, and which contains the ground of this connection. There must be a being as the common cause of the natural and moral world, a being who knows our characters of intelligence, and who, according to this intelligence imparts to us happiness. Such a being is God.

Thus from the practical reason there issue the ideas of immortality and of God, as we have already seen to be the case with the idea of freedom. The reality of the idea of freedom is derived from the possibility of a moral law; that of the idea of immortality is borrowed from the possibility of a perfect virtue; that of the idea of a God follows from the necessary demand of a perfect happiness. These three ideas, therefore, which the speculative reason has treated as problems that could not be solved, gain a firm basis in the province of the practical reason. Still they are not yet theoretical dogmas, but as Kant calls them practical postulates, necessary premises of moral action. My theoretical knowledge is not enlarged by them : I only know now that there are objects corresponding to these ideas, but of these objects I can know no more. Of God, for instance, we possess and know no more than this very conception; and if we should attempt to establish the theory of the supersensible grounded upon such categories, this would be to make theology like a magic lantern, with its phantasmagorical representations. Yet has the practical reason acquired for us a certainty respecting the objective reality of these ideas, which the theoretical reason had been obliged to leave undecided, and in this respect the practical reason has the primacy. This relation of the two faculties of knowledge is wisely established in relation to the destiny of men. Since the ideas of God and immortality are theoretically obscure to us, they do not defile our moral motives by fear and hope, but leave us free space to act through reverence for the moral law.

Thus far Kant's Critick of the Practical Reason. In connection with this we may here mention his *views of religion* as they appear in his treatise upon " *Religion within the Bounds of Pure Reason.*" The chief idea of this treatise is the referring of religion to morality. Between morality and religion there may be the twofold relation, that either morality is founded upon religion, or else religion upon morality. If the first relation were real, it would give us fear and hope as principles of moral action ; but this cannot be, and we are therefore left alone to the second. Morality leads necessarily to religion, because the highest good is a necessary ideal of the reason, and this can only be realized through a God; but in no way may religion first incite us to virtue, for the idea of God may never become a moral motive. Religion, according to Kant, is the recognition of all our duties as divine commands. It is revealed religion when I find in it the divine command, and thus learn my duty ; it is natural religion when I find in it my duty, and thus learn the divine command. The Church is an ethical community, which has for its end the fulfilment and the most perfect exhibition of moral commands,—a union of those who with united energies purpose to resist evil and advance morality. The Church, in so far as it is no object of a possible experience, is called the invisible Church, which, as such, is a simple idea of the union of all the righteous under the divine moral government of the world. The visible Church, on the other hand, is that which presents the kingdom of God upon earth, so far as this can be attained through men. The requisites, and hence also the characteristics of the true visible Church (which are divided according to the table of the categories since this Church is given in experience) are the following : (a) In respect of *quantity* the Church must be total or *universal ;* and though it may be divided in accidental opinions, yet must it be instituted upon such principles as will necessarily lead to a universal union in one single church. (b) The *quality* of the true visible Church is *purity,* as a union under no other than moral motives, since it is at the same time purified from the stupidness of superstition and the madness of fanaticism. (c) The *relation* of the members of the Church to each other rests upon the principle of freedom. The Church is, therefore, a *free state,* neither a hierarchy nor a democracy, but a voluntary, universal, and enduring union of heart. (d) In respect of *modality* the Church demands that its constitution should not be changed. The laws themselves may not change, though one may reserve to himself the privilege of changing some accidental arrangements which relate simply to the administration.—That alone which can establish a universal Church is the moral faith of the reason, for this alone can be shared by the convictions of every man. But, because of the peculiar weakness of human nature, we can never reckon enough on this pure faith to build a Church on it alone, for men are not easily convinced that the striving after virtue and an irreproachable life is every thing which God demands : they always suppose that they must offer to God a special service prescribed by tradition, in which it only comes to this—that he is served.

To establish a Church, we must therefore have a statutory faith historically grounded upon facts. This is the so-called faith of the Church. In every Church there are therefore two elements—the purely moral, or the faith of reason, and the historico-statutory, or the faith of the Church. It depends now upon the relation of the two elements whether a Church shall have any worth or not. The statutory element should ever be only the vehicle of the moral. Just so soon as this element becomes in itself an independent end, claiming an independent validity, will the Church become corrupt and irrational, and whenever the Church passes over to the pure faith of reason, does it approximate to the kingdom of God. Upon this principle we may distinguish the true from the spurious service of the kingdom of God, religion from priestcraft. A dogma has worth alone in so far as it has a moral content. The apostle Paul himself would with difficulty have given credit to the dicta of the faith of the Church without this moral faith. From the doctrine of the Trinity, *e. g.* taken literally, nothing actually practical can be derived. Whether we have to reverence in the Godhead three persons or ten makes no difference, if in both cases we have the same rules for our conduct of life. The Bible also, with its interpretation, must be considered in a moral point of view. The records of revelation must be interpreted in a sense which will harmonize with the universal rules of the religion of reason. Reason is in religious things the highest interpreter of the Bible. This interpretation in reference to some texts may seem forced, yet it must be preferred to any such literal interpretation as would contain nothing for morality, or perhaps go against every moral motive. That such a moral signification may always be found without ever entirely repudiating the literal sense, results from the fact that the foundation for a moral religion lay originally in the human reason. We need only to divest the representations of the Bible of their mythical dress (an attempt which Kant has himself made, by moral explanation of some of the weightiest doctrines), in order to attain a rational sense which shall be universally valid. The historical element of the sacred books is in itself of no account. The maturer the reason becomes, the more it can hold fast for itself the moral sense, so much the more unnecessary will be the statutory institutions of the faith of the Church. The transition of the faith of the Church to the pure faith of reason is the approximation to the kingdom of God, to which, however, we can only approach nearer and nearer in an infinite progress. The actual realization of the kingdom of God is the end of the world, the cessation of history.

III. Critick of the Faculty of Judgment.—The conception of this science Kant gives in the following manner. The two faculties of the human mind hitherto considered were the faculty of knowledge and that of desire. It was proved in the Critick of pure Reason, that the understanding only as faculty of knowledge included constitutive principles apriori; and it was shown in the Critick of Practical Reason, that the reason possesses constitutive principles apriori, simply in reference to the faculty of desire. Whether now the *faculty of judgment*, as the middle link between understanding and reason, can take its object—the feeling of pleasure and pain as the middle link between the faculty of knowledge and that of desire—and furnish it apriori with principles which shall be for themselves constitutive and not simply regulative: this is the point upon which the Critick of the Faculty of Judgment has to turn.

The faculty of judgment is the middle link between the understanding as the faculty of conceptions, and the reason as the faculty of principles. In this position it has the following functions: The speculative reason had taught us to consider the world only according to natural laws; the practical reason had inferred for us a moral world, in which every thing is determined through freedom. There was thus a gulf between the kingdom of nature and that of freedom, which could not be passed unless the faculty of judgment should furnish a conception which should unite the two sides. That it is entitled to do this lies in the very conception of the faculty of judgment. Since it is the faculty of conceiving the particular as contained under the universal, it thus refers the empirical manifoldness of nature to a supersensible, transcendental principle, which embraces in itself the ground for the unity of the manifold. The object of the faculty of judgment is, therefore, the conception of *design* in nature; for the evidence of this points to that supersensible unity which contains the ground for the actuality of an object. And since all design and every actualization of an end is connected with pleasure, we may farther explain the faculty of judgment by saying, that it contains the laws for the feeling of pleasure and pain.

The evidence of design in nature can be represented either subjectively or objectively. In the first case I perceive pleasure and pain, immediately through the representation of an object, before I have formed a conception of it; my delight, in this instance, can only be referred to a designed harmony of relation, between the form of an object, and my faculty of beholding. The faculty of judgment viewed thus subjectively, is called the *æsthetic faculty.* In the second case, I form to myself at the outset, a conception of the object, and then judge whether the form of the object corresponds to this conception. In order to find a flower that is beautiful to my beholding, I do not need to have a conception of the flower; but, if I would see a design in it, then a conception is necessary. The faculty of judgment, viewed as capacity to judge of these objective designs, is called the *teleological faculty.*

1. CRITICK OF THE ÆSTHETIC FACULTY OF JUDGMENT. (1.) *Analytic.*—The analytic of the æsthetic faculty of judgment is divided into two parts, the analytic of the *beautiful*, and the analytic of the *sublime.*

In order to discover what is required in naming an object *beautiful*, we must analyze the judgment of taste, as the faculty for deciding upon the beautiful. (a) In respect of quality, the beautiful is the object of a pure, uninterested satisfaction. This disinterestedness enables us to distinguish between the satisfaction in the beautiful, and the satisfaction in the agreeable and the good. In the agreeable and the good I am interested; my satisfaction in the agreeable is connected with a sensation of desire; my satisfaction in the good is, at the same time, a motive for my will to actualize it. My satisfaction in the beautiful alone is without interest. (b) In respect of quantity, the beautiful is that which universally pleases. In respect of the agreeable, every one decides that his satisfaction in it is only a personal one; but if any one should affirm of a picture, that it is beautiful, he would expect that not only he, but every other one, would also find it so. Nevertheless, this judgment of the taste does not arise from conceptions; its universal validity is therefore purely subjective. I do not judge that all the objects of a species are beautiful, but only that a certain specific object will appear beautiful to every beholder. All the judgments of taste are individual judgments. (c) In respect of relation, that is beautiful in which we find the form of design, without representing to ourselves any specific design. (d) In respect of modality, that is beautiful which is recognized without a conception, as the object of a necessary satisfaction. Of every representation, it is at least possible, that it may awaken pleasure. The representation of the agreeable awakens actual pleasure. The representation of the beautiful, on the other hand, awakens pleasure necessarily. The necessity which is conceived in an æsthetic judgment, is a necessity for determining every thing by a judgment, which can be viewed as an example of a universal rule, though the rule itself cannot be stated. The subjective principle which lies at the basis of the judgment of taste, is therefore a common sense, which determines what is pleasing, and what displeasing, only through feeling, and not through conception.

The *sublime* is that which is absolutely, or beyond all comparison, great, compared with which every thing else is small. But now in nature there is nothing which has no greater. The absolutely great is only the infinite, and the infinite is only to be met with in ourselves, as idea. The sublime, therefore, is not properly found in nature, but is only carried over to nature from our own minds. We call that sublime in nature, which awakens within us the idea of the infinite. As in the beautiful there is prominent reference to quality, so, in the sublime, the most important element of all, is quantity; and this quantity is either greatness of extension (the mathematically sublime), or greatness of power (the dynamically sublime). In the sublime there is a greater satisfaction in the formless, than in the form. The sublime excites a vigorous movement of the heart, and awakens pleasure only through pain, i. e. through the feeling that the energies of life are for the moment restrained. The satisfaction in the sublime is hence not so much a positive pleasure, but rather an amazement and awe, which may be called a negative pleasure.

The elements for an æsthetic judgment of the sublime are the same as in the feeling of the beautiful. (a) In respect of quantity, that is sublime which is absolutely great, in comparison with which every thing else is small. The æsthetic estimate of greatness does not lie, however, in numeration, but in the simple intuition of the subject. The greatness of an object of nature, which the imagination attempts in vain to comprehend, leads to a supersensible substratum, which is great beyond all the measures of the sense, and which has reference properly to the feeling of the sublime. It is not the object itself, as the surging sea, which is sublime, but rather the subject's frame of mind, in the estimation of this object. (b) In respect of quality, the sublime does not awaken pure pleasure, like the beautiful, but first pain, and through this, pleasure. The feeling of the insufficiency of our imagination, in the æsthetic estimate of greatness, gives rise to pain; but, on the other side, the consciousness of our independent reason, for which the faculty of imagination is inadequate, awakens pleasure. In this respect, therefore, that is sublime which immediately pleases us, through its opposition to the interest of the sense. (c) In respect of relation, the sublime suffers nature to appear as a power, indeed, but in reference to which, we have the consciousness of superiority. (d) In respect of modality, the judgments concerning the sublime are as necessarily valid, as those for the beautiful; only with this difference, that our judgment of the sublime finds an entrance to some minds, with greater difficulty than our judgment of the beautiful, since to perceive the sublime, culture, and developed moral ideas, are necessary.

(2.) *Dialectic.*—A dialectic of the æsthetic faculty of judgment, like every dialectic, is only possible where we can meet with judgments which lay claim to universality apriori. For dialectics consists in the opposition of such judgments. The antinomy of the principles of taste rests upon the two opposite elements of the judgment of taste, that it is purely subjective, and at the same time, lays claim to universal validity. Hence, the two common-place sayings: "there is no disputing about taste,"

12

and " there is a contest of taste." From these, we have the following antinomy. (*a*) Thesis: the judgment of taste cannot be grounded on conception, else might we dispute it. (*b*) Antithesis: the judgment of taste must be grounded on conception, else, notwithstanding its diversity, there could be no contest respecting it.—This antinomy, says Kant, is, however, only an apparent one, and disappears as soon as the two propositions are more accurately apprehended. - The thesis should be: the judgment of taste is not grounded upon a definite conception, and is not strictly demonstrable; the antithesis should be: this judgment is grounded upon a conception, though an indefinite one, viz., upon the conception of a supersensible substratum for the phenomenal. Thus apprehended, there is no longer any contradiction between the two propositions.

In the conclusion of the æsthetic faculty of judgment, we can now answer the question, whether the fitness of things to our faculty of judgment (their beauty and sublimity), lies in the things themselves, or in us? The æsthetic realism claims that the supreme cause of nature designed to produce things which should affect our imagination, as beautiful and sublime, and the organic forms of nature strongly support this view. But on the other hand, nature exhibits even in her merely mechanical forms, such a tendency to the beautiful, that we might believe that she could produce also the most beautiful organic forms through mechanism alone; and that thus the design would lie not in nature, but in our soul. This is the standpoint of idealism, upon which it becomes explicable how we can determine any thing apriori concerning beauty and sublimity. But the highest view of the æsthetical, is to use it as a symbol of the moral good. Thus Kant makes the theory of taste, like religion, to be a corollary of morality.

2. CRITICK OF THE TELEOLOGICAL FACULTY OF JUDGMENT.—In the foregoing, we have considered the subjective æsthetical design in the objects of nature. But the objects of nature have also a relation of design to each other. The teleological faculty of judgment has also to consider this faculty of design.

(1.) *Analytic of the Teleological Faculty of Judgment.*—The analytic has to determine the kinds of objective design. Objective, material design, is of two kinds, external, and internal. The external design is only relative, since it simply indicates a usefulness of one thing for another. Sand, for instance, which borders the sea shore, is of use in bearing pine forests. In order that animals can live upon the earth, the earth must produce nourishment for them, etc. These examples of external design, show that here the design never belongs to the means in itself, but only accidentally. We should never get a conception of the sand by saying that it is a means for pine forests; it is conceivable for itself, without any reference to the conception of design. The earth does not produce nourishment, because it is necessary that men should dwell upon it. In brief, this external or relative design may be conceived from the mechanism of nature alone. Not so the inner design of nature, which shows itself prominently in the organic products of nature. In an organic product of nature, every one of its parts is end, and every one, means or instrument. In the process of generation, the natural product appears as species, in growth it appears as individual, and in the process of complete formation, every part of the individual shows itself. This natural organism cannot be explained from mechanical causes, but only through final causes, or teleologically.

(2.) *Dialectic.*—The dialectic of the teleological faculty of judgment, has to adjust this opposition between this mechanism of nature and teleology. On the one side we have the thesis: every production of material things must be judged as possible, according to simple mechanical laws. On the other side we have the antithesis: certain products of material nature cannot be judged as possible, according to simple mechanical laws, but demand the conception of design for their explanation. If these two maxims are posited as constitutive (objective) principles for the possibility of the objects themselves, then do they contradict each other, but as simply regulative (subjective) principles for the investigation of nature, they are not contradictory. Earlier systems treated the conception of design in nature dogmatically,

and either affirmed or denied its essential existence in nature.
But we, convinced that teleology is only a regulative principle,
have nothing to do with the question whether an inner design belongs essentially to nature or not, but we only affirm that our
faculty of judgment must look upon nature as designed.   We
envisage the conception of design in nature, but leave it wholly
undecided whether to another understanding, which does not
think discursively like ours, nature may not be understood, without at all needing to bring in this conception of design.   Our understanding thinks discursively : it proceeds from the parts, and
comprehends the whole as the product of its parts; it cannot,
therefore, conceive the organic products of nature, where the
whole is the ground and the prius of the parts, except from the
point of view of the conception of design.   If there were, on the
other hand, an intuitive understanding, which could know the
particular and the parts as co-determined in the universal and
the whole ; such an understanding might conceive the whole of
nature out of one principle, and would not need the conception
of end.

If Kant had thoroughly carried out this conception of an intuitive understanding as well as the conception of an immanent
design in nature, he would have overcome, in principle, the stand-
point of subjective idealism, which he made numerous attempts, in
his critick of the faculty of judgment, to break through ; but these
ideas he only propounded, and left them to be positively carried
out by his successors.

SECTION XXXIX.

TRANSITION TO THE POST-KANTIAN PHILOSOPHY.

The Kantian philosophy soon gained in Germany an almost
undisputed rule.   The imposing boldness of its standpoint, the
novelty of its results, the applicability of its principles, the moral

severity of its view of the world, and above all, the spirit of freedom and moral autonomy which appeared in it, and which was so
directly counter to the efforts of that age, gained for it an assent
as enthusiastic as it was extended.   It aroused among all cultivated classes a wider interest and participation in philosophic
pursuits, than had ever appeared in an equal degree among any
people.   In a short time it had drawn to itself a very numerous
school : there were soon few German universities in which it had
not had its talented representatives, while in every department of
science and literature, especially in theology (it is the parent of
theological rationalism), and in natural rights, as also in belles-
lettres (*Schiller*), it began to exert its influence.   Yet most of the
writers who appeared in the Kantian school, confined themselves
to an exposition or popular application of the doctrine as Kant
had given it, and even the most talented and independent among
the defenders and improvers of the critical philosophy (*e. g
Reinhold*, 1758–1823 ; *Bardili*, 1761–1808 ; *Schulze, Beck,
Fries, Krug, Bouterweck*), only attempted to give a firmer basis
to the Kantian philosophy as they had received it, to obviate
some of its wants and deficiencies, and to carry out the standpoint
of transcendental idealism more purely and consistently.   Among
those who carried out the Kantian philosophy, only two men,
Fichte and *Herbart*, can be named, who made by their actual
advance an epoch in philosophy ; and among its opposers (*e. g.
Hamann, Herder*), only one, *Jacobi*, is of philosophic importance.
These three philosophers are hence the first objects for us to consider.   In order to a more accurate development of their principles, we preface a brief and general characteristic of their relation
to the Kantian philosophy.

1. Dogmatism had been critically annihilated by Kant; his
Critick of pure Reason had for its result the theoretical inde-
monstrableness of the three ideas of the reason, God, freedom, and
immortality.   True, these ideas which, from the standpoint of
theoretical knowledge, had been thrust out, Kant had introduced
again as postulates of the practical reason ; but as postulates, as
only practical premises, they possess no theoretic certainty, and

remain exposed to doubt.   In order to do away with this uncertainty, and this despairing of knowledge which had seemed to be the end of the Kantian philosophy, *Jacobi*, a younger cotemporary of Kant, placed himself upon the standpoint of the faith philosophy in opposition to the standpoint of criticism.   Though these highest ideas of the reason, the eternal and the divine, cannot be reached and proved by means of demonstration, yet is it the very essence of the divine that it is indemonstrable and unattainable for the understanding.   In order to be certain of the highest, of that which lies beyond the understanding, there is only one organ, viz., feeling.   In feeling, therefore, in immediate knowledge, in faith, Jacobi thought he had found that certainty which Kant had sought in vain on the basis of discursive thinking.

2. While Jacobi stood in an antithetic relation to the Kantian philosophy, *Fichte* appears as its immediate consequence. Fichte carried out to its consequence the Kantian dualism, according to which the Ego, as theoretic, is subjected to the external world, while as practical, it is its master, or, in other words, according to which the Ego stands related to the objective world, now receptively and again spontaneously.   He allowed the reason to be exclusively practical, as will alone, and spontaneity alone, and apprehended its theoretical and receptive relation to the objective world as only a circumscribed activity, as a limitation prescribed to itself by the reason.   But for the reason, so far as it is practical, there is nothing objective except as it is produced. The will knows no being but only an ought.   Hence the objective being of truth is universally denied, and the thing which is essentially unknown must fall away of itself as an empty shadow. " Every thing which is, is the Ego," is the principle of the Fichtian system, and represents at the same time the subjective idealism in its consequence and completion.

3. While the subjective idealism of Fichte was carried out in the objective idealism of Schelling, and the absolute idealism of Hegel, there arose cotemporaneously with these systems a third offshoot of the Kantian criticism, viz., the philosophy of *Herbart*. It had its subjective origin in the Kantian philosophy, but its ob-

jective and historic connection with Kant is slight. It breaks up all historic continuity, and holds an isolated position in the history of philosophy. Its general basis is Kantian, in so far as it makes for its problem a critical investigation of the subjective experience. We place it between Fichte and Schelling.

SECTION XL.

JACOBI.

FRIEDRICH HEINRICH JACOBI was born at Düsseldorf in 1743. His father destined him for a merchant. After he had studied in Geneva and become interested in philosophy, he entered his father's mercantile establishment, but afterwards abandoned this business, having been made chancellor of the exchequer and customs commissioner for Cleves and Berg, and also privy councillor at Düsseldorf. In this city, or at his neighboring estate of Pempelfort, he spent a great part of his life devoted to philosophy and his friends. In the year 1804 he was called to the newly-formed Academy of Sciences in Munich. In 1807 he was chosen president of this institution, a post which he filled till his death in 1819. Jacobi had a rich intellect and an amiable character. Besides being a philosopher, he was also a poet and citizen of the world ; and hence we find in his philosophizing an absence of strict logical arrangement and precise expression of thought. His writings are no systematic whole, but are occasional treatises written " rhapsodically and in grasshopper gait," for the most part in the form of letters, dialogues, and romances. " It was never my purpose," he says himself, " to set up a system for the schools. My writings have sprung from my innermost life, and were the result of that which had taken place within me. In a certain sense I did not make them voluntarily, but they were drawn out of me by a higher power irresistible to myself.' This want of an inner principle of classification and of a syste matic arrangement, renders a development of Jacobi's philosophy not easy. It may best be represented under the following three points of view :—1. Jacobi's polemic against mediate knowledge. 2. His principle of immediate knowledge. 3. His relation to the cotemporaneous philosophy, especially to the Kantian criticism.

1. Spinoza was the negative starting point of Jacobi's philosophizing. In his work "*On the Doctrine of Spinoza, in letters to Moses Mendelssohn*" (1785), he directed public attention again to the almost wholly forgotten philosophy of Spinoza. The correspondence originated thus : Jacobi made the discovery that Lessing was a Spinozist, and announces this to Mendelssohn. The latter will not believe it, and thence grew the farther historical and philosophical examination. The positive philosophic views which Jacobi exhibits in this treatise can be reduced to the following three principles : (1) Spinozism is fatalism and atheism. (2) Every path of philosophic demonstration leads to fatalism and atheism. (3) In order that we may not fall into these, we must set a limit to demonstrating, and recognize faith as the element of all metaphysic knowledge.

(1.) Spinozism is atheism, because, according to it, the cause of the world is no person—is no being working for an end, and endowed with reason and will—and hence is no God. It is fatalism, for, according to it, the human will regards itself only falsely as free.

(2.) This atheism and fatalism is, however, only the necessary consequence of all strictly demonstrative philosophizing. To conceive a thing, says Jacobi, is to refer a thing to its nearest cause ; it is to find a possible for an actual, the condition for a conditioned, the mediation for an immediate. We conceive only that which we can explain out of another. Hence our conceiving moves in a chain of conditioned conditions, and this connection forms a mechanism of nature, in whose investigation our understanding has its immeasurable field. However far we may carry conception and demonstration, we must hold, in reference to every object, to a still higher one which conditions it ; where this chain of the conditioned ceases, there do conception and demonstration also cease; till we give up demonstrating we can reach no infinite. If philosophy determines to apprehend the infinite with the finite understanding, then must it bring down the divine to the finite; and here is where every preceding philosophy has been entangled, while it is obviously an absurd undertaking to attempt to discover the conditions of the unconditioned, and make the absolutely necessary a possible, in order that we may be able to construct it. A God who could be proved is no God, for the ground of proof is ever above that which is to be proved; the latter has its whole reality from the former. If the existence of God should be proved, then God would be derived from a ground which were before and above him. Hence the paradox of Jacobi; it is for the interest of science that there be no God, no supernatural and no extra or supramundane being. Only upon the condition that nature alone is, and is therefore independent and all in all, can science hope to gain its goal of perfection, and become, like its object itself, all in all. Hence the result which Jacobi derives from the "Drama of the history of philosophy" is this :—" There is no other philosophy than that of Spinoza. He who considers all the works and acts of men to be the effect of natural mechanism, and who believes that intelligence is but an accompanying consciousness, which has only to act the part of a looker-on, cannot be contended with and cannot be helped-till we set him free from his philosophy. No philosophical conclusion can reach him, for what he denies cannot be philosophically proved, and what he proves cannot be philosophically denied." Whence then is help to come? " The understanding, taken by itself, is materialistic and irrational; it denies spirit and God. The reason taken by itself is idealistic, and has nothing to do with the understanding; it denies nature and makes itself God."

(3.) Hence we must seek another way of knowing the supersensible, which is faith. Jacobi calls this flight from cognition through conception to faith, the *salto mortale* of the human reason. Every certainty through a conception demands another certainty, but in faith we are led to an immediate certainty which needs no ground nor proof, and which is in fact absolutely exclusive of all proof.

12*

Such a confidence which does not arise from arguments, is called faith. We know the sensible as well as the supersensible only through faith. All human knowledge springs from revelation and faith.

These principles which Jacobi brought out in his letters concerning Spinoza, did not fail to arouse a universal opposition in the German philosophical world. It was charged upon him that he was an enemy of reason, a preacher of blind faith, a despiser of science and of philosophy, a fanatic and a papist. To rebut these attacks, and to justify his standpoint, he wrote in 1787, a year and a half after the first appearance of the work already named, his dialogue entitled "*David Hume, or Faith, Idealism, and Realism*," in which he developes more extensively and definitely his principle of faith or immediate knowledge.

2. Jacobi distinguished his faith at the outset from a blind credence in authority. A blind faith is that which supports itself on a foreign view, instead of on the grounds of reason. But this is not the case with his faith, which rather rests upon the innermost necessity of the subject itself. Still farther: his faith is not an arbitrary imagination: we can imagine to ourselves every thing possible, but in order to regard a thing as actual, there must be an inexplicable necessity of our feeling, which we cannot otherwise name than faith. Jacobi was not constant in his terminology, and hence did not always express himself alike in respect of the relation in which faith stood to the different sides of the human faculty of knowledge. In his earlier terminology he placed faith (or as he also called it, the power of faith), on the side of the sense or the receptivity, and let it stand opposed to the understanding and the reason, taking these two terms as equivalent expressions for the finite and immediate knowledge of previous philosophy; afterwards he followed Kant, and, distinguishing between the reason and the understanding, he called that reason which he had previously named sense and faith. According to him now, the faith or intuition of the reason is the organ for perceiving the supersensible. As such, it stands opposed to the understanding. There must be a higher faculty

which can learn, in a way inconceivable to sense and the under-standing, that which is true in and above the phenomena. Over against the explaining understanding stands the reason, or the natural faith of the reason, which does not explain, but positively reveals and unconditionally decides. As there is an intuition of the sense, so is there a rational intuition through the reason, and a demonstration has no more validity in respect of the latter than in respect of the former. Jacobi justifies his use of the term, in-tuition of the reason, from the want of any other suitable designa-tion. Language has no other expression to indicate the way in which that, which is unattainable to the sense, becomes appre-hended in the transcendental feeling. If any one affirms that he knows any thing, he may properly be required to state the origin of his knowledge, and in doing this, he must of necessity go back either to sensation or to feeling; the latter stands above the former as high as the human species above the brute. So I affirm, then, without hesitation, says Jacobi, that my philosophy starts from pure feeling, and declares the authority of this to be supreme. The faculty of feeling is the highest in man, and that alone which specifically distinguishes him from the brute. This faculty is one and the same with reason; or, reason may be said to find in it its single and only starting point.

Jacobi had the clearest consciousness of the opposition in which he stood, with this principle of immediate knowledge, to previous philosophy. In his introduction to his complete works, he says: " There had arisen since the time of Aristotle an in-creasing effort in philosophical schools, to subject the immediate knowledge to the mediate, to make that faculty of perception which originally establishes every thing, dependent on the faculty of re-flection, which is conditioned through abstraction; to subordinate the archetype to the copy, the essence to the word, the reason to the understanding, and, in fact, to make the former wholly disap-pear in the latter. Nothing is allowed to be true which is not capable of a double demonstration, in the intuition and in the conception, in the thing and in its image or word; the thing it-self, it is said, must truly lie and actually be known only in the word." But every philosophy which allows only the reflecting reason, must lose itself at length in an utter ignorance. Its end is nihilism.

3. From what has been already said, the position of Jacobi with his principle of faith, in relation to the Kantian philosophy, can, partly at least, be seen. Jacobi had separated himself from this philosophy, partly in the above-named dialogue "David Hume," (especially in an appendix to this, in which he discussed the transcendental Idealism), and partly in his essay " *On the attempt of criticism to bring the reason to the understanding* " (1801). His relation to it may be reduced to the following three general points :

(1.) Jacobi does not agree with Kant's theory of sensuous knowledge. In opposition to this theory he defends the standpoint of empiricism, affirms the truthfulness of the sense-perception, and denies the apriority of space and time, for which Kant contends in order to prove that objects as well as their relations are simply determinations of our own self, and do not at all exist externally to us. For, however much it may be affirmed that there is something corresponding to our notions as their cause, yet does it remain concealed what this something is. According to Kant, the laws of our beholding and thinking are without objective validity, our knowledge has no objective significance. But it is wrong to claim that in the phenomena there is nothing revealed of the hidden truth which lies behind them. With such a claim, it were far better to give up completely the unknown thing-in-itself, and carry out to its results the consequent idealism. " Logically, Kant is at fault, when he presupposes objects which make impressions on our soul. He is bound to teach the strictest idealism.

(2.) Yet Jacobi essentially agrees with Kant's critick of the understanding. Jacobi affirmed, as Kant had done, that the understanding is insufficient to know the supersensible, and that the highest ideas of the reason could be apprehended only in faith. Jacobi places Kant's great merit in having cleared away the ideas, which were simply the products of reflection and logical phantasms. " It is very easy for the understanding, when producing one notion from another, and thus gradually mounting up to ideas, to imagine that, by virtue of these, which, though they carry it beyond the intuitions of the sense, are nothing but logical phantasms, it has not only the faculty but the most decided determination to fly truly above the world of sense, and to gain by its flight a higher science independent of the intuition, a science of the supersensible. Kant discovers and destroys this error and self-deception. Thus there is gained, at least, a clear place for a *genuine* rationalism. This is Kant's truly great deed, his immortal merit. But the sound sense of our sage did not allow him to hide from himself that this clear place must disappear in a gulf, which would swallow up in itself all knowledge of the true, unless a God should interpose to hinder it. Here Kant's doctrine and mine meet."

(3.) But Jacobi does not fully agree with Kant, in wholly denying to the theoretical reason the faculty of objective knowledge. He blames Kant for complaining that the human reason cannot theoretically prove the reality of its ideas. He affirms that Kant is thus still entangled in the delusion, that the only reason why these ideas cannot be proved, is found in the nature of the ideas themselves, and not in the deficient nature of our knowledge. Kant therefore attempts to seek, in a practical way, a kind of scientific proof; a roundabout way, which, to every profound seeker, must seem folly, since every proof is as impossible as it is unnecessary.

Jacobi agreed better with Kant, than with the post-Kantian philosophy. The atheistic tendency of the latter was especially repulsive to him. " To Kant, that profound thinker and upright philosopher, the words God, freedom, immortality, and religion, signified the same as they have ever done to the sound human understanding; he in no way treats them as nothing but deception. He created offence by irresistibly showing the insufficiency of all proofs of speculative philosophy for these ideas. That which was wanting in the theoretical proof, he made up by the necessary postulates of a pure practical reason. With these, ac-

cording to Kant's assurance, philosophy was fully helped out of
her difficulty, and the goal, which had been always missed, actually reached.   But the first daughter of the critical philosophy
(Fichte's system) makes the living and working moral order itself to be God, a God expressly declared to be without consciousness and self-existence.   These frank words, spoken publicly and
without restraint, roused some attention, but the fear soon sub-
sided.   Presently astonishment ceased wholly, for the second
daughter of the critical philosophy (Schelling's system) gave up
entirely the distinction which the first had allowed to remain between natural and moral philosophy, necessity and freedom, and
without any further ado affirmed that the only existence is nature, and that there is nothing above; this second daughter is
Spinozism transfigured and reversed, an ideal materialism."   This
latter allusion to Schelling, connected as it was with other and
harder thrusts in the same essay, called out from this philosopher
the well-known answer : " *Schelling's Monument to the Treatise
on Divine Things*, 1812."

If we now take a critical survey of the philosophical stand-
point of Jacobi, we shall find its peculiarity to consist in the abstract separation of understanding and feeling.   These two Jacobi could not bring into harmony.   " There is light in my
heart," he says, " but it goes out whenever I attempt to bring it
into the understanding.   Which is the true luminary of these
two ?   That of the understanding, which, though it reveals fixed
forms, shows behind them only a baseless gulf?   Or that of the
heart, which points its light promisingly upwards, though determinate knowledge escapes it ?   Can the human spirit grasp the
truth unless it possesses these two luminaries united in one light?
And is this union conceivable except through a miracle ? "   If
now, in order to escape in a certain degree this contradiction between understanding and feeling, Jacobi gave to immediate
knowledge the place of mediate as finite knowledge, this was a
self-deception.   Even that knowledge, which is supposed to be
immediate, and which Jacobi regards as the peculiar organ for
knowing the supersensible, is also mediate, obliged to go through

a course of subjective mediations, and can only give itself out as immediate when it wholly forgets its own origin.

SECTION XLI.

FICHTE

JOHANN GOTTLIEB FICHTE was born at Rammenau, in Upper Lusatia, 1762. A nobleman of Silesia became interested in the boy, and having committed him first to the instruction of a clergyman, he afterwards placed him at the high school at Schulp-forte. In his eighteenth year, at Michaelmas, 1780, Fichte entered the university at Jena to study theology. He soon found himself attracted to philosophy, and became powerfully affected by the study of Spinoza. His pecuniary circumstances were straitened, but this only served to harden his will and his energy. In 1784 he became employed as a teacher in a certain family, and spent some time in this occupation with different families in Saxony. In 1787 he sought a place as country clergyman, but was refused on account of his religious opinions. He was now obliged to leave his fatherland, to which he clung with his whole soul. He repaired to Zurich, where, in 1788, he took a post as private tutor, and where also he became acquainted with his future wife, a sister's daughter of Klopstock. At Easter, 1790, he returned to Saxony and taught privately at Leipsic, where he became acquainted with the Kantian philosophy, by means of lessons which he was obliged to give to a student. In the spring of 1791 we find him as private tutor at Warsaw, and soon after in Königsberg, where he resorted, that he might become personally acquainted with the Kant he had learned to revere. Instead of a letter of recommendation he presented him his "*Critick of all Revelation*," a treatise which Fichte composed in eight days. In this he attempted to deduce, from the practical reason, the possibility of a revelation. This is not seen purely apriori, but only under an empirical condition ; we must consider humanity to be in a moral ruin so complete, that the moral law has lost all its influence upon the will and all morality is extinguished. In such a case we may expect that God, as moral governor of the world, would give man, through the sense, some pure moral impulses, and reveal himself as lawgiver to them through a special manifestation determined for this end, in the world of sense. In such a case a particular revelation were a postulate of the practical reason. Fichte sought also to determine apriori the possible content of such a revelation. Since we need to know nothing but God, freedom, and immortality, the revelation will contain naught but these, and these it must contain in a comprehensible form, yet so that the symbolical dress may lay no .claim to unlimited veneration. This treatise, which appeared anonymously in 1792, at once attracted the greatest attention, and was at first universally regarded as a work of Kant. It procured for its author, soon after, a call to the chair of philosophy at Jena, to succeed Reinhold, who then went to Kiel. Fichte received this appointment in 1793 at Zurich, where he had gone to consummate his marriage. At the same time he wrote and published,·also anonymously, his " *Aids to correct views of the French Revolution*," an essay which the governments never looked upon with favor. At Easter, 1794, he entered upon his new office, and soon saw his public call confirmed. Taking now a new standpoint, which transcended Kant, he sought to establish this, and carry it out in a series of writings (the *Wissenschaftslehre* appeared in 1794, the *Naturrecht* in 1796, and the *Sittenlehre* in 1798), by which he exerted a powerful influence upon the scientific movement in Germany, aided as he was in this by the fact that Jena was then one of the most flourishing of the German universities, and the resort of every vigorous head. With Goethe, Schiller, the brothers Schlegel, William von Humboldt, and Hufeland, Fichte was in close fellowship, though this was unfortunately broken after a few years. In 1795 he became associate editor of the "*Philosophical Journal*," which had been established by Niethammer. A fellow-laborer, Rector Forberg, at Saalfeld, offered for publication in this journal an article " to determine the conception of religion." Fichte advised the author not to publish it, but at length inserted it in the journal, prefacing it, however, with an introduction of his own " *On the ground of our faith in a divine government of the world*," in which he endeavored to remove, or at least soften, the views in the article which might give offence. Both the essays raised a great cry of atheism. The elector of Saxony confiscated the journal in his territory, and sent a requisition to the dukes Ernest, who held in common the university of Jena, to summon the author to trial and punishment. Fichte answered the edict of confiscation and attempted to justify himself to the public (1799), by his " *Appeal to the Public. An essay which it is requested may be read before it is confiscated ;*" while he defended his course to the government by an article entitled " *The Publishers of the Philosophical Journal justified from the charge of Atheism.*" The government of Weimar, being as anxious to spare him as it was to please the elector of Saxony, delayed its decision. But as Fichte, either with or without reason, had privately learned that the whole matter was to be settled by reprimanding the accused parties for their want of caution ; and, desiring either a civil acquittal or an open and proper satisfaction, he wrote a private letter to a member of the government, in which he desired his dismission in case of a reprimand, and which he closed with the intimation that many of his friends would leave the university with him, in order to establish together a new one in Germany. The government regarded this letter as an application for his discharge, indirectly declaring that the reprimand was unavoidable. Fichte, now an object of suspicion, both on account of his religious and political views, looked about him in vain for a place of refuge. The prince of Rudolstadt, to whom he turned, denied him his protection, and his arrival in Berlin (1799) attracted great notice. In Berlin, where he had much intercourse with Frederick Schlegel, and also with Schleiermacher and Novalis, his views became gradually modified ; the catastrophe at Jena had led him from the exclusive moral standpoint which he, resting upon Kant, had

hitherto held, to the sphere of religion; he now sought to recon
cile religion with his standpoint of the *Wissenshaftslehre*, and
turned himself to a certain mysticism (the second form of the
Fichtian theory). After he had privately taught a number of
years in Berlin, and had also held philosophical lectures for men
of culture, he was recommended (1805) by Beyme and Altenstein,
chancellor of state of Hardenberg, to a professorship of philosophy in Erlangen, an appointment which he received together
with a permit to return to Berlin in the winter, and hold there
his philosophical lectures before the public. Thus, in the winter
of 1807-8, while a French marshal was governor of Berlin, and
while his voice was often drowned by the hostile tumults of the
enemy through the streets, he delivered his famous "*Addresses to
the German nation.*" Fichte labored most assiduously for the
foundation of the Berlin university, for only by wholly trans-
forming the common education did he believe the regeneration of
Germany could be secured. As the new university was opened
1809, he was made in the first year dean of the philosophical
faculty, and in the second was invested with the dignity of rector.
In the "war of liberation," then breaking out, Fichte took the
liveliest participation by word and deed. His wife had contracted
a nervous fever by her care of the sick and wounded, and though
she recovered, he fell a victim to the same disease. He died Jan.
28, 1814, not having yet completed his fifty-second year.

In the following exposition of Fichte's philosophy, we distinguish between the two internally different periods of his philosophizing, that of Jena and that of Berlin. The first division will include
two parts—Fichte's theory of science and his practical philosophy.

I. The Fichtian Philosophy in its Original Form. 1.
The Theoretical Philosophy of Fichte, his Wissenschaftslehre, or Theory of Science.—It has already been shown (§ 39)
that the thoroughly-going subjective idealism of Fichte was only
the logical consequence of the Kantian standpoint. It was wholly
unavoidable that Fichte should entirely reject the Kantian essentially thing (*thing in itself*), which Kant had himself declared to
be unrecognizable though real, and that he should posit as a

proper act of the mind, that external influence which Kant had referred to the essentially thing. That the Ego alone is, and that which we regard as a limitation of the Ego by external objects, is rather the proper self-limitation of the Ego; this is the grand feature of the Fichtian as of every idealism.

Fichte himself supported the standpoint of this Theory of Science as follows: In every experience there is conjointly an Ego and a thing, the intelligence and its object. Which of these two sides must now be reduced to the other ? If the philosopher abstracts the Ego, he has remaining an essentially thing, and must then apprehend his representations or sensations as the products of this object ; if he abstracts the object, he has remaining an essentially Ego (an Ego *in itself*). The former is dogmatism, the latter idealism. Both are irreconcilable with each other, and there is no third way possible. We must therefore choose between the two. In order to decide between the two systems, we must note the following : (1) That the Ego appears in consciousness, wherefore the essentially thing is a pure invention, since in consciousness we have only that which is perceived ; (2.) Dogmatism must account for the origin of its representation through some essentially object, it must start from something which does not lie in the consciousness. But the effect of being is only being, and not representation. Hence idealism alone can be correct which does not start from being, but from intelligence. According to idealism, intelligence is only active, not passive, because it is a first and absolute : and on this account there belongs to it no being, but simply an acting. The forms of this acting, the system of the necessary mode in which intelligence acts, must be found from the essence of intelligence. If we should take the laws of intelligence from experience, as Kant did his categories, we fail in two respects : (1) We do not see why intelligence must so act, nor whether these laws are immanent laws of intelligence ; (2) We do not see how the object itself originates. Hence the fundamental principles of intelligence, as well as the objective world, must be derived from the Ego itself.

Fichte supposed that in these results he only expressed the

true sense of the Kantian philosophy. "Whatever my system may properly be, whether the genuine criticism thoroughly carried out, *as I believe it is*, or howsoever it be named, is of no account." His system, Fichte affirms, had the same view of the matter as Kant's, while the numerous followers of this philosopher had wholly mistaken and misunderstood their master's idealism. In the second introduction to the Theory of Science (1797), Fichte grants to these expounders of the Critick of pure Reason that it contains some passages where Kant would affirm that sensations must be given to the subject from without as the material conditions of objective reality; but shows that the innumerably repeated declarations of the Critick, that there could be no influence upon us of a real transcendental object outside of us, cannot at all be reconciled with these passages, if any thing other than a simple thought be understood as the ground of the sensations. "So long," adds Fichte, "as Kant does not expressly declare that he derives sensations from an impression of some essentially thing, or, to use his terminology, that sensation must be explained from a transcendental object existing externally to us: so long will I not believe what these expounders tell us of Kant. But if he should give such an explanation, I should sooner regard the Critick of Pure Reason to be a work of chance than of design." For such an explanation the aged Kant did not suffer him long to wait. In the *Intelligenzblatt der Allgemeinen Litteraturzeitung* (1799), he formally, and with much emphasis, rejects the Fichtian improvement of his system, and protests against every interpretation of his writings according to the conceit of any mind, while he maintains the literal interpretation of his theory as laid down in the Critick of Reason. Reinhold remarks upon all this: " Since the well known and public explanation of Kant respecting Fichte's philosophy, there can be no longer a doubt that Kant himself would represent his own system, and desire to have it represented by his readers, entirely otherwise than Fichte had represented and interpreted it. But from this it irresistibly follows, that Kant himself did not regard his system as illogical because it presupposed something external to the subjectivity. Nevertheless, it does not at all follow that Fichte erred when he declared that this system, with such a presupposition, must be illogical." So much for Reinhold. That Kant himself did not fail to see this inconclusiveness, is evident from the changes he introduced into the second edition of the Critick of Pure Reason, where he suffered the idealistic side of his system to fall back decidedly behind the empirical.

From what has been said, we can see the universal standpoint of the Theory of Science; the Ego is made a principle, and from the Ego every thing else is sought to be derived. It hardly needs to be remarked, that by this Ego we are to understand, not any individual, but the universal Ego, the universal rationality. The Ego and the individual, the pure and the empirical Ego, are wholly different conceptions.

We have still the following preface to make concerning the form of the Theory of Science. A theory of science, according to Fichte, must posit some supreme principle, from which every other must be derived. This supreme principle must be absolutely, and through itself, certain. If our human knowledge should be any thing but fragmentary, there must be such a supreme principle. But now, since such a principle does not admit of proof, every thing depends upon giving it a trial. Its test and demonstration can only be thus gained, viz., if we find a principle to which all science may be referred, then is this shown to be a fundamental principle. But besides the first fundamental principle, there are yet two others to be considered, the one of which is unconditioned as to its content, but as to its form, conditioned through and derived from the first fundamental principle; the other the reverse. The relation of these three principles to each other is, in fine, this, viz., that the second stands opposed to the first, while a third is the product of the two. Hence, according to this plan, the first absolute principle starts from the Ego, the second opposes to the Ego a thing or a non-Ego, and the third brings forward the Ego again in reaction against the thing or the non-Ego. This method of Fichte (thesis,—antithesis,—synthesis) is the same as Hegel subsequently adopted, and applied to the

whole system of philosophy, a union of the synthetical and analytical methods. We start with a fundamental synthesis, which
we analyze to produce its antitheses, in order to unite these antitheses again through a second synthesis. But in making this
second synthesis, our analysis discovers still farther antitheses,
which obliges us therefore to find another synthesis, and so onward in the process, till we come at length to antitheses which can
no longer be perfectly but only approximately connected.

We stand now upon the threshold of the *Theory of Science.*
It is divided into three parts. (1) General principles of a theory
of science. (2) Principles of theoretical knowledge. (3) Principles of practical science.

As has already been said, there are three *supreme* fundamental principles, one absolutely unconditioned, and two relatively
unconditioned.

(1.) *The absolutely first and absolutely unconditioned fundamental principle* ought to express that act of the mind which lies
at the basis of all consciousness, and alone makes consciousness
possible. Such is the principle of identity, A=A. This principle remains, and cannot be thought away, though every empirical
determination be removed. It is a fact of consciousness, and
must, therefore, be universally admitted : but at the same time it
is by no means conditioned, like every other empirical fact, but
unconditioned, because it is a free act. By affirming that this
principle is certain without any farther ground, we ascribe to ourselves the faculty of *positing* something absolutely. We do not,
therefore, affirm that A is, but only that if A is, then it is equal
to A. It is no matter now about the content of the principle, we
need only regard its form. The principle A=A is, therefore,
conditioned (hypothetically) as to its content, and unconditioned
only as to its form and its connection. If we would now have a
principle unconditioned in its content as well as in its connection,
we put Ego in the place of A, as we are fully entitled to do, since
the connection of subject and predicate contained in the judgment
A=A is posited in the Ego and through the Ego. Hence A=A
becomes transformed into Ego=Ego. This principle is uncondi-

tioned not only as to its connection, but also as to its content. While we could not, instead of $A=A$, say that A is, yet we can instead of $Ego=Ego$, say that Ego is. All the facts of the empirical consciousness find their ground of explanation in this, viz., that before any thing else is posited in the Ego, the Ego itself is there. This fact, that the Ego is absolutely posited and grounded on itself, is the basis of all acting in the human mind, and shows the pure character of activity in itself. The Ego *is*, because it posits itself, and it only is, because this simple positing of itself is wholly by itself. The being of the Ego is thus seen in the positing of the Ego, and on the other hand, the Ego is enabled *to posit* simply by virtue of its being. It is at the same time the acting, and the product of the action. I am, is the expression of the only possible deed. Logically considered we have, in the first principle of a Theory of Science, $A=A$, the logical law of identity. From the proposition $A=A$, we arrive at the proposition $Ego=Ego$. The latter proposition, however, does not derive its validity from the former, but contrarywise. The prius of all judgments is the Ego, which posits the connection of subject and predicate. The logical law of identity arises, therefore, from $Ego=Ego$. Metaphysically considered, we have in this same first principle of a Theory of Science, the category of *reality*. We obtain this category by abstracting every thing from the content, and reflecting simply upon the mode of acting of the human mind From the Ego, as the absolute subject, every category is derived

(2.) *The second fundamental principle*, conditioned in its content, and only unconditioned in its form, which is just as incapable as the first of demonstration or derivation, is also a fact of the empirical consciousness : it is the proposition non-A is not$=$A. This sentence is unconditioned in its form, because it is free act like the first, from which it cannot be derived ; but in its content, as to its matter it is conditioned, because if a non-A is posited, there must have previously been posited an A. Let us examine this principle more closely. In the first principle, $A=A$, the form of the act was a positing, while in this second principle it is an opposing. There is an absolute opposition, and this opposition, in its simple form, is an act absolutely possible, standing under no condition, limited by no higher ground. But as to its matter, the opposition presupposes a position; the non-A cannot be posited without the A. What non-A is, I do not through that yet know: I only know concerning non-A that it is the opposite of A: hence I only know what non-A is under the condition that I know A. But now A is posited through the Ego; there is originally nothing posited but the Ego, and nothing but this absolutely posited. Hence there can be an absolute opposition only to the Ego. That which is opposed to the Ego is the non-Ego. A non-Ego is absolutely opposed to the Ego, and this is the second fact of the empirical consciousness. In every thing ascribed to the Ego, the contrary, by virtue of this simple opposition, must be ascribed to the non Ego.—As we obtained from the first principle Ego=Ego, the logical law of identity, so now we have, from the second sentence Ego is not = non-Ego, the logical law of contradiction. And metaphysically,—since we wholly abstract the definite act of judgment, and, simply in the form of sequence, conclude not-being from opposite being,—we possess from this second principle the category of *negation*.

(3.) *The third principle*, conditioned in its form, is almost capable of proof, since it is determined by two others. At every step we approach the province where every thing can be proved. This third principle is conditioned in its form, and unconditioned only in its content: *i. e.* the problem, but not the solution of the act to be established through it, has been given through the two preceding principles. The solution is afforded unconditionally and absolutely by a decisive word of the reason. The problem to be solved by this third principle is this, viz., to adjust the contradiction contained in the two former ones. On the one side, the Ego is wholly suppressed by the non-Ego: there can be no positing of the Ego so far as the non-Ego is posited. On the other side, the non-Ego is only an Ego posited in the consciousness, and hence the Ego is not suppressed by the non-Ego. The Ego appearing on the one side to be suppressed, is not really suppressed. Such a result would be non-A=A. In order to remove this contradiction, which threatens to destroy the identity of our consciousness, and the only absolute foundation of our knowledge, we must find in x that which will justify both of the first two principles, and leave the identity of our consciousness undisturbed. The two opposites, the Ego and the non-Ego, should be united in the consciousness, should be alike posited without either excluding the other; they should be received in the identity of the proper consciousness. How shall being and not-being, reality and negation, be conceived together without destroying each other? They will reciprocally *limit* each other. Hence the unknown quantity x, whose terms we are seeking, stands for these limits: limitation is the sought-for act of the Ego, and as category in the thought, we have thus the category of determination or *limitation*. But in limitation, there is also given the category of *quantity*, for when we say that any thing is limited, we mean that its reality is through negation, not *wholly*, but only *partially* suppressed. Thus the conception of limit contains also the conception of divisibility, besides the conceptions of reality and negation. Through the act of limitation, the Ego as well as the non-Ego, is posited as divisible. Still farther, we see how a logical law follows from the third fundamental principle as well as from the first two. If we abstract the definite content, the Ego and the non-Ego, and leave remaining the simple form of the union of opposites through the conception of divisibility, we have then the logical *principle of the ground*, or foundation, which may be expressed in the formula: A in part = non-A, non-A in part = A. Wherever two opposites are alike in one characteristic, we consider the ground as a ground of relation, and wherever two similar things are opposite in one characteristic, we consider the ground as a ground of distinction.—With these three principles we have now exhausted the measure of that which is unconditioned and absolutely certain. We can embrace the three in the following formula:

I posit in the Ego a divisible non Ego over against the divisible Ego. No philosophy can go beyond this cognition, and every fundamental philosophy should go back to this. Just so far as it does this, it becomes science (*Wissenschaftslehre*).

13

Every thing which can appear in a system of knowledge, as well as a farther division of the Theory of Science itself, must be derived from this. The proposition that the Ego and the non-Ego reciprocally limit each other, may be divided into the following two : (1) the Ego posits itself as limited through the non-Ego (*i. e.* the Ego is in a cognitive (or passive) relation) ; (2) the Ego posits the non-Ego as limited through the Ego (*i. e.* the Ego is in an active relation). The former proposition is the basis of the theoretical, and the latter of the practical part of the Theory of Science. The latter part cannot, at the outset, be brought upon the stage ; for the non-Ego, which should be limited by the acting Ego, does not at the outset exist, and we must wait and see whether it will find, in the theoretical part, a reality.

The groundwork of theoretical knowledge advances through an uninterrupted series of antitheses and syntheses. The fundamental synthesis of the theoretical Theory of Science is the proposition : *the Ego posits itself as determined* (limited) *by the non-Ego.* If we analyze this sentence, we find in it two subordinate sentences which are reciprocally opposite. (1) The non-Ego as active determines the Ego, which thus far is passive ; but since all activity must start from the Ego, so (2) the Ego determines itself through an absolute activity. Herein is a contradiction, that the Ego should be at the same time active and passive. Since this contradiction would destroy the above proposition, and also suppress the unity of consciousness, we are forced to seek some point, some new synthesis, in which these given antitheses may be united. This synthesis is attained when we find that the conceptions of action and passion, which are contained under the categories of reality and negation, find their compensation and due adjustment in the conception of divisibility. The propositions : " the Ego determines," and " the Ego is determined," are reconciled in the proposition : " the Ego determines itself in part, and is determined in part." Both, however, should be considered as one and the same. Hence more accurately : as many parts of reality as the Ego posits in itself, so many parts of negation does it posit in the non-Ego ; and as many parts of reality as the Ego posits in the non-Ego, so many parts of negation does it posit in itself. This determination is *reciprocal determination*, or *reciprocal action*. Thus Fichte deduces the last of the three categories under Kant's general category of relation. In a similar way (viz., by finding a synthesis for apparent contradictions), he deduces the two other categories of this class, viz., that of cause, and that of substance. The process is thus : So far as the Ego is determined, and therefore passive, has the non-Ego reality. The category of reciprocal determination, to which we may ascribe indifferently either of the two sides, reality or negation, may, more strictly taken, imply that the Ego is passive, and the non-Ego active. The notion which expresses this relation is that of *causality*. That, to which activity is ascribed, is called *cause* (primal reality), and that to which passiveness is ascribed, is called *effect;* both, conceived in connection, may be termed a *working*. On the other side, the Ego determines itself. Herein is a contradiction ; (1) the Ego determines itself ; it is therefore that which determines, and is thus active ; (2) it determines itself ; it is therefore that which becomes determined, and is thus passive. Thus in one respect and in one action both reality and negation are ascribed to it. To resolve this contradiction, we must find a mode of action which is activity and passiveness in one ; the Ego must determine its passiveness through activity, and its activity through passiveness. This solution is attained by aid of the conception of quantity. In the Ego all reality is first of all posited as absolute quantum, as absolute totality, and thus far the Ego may be compared to a greatest circle which contains all the rest. A definite quantum of activity, or a limited sphere within this greatest circle of activity, is indeed a *reality;* but when compared with the totality of activity, is it also a *negation* of the totality or passiveness. Here we have found the mediation sought for ; it lies in the notion of *substance*. In so far as the Ego is considered as the whole circle, embracing the totality of all realities, is it substance ; but so far as it becomes posited in a determinate sphere of this circle, is it accidental. No accidence is conceivable without substance ; for, in order to know that any thing is a definite reality, it must first be referred to reality in general, or to substance. In every change we think of substance in the universal; accidence is something specific (determinate), which changes with every changing cause. *There is originally but one substance, the Ego ;* in this one substance all possible accidents, and therefore all possible realities, are posited. The Ego alone is the absolutely infinite. The Ego, as thinking and as acting, indicates a limitation. The Fichtian theory is accordingly Spinozism, only (as Jacobi strikingly called it) a reversed and idealistic Spinozism.

Let us look back a moment. The objectivity which Kant had allowed to exist Fichte has destroyed. There is *only* the Ego. But the Ego presupposes a non-Ego, and therefore a kind of object. How the Ego comes to posit such an object, must the theoretical Theory of Science now proceed to show.

There are two extreme views respecting the relation of the Ego to the non-Ego, according as we start from the conception of cause, or that of substance. (1) Starting from the conception of cause, we have posited through the passiveness of the Ego an activity of the non-Ego. This passiveness of the Ego must have some ground. This cannot lie in the Ego, which in itself posits only activity. Consequently it lies in the non-Ego. Here the distinction between action and passion is apprehended, not simply as quantitative (*i. e.,* viewing the passiveness as a diminished activity), but the passion is in quality opposed to the action; a presupposed activity of the non-Ego is, therefore, a real ground of the passiveness in the Ego. (2) Starting from the conception of substance, we have posited a passiveness of the Ego through its own activity. Here the passiveness in respect of quality is the same as activity, it being only a diminished activity. While, therefore, according to the first view, the passive Ego has a ground distinct in quality from the Ego, and thus a real ground, yet here its ground is only a diminished activity of the Ego, distinct only in quantity from the Ego, and is thus an ideal ground. The former view is dogmatic realism, the latter is dogmatic idealism. The latter affirms: all reality of the non-

Ego is only a reality given it from the Ego; the former declares: nothing can be given, unless there be something to receive, unless an independent reality of the non-Ego, as thing in itself, be pre-supposed. Both views present thus a contradiction, which can only be removed by a new synthesis. Fichte attempted this syn-thesis of idealism and realism, by bringing out a mediating sys-tem of critical idealism. For this purpose he sought to show that the ideal ground and the real ground are one and the same. Neither is the simple activity of the Ego a ground for the reality of the non-Ego, nor is the simple activity of the non-Ego a ground for the passiveness in the Ego. Both must be conceived together in this way, viz., the activity of the Ego meets a *hin-drance*, which is set up against it, not without some assistance of the Ego, and which circumscribes and reflects in itself this activ-ity of the Ego. The hindrance is found when the subjective can be no farther extended, and the expanding activity of the Ego is driven back into itself, producing as its result self-limita-tion. What we call objects are nothing other than the different impinging of the activity of the Ego on some inconceivable hin-drance, and these determinations of the Ego, we carry over to something external to ourselves, and represent them to ourselves as space filling matter. That which Fichte calls a hindrance through the non-Ego, is thus in fact the same as Kant calls thing essentially, the only difference being that with Fichte it is made subjective. From this point Fichte then deduces the subjective activities of the Ego, which mediate, or seek to mediate, theoret-ically, the Ego with the non-Ego—as imagination, representation (sensation, intuition, feeling), understanding, faculty of judgment, reason; and in connection with this he brought out the subjective projections of the intuition, space, and time.

We have now reached the third part of the Theory of Sci-ence, viz., *the foundation of the practical*. We have seen that the Ego represents. But that it may represent does not depend upon the Ego alone, but is determined by something external to it. We could in no way conceive of a representation, except through the presupposition that the Ego finds some hindrance to its undetermined and unlimited activity. Accordingly the Ego, as intelligence, is universally dependent upon an indefinite, and hitherto wholly indefinable non-Ego, and only through and by means of such non-Ego, is it intelligence. A finite being is only finite as intelligence. These limits, however, we shall break through. The practical law which unites the finite Ego with the infinite, can depend upon nothing external to ourselves. The Ego, according to all its determinations, should be posited absolutely through itself, and hence should be wholly independent of every possible non-Ego. Consequently, the absolute Ego and the intelligent Ego, both of which should constitute but one, are opposed to each other. This contradiction is obviated, when we see that because the absolute Ego is capable of no passiveness, but is absolute activity, therefore the Ego determines, through itself, that hitherto unknown non-Ego, to which the hindrance has been ascribed. The limits which the Ego, as theoretic, has set over against itself in the non-Ego, it must, as practical, seek to destroy, and absorb again the non-Ego in itself (or conceive it as the self-limitation of the Ego). The Kantian primacy of the practical reason is here made a truth. The transition of the theoretical part into the practical, the necessity of advancing from the one to the other, Fichte represents more closely thus:— The theoretical Theory of Science had to do with the mediation of the Ego, and the non-Ego. For this end it introduced one connecting link after another, without ever attaining its end. Then enters the reason with the absolute and decisive word : " there ought to be no non-Ego, since the non-Ego can in no way be united with the Ego ; " and with this the knot is cut, though not untied. Thus it is the incongruity between the absolute (practical) Ego, and the finite (intelligent) Ego, which is carried over beyond the theoretical province into the practical. True, this incongruity does not wholly disappear, even in the practical province, where the act is only an infinite striving to surpass the limits of the non-Ego. The Ego, so far as it is practical, has, indeed, the tendency to pass beyond the actual world, and establish an ideal world, as it would be were every reality posited by the absolute Ego; but this striving is always confined to the finite partly through itself, because it goes out towards objects, and objects are finite, and partly through the resistance of the sensible world. We ought to seek to reach the infinite, but we cannot do it; this striving and inability is the impress of our destiny for eternity.

Thus—and in these words Fichte brings together the result of the Theory of Science—the whole being of finite rational natures is comprehended and exhausted: an original idea of our absolute being; an effort to reflect upon ourselves, in order to gain this idea; a limitation, not of this striving, but of our own existence, which first becomes actual through this limitation, or through an opposite principle, a non-Ego, or our finiteness; a self-consciousness, and especially a consciousness of our practical strivings; a determination accordingly of our representations, and through these of our actions; a constant widening of our limits into the infinite.

2. FICHTE'S PRACTICAL PHILOSOPHY.—The principles which Fichte had developed in his Theory of Science he applied to practical life, especially to the theory of rights and morals. He sought to deduce here every thing with methodical rigidness, without admitting any thing which could not be proved from experience. Thus, in the theory of rights and of morals, he will not presuppose a plurality of persons, but first deduces this: even that the man has a body is first demonstrated, though, to be sure, not stringently.

The Theory of Rights (*the rights of nature*) Fichte founds upon the conception of the individual. First, he deduces the conception of rights, and as follows:—A finite rational being cannot posit itself without ascribing to itself a free activity. Through this positing of its faculties to a free activity, this rational being posits an external world of sense, for it can ascribe to itself no activity till it has posited an object towards which this activity may be directed. Still farther, this free activity of a rational being presupposes other rational beings, for without these it would never be conscious that it was free. We have therefore a plu-

rality of free individuals, each one of whom has a sphere of free
activity. This co-existence of free individuals is not possible
without a relation of rights. Since no one with freedom passes
beyond his sphere, and each one therefore limits himself, they recognize each other as rational and free. This relation of a reciprocal
acting through intelligence and freedom between rational beings,
according to which each one has his freedom limited by the conception of the possibility of the other's freedom, under the condition also that this other limits his own freedom also through
that of the first, is called a *relation of rights.* The supreme
maxim of a theory of rights is therefore this : limit thy freedom
through the conception of the freedom of every other person with
whom thou canst be connected. After Fichte has attempted the
application of this conception of rights, and for this end has deduced the corporeity, the anthropological side of man, he passes
over to a proper *theory of rights.* The theory of rights may be
divided into three parts. (1) Rights which belong to the simple
conception of person are called *original rights.* The original
right is the absolute right of the person to be only a cause in the
sensible world, though he may be absolutely (in other relations
than to the sense) an effect. In this are contained, (*a*) the right
of personal (bodily) freedom, and (*b*) the right of property. But
every relation of rights between individual persons is conditioned
through each one's recognition of the rights of the other. Each
one must limit the quantum of his free acts for the sake of the
freedom of the other, and only so far as the other has respect to
my freedom need I have regard to his. In case, therefore, the
other does not respect my original rights, some mechanical necessity must be sought in order to secure the rights of person, and
this involves (2) the *Right of Coercion.* The laws of punishment
have their end in securing that the opposite of that which is in
tended shall follow every unrighteous aim, that every vicious pur
pose shall be destroyed, and the right in its integrity be estab
lished. To establish such a law of coercion, and to secure a uni
versal coercive power, the free individuals must enter into covenant among themselves. Such a covenant is only possible on the

ground of a common nature.   Natural right, *i. e.* the rightful relation between man and man, presupposes thus (3) a *civil right*, viz.,
(*a*) a free covenant, a compact of citizens by which the free individuals guarantee to each other their reciprocal rights; (*b*) positive
laws, a civil legislation, through which the common will of all becomes law; (*c*) an executive force, a civil power which executes
the common will, and in which, therefore, the private will and the
common will are synthetically united.   The particular view of
Fichte's theory of rights is this: on the one side there is the state
as reason demands (philosophical theory of rights), and on the
other side the state as it actually is (theory of positive rights and
of the state).   But now comes up the problem, to make the actual
state ever more and more conformable to the state of reason.
The science which has this approximation for its aim, is polity.
We can demand of no actual state a perfect conformity to the
idea of a state.   Every state constitution is according to right, if
it only leaves possible an advancement to a better state, and the
only constitution wholly contrary to right is that whose end is to
hold every thing just as it is.

The absolute Ego of the Theory of Science is separated in the
Theory of Rights into an infinite number of persons with rights:
to bring it out again in its unity is the problem of *Ethics*.   Right
and morals are essentially different.   Right is the external necessity to omit or to do something in order not to infringe upon the
freedom of another; the inner necessity to do or omit something wholly independent of external ends, constitutes the moral
nature of man.   And as the theory of rights arose from the conflict
of the impulse of freedom in one subject with the impulse of freedom in another subject, so does the theory of morals or ethics arise
from such a conflict, which, in the present case, is not external but
internal, between two impulses in one and the same person. (1) The
rational being is impelled towards absolute independence, and
strives after freedom for the sake of freedom.   This fundamental
impulse may be called the pure impulse, and it furnishes the
formal principle of ethics, the principle of absolute autonomy, of
absolute indeterminableness through anything external to the Ego.

13*

But (2) as the rational being is actually empirical and finite, as it by nature posits over against itself a non-Ego and posits itself as corporeal, so there is found beside the pure impulse another, the impulse of nature, which makes for its end not freedom but enjoyment. This impulse of nature furnishes the material, utilitarian (eudœmoniacal) principle of striving after a connected enjoyment. Both impulses, which from a transcendental standpoint are one and the same original impulse of the human being, strive after unity, and furnish a third impulse which is a mingling of the two. The pure impulse gives the form, and the natural impulse the content of an action. It is true that sensuous objects will be chosen, but by virtue of the pure impulse these are modified so as to conform to the absolute Ego. This mingled impulse is now the moral impulse. It mediates the pure and the natural impulse. But since these two lie infinitely apart, the approximation of the natural to the pure impulse is an infinite progression. The intent in an action is directed towards a complete freeing from nature, and it is only the result of our limitation that the act should remain still conformable to the natural impulse. Since the Ego can never be independent so long as it is Ego, the final aim of the rational being lies in infinity. There must be a course in whose progress the Ego can conceive itself as approximating towards absolute independence. This course is determined in infinity in the idea; there is, therefore, no possible case in which it is not determined what the pure impulse should demand. We might name this course the moral determination (destiny) of the finite rational being. *The principle of ethics is, therefore: Always fulfil thy destiny!* That which is in every moment conformable to our moral destiny, is at the same time demanded by our natural impulse, though it does not follow that every thing which the latter demands agrees therefore with the former. I ought to act only when conscious that something is duty, and I ought to discharge the duty for its own sake. The blind motives of sympathy, love of mankind, &c., have not, as mere impulses of nature, morality. The moral impulse has causality as having none, for it demands be free! Through the conception of the absolute ought, is the rational being absolutely independent, and is represented thus only when acting from duty. The formal condition of the morality of our actions, is: act always according to the best conviction of thy duty; or, act according to thy conscience. The absolute criterion of the correctness of our conviction of duty is a feeling of truth and certainty. This immediate feeling never deceives, for it only exists with the perfect harmony of our empirical Ego with that which is pure and original. From this point Fichte developes his particular ethics, or theory of duties, which, however, we must here pass by.

Fichte's *theory of religion* is developed in the above mentioned treatise: " *On the ground of our faith in a divine government of the world,*" and in the writings which he subsequently put forth in its defence. The moral government of the world, says Fichte, we assume to be the divine. This divine government becomes living and actual in us through right-doing: it is presupposed in every one of our actions which are only performed in the presupposition that the moral end is attainable in the world of sense. The faith in such an order of the world comprises the whole of faith, for this living and active moral order is God; we need no other God, and can comprehend no other. There is no ground in the reason to go out of this moral order of the world, and by concluding from design to a designer, affirm a separate being as its cause. Is, then, this order an accidental one? It is the absolute First of all objective knowledge. But now if you should be allowed to draw the conclusion that there is a God as a separate being, what have you gained by this? This being should be distinct from you and the world, it should work in the latter according to conceptions; it should, therefore, be capable of conceptions, and possess personality and consciousness. But what do you call personality and consciousness? Certainly that which you have found in yourself, which you have learned to know in yourself, and which you have characterized with such a name. But that you cannot conceive of this without limitation and finiteness, you might see by the slightest attention to the construction of this conception. By attaching, therefore, such a predicate to this being, you bring it down to a finite, and make it a being like your-self; you have not conceived God as you intended to do, but have only multiplied yourself in thought. The conception of God, as a separate substance, is impossible and contradictory. God has essential existence only as such a moral order of the world. Every belief in a divine being, which contains any thing more than the conception of the moral order of the world, is an abomination to me, and in the highest degree unworthy of a rational being.—Religion and morality are, on this standpoint, as on that of Kant, naturally one; both are an apprehending of the supersensible, the former through action and the latter through faith. This "Religion of joyous right-doing," Fichte farther carried out in the writings which he put forth to rebut the charge of atheism. He affirms that nothing but the principles of the new philosophy could restore the degenerate religious sense among men, and bring to light the inner essence of the Christian doctrine. Especially he seeks to show this in his "Appeal" to the public. In this he says: to furnish an answer to the questions: what is good? what is true? is the aim of my philosophical system. We must start with the affirmation that there is something absolutely true and good; that there is something which can hold and bind the free flight of thought. There is a voice in man which cannot be silenced, which affirms that there is a duty, and that it must be done simply for its own sake. Resting on this basis, there is opened to us an entirely new world in our being; we attain a higher existence, which is independent of all nature, and is grounded simply in ourselves. I would call this absolute self-sat-isfaction of the reason, this perfect freedom from all dependence, blessedness. As the single but unerring means of blessedness, my conscience points me to the fulfilment of duty. I am, therefore, impressed by the unshaken conviction, that there is a rule and fixed order, according to which the purely moral disposition neces-sarily makes blessed. It is absolutely necessary, and it is the essential element in religion, that the man who maintains the dig-nity of his reason, will repose on the faith in this order of a moral world, will regard each one of his duties as an enactment of this order, and will joyfully submit himself to, and find bliss in, every consequence of his duty. Thou shalt know God if I can only beget in thee a dutiful character, and though to others of us thou mayest seem to be still in the world of sense, yet for thyself art thou already a partaker of eternal life.

II. THE LATER FORM OF FICHTE'S PHILOSOPHY.—Every thing of importance which Fichte accomplished as a speculative philosopher, is contained in the Theory of Science as above considered. Subsequently, after his departure from Jena, his system gradually became modified, and from different causes. Partly, because it was difficult to maintain the rigid idealism of the Theory of Science; partly, because Schelling's natural philosophy, which now appeared, was not without an influence upon Fichte's thinking, though the latter denied this and became involved in a bitter controversy with Schelling; and, partly, his outward relations, which were far from being happy, contributed to modify his view of the world. Fichte's writings, in this second period, are for the most part popular, and intended for a mixed class of readers. They all bear the impress of his acute mind, and of his exalted manly character, but lack the originality and the scientific sequence of his earlier productions. Those of them which are scientific do not satisfy the demands which he himself had previously laid down with so much strictness, both for himself and others, in respect of genetic construction and philosophical method. His doctrine at this time seems rather as a web, of his old subjective idealistic conceptions and the newly added objective idealism, so loosely connected that Schelling might call it the completest syncretism and eclecticism. His new standpoint is chiefly distinguished from his old by his attempt to merge his subjective idealism into an objective pantheism (in accordance with the new Platonism), to transmute the Ego of his earlier philosophy into the absolute, or the thought of God. God, whose conception he had formerly placed only at the end of his system, in the doubtful form of a moral order of the world, becomes to him now the absolute beginning, and single element of his philosophy. This gave to his philosophy an entirely new color. The moral severity gives place to a religious mildness; instead of the Ego and the Ought, life and love are now the chief features of his philosophy; in place of the exact dialectic of the Theory of Science, he now makes choice of mystical and metaphorical modes of expression.

This second period of Fichte's philosophy is especially characterized by its inclination to religion and Christianity, as exhibited most prominently in the essay "*Direction to a Blessed Life.*" Fichte here affirms that his new doctrine is exactly that of Christianity, and especially of the Gospel according to John. He would make this gospel alone the clear foundation of Christian truth, since the other apostles remained half Jews after their conversion, and adhered to the fundamental error of Judaism, that the world had a creation in time. Fichte lays great weight upon the first part of John's prologue, where the formation of the world out of nothing is confuted, and a true view laid down of a revelation co-eternal with God, and necessarily given with his being. That which this prologue says of the incarnation of the Logos in the person of Jesus, has, according to Fichte, only a historic validity. The absolute and eternally true standpoint is, that at all times, and in every one, without exception, who is vitally sensible of his union with God, and who actually and in fact yields up his whole individual life to the divine life within him,—the eternal word becomes flesh in the same way as in Jesus Christ and holds a personal, sensible, and human existence. The whole communion of believers, the first-born alike with the later born, coincides in the Godhead, the common source of life for all. And so then, Christianity having gained its end, disappears again in the eternal truth, and affirms that every man should come to a union with God. So long as man desires to be himself any thing whatsoever, God does not come to him, for no man can become God. But just so soon as he purely, wholly, and radically gives up himself, God alone remains, and is all and in all. The man himself can beget no God, but he can give up himself as a proper negation, and thus he disappears in God.

The result of his advanced philosophizing, Fichte has briefly and clearly comprehended in the following lines, which we extract from two posthumous sonnets :

The Eternal One
Lives in my life and sees in my beholding.
Nought is but God, and God is nought but life.
Clearly the vail of things rises before thee ;
It is thyself, what though the mortal die
And hence there lives but God in thine endeavors,
If thou wilt look through that which lives beyond this death,
The vail of things shall seem to thee as vail,
And unveiled thou shalt look upon the life divine.

———•♦•———

SECTION XLII.

HERBART.

A peculiar, and in many respects noticeable, carrying out of the Kantian philosophy, was attempted by *Johann Friedrich Herbart,* who was born at Oldenburg in 1776, chosen professor of philosophy in Göttingen in 1805 ; made Kant's successor at Königsberg in 1808, and recalled to Göttingen in 1833, where he died in 1841. His philosophy, instead of making, like most other systems, for its principle, an idea of the reason, followed the direction of Kant, and expended itself mainly in a critical examination of the subjective experience. It is essentially a criticism, but with results which are peculiar, and which differ wholly from those of Kant. Its fundamental position in the history of philosophy is an isolated one ; instead of regarding antecedent systems as elements of a true philosophy, it looks upon almost all of them as failures. It is especially hostile to the post-Kantian German philosophy, and most of all to Schelling's philosophy of nature, in which it could only behold a phantom and a delusion ; sooner than come in contact with this, it would join Hegelianism, of which it is the opposite pole. We will give a brief exposition f its prominent thoughts.

1. The Basis and Starting-point of Philosophy is, accord
ing to Herbart, the common view of things, or a knowledge which
shall accord with experience.   A philosophical system is in reality nothing but an attempt by which a thinker strives to solve certain questions which present themselves before him.   Every question brought up in philosophy should refer itself singly and solely
to that which is given, and must arise from this source alone, because there is no other original field of certainty, for men, than
experience alone.   Every philosophy should begin with it.   The
thinking should yield itself to experience, which should lead it,
and not be led by it.   Experience, therefore, is the only object
and basis of philosophy ; that which is not given cannot be an object of thought, and it is impossible to establish any knowledge
which transcends the limits of experience.

2. The first act of Philosophy.—Though the material furnished by experience is the basis of philosophy, yet, since it is
furnished, it stands outside of philosophy.   The question arises,
what is the first act or beginning of philosophy ?   The thinking
should first separate itself from experience, that it may clearly
see the difficulties of its undertaking.   *The beginning of philosophy*, where the thinking rises above that which is given, is accordingly doubt or *scepticism*.   Scepticism is twofold, a lower
and a higher.   The lower scepticism simply doubts that things
are so constituted as they appear to us to be ; the higher scepticism passes beyond the form of the phenomenon, and inquires
whether in reality any thing there exists.   It doubts *e. g.* the succession in time ; it asks in reference to the forms of the objects
of nature which exhibit design, whether the design is perceived,
or only attached to them in the thought, &c.   Thus the problems
which form the content of metaphysics, are gradually brought
out.   The result of scepticism is therefore not negative, but positive.   Doubt is nothing but the thinking upon those conceptions
of experience which are the material of philosophy.   Through this
reflection, scepticism leads us to the knowledge that these conceptions of experience, though they refer to something given, yet
contain no conceivable content free from logical incongruities.

3. REMODELLING OF THE CONCEPTIONS OF EXPERIENCE.—Metaphysics, according to Herbart, is the science of that which is conceivable in experience. Our view thus far has been a twofold one. On the one side we hold fast to the opinion that the single basis of philosophy is experience, and on the other side, scepticism has shaken the credibility of experience. The point now is to transform this scepticism into a definite knowledge of metaphysical problems. Conceptions from experience crowd'upon us, which cannot be thoughts, *i. e.* they may indeed be thought by the ordinary understanding, but this thinking is obscure and confused, and does not separate nor compare opposing characteristics. But an acute process of thought, a logical analysis, will find in the conceptions of experience (*e.g.* space, time, becoming, motion, &c.) contradictions and characteristics, which are totally inconsistent with each other. What now is to be done ? We may not reject these conceptions, for they are given, and beyond the given we cannot step ; we cannot retain them, for they are inconceivable and cannot logically be established. The only way of escape which remains to us is to remodel them. *To remodel the conceptions of experience*, to eliminate their contradictions, is the proper act of speculation. Scepticism has brought to light the more definite problems which involve a contradiction, and whose solution it therefore belongs to metaphysics to attempt ; the most important of these are the problems of inherence, change, and the Ego.

The relation between Herbart and Hegel is very clear at this point. Both are agreed respecting the contradictory nature of the determinations of thought, and the conceptions of experience. But from this point they separate. It is the nature of these conceptions as of every thing, says Hegel, to be an inner contradiction ; becoming, for instance, is essentially the unity of being, and not being, &c. This is impossible, says Herbart, on the other side, so long as the principle of contradiction is valid ; if the conceptions of experience contain inner contradictions, this is not the fault of the objective world, but of the representing subject who must rectify his false apprehension by remodelling these conceptions, and eliminating the contradiction. Herbart thus charges the

philosophy of Hegel with empiricism, because it receives from experience these contradictory conceptions unchanged, and not only
regards these as established, but even goes so far as to metamor-
phose logic on their account, and this simply because they are
given in experience, though their contradictory nature is clearly
seen.　Hegel and Herbart stand related to each other as Heraclitus and Parmenides (*cf.* § § VI. and VII.)

4. HERBART'S REALS.—From this point Herbart reaches his
" reals " (*Realen*) as follows : To discover the contradictions, he
says, in all our conceptions of experience, might lead us to absolute scepticism, and to despair of the truth.　But here we re-
member that if the existence of every thing real be denied, then
the appearance, sensation, representation, and thought itself
would be destroyed.　We perceive, therefore, just as strong an
indication of being as of appearance.　We cannot, indeed, ascribe to the given any true and essential being *per se*, it is not
per se alone, but only on, or in, or through something other.
The truly being is an absolute being, which as such excludes
every thing relative and dependent ; it is *absolute position*,
which it is not for us first to posit, but only to recognize.　In so
far as this being is attributed to any thing, this latter possesses
reality.　The truly being is, therefore, ever a *quale*, a something
which is considered as being.　In order now that this posited
may correspond to the conditions which lie in the conception of
absolute position, the *what* of the real must be thought (*a*) as
absolutely positive or affirmative, *i. e.* without any negation or
limitation, which might destroy again the absoluteness ; (*b*) as absolutely simple, *i. e.* in no way, as a multiplicity or admitting of
inner antitheses ; (*c*) as indeterminate by any conceptions of greatness, *i. e.* not as a quantum which may be divided and extended
in time and space ; hence, also, not as a constant greatness or continuity.　But we must never forget that this being or this absolute
reality is not simply something thought, but is something independent and resting on itself, and hence it is simply to be recognized by the thinking.　The conception of this thinking lies at
the basis of all Herbart's metaphysics.　Take an example of this.

The first problem to be solved in metaphysics is the problem of inherence, or the thing with its characteristics. Every perceptible thing represents itself to the senses as a complex of several characteristics. But all the attributes of a thing which are given in perception are relative. We say *e. g.* that sound is a property of a certain body. It sounds—but it cannot do this without air; what now becomes of this property in a space without air? Again, we say that a body is heavy, but it is only so on the earth. Or again, that a body is colored, but light is necessary for this; what now becomes of such a property in darkness? Still farther, a multiplicity of properties is incompatible with the unity of an object. If you ask *what* is this thing, you are answered with the sum of its characteristics; it is soft, white, full-sounding, heavy,—but your question was of one, not of many. The answer only affirms what the thing has, not what it is. Moreover, the list of characteristics is always incomplete. The what of a thing can therefore lie neither in the individual given properties, nor in their unity. In determining what a thing is, we have only this answer remaining, viz., the thing is that unknown, which we must posit before we can posit any thing as lying in the given properties; in a word, it is the substance. For if, in order to see what the thing purely and essentially is, we take away the characteristics which it may have, we find that nothing more remains, and we perceive that what we considered as the real thing was only a complex of characteristics, and the union of these in one whole. But since every appearance indicates a definite reality, and thus since there must be as much reality as there is appearance, we have to consider the reality, which lies at the basis of the thing, with its characteristics, as a complex of many simple substances or monads, and whose quality is different in different instances. When our experience has led us to a repeated grouping together of these monads, we call the group a thing. Let us now briefly look at the formation of those fundamental conceptions of metaphysics, which involve the same thoughts through the fundamental conception of being. First, there is the conception of causality, which cannot be maintained

in its ordinary form. All that we can perceive in the act is succession in time, and not the necessary connection of cause with
effect. The cause in itself can be neither transcendent nor immanent; it cannot be transcendent, because a real influence of
one real thing upon another, contradicts the conception of the
absolute reality; nor immanent, for then the substance must be
thought as one with its characteristics, which contradicts the investigations concerning a thing with its characteristics. We can
just as little find in the conception of the real an answer to the
question, how one determinate being can be brought into contact
with another, for the real is the absolute unchangeable. We can
therefore only explain the conception of causality on the ground
that the different reals which lie at the basis of the characteristics are conceived, each one for itself, as cause of the phenomenon; there being just as many causes as there are phenomena.
The problem of change, is intimately connected with the conception of cause. Since, however, according to Herbart, there is no
inner change, no self-determination, no becoming and no life; since
the monads are, and remain in themselves unchangeable, they do
not therefore *become* different in respect of quality, but they *are*
originally different one from another, and each one exhibits its
equality without ever any change. The problem of change can
thus only be solved through the theory of the disturbance and
self-preservation of these essences. But if that which we call
not simply an apparent but an actual event, in the essence of the
monads, may be reduced to a "self-preservation," as the last
gleam of an activity and life, still we have the question ever remaining, how to explain the appearance of change. For this it
is necessary to bring in two auxiliary conceptions; first, that of
accidental views, and second, that of intellectual spaces. The
accidental views, an expression taken from mathematics, signify,
in reference to the problem before us this much, viz., one and the
same conception may often be considered in very different relations to some other essence, without the slightest change in its
own essence, *e. g.* a straight line may be considered as radius or
as tangent, and a tone as harmonious or discordant. By help of

these accidental views, we may now regard that which actually results in the monad, when other monads, opposite in quality, come in contact with it, as on the one side an actual occurrence, though on the other side, no actual change can be imputed to the original condition of the monads (a gray color, *e. g.* seems comparatively white by the side of black, and comparatively black by the side of white, without changing at all its quality). A further auxiliary conception is that of intellectual space, which arises when we must consider these essences as at the same time together and not together. By means of this conception we can eliminate the contradictions from the conception of movement. Lastly, it can be seen that the conception of matter and that of the Ego (in psychologically explaining which, the rest of the metaphysics is occupied) are, like the preceding ones, no less contradictory in themselves than they are irreconcilable with the fundamental conception of the real; for neither can an extended being, like matter, be formed out of spaceless monads—and with matter, therefore, fall also the ordinary conceptions of space and time—nor can we admit, without transformation, the conception of the Ego, since it exhibits the contradictory conception of a thing with many and changing characteristics (conditions, powers, faculties, &c.)

We are reminded by Herbart's "*reals*" of the atomic theory of the atomists (*cf.* § IX. 2), of the Eleatic theory of the one being (*cf.* § VI.), and of Leibnitz's monadology. His reals however are distinguished from the atoms by not possessing impenetrability. The monads of Herbart may be just as well represented in the same space as a mathematical point may be conceived as accurately coexisting with another in the same place. In this respect the "real" of Herbart has a far greater similarity to the "one" of the Eleatics. Both are simple, and to be conceived in intellectual spaces, but the essential difference is, that Herbart's substances exist in numbers distinct from one another, and even from opposites among themselves. Herbart's simple quantities have already been compared to the monads of Leibnitz, but these latter have essentially a power of representation; they are essences with inner circumstances, while, according to Herbart, representation, just as little as every other circumstance, belongs to the essence itself.

5. PSYCHOLOGY is connected with metaphysics. The Ego is primarily a metaphysical problem, and comes in this respect under the category of the thing with its characteristics. It is a real with many properties changing circumstances, powers, faculties, activities, &c., and thus is not without contradictions. But then the Ego is a psychological principle, and here those contradictions may be considered which lie in the ideality of subject and object. The subject posits itself and is therefore itself object. But this posited object is nothing other than the positing subject. Thus the Ego is, as Fichte says, subject-object, and, as such, full of the hardest contradictions, for subject and object will never be affirmed as one and the same without contradiction. But now if the Ego is given it cannot be thrown away, but must be purified from its contradictions. This occurs whenever the Ego is conceived as that which represents, and the different sensations, thoughts, &c. are embraced under the common conception of changing appearance. The solution of this problem is similar to that of inherence. As in the latter problem the thing was apprehended as a complex of as many reals as it has characteristics, just so here the Ego; but with the Ego inner circumstances and representations correspond to the characteristics. Thus that which we are accustomed to name Ego is nothing other than the soul. The soul as a monad, as absolutely being, is therefore simple, eternal, indissoluble, from which we may conclude its eternal existence. From this standpoint Herbart combats the ordinary course of psychology which ascribes certain powers and faculties to the soul. That which stands out in the soul is nothing other than self-preservation, which can only be manifold and changing in opposition to other reals. The causes of changing circumstances are therefore these other reals, which come variously in conflict with the soul-monad, and thus produce that apparently infinite manifoldness of sensations, representations, and affections. This theory of self-preservation lies at the basis of all Herbart's psychology. That which psychology ordinarily calls feeling, thinking, representing,

&c., are only specific differences in the self-preservation of the soul; they indicate no proper condition of the inner real essence itself, but only relations between the reals, relations, which, coming up together at the same time from different sides, are partly suppressed, partly forwarded, and partly modified Consciousness is the sum of those relations in which the soul stands to other essences. But the relations to the objects, and hence to the representations corresponding to these, are not all equally strong; one presses, restricts, and obscures another, a relation of equilibrium which can be calculated according to the doctrine of statics. But the suppressed representations do not wholly disappear, but waiting on the threshold of consciousness for the favorable moment when they shall be permitted again to arise, they join themselves with kindred representations, and press forward with united energies. This movement of the representations (sketched in a masterly manner by Herbart) may be calculated according to the rules of mathematics, and this is Herbart's well known application of mathematics to the empirical theory of the soul. The representations which were pressed back, which wait on the threshold of consciousness and only work in the darkness, and of which we are only half conscious, are feelings. They express themselves as desires, according as their struggle forward is more or less successful. Desire becomes will when united with the hope of success. The will is no separate faculty of the mind, but consists only in the relation of the dominant representations to the others. The power of deciding and the character of a man, prominently depend upon the constant presence in the consciousness of a certain number of representations, while other representations are weakened, or denied an entrance over the threshold of consciousness.

6. THE IMPORTANCE OF HERBART'S PHILOSOPHY.—Herbart's philosophy is important mainly for its metaphysics and psychology. In the other spheres and activities of the human mind, *e. g.* rights, morality, the state, art, religion, his philosophy is mostly barren of results, and though there are not wanting here striking observations, yet these have no connection with the speculative principles of the system. Herbart fundamentally isolates the different phil-

osophical sciences, distinguishing especially and in the strictest manner between theoretical and practical philosophy. He charges the effort after unity in philosophy, with occasioning the greatest errors; for logical, metaphysical, and æsthetic forms are entirely diverse. Ethics and æsthetics have to do with objects in which an immediate evidence appears, but this is foreign to the whole nature of metaphysics, which can only gain its knowledge as errors have been removed. Æsthetic judgments on which practical philosophy rests, are independent of the reality of any object, and appear with immediate certainty in the midst of the strongest metaphysical doubts. Moral elements, says Herbart, are pleasing and displeasing relations of the will. He thus grounds the whole practical philosophy upon æsthetic judgments. The æsthetic judgment is an involuntary and immediate judgment, which attaches to certain objects, without proof, the predicates of goodness and badness.—Here is seen the greatest difference between Herbart and Kant.

We may characterize, on the whole, the philosophy of Herbart as a carrying out of the monadology of Leibnitz, full of enduring acuteness, but without any inner fruitfulness or capacity of development.

SECTION XLIII.

SCHELLING.

Schelling sprang from *Fichte.* We may pass on to an exposition of his philosophy without any farther introduction, since that which it contains from Fichte forms a part of its historical development, and will therefore be treated of as this is unfolded.

Friedrich Wilhelm Joseph *Schelling* was born at Leonberg, in W rtemberg, January 27th, 1775. With a very precocious development, he entered the theological seminary at Tübingen in his fifteenth year, and devoted himself partly to philology and mythology, but especially to Kant's philosophy. During his course as a student, he was in personal connection with Hölderlin and Hegel. Schelling came before the world as an author very early. In 1792 appeared his graduating treatise on the third chapter of Genesis, in which he gave an interesting philosophical signification to the Mosaic account of the fall. In the following year, 1793, he published in *Paulus'* Memorabilia an essay of a kindred nature " *On the Myths and Philosophemes of the Ancient World.*" To the last year of his abode at Tübingen belong the two philosophical writings : " *On the Possibility of a Form for Philosophy,*" and " *On the Ego as a Principle of Philosophy, or on the Unconditioned in Human Knowledge.*" After completing his university studies, Schelling went to Leipsic as tutor to the Baron von Riedesel, but soon afterwards repaired to Jena, where he became the pupil and co-laborer of Fichte. After Fichte's departure from Jena, he became himself, 1798, teacher of philosophy there, and now began, removing himself from Fichte's standpoint, to develope more and more his own peculiar views. He published in Jena the *Journal of Speculative Physics*, and also in company with Hegel, *the Critical Journal.* In the year 1803 he went to Würzburg as professor *ordinarius* of philosophy. In 1807 he repaired to Munich as member *ordinarius* of the newly established academy of sciences there. The year after he became general secretary of the Academy of the plastic arts, and subsequently, when the university professorship was established at Munich, he became its incumbent. After the death of Jacobi, he was chosen president of the Munich Academy. In 1841 he removed to Berlin, where he has sometimes held lectures. For the last ten years Schelling has written nothing of importance, although he has repeatedly promised an exposition of his present system. By far the greater portion of his writings belongs to his early life. Schelling's philosophy is no completed system of which his separate works are the constituent elements ; but, like Plato's, it has a historical development, a course of formative steps which the philosopher has passed through in his

14

own life. Instead of systematically elaborating the separate
sciences from the standpoint of his principle, Schelling has gone
back repeatedly to the beginning again, seeking ever for new
foundations and new standpoints, connecting these for the most part
(like Plato) with some antecedent philosophemes, (Fichte, Spinoza, New Platonism, Leibnitz, Jacob Bœhme, Gnosticism,) which
in their order he attempted to interweave with his system. We
must modify accordingly our exposition of Schelling's Philosophy,
and take up its different periods, separated according to the different groups of his writings.*

I. First Period. Schelling's Procession from Fichte.

Schelling's starting point was Fichte, whom he decidedly followed in his earliest writings. In his essay, " *On the Possibility
of a Form of Philosophy*," he shows the necessity of that supreme
principle which Fichte had first propounded. In his essay, " *On
the Ego*," Schelling shows that the ultimate ground of our knowledge can only lie in the Ego, and hence that every true philosophy
must be idealism. If our knowledge shall possess reality, there
must be one point in which ideality and reality, thought and being, can identically coincide ; and if outside of our knowledge,
there were something higher which conditioned it, if itself were
not the highest, then it could not be absolute. Fichte regarded
this essay as a commentary on his *Theory of Science ;* yet it contains already indications of Schelling's subsequent standpoint, in
its expressly affirming the unity of all knowledge, the necessity
that in the end all the different sciences shall become merged into
one. In the " *Letters on Dogmatism and Criticism*," 1795,
Schelling combatted the notions of those Kantians who had left
the critical and idealistic standpoint of their master, and fallen
back again into the old dogmatism. It was also on the stand-
point of Fichte that Schelling published in Niethammer's and
Fichte's Journal, 1797–98, a series of articles, in which he gave
a survey of the recent philosophical literature. Here he begins

* Schelling died August 20th, 1854, at Ragaz, Switzerland, whither he
had gone for the benefit of his health, which had long been declining.—
Translator.

to turn his attention towards a philosophical deduction of nature, though he still remains on the standpoint of Fichte when he deduces nature wholly from the essence of the Ego. In the essay which was composed soon after, and entitled "*Ideas for a philosophy of Nature*," 1797, and the one "*On the World-soul*," 1798, he gradually unfolded more clearly his views. The chief points which are brought out in the two last named essays are the following: The first origin of the conception of matter springs from nature and the intuition of the human mind. The mind is the union of an unlimited and a limiting energy. If there were no limit to the mind, consciousness would be just as impossible as if the mind were totally and absolutely limited. Feeling, perception and knowledge are only conceivable, as the energy which strives for the unlimited becomes limited through its opposite, and as this latter becomes itself freed from its limitations. The actual mind or heart consists only in the antagonism of these two energies, and hence only in their ever approximate or relative unity. Just so is it in nature. Matter as such is not the first, for the forces of which it is the unity are before it. Matter is only to be apprehended as the ever becoming product of attraction and repulsion; it is not, therefore, a mere inert grossness, as we are apt to represent it, but these forces are its original. But force in the material is like something immaterial. Force in nature is that which we may compare to mind. Since now the mind or heart exhibits precisely the same conflict, as matter, of opposite forces, we must unite the two in a higher identity. But the organ of the mind for apprehending nature is the intuition which takes, as object of the external sense, the space which has been filled and limited by the attracting and repelling forces. Thus Schelling was led to the conclusion that *the same absolute* appears in nature as in mind, and that the harmony of these is something more than a thought in reference to them. " Or if you affirm that we only *carry over* such an idea to nature, then have you utterly failed to apprehend the only nature which there can be to us. For our view of nature is not that it accidentally meets the laws of our mind—(perhaps through the mediation of a third)—but that it necessarily and originally not only expresses, but itself realizes, the laws of our mind, and that it is nature, and is called such only in so far as it does this." " Nature should be the visible mind, and mind invisible nature. Here, therefore, in the absolute ideality of the mind *within* us, and nature *without* us, must we solve the problem how it is possible for a nature outside of us to be." This thought, that nature or matter is just as much the áctual unity of an attracting and a repelling force, as the mind or heart is the unity of an unlimited and a limiting tendency, and that the repelling force in matter corresponds to the positive or unlimited activity of the mind, while the attracting force corresponds to the mind's negative or limiting activity—this identical deduction of matter from the essence of the Ego, is very prominent in all that Schelling wrote upon natural philosophy during this period. Nature thus appears as a copy (*Doppelbild*) of the mind, which the mind itself produces, in order to return, by its means, to pure self-intuition, to self-consciousness. Hence we have the successive stages of nature, in which all the stations of the mind in its way to self-consciousness are externally established. It is especially in the organic world that the mind can behold its own self-production. Hence, in every thing organic, there is something symbolical, every plant bears some feature of the soul. The chief characteristics of an organic formation,—the self-forming process from within outwards, the conformity to some end, the change of interpenetration of form and matter—are equally chief features of the mind. Since now there exists in our mind an endless striving to organize itself, so there must also be manifested in the external world a universal tendency to organization. The whole universe may thus be called a kind of organization which has formed itself from a centre, rising ever from a lower to a higher stage. From such a point of view, the natural philosopher will make it his chief effort to bring to a unity in his contemplations that life of nature, which by many researches into physical science had been separated into numberless different powers. "It is a needless trouble which many have given themselves, to show how very different is the working of fire and electricity, for every one knows this who has ever seen or heard of the two. But our mind strives after unity in the system of its knowledge; it will not endure that there should be pressed upon it a separate principle for every single phenomenon, and it will only believe that it sees nature where it can discover the greatest simplicity of laws in the greatest multiplicity of phenomena, and the highest frugality of means in the highest prodigality of effects. Therefore, every thought, even that which is now rough and crude, merits attention so soon as it tends towards the simplifying of principles, and if it serves no other end, it at least strengthens the impulse to investigate and trace out the hidden process of nature." The special tendency of the scientific investigation of nature which prevailed at that time, was to make a duality of forces the predominant element in the life of nature. In mechanics, the Kantian theory of the opposition of attraction and repulsion was adopted; in chemistry, by apprehending electricity as positive and negative, its phenomenon was brought near that of magnetism; in physiology there was the opposition of irritability and sensibility, &c. In opposition to these dualities, Schelling now insisted upon the unity of every thing opposite, the unity of all dualities, and this not simply as an abstract unity, but as a concrete identity, as the harmonious coworking of the heterogeneous. The world is the actual unity of a positive and a negative principle, " and these two conflicting forces taken together, or represented in their conflict, lead to the idea of an organizing principle which makes of the world a system, in other words, to the idea of a world-soul."

In his above-cited essay on " *the world-soul*," Schelling took the great step forward of apprehending nature as entirely autonomic. In the world-soul nature has a peculiar principle which dwells within it, and works according to conception. In this way the objective world was recognized as the independent life of nature in a manner which the logical idealism of Fichte would not permit. Schelling proceeeded still farther in this direction, and distinguished definitely, as the two sides of philosophy, the philosophy of nature and a transcendental philosophy. By placing a philosophy of nature by the side of idealism, Schelling passed decidedly beyond the standpoint of science, and we thus enter a second stadium of his philosophizing, though his method still remained that of Fichte, and he continued to believe that he was speculating in the spirit of the *Theory of Science.*

II. SECOND PERIOD. STANDPOINT OF THE DISTINGUISHING BETWEEN THE PHILOSOPHY OF NATURE AND OF MIND.

This standpoint of Schelling is chiefly carried out in the following works :—" *First Draft of a System of Natural Philosophy*," 1799 ; an introduction to this, 1799 ; articles in the "*Journal of Speculative Physics*," 1800, 1801 ; *System of Transcendental Idealism*," 1800. Schelling thus distinguishes the two sides of philosophy. All knowledge rests upon the harmony of a subject with an object. That which is simply objective is natural, and that which is simply subjective is the Ego or intelligence. There are two possible ways of uniting these two sides : we may either make nature first, and inquire how it is that intelligence is associated with it (natural philosophy) ; or we may make the subject first, and inquire how do objects proceed from the subject (transcendental philosophy). The end of all philosophy must be to make either an intelligence out of nature, or a nature out of intelligence. As the transcendental philosophy has to subject the real to the ideal, so must natural philosophy attempt to explain the ideal from the real. Both, however, are only the two poles of one and the same knowledge which reciprocally attract each other ; hence, if we start from either pole, we are necessarily drawn towards the other.

1. NATURAL PHILOSOPHY.—To philosophize concerning nature is, in a certain sense, to create nature—to raise it from the dead mechanism in which it had seemed confined, to inspire it with freedom, and transpose it into a properly free development. And what, then, is matter, other than mind which has become extinct? According to this view, since nature is only the visible organism of our understanding, it can produce nothing but what is conformable to a rule and an end. But you radically destroy every idea of nature just so soon as you allow its design to have come to it from without, by passing over from the understanding of any

being. The complete exhibition of the intellectual world in the laws and forms of the phenomenal world, and, on the other hand, the complete conception of these laws and forms from the intellectual world, and therefore the exhibition of the ideality of nature with the ideal world, is the work of natural philosophy. Immediate experience is indeed its starting point; we know originally nothing except through experience; but just as soon as I gain an insight into the inner necessity of a principle of experience, it becomes a principle apriori. Natural philosophy is empiricism extended until it becomes absolute.

Schelling expresses himself as follows, concerning the chief principles of a philosophy of nature. Nature is a suspension (*Schweben*) between productivity and product, which is always passing over into definite forms and products, just as it is always productively passing beyond these. This suspension indicates a duality of principles, through which nature is held in a constant activity, and hindered from exhausting itself in its products. A universal duality is thus the principle of every explanation of nature; it is the first principle of a philosophic theory of nature, to end in all nature with polarity and dualism. On the other hand, the final cause of all our contemplation of nature is to know that absolute unity which comprehends the whole, and which suffers only one side of itself to be known in nature. Nature is, as it were, the instrument of this absolute unity, through which it eternally executes and actualizes that which is prefigured in the absolute understanding. The whole absolute is therefore cognizable in nature, though phenomenal nature only exhibits in a succession, and produces in an endless development, that which the true or real nature eternally possesses. Schelling treats of natural philosophy in three sections : (1) the proof that nature, in its original products, is *organic ;* (2) the conditions of an *inorganic* nature; (3) the reciprocal determination of organic and inorganic nature.

(1.) *Organic nature* Schelling thus deduces : Nature absolutely apprehended is nothing other than infinite activity, infinite productivity. If this were unhindered in expressing itself, it would at once, with infinite celerity, produce an absolute product, which would allow no explanation for empirical nature. If this latter may be explained—if there may be finite products, we must consider the productive activity of nature as restrained by an opposite, a retarding activity, which lies in nature itself. Thus arises a series of finite products. But since the absolute productivity of nature tends towards an absolute product, these individual products are only apparent ones, beyond each one of which nature herself advances, in order to satisfy the absoluteness of her inner productivity through an infinite series of individual products. In this eternal producing of finite products, nature shows itself as a living antagonism of two opposite forces, a productive and a retarding tendency. And, indeed, the working of this latter is infinitely manifold; the original productive impulse of nature has not only to combat a simple restraint, but it must struggle with an infinity of reactions, which may be called original qualities. Hence every organic being is the permanent expression for a conflict of reciprocally destroying and limiting actions of nature. And from this, viz., from the original limitation and infinite restraint of the formative impulse of nature, we see the reason why every organization, instead of attaining to an absolute product, only reproduces itself *ad infinitum*. Upon this rests the special significance for the organic world, of the distinction of sex. The distinction of sex fixes the organic products of nature, it restrains them within their own processes of development, and suffers them only to produce the same again. But in this production nature has no regard for the individual, but only for the species. The individual is contrary to nature; nature desires the absolute, and its constant effort is to represent this. Individual products, therefore, in which the activity of nature is brought to a stand, can only be regarded as abortive attempts to represent the absolute. Hence the individual must be the means, and the species the end of nature. Just so soon as the species is secured, nature abandons the individuals and labors for their destruction. Schelling divides the dynamic scale of organic nature according to the three grand functions of the organic world:

(a) Formative impulse (reproductive energy); (b) Irritability; (c) Sensibility. Highest in rank are those organisms in which sensibility has the preponderance over irritability; a lower rank is held by those where irritability preponderates, and lower still are those where reproduction first comes out in its entire perfection, while sensibility and irritability are almost extinct. Yet these three powers are interwoven together in all nature, and hence there is but one organization, descending through all nature from man to the plant.

(2.) *Inorganic nature* offers the antithesis to organic. The existence and essence of inorganic nature are conditioned through the existence and essence of organic nature. While the powers of organic nature are productive, those of inorganic nature are not productive. While organic nature aims only to establish the species, inorganic nature regards only the individual, and offers no reproduction of the species through the individual. It possesses a great multitude of materials, but can only use these materials in the way of conjoining or separating. In a word, inorganic nature is simply a mass held together by some external cause as gravity. Yet it, like organic nature, has its gradations. The power of reproduction in the latter has its counterpart in the chemical process in the former; that which in the one case is irritability, in the other is electricity; and sensibility, which is the highest stage of organic life, corresponds to the universal magnetism, the highest stage of the inorganic.

(3.) *The reciprocal determination of the organic and inorganic world*, is made clear by what has already been said. The result to which every genuine philosophy of nature must come, is that the distinction between organic and inorganic nature is only in nature as object, and that nature, as originally productive, waves over both. If the functions of an organism are only possible on the condition that there is a definite external world, and an organic world, then must the external world and the organic world have a common origin. This can only be explained on the ground that inorganic nature presupposes in order to its existence a higher dynamical order of things, to which it is subject. There must be a third, which can unite again organic and inorganic nature; which can be a medium, holding the continuity between the two. Both must be identified in some ultimate cause, through which, as through one common soul of nature (world-soul), both the organic and inorganic, *i. e.* universal nature, is inspired; in some common principle, which, fluctuating between inorganic and organic nature, and maintaining the continuity of the two, contains the first cause of all changes in the one, and the ultimate ground of all activity in the other. We have here the idea of a universal organism. That it is one and the same organization which unites in one the organic and inorganic world, would appear from what has already been said of the parallel gradations of the two worlds. That which in universal nature is the cause of magnetism, is in organic nature the cause of sensibility, and the latter is only a higher potency of the former. Just as in the organic world through sensibility, so in universal nature through magnetism, there arises a duality from the ideality. In this way organic nature appears only as a higher stage of the inorganic; the very same dualism which is seen in magnetic polarity, electrical phenomena, and chemical differences, displays itself also in the organic world.

2. TRANSCENDENTAL PHILOSOPHY.—Transcendental philosophy is the philosophy of nature become subjective. The whole succession of objects thus far described, becomes now repeated as a successive development of the beholding subject. It is the peculiarity of transcendental idealism, that so soon as it is once admitted, it requires that the origin of all knowledge shall be sought for anew; that the truth which has long been considered as established, should be subjected to a new examination, and that this examination should proceed under at least an entirely new form. All parts of philosophy must be exhibited in one continuity, and the whole of philosophy must be regarded as that which it is, viz., the advancing history of consciousness, which can use only as monuments or documents that which is laid down in experience. (Schelling's transcendental idealism is, in this respect, the forerunner to Hegel's *Phœnomenology*, which pursues a similar

course). The exhibition of this connection is properly a succession of intuitions through which the Ego raises itself to consciousness in the highest potency. Neither transcendental philosophy nor the philosophy of nature, can alone represent the parallelism between nature and intelligence; but, in order to this, both sciences must be united, the former being considered as a necessary counterpart to the other. The division of transcendental philosophy follows from its problem, to seek anew the origin of all knowledge, and to subject to a new examination every previous judgment which had been held to be established truth. The pre-judgments of the common understanding are principally two: (1) That a world of objects exist independent of, and outside of, ourselves, and are represented to us just as they are. To explain this pre-judgment, is the problem of the first part of the transcendental philosophy (*theoretical philosophy*). (2) That we can produce an effect upon the objective world according to representations which arise freely within us. The solution of this problem is *practical philosophy*. But, with these two problems we find ourselves entangled, (3) in a contradiction. How is it possible that our thought should ever rule over the world of sense, if the representation is conditional in its origin by the objective? The solution of this problem, which is the highest of transcendental philosophy, is the answer to the question: how can the representations be conceived as directing themselves according to the objects, and at the same time the objects be conceived as directing themselves according to the representations? This is only conceivable on the ground that the activity through which the objective world is produced, is originally identical with that which utters itself in the will. To show this identity of conscious and unconscious activity, is the problem of the third part of transcendental philosophy, or the science of ends in nature and of art. The three parts of the transcendental philosophy correspond thus entirely to the three criticks of Kant.

(1.) *The theoretical philosophy* starts from the highest principle of knowledge, the self-consciousness, and from this point developes the history of self-consciousness, according to its most

prominent epochs and stations, viz., sensation, intuition, productive intuition (which produces matter)—outer and inner intuition
(from which space and time, and all Kant's categories may be
derived), abstraction (by which the intelligence distinguishes
itself from its products)—absolute abstraction, or absolute act
of will. With the act of the will there is spread before us,

(2). *The Field of Practical Philosophy.*—In practical philosophy the Ego is no longer beholding, *i. e.* consciousless, but
is consciously producing, *i. e.* realizing. As a whole, nature developes itself from the original act of self-consciousness, so from
the second act, or the act of free self-determination, there is produced a second nature, to find the origin for which is the object
of practical philosophy. In his exposition of the practical philosophy, Schelling follows almost wholly the theory of Fichte,
but closes this section with some remarkable expressions respecting the philosophy of history. History, as a whole, is, according
to him, a gradual and self-disclosing revelation of the absolute, a
progressing demonstration of the existence of a God. The history of this revelation may be divided into three periods. The
first is that in which the overruling power was apprehended only
as destiny, *i. e.* as a blind power, cold and consciousless, which
brings the greatest and most glorious things of earth to ruin; it
is marked by the decay of the magnificence and wonders of the
ancient world, and the fall of the noblest manhood that has ever
bloomed. The second period of history is that in which this destiny manifests itself as nature, and the hidden law seems changed
into a manifest law of nature, which compels freedom and every
choice to submit to and serve a plan of nature. This period
seems to begin with the spread of the great Roman republic.
The third period will be that where what has previously been regarded as destiny and nature, will develope itself as Providence.
When this period shall begin, we cannot say; we can only affirm
that if it be, then God will be seen also to be.

(3.) *Philosophy of Art.*—The problem of transcendental
philosophy is to harmonize the subjective and the objective. In
history, with which practical philosophy closes, the identity of

the two is not exhibited, but only approximated in an infinite
progress. But now the Ego must attain a position where it can
actually look upon this identity, which constitutes its inner essence. If now all conscious activity exhibits design, then a conscious and consciousless activity can only coincide in a product,
which, though it exhibits design, was yet produced without design. Such a product is nature ; we have here the principle of
all *teleology*, in which alone the solution of the given problem
can be sought. The peculiarity of nature is this, viz., that
though it exhibits itself as nothing but a blind mechanism, it yet
displays design, and represents an identity of the conscious subjective, and the consciousless objective activity ; in it the Ego
beholds its own most peculiar essence, which consists alone in this
identity. But in nature the Ego beholds this identity, not as
something objective, which has a being only outside of it, but
also as that whose principle lies within the Ego itself. This beholding is the art-intuition. As the production of nature is consciousless, though similar to that which is conscious, so the æsthetic production of the artist is a conscious production, similar
to that which is consciousless. *Æsthetics* must therefore be
joined to teleology. That contradiction between the conscious
and the consciousless, which moves forward untiringly in history,
and which is unconsciously reconciled in nature, finds its conscious reconciliation in a work of art. In a work of art, the intelligence attains a perfect intuition of itself. The feeling which
accompanies this intuition, is the feeling of an endless satisfaction ; all contradictions being resolved, and every riddle explained. The unknown, which unexpectedly harmonizes the objective and the conscious activity, is nothing other than that absolute and unchangeable identity, to which every existence must
be referred. In the artist it lays aside the veil, which elsewhere
surrounds it, and irresistibly impels him to complete his work.
Thus there is no other eternal revelation but art, and this is also
the miracle which should convince us of the reality of that supreme, which is never itself objective, but is the cause of all objective. Hence art holds a higher rank than philosophy, for only

in art has the intellectual intuition objectivity. There is nothing, therefore, higher to the philosopher than art, because this
opens before him, as it were, the holy of holies, where that which
is separate in nature and history, and which in life and action, as
in thought, must ever diverge, burns, as it were, in one flame, in
an eternal and original union. From this we see also both the
fact and the reason for it, that philosophy, as philosophy, can
never be universally valid. Art is that alone to which is given
an absolute objectivity, and it is through this alone that nature,
consciously productive, concludes and completes itself within itself.

The "*Transcendental Idealism*" is the last work which
Schelling wrote after the method of Fichte. In its principle he
goes decidedly beyond the standpoint of Fichte. That which
was with Fichte the inconceivable limit of the Ego, Schelling
derives as a necessary duality, from the simple essence of the
Ego. While Fichte had regarded the union of subject and object, only as an infinite progression towards that which ought to
be, Schelling looked upon it as actually accomplished in a work
of art. With Fichte God was apprehended only as the object of
a moral faith, but with Schelling he was looked upon as the immediate object of the æsthetic intuition. This difference between
the two could not long be concealed from Schelling. He was
obliged to see that he no longer stood upon the basis of subjective idealism, but that his real position was that of objective idealism. If he had already gone beyond Fichte in setting the philosophy of nature and transcendental philosophy opposite to each
other, it was perfectly consistent for him now to go one step farther, and, placing himself on the point of indifference between
the two, make the identity of the ideal and the real, of thought
and being, as his principle. This principle *Spinoza* had already
possessed before him. To this philosophy of identity Schelling
now found himself peculiarly attracted. Instead of following
Fichte's method, he now availed himself of that of Spinoza, the
mathematical, to which he ascribed the greatest evidence of proof.

III. Third Period: Period of Spinozism, or the Indifference of the Ideal and the Real.

The principal writings of this period are :—" *Exposition of my System of Philosophy*" (Journal for Speculative Physics, ii. 2); the second edition, with additions, of the " *Ideas for a Philosophy of Nature*," 1803; the dialogue, " *Bruno, or concerning the Divine and the Natural Principle of Things*," 1802 ; " *Lectures on the Method of Academical Study*," 1803; three numbers of a " *New Journal for Speculative Physics*," 1802–3. The characteristic of the new standpoint of Schelling, to which we now arrive, is perfectly exhibited in the definition of reason, which he places at the head of the first of the above-named writings; I give to reason the name absolute, or the reason in so far as it is conceived as the total *indifference of the subjective and the objective*. To think of reason is demanded of every man ; to think of it as absolute, and thus to reach the standpoint which I require, every thing must be abstracted from the thinking subject. To him who makes this abstraction, reason immediately ceases to be something subjective, as most men represent it ; neither can it be conceived as something objective, since an objective, or that which is thought, is only possible in opposition to that which thinks. We thus rise through this abstraction to the reality of things (*zum wahren an-sich*), which reality is precisely in the indifference point of the subjective and the objective. The standpoint of philosophy is the standpoint of reason ; its knowledge is a knowledge of things as they are in themselves, *i. e.* as they are in the reason. It is the nature of philosophy to destroy every distinction which the imagination has mingled with the thinking, and to see in things only that through which they express the absolute reason, not regarding in them that which is simply an object for that reflection which expends itself on the laws of mechanism and in time. Besides reason there is nothing, and in it is every thing. Reason is the absolute. All objections to this principle can only arise from the fact, that men are in the habit of looking at things not as they are in reason, but as they appear. Every thing which is, is in essence like the reason, and is one with it. It is not the reason which posits something external to itself, but only the false use of reason, which is connected with the

incapacity of forgetting the subjective in itself. The reason is
absolutely *one* and like itself. The highest law for the being
of reason, and since there is nothing besides reason, the highest law for all being, is the law of identity. Between subject
and object therefore—since it is one and the same absolute
identity which displays itself in both—there can be no difference except a *quantitative* difference (a difference of more or
less), so that nothing is either simple object or simple subject, but
in all things subject and object are united, this union being in
different proportions, so that sometimes the subject and sometimes
the object has the preponderance. But since the absolute is pure
identity of subject and object, there can be no quantitative difference except outside of the identity, *i. e.* in the finite. As the
fundamental form of the infinite is A=A, so the scheme of the
finite is A=B (*i. e.* the union of a subjective with another objective in a different proportion). But, in reality, nothing is finite,
because the identity is the only reality. So far as there is difference in individual things, the identity exists in the form of indifference. If we could see together every thing which is, we should
find in all the pure identity, because we should find in all a perfect
quantitative equilibrium of subjectivity and objectivity. True,
we find, in looking at individual objects, that sometimes the preponderance is on one side and sometimes on the other, but in the
whole this is compensated. The absolute identity is the absolute
totality, the universe itself. There is in reality (*an-sich*) no individual being or thing. There is in reality nothing beyond the
totality; and if any thing beyond this is beheld, this can only
happen by virtue of an arbitrary separation of the individual from
the whole, which is done through reflection, and is the source of
every error. The absolute identity is essentially the same in
every part of the universe. Hence the universe may be conceived
under the figure of a line, in the centre of which is the A=A,
while at the end on one side is $\overset{+}{A}$=B, *i. e.* a transcendence of the
subjective, and at the end on the other side is A=$\overset{+}{B}$, *i. e.* a transcendence of the objective, though this must be conceived so that a

relative identity may exist even in these extremes. The one side is the real or nature, the other side is the ideal. The real side developes itself according to three potences (a potence, or power, indicates a definite quantitative difference of subjectivity and objectivity). (1) The first potence is matter and weight—the greatest preponderance of the object. (2) The second potence is light (A^2), an inner—as weight is an outer—intuition of nature. The light is a higher rising of the subjective. It is the absolute identity itself. (3) The third potence is organism (A^3), the common product of light and weight. Organism is just as original as matter. Inorganic nature, as such, does not exist : it is actually organized, and is, as it were, the universal germ out of which organization proceeds. The organization of every globe is but the inner evolution of the globe itself; the earth itself, by its own evolving, becomes animal and plant. The organic world has not formed itself out of the inorganic, but has been at least potentially present in it from the beginning. That matter which lies before us, apparently inorganic, is the residuum of organic metamorphoses, which could not become organic. The human brain is the highest bloom of the whole organic metamorphosis of the earth. From the above, Schelling adds, it must be perceived that we affirm an inner identity of all things, and a potential presence of every thing in every other, and therefore even the so-called dead matter may be viewed only as a sleeping-world of animals and plants, which, in some period, the absolute identity may animate and raise to life. At this point Schelling stops suddenly, without developing further the three potences of the ideal series, corresponding to those of the real. Elsewhere he completes the work by setting up the following three potences of the ideal series : (1) Knowledge, the potence of reflection ; (2) Action, the potence of subsumption ; (3) the Reason as the unity of reflection and subsumption. These three potences represent themselves : (1) as the true, the imprinting of the matter in the form ; (2) as the good, or the imprinting of the form in the matter ; (3) as the beautiful, or the work of art, the absolute blending together of form and matter.

Schelling sought also to furnish himself with a new method for knowing the absolute identity. Neither the analytic nor the synthetical method seems to him suitable for this, since both are only a finite knowledge. Gradually, also, he abandoned the mathematical method. The logical forms of the ordinary method of knowledge, and even the ordinary metaphysical categories, were now insufficient for him. Schelling now places the intellectual intuition as the starting point of true knowledge. Intuition, in general, is an equal positing of thought and being. When I behold an object, the being of the object and my thought of the object is for me absolutely the same. But in the ordinary intuition, some separate sensible being is posited as one with the thought. But in the intellectual or rational intuition, being in general, and every being is made identical with the thought, and the absolute *subject-object* is beheld. The intellectual intuition is absolute knowledge, and as such it can only be conceived as that in which thought and being are not opposed to each other. It is the beginning and the first step towards philosophy to behold, immediately and intellectually within thyself, that same indifference of the ideal and the real which thou beholdest projected as it were from thyself in space and time. This absolutely absolute mode of knowledge is wholly and entirely in the absolute itself. That it can never become taught is clear. It cannot, moreover, be seen why philosophy is bound to have special regard to the unattainable. It seems much more fitting to make so complete a separation on every side between the entrance to philosophy and the common knowledge, that no road nor track shall lead from the latter to the former. The absolute mode of knowledge, like the truth which it contains, has no true opposition outside of itself, and as it cannot be demonstrated by any intelligent being, so nothing can be set up in opposition to it by any.—Schelling has attempted to bring the intellectual intuition into a method, and has named this method construction. The possibility and the necessity of the constructive method is based upon the fact that the absolute is in all, and that all is the absolute. Construction is nothing other than the proving that the whole is absolutely expressed in every particular relation and object. To construe an object, philosophically, is to prove that in this object the whole inner structure of the absolute repeats itself.

In Schelling's "*Lectures on the Method of Academical Study*" (delivered in 1802, and published in 1803), he sought to treat encyclopædiacally, every philosophical discipline from the given standpoint of identity or indifference. They furnish a connected and popular exposition of the outlines of his philosophy, in the form of a critical modelling of the studies of the university course. The most noticeable feature in them is Schelling's attempt at a historical construction of Christianity. The incarnation of God is an incarnation from eternity. The eternal Son of God, born from the essence of the father of all things, is the finite itself, as it is in the eternal intuition of God. Christ is only the historical and phenomenal pinnacle of the incarnation ; as an individual, he is a person wholly conceivable from the circumstances of the age in which he appeared. Since God is eternally outside of all time, it is inconceivable that he should have assumed a human nature at any definite moment of time. The temporal form of Christianity, the exoteric Christianity does not correspond to its idea, and has its perfection yet to be hoped for. A chief hindrance to the perfection of Christianity, was, and is the so-called Bible, which, moreover, is far inferior to other religious writings, in a genuine religious content. The future must bring a new birth of the esoteric Christianity, or a new and higher form of religion, in which philosophy, religion and poesy shall melt together in unity.—This latter remark contains already an intimation of the "*Philosophy of Revelation*," a work subsequently written by Schelling, and which exhibited many of the principles current in the age of the apostle John. In the work we are now considering, there are also many other points which correspond to this later standpoint of Schelling. Thus he places at the summit of history a kind of golden age. It is inconceivable, he says, that man as he now appears, should have raised himself through himself from instinct to consciousness, from animality to rationality. Another human race, must, therefore, have preceded the present, which the old saga have immortalized under the form of gods and heroes.   The first origin of religion and culture is only conceivable through the instruction of higher natures.   I hold the condition of culture as the first condition of the human race, and considerer the first foundation of states, sciences, religion and arts as cotemporary, or rather as one thing : so that all these were not truly separate, but in the completest interpenetration, as it will be again in the final consummation.   Schelling is no more than consistent when he accordingly apprehends the symbols of mythology which we meet with at the beginning of history, as disclosures of the highest wisdom.   There is here also a step towards his subsequent " *Philosophy of Mythology.*"

The mystical element revealed in these expressions of Schelling gained continually a greater prominence with him.   Its growth was partly connected with his fruitless search after an absolute method, and a fitting form in which he might have satisfactorily expressed his philosophic intuitions.   All noble mysticism rests on the incapacity of adequately expressing an infinite content in the form of a conception.   So Schelling, after he had been restlessly tossed about in every method, soon gave up also his method of construction, and abandoned himself wholly to the unlimited current of his fancy.   But though this was partly the cause of his mysticism, it is also true that his philosophical standpoint was gradually undergoing a change.   From the speculative science of nature, he was gradually passing over more and more into the philosophy of mind, by which the determination of the absolute in his conception became changed.   While he had previously determined the absolute as the indifference of the ideal and the real, he now gives a preponderance to the ideal over the real, and makes ideality the fundamental determination of the absolute.   The first is the ideal; secondly, the ideal determines itself in itself to the real, and the real as such is the third.   The earlier harmony of mind and matter is dissolved : matter appears now as the negative of mind.   Since Schelling in this way distinguishes the universe from the absolute as its counterpart, we see that he leaves decidedly the basis of Spinozism on which he had previously stood, and places himself on a new standpoint.

IV. FOURTH PERIOD: THE DIRECTION OF SCHELLING'S PHI-LOSOPHY AS MYSTICAL AND ALLIED TO NEW-PLATONISM.

The writings of this period are :—" *Philosophy and Religion*," 1804. " *Exposition of the true relation of the Philosophy of Nature to the improved Theory of Fichte*," 1806; " *Medical Annual* " (published in company with *Marcus*) 1805–1808.—As has already been said, the absolute and the universe were, on the standpoint of indifference, identical. Nature and history were immediate manifestations of the absolute. But now Schelling lays stress upon the difference between the two, and the independence of the world. This he expresses in a striking way in the first of the above named writings, by placing the origin of the world wholly after the manner of New-Platonism, in a breaking away or a falling off from the absolute. From the absolute to the actual, there is no abiding transition ; the origin of the sensible world is only conceivable as a complete breaking off *per saltum* from the abso-lute. The absolute is the only real, finite things are not real ; they can, therefore, have their ground in no reality imparted to them from the absolute, but only in a separation and complete falling away from the absolute. The reconciliation of this fall, and the manifestation of God made complete, is the final cause of history. With this idea there are also connected other represen-tations borrowed from New-Platonism, which Schelling brings out in the same work. He speaks in it of the descent of the soul from intellectuality, to the world of sense, and like the Platonic myth he allows this fall of souls to be a punishment for their self-hood (pride); he speaks also in connection with this of a regenera-tion, or transmigration of souls, by which they either begin a higher life on a better sphere, or intoxicated with matter, they are driven down to a still lower abode, according as they have in the present life laid aside more or less of their selfhood, and become purified in a greater or less degree, to an identity with the infi-nite ; but we are especially reminded of New-Platonism by the high place and the mystical and symbolical significance, which Schelling gives in this work to the Greek mysteries (as did Bruno), and the view that if religion would be held in its pure ideality, it can only exist as exoteric, or in the form of mysteries.—This notion of a higher blending together of religion and philosophy goes through all the writings of this period. All true experience, says Schelling in the " *Medical Annual*," is religious. The existence of God is an empirical truth, and the ground of all experience. True, religion is not philosophy, but the philosophy which does not unite in sacred harmony, religion with science, were unworthy of the name. True, I know something higher than science. And if science has only these two ways open before it to knowledge, viz., that of analysis or abstraction, and that of synthetic deriva-tion, then we deny all science of the absolute. Speculation is every thing, *i. e.* a beholding, a contemplation of that which is in God. Science itself has worth only so far as it is speculative, *i. e.* only so far as it is a contemplation of God as he is. But the time will come when the sciences shall more and more cease, and immediate knowledge take their place. The mortal eye closes only in the highest science, where it is no longer the man who sees, but the eternal beholding which has now become seeing in him.

With this theosophic view of the world, Schelling was led to pay attention to the earlier mystics. He began to study their writings. He answered the charge of mysticism in his controversy with Fichte as follows :—Among the learned of the last century, there was a tacit agreement never to go beyond a certain height, and, therefore, the genuine spirit of science was given up to the unlearned. These, because they were uneducated and had drawn upon themselves the jealousy of the learned, were called fanat-ics. But many a philosopher by profession might well have ex-changed all his rhetoric for the fulness of mind and heart which abound in the writings of such fanatics. Therefore I am not ashamed of the name of such a fanatic. I will even seek to make this reproach true ; if I have not hitherto studied the writings of these men correctly, it has been owing to negligence.

Schelling did not omit to verify these words. There were some special mental affinities between himself and *Jacob Boehme,* with whom he now became more and more closely joined. A study of his writings is indeed indicated in Schelling's works of the present period. One of the most famous of Schelling's writings, his theory of freedom, which appeared after this (" *Philosophische Untersuchungen über das Wesen der menschlichen Freiheit*," 1809), is composed entirely in the spirit of Jacob Boehme. We begin with it a new period of Schelling's philosophizing, where *the will* is affirmed as the essence of God, and we have thus a new definition of the absolute differing from every previous one.

V. FIFTH PERIOD :—ATTEMPT AT A THEOGONY AND COSMOGONY AFTER THE MANNER OF JACOB BOEHME.

Schelling had much in common with Jacob Boehme. Both considered the speculative cognition as a kind of immediate intuition. Both made use of forms which mingled the abstract and the sensuous, and interpenetrated the definiteness of logic with the coloring of fancy. Both, in fine, were speculatively in close contact. The self-duplication of the absolute was a fundamental thought of Boehme. He started with the principle, that the divine essence was the indeterminable, infinite, and inconceivable, the absence of ground (*Ungrund*). This absence of ground now projects itself in a proper feeling of its abstract and infinite essence, into the finite, *i. e.* into a ground, or the centre of nature, in the dark womb of which qualities are produced, from whose harsh collision the lightning streams forth, which, as mind or principle of light, is destined to rule and explain the struggling powers of nature, so that the God who has been raised from the absence of ground through a ground to the light of the mind, may henceforth move in an eternal kingdom of joy. This theogony of Jacob Boehme is in striking accord with the present standpoint of Schelling. As Boehme had apprehended the absolute as the indeterminable absence of ground, so had Schelling in his earlier writings apprehended it as indifference. As Boehme had distinguished this absence of ground from a ground, or from nature and from God, as the light of minds, so had Schelling, in the writings of the last period, apprehended the absolute as a self-renunciation, and a re-

turn back from this renunciation into a higher unity with itself.
We have here the three chief elements of that history of God,
around which Schelling's essay on freedom turns: (1) God as
indifference, or the absence of ground; (2) God as duplication
into ground and existence, real and ideal; (3) Reconciliation of
this duplication, and elevation of the original indifference to identity. The first element of the divine life is that of pure indifference, or indistinguishableness. This, which precedes every thing
existing, may be called the original ground, or the absence of
ground. The absence of ground is not a product of opposites,
nor are they contained *implicite* in it, but it is a proper essence
separate from every opposite, and having no predicate but that of
predicatelessness. Real and ideal, darkness and light, can never
be predicated of the absence of ground as opposites; they can
only be affirmed of it as not-opposites in a neither-nor. From
this indifference now rises the duality: the absence of ground
separates into two co-eternal beginnings, so that ground and existence may become one through love, and the indeterminable and
lifeless indifference may rise to a determinate and living identity.
Since nothing is before or external to God, he must have the
ground of his existence in himself. But this ground is not simply logical, as conception, but real, as something which is actually to be distinguished in God from existence; it is nature in God,
an essence inseparable indeed from him, but yet distinct. Hence
we cannot assign to this ground understanding and will, but only
desire after this; it is the longing to produce itself. But in that
this ground moves in its longing according to obscure and uncertain laws like a swelling sea, there is, self-begotten in God,
another and reflexive motion, an inner representation by which he
beholds himself in his image. This representation is the eternal
word in God, which rises as light in the darkness of the ground,
and endows its blind longing with understanding. This understanding, united with the ground, becomes pre-creating will. Its
work is to give order to nature, and to regulate the hitherto un-
regulated ground; and from this explanation of the real through
the ideal, comes the creation of the world. · The development of

the world has two stadia : (1) the travail of light, or the progressive development of nature to man ; (2) the travail of mind, or the development of mind in history.

(1.) The progressive development of nature proceeds from a conflict of the ground with the understanding. The ground originally sought to produce every thing solely from itself, but its products had no consistence without the understanding, and went again to the ground, a creation which we see exhibited in the extinct classes of animals and plants of the pre-Adamite world. But consecutively and gradually, the ground admitted the work of the understanding, and every such step towards light is indicated by a new class of nature's beings. In every creature of nature we must, therefore, distinguish two principles : first, the obscure principle through which the creatures of nature are separate from God, and have a particular will ; second, the divine principle of the understanding, of the universal will. With irrational creatures of nature, however, these two principles are not yet brought to unity ; but the particular will is simple seeking and desire, while the universal will, without the individual will, reigns as an external power of nature, as controlling instinct.

(2.) The two principles, the particular and the universal will, are first united in man as they are in the absolute : but in God they are united inseparably, and in man separably, for otherwise God could not reveal himself in man. It is even this separableness of the universal will, and the particular will, which makes good and evil possible. The good is the subjection of the particular will to the universal will, and the reverse of this right relation is evil. Human freedom consists in this possibility of good and evil. The empirical man, however, is not free, but his whole empirical condition is posited by a previous act of intelligence. The man must act just as he does, but is nevertheless free, because he has from eternity freely made himself that which he now necessarily is. The history of the human race is founded for the most part on the struggle of the individual will with the universal will, as the history of nature is founded on the struggle of the ground with the understanding. The different stages

15

through which evil, as a historical power, takes its way in conflict with love, constitute the periods of the world's history. Christianity is the centre of history: in Christ, the principle of love came in personal contact with incarnate evil: Christ was the mediator to reconcile on the highest stage the creation with God; for that which is personal can alone redeem the personal. The end of history is the reconciliation of the particular will and love, the prevalence of the universal will, so that God shall be all in all. The original indifference is thus elevated to identity.

Schelling has given a farther justification of this his idea of God, in his controversial pamphlet against Jacobi, (1812). The charge of naturalism which Jacobi made against him, he sought to refute by showing how the true idea of God was a union of naturalism and theism. Naturalism seeks to conceive of God as ground of the world (immanent), while theism would view him as the world's cause (transcendent): the true course is to unite both determinations. God is at the same time ground and cause. It no way contradicts the conception of God to affirm that, so far as he reveals himself, he developes himself from himself, advancing from the imperfect to the perfect: the imperfect is in fact the perfect itself, only in a state of becoming. It is necessary that this becoming should be by stages, in order that the fulness of the perfect may appear on all sides. If there were no obscure ground, no nature, no negative principle in God, we could not speak of a consciousness of God. So long as the God of modern theism remains the simple essence which ought to be purely essential, but which in fact is without essence, so long as an actual twofoldness is not recognized in God, and a limiting and denying energy (a nature, a negative principle) is not placed in opposition to the extending and affirming energy in God, so long will science be entitled to make its denial of a personal God. It is universally and essentially impossible to conceive of a being with consciousness, which has not been brought into limit by some denying energy within himself—as universally and essentially impossible as to conceive of a circle without a centre.

VI. Since the essay against Jacobi, which in its philosophical content accords mainly with his theory of freedom, Schelling has not made public any thing of importance. He has often announced a work entitled " *Die Weltalter*," which should contain a complete and elaborate exposition of his philosophy, but has always withdrawn it before its appearance. *Paulus* has surreptitiously brought his later Berlin lectures before the public in a manner for which he has been greatly blamed: but since this publication is not recognized by Schelling himself, it cannot be used as an authentic source of knowledge of his philosophy. During this long period, Schelling has published only two articles of a philosophical content : " *On the Deities of Samothracos*," 1815, and a " *Critical Preface* " to *Becker's* translation of a preface of *Cousin*, 1834. Both articles are very characteristic of the present standpoint of Schelling's philosophizing—he himself calls his present philosophy *Positive Philosophy, or the Philosophy of Mythology and Revelation*,—but as they give only intimations of this, and do not reach a complete exposition, they do not admit of being used for our purpose.

SECTION XLIV.

TRANSITION TO HEGEL.

The great want of Schelling's philosophizing, was its inability to furnish a suitable form for the philosophic content. Schelling went through the list of all methods, and at last abandoned all. But this absence of method into which he ultimately sank, contradicted the very principle of his philosophizing. If thought and being are identical, yet form and content cannot be indifferent in respect to each other. On the standpoint of absolute knowledge, there must be found for the absolute content an absolute form, which shall be identical with the content. This is the position assumed by *Hegel*. Hegel has fused the content of Schelling's philosophy by means of the *absolute method*.

Hegel sprang as truly from Fichte as from Schelling; the origin of his system is found in both. His method is essentially that of Fichte, but his general philosophical standpoint is Schelling's. He has combined both Fichte and Schelling.

Hegel has himself, in his "*Phenomenology*," the first work in which he appeared as a philosopher on his own hook, having previously been considered as an adherent of Schelling—clearly expressed his difference from Schelling, which he comprehensively affirms in the following three hits (*Schlagworte*):—In Schelling's philosophy, the absolute is, as it were, shot out of a pistol; it is only the night in which every cow looks black; when it is widened to a system, it is like the course of a painter, who has on his palette but two colors, red and green, and who would cover a surface with the former when a historical piece was demanded, and with the latter when a landscape was required. The first of these charges refers to the mode of attaining the idea of the absolute, viz., immediately, through intellectual intuition; this leap Hegel changes, in his *Phenomenology*, to a regular transit, proceeding step by step. The second charge relates to the way in which the absolute thus gained is conceived and expressed, viz., simply as the absence of all finite distinctions, and not as the immanent positing of a system of distinctions within itself. Hegel declares that every thing depends upon apprehending and expressing the true not as substance (*i. e.* as negation of determinateness), but as subject (as a positing and producing of finite distinction). The third charge has to do with Schelling's manner of carrying out his principle through the concrete content of the facts given in the natural and intellectual worlds, viz., by the application of a ready-made schema (the opposition of the ideal and the real) to the objects, instead of suffering them to unfold and separate themselves from themselves. The school of Schelling was especially given to this schematizing formalism, and that which Hegel remarks, in the introduction to his *Phenomenology*, may very well be applied to it: "If the formalism of a philosophy of nature should happen to teach that the understanding is electricity, or that the animate is nitrogen, the inexperienced might look upon such instructions with deep amazement, and perhaps revere them as displaying the marks of profound genius. But the trick of such a wisdom is as readily learned as it is easily practised; its repetition is as insufferable as the repetition of a discovered feat of legerdemain. This method of affixing to every thing heavenly and earthly, to all natural and intellectual forms, the two determinations of the universal scheme, makes the universe like a grocer's shop, in which a row of closed jars stand with their labels pasted on them.

The point, therefore, of greatest difference between Schelling and Hegel is their philosophical method, and this at the same time forms the bond of close connection which unites Hegel with Fichte. Thesis, antithesis, synthesis—this was the method by which Fichte had sought to deduce all being from the Ego, and in precisely the same way Hegel deduces all being—the intellectual and natural universe—from the thought, only with this difference, that with him that which was idealistically deduced had at the same time an objective reality. While the practical idealism of Fichte stood related to the objective world as a producer, and the ordinary empiricism as a beholder, yet with Hegel the speculative (conceiving) reason is at the same time productive and beholding. I produce (for myself) that which is (in itself) without my producing. The result of philosophy, says Hegel, is the thought which is by itself, and which comprehends in itself the universe, and changes it into an intelligent world. To raise all being to being in the consciousness, to knowledge, is the problem and the goal of philozophizing, and this goal is reached when the mind has become able to beget the whole objective world from itself.

In his first great work, the "*Phenomenology of the Mind*," Hegel sought to establish the standpoint of absolute knowledge or absolute idealism. He furnishes in this work a history of the phenomenal consciousness (whence its title), a development of the formative epochs of the consciousness in its progress to philosophical knowledge. The inner development of consciousness consists in this, viz., that the peculiar condition in which it finds

itself becomes objectified (or conscious), and through this knowledge of its own being the consciousness rises ever a new step to
a higher condition. The "*Phenomenology*" seeks to show how,
and out of what necessity the consciousness advances from step to
step, from reality to being *per se* (*vom Ansich zum Fürsich*),
from being to knowledge. The author begins with the immediate
consciousness as the lowest step. He entitled this section: "*The
Sensuous Certainty, or the This and the Mine.*" At this stage
the question is asked the Ego : what is *this*, or what is *here ?* and
it answers, *e. g.* the tree; and to the question, what is *now ?* it
answers now is the night. But if we turn ourselves around, *here*
is not a tree but a house ; and if we write down the second answer,
and look at it again after a little time, we find that *now* is no
longer night but mid-day. The *this* becomes, therefore, a not-
this, *i. e.* a universal. And very naturally; for if I say : this
piece of paper, yet each and every paper is a this piece of paper,
and I have only said the universal. By such inner dialectics the
whole field of the immediate certainty of the sense in perception
is gone over. In this way—since every formative step (every
form) of the consciousness of the philosophizing subject is involved in contradictions, and is carried by this immanent dialectics to a higher form of consciousness—this process of development goes on till the contradiction is destroyed, *i. e.* till all
strangeness between subject and object disappears, and the mind
rises to a perfect self-knowledge and self-certainty. To characterize briefly the different steps of this process, we might say that
the consciousness is first found as a certainty of the sense, or as
the *this* and the *mine ;* next as perception, which apprehends the
objective as a thing with its properties ; and then as understanding, *i. e.* apprehending the objects as being reflected in itself, or
distinguishing between power and expression, being and manifestation, outer and inner. From this point the consciousness, which
has only recognized itself, its own pure being in its objects and
their determinations, and for which therefore every other thing
than itself has, as such, no significance, becomes the self-like Ego,
and rises to the truth and certainty of itself to self-consciousness

The self-consciousness become universal, or as reason, now traverses also a series of development-steps, until it manifests itself as spirit, as the reason which, in accord with all rationality, and satisfied with the rational world without, extends itself over the natural and intellectual universe as *its* kingdom, in which it finds itself at home. Mind now passes through its stages of unconstrained morality, culture and refinement, ethics and the ethical view of the world to religion; and religion itself in its perfection, as revealed religion becomes absolute knowledge. At this last stage being and thought are no more separate, being is no longer an object for the thought, but the thought itself is the object of the thought. Science is nothing other than the true knowledge of the mind concerning itself. In the conclusion of the " *Phenomenology*," Hegel casts the following retrospect on the course which he has laid down : " The goal which is to be reached, viz., absolute knowledge, or the mind knowing itself as mind, requires us to take notice of minds as they are in themselves, and the organization of their kingdom. These elements are preserved, and furnished to us either by history, where we look at the side of the mind's free existence as it accidentally appears, or by the science of phenomenal knowledge, where we look at the side of the mind's ideal organization. These two sources taken together, as the ideal history, give us the real history and the true being of the absolute spirit, the actuality, truth, and certainty of his throne, without which he were lifeless and alone; only ' from the cup of this kingdom of minds does there stream forth for him his infinity.' "

SECTION XLV.

HEGEL.

George Wilhelm Friedrich Hegel was born at Stuttgart, the 27th of August, 1770. In his eighteenth year he entered the university of Tubingen, in order to devote himself to the study of theology. During his course of study here, he attracted no marked attention; Schelling, who was his junior in years, shone far beyond all his cotemporaries. After leaving Tübingen, he took a situation as private tutor, first in Switzerland, and afterwards in Frankfort-on-the-Main till 1801, when he settled down at Jena. At first he was regarded as a disciple, and defender of Schelling's philosophy, and as such he wrote in 1801 his first minor treatise on the " *Difference between Fichte and Schelling.*" Soon afterwards he became associated with Schelling in publishing the " *Critical Journal of Philosophy,*" 1802–3, for which he furnished a number of important articles. His labors as an academical teacher met at first with but little encouragement; he gave his first lecture to only four hearers. Yet in 1806 he became professor in the university, though the political catastrophe in which the country was soon afterwards involved, deprived him again of the place. Amid the cannon's thunder of the battle of Jena, he finished " *the Phenomenology of the Mind,*" his first great and independent work, the crown of his Jena labors. He was subsequently in the habit of calling this book which appeared in 1807, his " voyage of discovery." From Jena, Hegel for want of the means of subsistence went to Bamberg, where for two years he was editor of a political journal published there. In the fall of 1808, he became rector of the gymnasium at Nuremberg. In this situation he wrote his *Logic,* 1812–16. All his works were produced slowly, and he first properly began his literary activity as Schelling finished his. In 1816, he received a call to a professorship of philosophy at Heidelberg, where in 1817 he published his " *Encyclopædia of the philosophical sciences,*" in which for the first time he showed the whole circuit of his system. But his peculiar fame, and his far-reaching activity, dates first from his call to Berlin in 1818. It was at Berlin that he surrounded himself with an extensive and very actively scientific school, and where through his connection with the Prussian government he gained a political influence and acquired a reputation for his philosophy, as *the* philosophy of the State, though this neither speaks favorably for its inner purity, nor its moral credit. Yet in his

"*Philosophy of Rights*," which appeared in 1821 (a time, to be sure, when the Prussian State had not yet shown any decidedly anti-constitutional tendency), Hegel does not deny the political demands of the present age; he declares in favor of popular representation, freedom of the press, and publicity of judicial proceedings, trial by jury, and an administrative independence of corporations.

In Berlin, Hegel gave lectures upon almost every branch of philosophy, and these have been published by his disciples and friends after his death. His manner as a lecturer was stammering, clumsy, and unadorned, but was still not without a peculiar attraction as the immediate expression of profound thoughtfulness. His social intercourse was more with the uncultivated than with the learned; he was not fond of shining as a genius in social circles. In 1829 he became rector of the university, an office which he administered in a more practical manner than Fichte had done. Hegel died with the cholera, Nov. 14th, 1831, the day also of Leibnitz's death. He rests in the same churchyard with Solger and Fichte, near by the latter, and not far from the former. His writings and lectures form seventeen volumes which have appeared since 1832: Vol. I. Minor Articles; II. Phenomenology; III–V. Logic; VI.–VII. Encyclopædia; VIII. Philosphy of Rights; IX. Philosophy of History; X. Æsthetics; XI.–XII. Philosophy of Religion; XIII.–XV. History of Philosophy; XVI–XVII. Miscellanies. His life has been written by Rosenkranz.

Hegel's system may be divided in a number of ways. The best mode is by connecting it with Schelling. Schellings's absolute was the identity or the indifference point of the ideal and the real. From this Hegel's threefold division immediately follows. (1) The exposition of the indifference point, the development of the pure conceptions or determinations in thought, which lie at the basis of all natural and intellectual life; in other words, the logical unfolding of the absolute,—*the science of logic.* (2) The development of the real world or of nature—*natural philosophy.* (3) The development of the ideal world, or of mind as it shows itself concretely in right, morals, the state, art, religion, and

15*

science.—*Philosophy of Mind.* These three parts of the system represent the three elements of the absolute method, thesis, antithesis, synthesis. The absolute is at first pure, and immaterial thought; secondly, it is differentiation (*Andersseyn*) of the pure thought or its diremption (*verzerrung*) in space and time—nature; thirdly, it returns from this self-estrangement to itself, destroys the differentiation of nature, and thus becomes actual self-knowing thought or mind.

I. SCIENCE OF LOGIC.—The Hegelian logic is the scientific exposition and development of the pure conceptions of reason, those conceptions or categories which lie at the basis of all thought and being, and which determine the subjective knowledge as truly as they form the indwelling soul of the objective reality; in a word, those ideas in which the ideal and the real have their point of coincidence. The domain of logic, says Hegel, is the truth, as it is *per se* in its native character. It is as Hegel himself figuratively expresses it, the representation of God as he is in his eternal being, before the creation of the world or a finite mind. In this respect it is, to be sure, a domain of shadows; but these shadows are, on the other hand, those simple essences freed from all sensuous matters, in whose diamond net the whole universe is constructed.

Different philosophers had already made a thankworthy beginning towards collecting and examining the pure conceptions of the reason, as Aristotle in his categories, Wolff in his ontology, and Kant in his transcendental analytics. But they had neither completely collected, nor critically sifted, nor (Kant excepted) derived them from one principle, but had only taken them up empirically, and treated them lexicologically. But in opposition to this course, Hegel attempted, (1) to completely collect the pure art-conceptions; (2) to critically sift them (*i. e.* to exclude every thing but pure thought); and (3)—which is the most characteristic peculiarity of the Hegelian logic—to derive these dialectically from one another, and carry them out to an internally connected system of pure reason. Hegel starts with the view, that in every conception of the reason, every other is contained *impli-*

cite, and may be dialectically developed from it. Fichte had already claimed that the reason must deduce the whole system of knowledge purely from itself, without any thing taken for granted; that some principle must be sought which should be of itself certain, and need no farther proof, and from which every thing else could be derived. Hegel holds fast to this thought. Starting from the simplest conception of reason, that of pure being, which needs no farther establishing, he seeks from this, by advancing from one conception ever to another and a richer one, to deduce the whole system of the pure knowledge of reason. The lever of this development is the dialectical method.

Hegel's dialectical method is partly taken from Plato, and partly from Fichte. The conception of negation is Platonic. All negation, says Hegel, is position, affirmation. If a conception is negated, the result is not the pure nothing—a pure negative, but a concrete positive; there results a new conception which extends around the negation of the preceding one. The negation of the one *e. g.* is the conception of the many. In this way Hegel makes negation a vehicle for dialectical progress. Every pre-supposed conception is denied, and from its negation a higher and richer conception is gained. This is connected with the method of Fichte, which posits a fundamental synthesis; and by analyzing this, seeks its antitheses, and then unites again these antitheses through a second synthesis,—*e. g.* being, nothing, becoming, quality, quantity, measure, &c. This method, which is at the same time analytical and synthetical, Hegel has carried through the whole system of science.

We now proceed to a brief survey of the Hegelian Logic. It is divided into three parts; the doctrine of *being*, the doctrine of *essence*, and the doctrine of *conception*.

1. THE DOCTRINE OF BEING. (1.) *Quality.*—Science begins with the immediate and indeterminate conception of *being*. This, in its want of content and emptiness, is nothing more than a pure negation, a *nothing*. These two conceptions are thus as absolutely identical as they are absolutely opposed; each of the two disappears immediately in its contrary. This oscillation of the two is the pure *becoming*,

which, if it be a transition from nothing to being, we call *arising,* or, in the reverse case, we call it a *departing.* The still and simple precipitate of this process of arising and departing, is *existence (Daseyn).* Existence is being with a determinateness, or it is *quality ;* more closely, it is *reality* or limited existence. Limited existence excludes every other from itself. This reference to itself, which is seen through its negative relation to every other, we call being *per se (Fürsichseyn).* Being *per se* which refers itself only to itself, and repels every other from itself, is *the one.* But, by means of this repelling, the one posits immediately *many* ones. But the many ones are not distinguished from each other. One is what the other is. The many are therefore one. But the one is just as truly the manifold. For its exclusion is the positing of its contrary, or it posits itself thereby as manifold. By this dialectic of *attraction* and *repulsion,* quality passes over into quantity : for indifference in respect of distinction or qualitative determinateness is *quantity.*

(2.) *Quantity.*—Quantity is determination of greatness, which, as such, is indifferent in respect of quality. In so far as the *greatness* contains many ones distinguishably within itself, it is a *discrete,* or has the element of *discretion ;* but on the other hand, in so far as the many ones are similar, and the greatness is thus indistinguishable, it is *continuous,* or has the element of *continuity.* Each of these two determinations is at the same time identical with the other ; discretion cannot be conceived without continuity, nor continuity without discretion. The existence of quantity, or the limited quantity, is the *quantum.* The quantum has also manifoldness and unity in itself ; it is the enumeration of the unities, *i. e. number.* Corresponding to the quantum or the extensive greatness, is the intensive greatness or *the degree.* With the conception of degree, so far as degree is simple determinateness, quantity approaches quality again. The unity of quantity and quality is *the measure.*

(3.) *The measure* is a qualitative quantum, a quantum on which the quality is dependent. An example of quantity determining the quality of a definite object is found in the temperature of water, which decides whether the water shall remain water or turn to ice or steam. Here the quantum of heat actually constitutes the quality of the water. Quality and quantity are, therefore, ideal determinations, perpetually turning around *on* one being, on a *third*, which is distinguished from the immediate what and how much (quality and quantity) of a thing. This third is the *essence*, which is the negation of every thing immediate, or quality independent of the immediate being. Essence is being *in se*, being divided in itself, a self-separation of being. Hence the twofoldness of all determinations of essence.

2. The Doctrine of Essence. (1.) *The Essence as such*. The essence as reflected being is the reference to itself only as it is a reference to something other. We apply to this being the term reflected analogously with the reflection of light, which, when it falls on a mirror, is thrown back by it. As now the reflected light is, through its reference to another object, something mediated or posited, so the reflected being is that which is shown to be mediated or grounded through another. From the fact that philosophy makes its problem to know the essence of things, the immediate being of things is represented as a covering or curtain behind which the essence is concealed. If, therefore, we speak of the essence of an object, the immediate being standing over against the essence (for without this the essence cannot be conceived), is set down to a mere negative, to an *appearance*. The being appears in the essence. The essence is, therefore, the being as *appearance in itself*. The essence when conceived in distinction from the appearance, gives the conception of the *essential*, and that which only appears in the essence, is the essenceless, or the *unessential*. But since the essential has a being only in distinction from the unessential, it follows that the latter is essential to the former, which needs its unessential just as much as the unessential needs it. Each of the two, therefore, appears in the other, or there takes place between them a reciprocal reference which we call *reflection*. We have, therefore, to do in this whole sphere with determinations of reflection, with determinations, each one of which refers to the other, and cannot be conceived without it

(*e. g.* positive and negative, ground and sequence, thing and properties, content and form, power and expression). We have, therefore, in the development of the essence, those same determinations which we found in the development of being, only no longer in an immediate, but in a reflected form. Instead of being and nothing, we have now the forms of the positive and negative; instead of the there-existent (*Daseyn*), we now have existence.

Essence is reflected being, a reference to itself, which, however, is mediated through a reference to something other which appears in it. This reflected reference to itself we call *identity* (which is unsatisfactorily and abstractly expressed in the so-called first principle of thought, that $A=A$). This identity, as a negativity referring itself to itself, as a repulsion of its own from itself, contains essentially the determination of *distinction*. The immediate and external distinction is the *difference*. The essential distinction, the distinction in itself, is the *antithesis* (*positive and negative*). The self-opposition of the essence is the *contradiction*. The antithesis of identity and distinction is put in agreement in the conception of the ground. Since now the essence distinguishes itself from itself, there is the essence as identical with itself or the *ground*, and the essence as distinguished from itself or the *sequence*. In the category of ground and sequence the same thing, *i. e.* the essence, is twice posited; the grounded and the ground are one and the same content, which makes it difficult to define the ground except through the sequence, or the sequence except through the ground. The two can, therefore, be divided only by a powerful abstraction; but because the two are identical, it is peculiarly a formalism to apply this category. If reflection would inquire after a ground, it is because it would see the thing as it were in a twofold relation, once in its immediateness, and then as posited through a ground.

(2.) *Essence and Phenomenon.*—The *phenomenon* is the appearance which the essence fills, and which is hence no longer essenceless. There is no appearance without essence, and no essence which may not enter into phenomenon. It is one and the same content which at one time is taken as essence, and at another as phenomenon. In the phenomenal essence we recognize the positive element which has hitherto been called ground, but which we now name *content*, and the negative element which we call the *form*. Every essence is a unity of content and form, *i. e. it exists*. In distinction from immediate being, we call that being which has proceeded from some ground, *existence*, *i. e.* grounded being. When we view the essence as existing, we call it *thing*. In the relation of a thing to its *properties* we have a repetition of the relation of form and content. The properties show us the thing in respect of its form, but it is thing in respect of its content. The relation between the thing and its properties is commonly indicated by the verb *to have* (*e. g.* the thing *has* properties), in order to distinguish between the two. The essence as a negative reference to itself, and as repelling itself from itself in order to a reflection in an *alterum*, is *power* and *expression*. In this category, like all the other categories of essence, one and the same content is posited twice. The power can only be explained from the expression, and the expression only from the power; consequently every explanation of which this category avails itself, is tautological. To regard power as uncognizable, is only a self-deception of the understanding respecting its own doing.—A higher expression for the category of power and expression is the category of *inner* and *outer*. The latter category stands higher than the former, because power needs some solicitation to express itself, but the inner is the essence spontaneously manifesting itself. Both of these, the inner and the outer, are also identical; neither is without the other. That, *e. g.* which the man is internally in respect of his character, is he also externally in his action. The truth of this relation will be, therefore, the identity of inner and outer, of essence and phenomenon, viz. :

(3.) *Actuality.*—Actuality must be added as a *third* to being and existence. In the actuality, the phenomenon is a complete and adequate manifestation of the essence. The true actuality is, therefore (in opposition to *possibility* and *contingency*), a necessary being, a rational *necessity*. The well-known Hegelian sentence that every thing is rational, and every thing rational is

actual, is seen in this apprehension of " actuality " to be a simple
tautology.   The necessary, when posited as its own ground, identical with itself, is *substance.*   The phenomenal side, the unessential in the substance, and the contingent in the necessary, are *accidences.*   These are no longer related to the substance, as the
phenomenon to the essence, or the outer to the inner, *i. e.* as an
adequate manifestation ; they are only transitory affections of the
substance, accidentally changing phenomenal forms, like sea waves
on the water of the sea.   They are not produced by the substance,
but are rather destroyed in it.   The relation of substance leads to
the relation of *cause.*   In the relation of cause there is one and
the same thing posited on the one side as *cause,* and on the other
side as *effect.*   The cause of warmth is warmth, and its effect is
again warmth.   The effect is a higher conception than the accidence, since it actually stands over against the cause, and the cause
itself passes over into effect.   So far, however, as each side in the
relation of cause presupposes the other, we shall find the true
relation one in which each side is at the same time cause and effect,
i. e. reciprocal action.   Reciprocal action is a higher relation
than causality, because there is no pure causality.   There is no
effect without counteraction.   We leave the province of essence
with the category of reciprocal action.   All the categories of
essence had shown themselves as a duplex of two sides, but when
we come to the category of reciprocal action, the opposition between cause and effect is destroyed, and they meet together ; unity
thus takes again the place of duplicity.   We have, therefore,
again a being which coincides with mediate being.   This unity of
being and essence, this inner or realized necessity, is the conception.

3. THE DOCTRINE OF THE CONCEPTION.—A conception is a
rational necessity.   We can only have a conception of that whose
true necessity we have recognized.   The conception is, therefore,
the truly actual, the peculiar essence ; because it states as well
that which is actual as that which should be.

(1.) *The subjective conception* contains the elements of *universality* (the conception of species), *particularity* (ground of
classification, logical difference), and *individuality* (species—logi-

cal difference). The conception is therefore a unity of that which is distinct. The self-separation of the conception is the *judgment*. In the judgment, the conception appears as self-excluding duality. The twofoldness is seen in the difference between subject and predicate, and the unity in the copula. Progress in the different forms of judgment, consists in this, viz., that the copula fills itself more and more with the conception. But thus the judgment passes over into the *conclusion* or inference, *i. e.* to the conception which is identical with itself through the conception. In the inference one conception is concluded with a third through a second. The different figures of the conclusion are the different steps in the self-mediation of the conception. The conception *is* when it mediates itself with itself and the conclusion is no longer subjective; it is no longer my act, but an objective relation is fulfilled in it.

(2.) *Objectivity* is a reality *only* of the conception. The objective conception has·three steps,—*Mechanism*, or the indifferent relation of objects to each other; *Chemism*, or the interpenetration of objects and their neutralization; *Teleology*, or the inner design of objects. The end accomplishing itself or the self-end is,

(3.) *The idea.*—The idea is the highest logical definition of the absolute. The immediate existence of the idea, we call *life*, or process of life. Every thing living is self-end immanent-end. The idea posited in its difference as a relation of objective and subjective, is the *true* and *good*. The true is the objective rationality subjectively posited; the good is the subjective rationality carried into the objectivity. Both conceptions together constitute the *absolute idea*, which *is* just as truly as it *should* be, *i. e.* the good is just as truly actualized as the true is living and self-realizing.

The absolute and full idea *is in space*, because it discharges itself from itself, as its reflection; this its being in space is *Nature*.

II. The Science of Nature.—Nature is the idea in the form of differentiation. It is the idea externalizing itself; it is the mind estranged from itself. The unity of the conception is therefore concealed in nature, and since philosophy makes it its problem to seek out the intelligence which is hidden in nature, and to pursue the process by which nature loses its own character and becomes mind, it should not forget that the essence of nature consists in being which has externalized itself, and that the products of nature neither have a reference to themselves, nor correspond to the conception, but grow up in unrestrained and unbridled contingency. Nature is a bacchanalian god who neither bridles nor checks himself. It therefore represents no ideal succession, rising ever in regular order, but, on the contrary, it every where obliterates all essential limits by its doubtful structures, which always defy every fixed classification. Because it is impossible to throw the determinations of the conception over nature, natural philosophy is forced at every point, as it were, to capitulate between the world of concrete individual structures, and the regulative of the speculative idea.

Natural philosophy has its beginning, its course, and its end. It begins with the first or immediate determination of nature, with the abstract universality of its being *extra se*, space and matter; its end is the dissevering of the mind from nature in the form of a rational and self-conscious individuality—man; the problem which it has to solve is, to show the intermediate link between these two extremes, and to follow out successively the increasingly successful struggles of nature to raise itself to self-consciousness, to man. In this process, nature passes through three principal stages.

1. MECHANICS, or matter and an ideal system of matter. Matter is the being *extra se* (*Aussersichseyn*) of nature, in its most universal form. Yet it shows at the outset that tendency to being *per se* which forms the guiding thread of natural philosophy—gravity. Gravity is the being *in se* (*Insichseyn*) of matter; it is the desire of matter to come to itself, and shows the first trace of subjectivity. The centre of gravity of a body is *the one* which it seeks. This same tendency of bringing all the manifold unto being *per se* lies at the basis of the solar system and of universal gravitation. The centrality which is the fundamental con-

ception of gravity, becomes here a system, which is in fact a rational system so far as the form of the orbit, the rapidity of motion, or the time of revolution may be referred to mathematical laws.

2. PHYSICS.—But matter possesses no individuality. Even in astronomy it is not the bodies themselves, but only their geometrical relations which interest us. We have here at the outset to treat of quantitative and not yet of qualitative determinations. Yet in the solar system, matter has found its centre, itself. Its abstract and hollow being *in se* has resolved itself into form. Matter now, as possessing a quality, is an object of *physics*. In physics we have to do with matter which has particularized itself in a body, in an individuality. To this province belongs inorganic nature, its forms and reciprocal references.

3. ORGANICS.—Inorganic nature, which was the object of physics, destroys itself in the chemical process. In the chemical process, the inorganic body loses all its properties (cohesion, color, shining, sound, transparency, &c.), and thus shows the evanescence of its existence and that relativity which is its being. This chemical process is overcome by the organic, the living process of nature. True, the living body is ever on the point of passing over to the chemical process; oxygen, hydrogen and salt, are always entering into a living organism, but their chemical action is always overcome; the living body resists the chemical process till it dies. Life is self-preservation, self-end. While therefore nature in physics had risen to individuality, in organics, it progresses to subjectivity. The idea, as life, represents itself in three stages.

(1.) The general image of life in *geological* organism, or the *mineral kingdom*. Yet the mineral kingdom is the result, and the residuum of a process of life and formation already passed. The primitive rock is the stiffened crystal of life, and the geological earth is a giant corpse. The present life which produces itself eternally anew, breaks forth as the first moving of subjectivity,

(2.) In the organism of *plants* or the *vegetable kingdom*. The plant rises indeed to a formative process, to a process of assimila-

tion, and to a process of species. But it is not yet a totality perfectly organized in itself. Each part of the plant is the whole individual, each twig is the whole tree. The parts are related indifferently to each other; the crown can become a root, and the root
a crown. The plant, therefore, does not yet attain a true being
in se of individuality; for, in order that this may be attained, an
absolute unity of the individual is necessary. This unity, which
constitutes an individual and concrete subjectivity, is first seen in

(3.) The *animal* organism, the *animal kingdom.* An uninterrupted intus-susception, free motion and sensation, are first
found in the animal organism. In its higher forms we find an
inner warmth and a voice. In its highest form, man, nature, or
rather the spirit, which works through nature, apprehends itself
as conscious individuality, as Ego. The spirit thus become a free
and rational self, has now completed its self-emancipation from
nature.

III. PHILOSOPHY OF MIND.—1. THE SUBJECTIVE MIND.—
The mind is the truth of nature; it is being removed from its
estrangement, and become identical with itself. Its formal essence, therefore, is freedom, the possibility of abstracting itself
from every thing else; its material essence is the capacity of
manifesting itself as mind, as a conscious rationality,—of positing
the intellectual universe as its kingdom, and of building a structure of objective rationality. In order, however, to know itself,
and every thing rational,—in order to posit nature more and more
negatively, the mind, like nature, must pass through a series of
stages or emancipative acts. As it comes from nature and rises
from its externality to being, *per se*, it is at first soul or spirit of
nature, and as such, it is an object of *anthropology* in a strict
sense. As this spirit of nature, it sympathizes with the general
planetary life of the earth, and is in this respect subject to diversity of climate, and change of seasons and days; it sympathizes
with the geographical portion of the world which it occupies, *i. e.,*
it is related to a diversity of race; still farther, it bears a national type, and is moreover determined by mode of life, formation of the body, &c., while these natural conditions work also

upon its intelligent and moral character. Lastly, we must here take notice of the way in which nature has determined the individual subject, *i. e.* his natural temperament, character, idiosyncrasy, &c. To this belong the natural changes of life, age, sexual relation, sleep, and waking. In all this the mind is still buried in nature, and this middle condition between being *per se* and the sleep of nature, is sensation, the hollow forming of the mind in its unconscious and unenlightened (*verstandlos*) individuality. A higher stage of sensation is feeling, *i. e.* sensation *in se*, where being *per se* appears; feeling in its completed form is self-feeling. Since the subject, in self-feeling, is buried in the peculiarity of his sensations, but at the same time concludes himself with himself, as a subjective one, the self-feeling is seen to be the preliminary step to consciousness. The Ego now appears as the shaft in which all these sensations, representations, cognitions and thoughts are preserved, which is with them all, and constitutes the centre in which they all come together. The mind as conscious, as a conscious being *per se*, as Ego, is the object of the *phenomenology* of consciousness.

The mind was individual, so long as it was interwoven with nature; it is consciousness or Ego when it has divested itself of nature. When distinguishing itself from nature, the mind withdraws itself into itself, and that with which it was formerly interwoven, and which gave it a peculiar (earthly, national, &c.) determination, stands now distinct from it, as its external world (earth, people, &c). The awaking of the Ego is thus the act by which the objective world, as such, is created; while on the other hand, the Ego awakens to a conscious subjectivity only *in* the objective world, and in distinction from it. The Ego, over against the objective world, is consciousness in the strict sense of the word. Consciousness becomes self-consciousness by passing through the stages of immediate sensuous consciousness, perception, and understanding, and convincing itself in this its formative history, that it has only to do with itself, while it believed that it had to do with something objective. Again, self-consciousness becomes universal or rational self-consciousness, as follows: In its strivings to stamp the impress of the Ego upon the objective, and thus make the objective subjective, it falls in conflict with other self-consciousnesses, and begins a war of extermination against them, but rises from this *bellum omnium contra omnes*, as common consciousness, as the finding of the proper mean between command and obedience, *i. e.* as truly universal, *i. e.* rational self-consciousness. The rational self-consciousness is actually free, because, when related to another, it is really related to itself, and in all is still with itself; it has emancipated itself from nature. We have now mind as mind, divested of its naturalness and subjectivity, and as such, it is an object of *Pneumatology.*

Mind is at first theoretical mind, or intelligence, and then practical mind, or will. It is theoretical in that it has to do with the rational as something given, and now posits it as its own; it is practical in that it immediately wills the subjective content (truth), which it has as its own, to be freed from its one-sided subjective form, and transformed into an objective. The practical mind is, so far, the truth of the theoretical. The theoretical mind, in its way to the practical, passes through the stages of intuition, representation, and thought; and the will on its side forms itself into a free will through impulse, desire, and inclination. The free will, as having a being in space (*Daseyn*), is the *objective mind,* right, and the state. In right, morals and the state, the freedom and rationality, which are chosen by the will, take on an objective form. Every natural determination and impulse now becomes moralized, and comes up to view again as ethical institute, as right and duty (the sexual impulse now appears as marriage, and the impulse of revenge as civil punishment, &c.)

2. THE OBJECTIVE MIND.—(1.) The immediate objective being (*Daseyn*) of the free will is *the right.* The individual, so far as he is capable of rights, so far as he has rights and exercises them, is a person. The maxim of right is, therefore, be a person and have respect to other persons. The person allows himself an external sphere for his freedom, a substratum in which he can exercise his will: as property, possession. As person I have the right of possession, the absolute right of appropriation, the right to cast

my will over every thing, which thereby becomes mine. But there exist other persons besides myself. My right is, therefore, limited through the right of others. There thus arises a conflict between will and will, which is settled in a compact, in a common will. The relation of compact is the first step towards the state, but only the *first* step, for if we should define the state as a com-pact of all with all, this would sink it in the category of private rights and private property. It does not depend upon the will of the individual whether he will live in the state or not. The relation of compact refers to private property. In a compact, therefore, two wills merge themselves in a common will, which as such becomes a right. But just here lies also the possibility of a conflict between the individual will and the right or the universal will. The separation of the two is a wrong (civil wrong, fraud, crime). This separation demands a reconciliation, a restoration of the right or the universal will from its momentary suppression or negation by the particular will. The right restoring itself in respect of the particular will, and establishing a negation of the wrong, is punishment. Those theories, which found the right of punishment in some end of warning or improvement, mistake the essence of punishment. Threatening, warning, &c., are finite ends, *i. e.* means, and moreover uncertain means : but an act of righteousness should not be made a means; righteousness is not exercised in order that any thing other than itself shall be gained. The fulfilment and self-manifestation of righteousness is absolute end, self-end. The particular views we have mentioned, can only be considered in reference to the mode of punishment. The pun-ishment which is inflicted on a criminal, is *his* right, *his* ration-ality, *his* law, beneath which he should be subsumed. His act comes back upon himself. Hegel also defends capital punishment whose abolition seemed to him as an untimely sentimentalism.

(2.) The removal of the opposition of the universal and par-ticular will in the subject constitutes *morality*. In morality the freedom of the will is carried forward to a self-determination of' the subjectivity, and the abstract right becomes duty and virtue. The moral standpoint is the standpoint of conscience, it is the right of the subjective will, the right of a free ethical decision. In the consideration of strict right, it is no inquiry what my principle or my view might be, but in morality the question is at once directed towards the purpose and moving spring of the will. Hegel calls this standpoint of moral reflection and dutiful action for a reason—morality, in distinction from a substantial, unconditioned and unreflecting ethics. This standpoint has three elements; (1) the element of resolution (*vorsatz*), where we consider the inner determination of the acting subject, that which allows an act to be ascribed only to me, and the blame of it to rest only on my will (imputation); (2) the element of purpose, where the completed act is regarded not according to its consequences, but according to its relative worth in reference to myself. The resolution was still internal; but now the act is completed, and I must suffer myself to judge according to the constituents of the act, because I must have known the circumstances under which I acted; (3) the element of the good, where the act is judged according to its universal worth. The good is peculiarly the reconciliation of the particular subjective will with the universal will, or with the conception of the will; in other words, to will the rational is good. Opposed to this is evil, or the elevation of the subjective will against the universal, the attempt to set up the peculiar and individual choice as absolute; in other words, to will the irrational is evil.

(3.) In morality we had conscience and the abstract good (the good which ought to be) standing over against each other. The concrete identity of the two, the union of subjective and objective good, is *ethics*. In the ethical the good has become actualized in an existing world, and a nature of self-consciousness.

The ethical mind is seen at first immediately, or in a natural form, as marriage and the *family*. Three elements meet together in marriage, which should not be separated, and which are so often and so wrongly isolated. Marriage is (1) a sexual relation, and is founded upon a difference of sex; it is, therefore, something other than Platonic love or monkish asceticism; (2) it is a civil contract; (3) it is love. Yet Hegel lays no great stress upon this subjective element in concluding upon marriage, for a reciprocal affection will spring up in the married life. It is more ethical when a determination to marry is first, and a definite personal affection follows afterwards, for marriage is most prominently duty Hegel would, therefore, place the greatest obstacles in the way of a dissolution of marriage. He has also developed and described in other respects the family state with a profound ethical feeling.

Since the family becomes separated into a multitude of families, it is a *civil society*, in which the members, though still independent individuals, are bound in unity by their wants, by the constitution of rights as a means of security for person and property, and by an outward administrative arrangement. Hegel distinguished the civil society from the state in opposition to most modern theorists upon the subject, who, regarding it as the great end of the state to give security of property and of personal freedom, reduced the state to a civil society. But on such a standpoint which would make the state wholly of wants and of rights, it is impossible, *e. g.* to conceive of war. On the ground of civil society each one stands for himself, is independent, and makes himself as end, while every thing else is a means for him. But the state, on the contrary, knows no independent individuals, each one of whom may regard and pursue only his own well-being; but in the state, the whole is the end, and the individual is the means.—For the administration of justice, Hegel, in opposition to those of our time who deny the right of legislation, would have written and intelligible laws, which should be within reach of every one; still farther, justice should be administered by a public trial by jury.—In respect of the organization of civil society, Hegel expresses a great preference for a corporation. Sanctity of marriage, he says, and honor in corporations, are the two elements around which the disorganization of civil society turns.

Civil society passes over into the *state* since the interest of the individual loses itself in the idea of an ethical whole. The state is the ethical idea actualized, it is the ethical mind as it rules over the action and knowledge of the individuals conceived in it. Finally the states themselves, since they appear as individuals in

16

an attracting or repelling relation to each other, represent, in their
destiny, in their rise and fall, the process of the *world's history.*

In his apprehension of the state, Hegel approached very near
the ancient notion, which merged the individual and the right of
individuality, wholly in the will of the state. He held fast to the
omnipotence of the state in the ancient sense. Hence his resistance to modern liberalism, which would allow individuals to postulate, to criticize, and to will according to their improved knowledge. The state is with Hegel the rational and ethical substance
in which the individual has to live, it is the existing reason to
which the individual has to submit himself with a free view. He
regarded a limited monarchy as the best form of government, after
the manner of the English constitution, to which Hegel was
especially inclined, and in reference to which he uttered his well-
known saying that the king was but the dot upon the i. There
must be an individual, Hegel supposes, who can *affirm* for the
state, who can prefix an "*I will*" to the resolves of the state, and
who can be the head of a formal decision. The personality of a
state, he says, "is only actual as a person, as monarch." Hence
Hegel defends hereditary monarchy, but he places the nobility by
its side as a mediating element between people and prince—not
indeed to control or limit the government, nor to maintain the
rights of the people, but only that the people may experience that
there is a good rule, that the consciousness of the people may be
with the government and that the state may enter into the subjective consciousness of the people.

States and the minds of individual races pour their currents
into the stream of the world's history. The strife, the victory,
and the subjection of the spirits of individual races, and the passing over of the world spirit from one people to another, is the content of the world's history. The development of the world's history is generally connected with some ruling race, which carries
in itself the world spirit in its present stage of development, and
in distinction from which the spirits of other races have no rights.
Thus these race-spirits stand around the throne of the absolute

spirit, as the executors of its actualization, as the witnesses and adornment of its glory.

3. THE ABSOLUTE MIND.—(1.) *Æsthetics.* The absolute mind is immediately present to the sensuous intuition as the beautiful or as art. The beautiful is the appearance of the idea through a sensible medium (a crystal, color, tone, poetry) ; it is the idea actualized in the form of a limited phenomenon. To the beautiful (and to its subordinate kinds, the simply beautiful, the sublime, and the comical) two factors always belong, thought and matter ; but both these are inseparable from each other ; the matter is the outer phenomenon of the thought, and should express nothing but the thought which inspires it and shines through it. The different ways in which matter and form are connected, furnish the different forms of art. In the symbolic form of art the matter preponderates ; the thought presses through it, and brings out the ideal only with difficulty. In the classic form of art, the ideal has attained its adequate existence in the matter ; content and form are absolutely befitting each other. Lastly, in romantic art, the mind preponderates, and the matter is a mere appearance and sign through which the mind every where breaks out, and struggles up above the material. The system of particular arts is connected with the different forms of art ; but the distinction of one particular art from another, depends especially upon the difference of the material.

(*a.*) The beginning of art is *Architecture.* It belongs essentially to the symbolic form of art, since in it the sensible matter far preponderates, and it first seeks the true conformity between content and form. Its material is stone, which it fashions according to the laws of gravity. Hence it has the character of magnitude, of silent earnestness, of oriental sublimity.

(*b.*) *Sculpture.*—The material of this art is also stone, but it advances from the inorganic to the organic. It gives the stone a bodily form, and makes it only a serving vehicle of the thought. In sculpture, the material, the stone, since it represents the body, that building of the soul, in its clearness and beauty, disappears wholly in the ideal; there is nothing left of the material which does not serve the idea.

(*c.*) *Painting.*—This is pre-eminently a romantic art. It represents, as sculpture cannot do, the life of the soul, the look, the disposition, the heart. Its medium is no longer a coarse material substratum, but the colored surface, and the soul-like play of light; it gives the *appearance* only of complete spacial dimension. Hence it is able to represent in a complete dramatic movement the whole scale of feelings, conditions of heart, and actions.

(*d.*) *Music.*—This leaves out all relation of space. Its material is sound, the vibration of a sonorous body. It leaves, therefore, the field of sensuous intuition, and works exclusively upon the sensation. Its basis is the breast of the sensitive soul. Music is the most subjective art.

(*e.*) Lastly in *Poetry*, or the speaking art, is the tongue of art loosed; poetry can represent every thing. Its material is not the mere sound, but the sound as word, as the sign of a representation, as the expression of reason. But this material cannot be formed at random, but only in verse according to certain rhythmical and musical laws. In poetry, all other arts return again; as epic, representing in a pleasing and extended narrative the figurative history of races, it corresponds to the plastic arts; as lyric, expressing some inner condition of soul, it corresponds to music; as dramatic poetry, exhibiting the struggles between characters acting out of directly opposite interests, it is the union of both these arts.

(2.) *Philosophy of Religion.*—Poetry forms the transition from art to religion. In art the idea was present for the intuition, in religion it is present for the representation. The content of every religion is the reconciliation of the finite with the infinite, of the subject with God. All religions seek a union of the divine and the human. This was done in the crudest form by

(*a.*) The natural religions of the oriental world. God is, with them, but a power of nature, a substance of nature, in comparison with which the finite and the individual disappear as nothing.

(*b.*) A higher idea of God is attained by the religions of spiritual individuality, in which the divine is looked upon as subject,—as an exalted subjectivity, full of power and wisdom in Judaism, the religion of sublimity ; as a circle of plastic divine forms in the Grecian religion, the religion of beauty; as an absolute end of the state in the Roman religion, the religion of the understanding or of design.

(*c.*) The revealed or Christian religion first establishes a positive reconciliation between God and the world, by beholding the actual unity of the divine and the human in the person of Christ, the God-man, and apprehending God as triune, *i. e.* as Himself, as incarnate, and as returning from this incarnation to Himself. The intellectual content of revealed religion, or of Christianity, is thus the same as that of speculative philosophy; the only difference being, that in the one case the content is represented in the form of the representation, in the form of a history ; while, in the other, it appears in the form of the conception. Stripped of its form of religious representation, we have now the standpoint of

(3.) *The Absolute Philosophy*, or the thought knowing itself as all truth, and reproducing the whole natural and intellectual universe from itself, having the system of philosophy for its development—a closed circle of circles.

With Hegel closes the history of philosophy. The philosophical developments which have succeeded him, and which are partly a carrying out of his system, and partly the attempt to lay a new basis for philosophy, belong to the present, and not yet to history.

THE END